OXFORD WORLD'S

# THE TWO FUND
# PROBLEMS OF

ARTHUR SCHOPENHAUER was born on 22 February 1788 in the
Hanseatic free city of Danzig (now Gdansk, Poland). His father
was a successful merchant and one of Danzig's leading citizens.
The family moved to Hamburg to escape the city's annexation by
Prussia in 1793. Schopenhauer spent two years in France from 1797
to 1799, and after four years in private school and a sixteen-month
tour of Europe was preparing to begin an apprenticeship with a
Hamburg merchant when, in April 1805, his father suddenly died.
After two years Schopenhauer abandoned his apprenticeship and
enrolled at the University of Göttingen where he studied Plato and
Kant. He began reading Eastern philosophy and became the first
Western philosopher to integrate Eastern thinking in his work.
His masterpiece, *The World as Will and Representation*, appeared in
December 1818. He joined the University of Berlin as lecturer in the
philosophy faculty, where he clashed with Hegel, a fellow member
of the faculty. He published *On the Will in Nature* in 1836, and *The
Two Fundamental Problems of Ethics* in 1840, with a vitriolic preface
criticizing the Royal Danish Society who had denied a prize to his
second essay. In 1844 Schopenhauer published a second edition of
*The World as Will and Representation*, adding a second volume of
fifty essays. A two-volume collection of essays entitled *Parerga and
Paralipomena* appeared in 1851. Schopenhauer died in Frankfurt in
September 1860, after a short illness.

DAVID E. CARTWRIGHT is Professor of Philosophy at the University
of Wisconsin–Whitewater. He has written widely on Schopenhauer
and is the author of the *Historical Dictionary of Schopenhauer's
Philosophy* (2005) and *Schopenhauer: A Biography* (2010).

EDWARD E. ERDMANN is Assistant Professor in Languages and
Literatures, University of Wisconsin–Whitewater.

CHRISTOPHER JANAWAY is Professor of Philosophy at the University
of Southampton. He is the author of *Self and World in Schopenhauer's
Philosophy* (1989), *Schopenhauer: A Very Short Introduction* (2002),
and editor of *The Cambridge Companion to Schopenhauer* (1999).

# OXFORD WORLD'S CLASSICS

*For over 100 years Oxford World's Classics have brought
readers closer to the world's great literature. Now with over 700
titles—from the 4,000-year-old myths of Mesopotamia to the
twentieth century's greatest novels—the series makes available
lesser-known as well as celebrated writing.*

*The pocket-sized hardbacks of the early years contained
introductions by Virginia Woolf, T. S. Eliot, Graham Greene,
and other literary figures which enriched the experience of reading.
Today the series is recognized for its fine scholarship and
reliability in texts that span world literature, drama and poetry,
religion, philosophy, and politics. Each edition includes perceptive
commentary and essential background information to meet the
changing needs of readers.*

OXFORD WORLD'S CLASSICS

ARTHUR SCHOPENHAUER

# The Two Fundamental Problems of Ethics

*Translated with Notes by*
DAVID E. CARTWRIGHT and
EDWARD E. ERDMANN

*With an Introduction by*
CHRISTOPHER JANAWAY

OXFORD
UNIVERSITY PRESS

# OXFORD

UNIVERSITY PRESS

Great Clarendon Street, Oxford ox2 6DP

Oxford University Press is a department of the University of Oxford.
It furthers the University's objective of excellence in research, scholarship,
and education by publishing worldwide in

Oxford New York

Auckland Cape Town Dar es Salaam Hong Kong Karachi
Kuala Lumpur Madrid Melbourne Mexico City Nairobi
New Delhi Shanghai Taipei Toronto

With offices in

Argentina Austria Brazil Chile Czech Republic France Greece
Guatemala Hungary Italy Japan Poland Portugal Singapore
South Korea Switzerland Thailand Turkey Ukraine Vietnam

Oxford is a registered trade mark of Oxford University Press
in the UK and in certain other countries

Published in the United States
by Oxford University Press Inc., New York

Translation, Note on the Text and Translation, Select Bibliography, Chronology,
Explanatory Notes © David E. Cartwright and Edward E. Erdmann 2010

Introduction © Christopher Janaway 2010

The moral rights of the authors have been asserted
Database right Oxford University Press (maker)

First published as an Oxford World's Classics paperback 2010

British Library Cataloguing in Publication Data

Data available

Library of Congress Cataloging in Publication Data

Library of Congress Control Number: 2009942573

Typeset by Glyph International, Bangalore, India
Printed in Great Britain
on acid-free paper by
Clays Ltd, Elcograf S.p.A.

ISBN 978-0-19-929722-1

`12

# ACKNOWLEDGEMENTS

WE have been extraordinarily fortunate to have received funds from a National Endowment for the Humanities Collaborative Research Grant, which support made possible the time to complete this and other translations of Schopenhauer's work. Of course, any views, findings, conclusions, or recommendations expressed in this publication do not necessarily reflect those of the National Endowment for the Humanities. To be sure, the guidance and efforts of Denise Ehlen, Director of Research and Sponsored Programs, and her staff at the University of Wisconsin–Whitewater made it possible for us to secure this grant. Yet Mary Pinkerton and the College of Letters and Sciences Professional Development Committee also helped with essential support. But in uncountable ways over the years our colleagues in the Departments of Philosophy and Religious Studies and Languages and Literatures have encouraged and supported all our efforts and tolerated our puns — no matter how low, or erudite, or just downright obscure.

As always, our colleagues and friends have been helpful. We are eager to credit the capable help of reference librarians Barbara Bren and Martha Stephenson, who met our questions about Schopenhauer's obscure allusions to scholarly and general culture with good humour and consistent success. Among those in the Department of Languages and Literatures, Joseph Hogan has always risen to the challenge of our untimely calls about Schopenhauer's allusions; Jian Guo has instructively helped with Chinese thought and language; Peter Hoff patiently helped with Schopenhauer's Spanish, and Matthew Lange kept us from blundering over *eine jede*. Then, too, on occasion, a learned friend, Richard Larson, exchanged suggestions for accurate translation for *ein Bier*.

Full credit for the opportunity for this translation goes to Christopher Janaway of the University of Southampton, who initiated and secured the contract for its publication. We also extend our thanks to Judith Luna, Jeff New, and Claire Thompson of Oxford University Press for their guidance and editorial care with this project.

With our loving gratitude, we dedicate this translation to Carol Lohry Cartwright and to Aureljean Gustafson-Erdmann.

# CONTENTS

# CONTENTS

## THE TWO FUNDAMENTAL PROBLEMS OF ETHICS

# INTRODUCTION

In 1840 Arthur Schopenhauer published two essays which, he claimed, 'mutually contribute to the completion of a system of the fundamental truths of ethics' (p. 5), and placed them together in a single volume (whose title-page was dated 1841). Both essays started life as submissions to prize competitions set by scholarly academies, one in Norway, which posed the question: 'Can the freedom of the human will be demonstrated from self-consciousness?'; the other in Denmark, with the rather more cumbersome question: 'Are the source and basis of morals to be sought in an idea of morality which is immediately contained in conscience, and in the analysis of the remaining fundamental moral notions originating from this, or in another cognitive principle?' — or, in short: What is the foundation of morals? Schopenhauer consistently referred to both his contributions as prize essays, even though only the first actually received a prize. The second essay, despite being the sole entry for the Danish competition, fell foul of a damning judgement, in part because of its rudeness towards Hegel and Fichte, the 'supreme philosophers' whose influence still shaped much of the academic establishment. Schopenhauer never forgave the Danish academy for this rejection, and filled the preface to *The Two Fundamental Problems of Ethics* with torrid condemnation, ridicule of Hegel, and a passionate defence of his own essay. The same attitudes are repeated, with a little more restraint but manifesting the same characteristic obstinacy, in the preface to the second edition of the book, which appeared with some additions and revisions in 1860, the last year of Schopenhauer's life, and which is essentially the edition that forms the basis for the present translation.

The degree of Schopenhauer's gratitude towards the Norwegian academics who awarded him a prize and membership of their society, and the sting of his rejection by their Danish counterparts, can perhaps be gauged from the course of his career as a philosopher to date. He was no longer young when he entered these essay competitions, but was still in search of recognition. Born in 1788, he had published his doctoral dissertation *On the Fourfold Root of the Principle of Sufficient Reason* in 1813, and after four years of intense work had produced a monumental book titled *The World as Will and Representation*. In this wide-ranging and ambitious work he dismissed all German philosophy after Kant as an aberration, insisted on regarding human beings ahistorically, refused them any higher 'dignity' than other parts of nature, claimed their essence to be a blind, irrational striving, effectively denied any possibility of moral or social progress, and praised mystical self-denial in face of the essential 'nothingness' of our ordinary existence. All of this set him already at odds with the predominantly Hegelian tenor of much academic life in Germany. Schopenhauer's would-be career as a university lecturer foundered at its outset during the 1820s, his productivity declined, and it was not until 1836, when he had reached his late forties, that he published a shorter book called *On the Will in Nature*, which was designed as a supplement to certain central aspects of *The World as Will and Representation*, but did nothing to alter the general neglect of Schopenhauer's work or diminish his bitter contempt for the age in which he lived.

Hegel had died in 1831, and his predecessor Fichte as early as 1813. Schopenhauer regarded Fichte (some of whose lectures he had attended as a student in Berlin) as a verbose, pretentious windbag, and takes a number of opportunities in the essays to try and persuade the reader of this by subjecting examples from Fichte's works to witty fun-poking. Hegel was, for him, a more sinister figure, a manipulative charlatan playing to a gullible public—the kind of scene portrayed by the Spanish satirist Gracián in a long excerpt translated in the preface to the first edition of the essays, where a showman hoodwinks the crowd by talking up a donkey as a magnificent eagle and a tiny man as a giant. By the time of the second edition Schopenhauer still cannot resist gloating that 'these supreme philosophers have, indeed, sunk very low in public estimation, and Hegel in particular fast approaches the contempt that awaits him in posterity' (p. 31). Schopenhauer is equally critical of the German intellectual public for being, as he sees it, taken in by pompous and vacuous terminology. Nor does he tire of berating the chorus of university professors, 'who with serious mien reiterate in public lectures about the infinite, about the absolute, and about so many other things of which they can know absolutely nothing' (p. 160) and who make their living stringing out the same old terminology, ruining the minds of the young. However, this antagonistic and embattled posture, though prevalent in Schopenhauer's writings, is by no means their only or most impressive aspect. In the essays on ethics we find a highly educated, inquisitive, and scholarly mind, at home in many languages, familiar with Western philosophy from the ancient Greeks onwards, through medieval Christian debates about free will and divine grace, to the Renaissance, the Enlightenment, and his own day, well read about scientific advances, knowledgeable about recent research on the thought of India and China, in tune with the news, and able to quote aptly from poetry of all periods. All of this richness is held together by a prose stylist who can construct majestic sentences of classical structure and yet imbue them with a lively and down-to-earth sense of argumentative purpose and intellectual honesty.

The core of the 'system of ethics' formed by the essays in *The Two Fundamental Problems of Ethics* is an account of what grounds our descriptions of human actions, and of human beings themselves, as morally good or morally bad. Many attempts have been made to find a theoretical foundation for these evaluative descriptions, but Schopenhauer claims that the solution, the true grounding of ethics, is that actions of moral worth are those that proceed from *compassion* towards some being other than ourselves. All virtues of character stem from two primary virtues, voluntary justice and loving kindness, and these are both forms of compassion. If one is acting justly—in the properly virtuous sense, not merely obeying laws self-interestedly for fear of punishment—then the incentive of one's action is purely and simply the prevention of harm or suffering to others, or the preservation of their well-being; if one is acting out of loving kindness, one's incentive is actively to promote the well-being of others or actively to assuage their suffering. All beings that suffer are worthy objects of compassion for us, including non-human animals, towards which the Western tradition of ethics has been shamefully neglectful, in Schopenhauer's eyes. We have greater similarity with other animals than previous moral theorists have been prepared to recognize. The fact of our having reason, the ability to form and manipulate abstract concepts in thought, merely means that we can act on more complicated motives than other animals, who are restricted to the perception of objects in the here and now. But that is not the basis for any difference in kind in the significance of our suffering, and the outlook of a morally good person will implicitly recognize that the same essence 'exists in every living being and . . . shines forth with inscrutable significance from all eyes which see the light of the sun' (p. 173). This recognition, and the resulting disposition to act compassionately, is the foundation of morals.

What does Schopenhauer mean by a foundation of morals? First we should note that he distinguishes between 'morals' (*Moral* in German) and 'morality' (*Moralität*). He comments that 'that which is theoretically and abstractly *morals* itself is practically and substantially *morality*' (p. 8). Morality, then, is a set of beliefs, attitudes, actions, and character-traits, as they occur in practice in human societies. 'Morals' is the name of the theoretical discipline that studies morality and attempts to explain its foundations. So Schopenhauer uses 'morals' to all intents and purposes as equivalent to 'ethics', 'moral theory', or 'moral philosophy'—with the qualification that religions that are not strictly philosophical have also propounded 'morals', of which Schopenhauer is critical on a number of counts: for example, that theology should have no place within philosophy, and that the fine morals set up by Christianity, for example, have failed to prevent gross instances of suffering and cruelty such as the Inquisition, religious wars, and the slave trade. Schopenhauer thinks that theorists have found it easy to agree about the 'what' of morality, but have always struggled over the 'why'. Morality is encapsulated in the simple principle: 'Harm no one; rather, help everyone as much as you can' (which Schopenhauer always gives in Latin: *Neminem laede, imo omnes, quantum potes, juva*—see pp. 150–1, 170, 173). Actions that express this maxim are moral actions, and agents that tend to act in ways expressive of it have morally good characters; the task of philosophical morals is to find the ground of this principle, to answer the question why one should act morally, and what force the outlook of a morally good character has against the prevalent incentives of egoism and malice.

For Schopenhauer every human being (and every animal too) has a central egoistic incentive: by nature a human being strives for ends and 'wills unconditionally to preserve his existence; wills it unconditionally free of pains . . . wills the greatest possible amount of well-being, and wills every pleasure of which he is capable' (p. 202). Humans are also susceptible to malice, which is an incentive to harm others. Acting egoistically, I may cause harm to another being on the way to attaining my own ends, but am not really oriented towards the other except as a means; but if I act maliciously, I want the other to suffer as such, and can even sacrifice my own well-being in pursuit of this aim. Because it is in competition with these anti-moral incentives, compassionate action, the only truly morally good action, is something of a rarity in human life, according to Schopenhauer. Its occurrence is even, he says, something 'mysterious', yet he requires us to accept the premise that it is a fact of human life. The sceptical position that no action is ever purely directed towards the alleviation of others' suffering or the enhancement of their well-being would, says Schopenhauer, leave ethics as a science with no real object. But to maintain that position one would have to find an egoistic or malicious motive behind every human action, even those such as Schopenhauer's favourite example, the self-sacrifice in battle of the medieval Swiss hero, Arnold von Winkelried.

Another sceptical attack on the possibility of morality might be thought to lie in the problematic nature of the assumption of free will. If there is no free will, then how are we responsible for our actions? And without responsibility, what becomes of morality? In the first of his two essays Schopenhauer confronts this squarely by arguing that there is indeed no freedom with respect to our particular acts of will, but that we are none the less justified in taking ourselves to be responsible, in feeling the sting of conscience, and blaming others as morally bad. Our self-consciousness cannot reveal to us the freedom of our will, because it is incapable of recognizing what causes us to will certain things and not others. Self-consciousness can tell us that we can act in certain ways *if we will* so to act. But it is an illusion, albeit an almost inevitable one, to take this for freedom of the will proper. My self-consciousness (to answer the question set by the Norwegian academicians) *cannot* decide for me the crucial question whether it was possible for me to will, in the very same circumstances, something other than I did in fact will on some occasion. On the other hand, if we regard ourselves objectively, then our willed actions, like everything else that happens in the world of objects, must be seen as causally necessitated. Schopenhauer details three kinds of cause that form a continuum throughout nature. First there is simple cause and effect, to which Newtonian principles apply, and which obtains in nature at the level of mechanics, physics, and chemistry; then, at the biological level, there is stimulus and response, where the degree of the effect is not proportional to the degree of the cause (increased heat or water will make plants grow faster up to a point, but beyond that point a very small change produces catastrophically different effects); and finally there is a kind of cause to which only animals, including humans, are subject, where the effect is mediated by cognition. These beings with minds can be motivated to act by their experiences. But that is just as much a case of cause and effect as anything else in the natural world. The connection between cause and effect becomes harder to grasp as we ascend from the impacts of billiard balls, through chemical and biological processes, to the overt behaviour of animals; but the essence—for Schopenhauer, the necessary connection of an effect with its cause—does not vary through the spectrum of cases.

An experience that occurs and moves me to act in such a way as to bring about a change in the world is, in Schopenhauer's vocabulary, a *motive*. Motives impact on my character and result in my willing some particular action, and if we assume both causal factors, the motive and my character, to be unchanged a second time around, then I could not do otherwise. It is a mere illusion to suppose that a different act of willing could have occurred in the same circumstances. However, we have an unshakeable sense of agency, a 'certainty that we ourselves are the *doers of our deeds*' (p. 112), and on this is founded our feeling of responsibility or accountability, which is not removed even by the conviction that we could not have acted otherwise. Schopenhauer suggests that I feel responsible for my character itself, for my being such that these particular actions have issued from me. What I *do* issues inescapably from what I *am*, and the feeling of guilt that results from my actions is ultimately explicable as guilt about my very being as an individual.

Character, for Schopenhauer, is distinctive to each individual, inborn and unchangeable. Any part of the natural world has its character—dispositions to behave in fixed ways on the occasion of causal influences—and the individual human being is no exception. Water will always boil at 100°C at sea level, fall headlong over a cliff-edge, and remain at rest in a stable receptacle. A human being will likewise always will, and act, in a particular way in a particular causal environment. The causes in our case include cognition of the physical world, conceptual classification, and reasoning, but this just makes for a vastly more complicated and less easily fathomable causal environment. It makes no difference to the basic pattern: an event takes place, which is the product of occurrent causal influences plus an unchanging, intrinsic disposition or nature. The great moral differences between human beings, of which Schopenhauer gives vivid examples, are put down to differences in their enduring natures. Each of us is to some extent egoistic, malicious, and compassionate by nature; that is to say, each of us has unchangeable dispositions to will our own well-being, to will the suffering of others, and to will the well-being of others and prevent or alleviate their suffering. The moral difference between human beings lies in the proportion in which these dispositions stand to one another. As a result, it is an error to suppose that one can bring about a fundamental moral change in someone by education. One can change the head, but not the heart, as Schopenhauer puts it. One can, for instance, teach an egoistic individual different concepts and arguments that will lead him or her to be egoistic in a more socially acceptable way. The person's will pursues its ends unalterably, and all one can do is channel it by providing it with alternative means to those ends — 'But no one can be talked out of egoism or malice any more than the cat can be of its inclination to mousing' (p. 255). Hence Schopenhauer's ethics is not a set of prescriptions (though 'preaching morals is easy...', as it says in the motto to the second essay (p. 121)). Rather, its task is to give a descriptive account of what constitutes moral goodness and explain its foundation: thus 'preaching morals is easy, grounding morals hard.'

A fair proportion of both these essays, but especially of *On the Basis of Morals*, comprises a dialogue with the philosophy of Immanuel Kant (1724–1804). Schopenhauer had already devoted one-fifth of his large work *The World as Will and Representation* to a critique of Kant's philosophy, in an Appendix prefaced with Voltaire's saying: 'It is the privilege of the true genius, and especially of the genius who opens up a pathway, to make great mistakes with impunity.' Schopenhauer admires Kant and adopts (or, as often as not, adapts) many of his concepts, but he is equally keen to remedy many of what he sees as his errors — and he thinks the latter predominate in the case of ethics. The second chapter of *On the Basis of Morals* is an extended critical essay on Kant's ethics, the teaching that had dominated the subject for the previous sixty years at Schopenhauer's time of writing, and that he argues must be cleared away so that a new start can be made. Kant's chief mistake, according to Schopenhauer, is his governing assumption that ethics must have an imperative form. Why are we

justified in thinking that we are to be commanded to act in certain
ways? How could such commands have an unconditional authority?
Where would the commands come from? In Schopenhauer's diagnosis
the genealogy of this notion is theological: the Judaeo-Christian God
could be pictured as issuing ten commandments which had the force
of laws that must be obeyed—but Kant expressly and rightly, in
Schopenhauer's view, forbids himself from giving an old-fashioned
theological foundation to ethics. If there is to be philosophical theology at all, it must be secondary to an independently grounded ethics.
Schopenhauer argues, then, that the assumption that ethics is about
a special kind of imperative, and an unconditional duty or 'ought', is
founded either on a surreptitious remnant of theology or on nothing.
Either way, it should not be admitted as an assumption in philosophical ethics. This criticism is quite far-reaching: the Kantian idea
that ethics is about a specially binding kind of obligation, and the
assumption that being morally good is a matter of following or giving
oneself some kind of law, are all called into question.

In light of this criticism, it might be questioned how we are to con-
strue Schopenhauer's principle of morality whose two parts, 'Harm
no one' and 'Help everyone', are also imperatives. Schopenhauer
takes the line that his moral principle is a summation of what is
already expressed in moral actions, and that what makes one's actions
moral is their issuing from a morally good character. One cannot be
commanded to be moral, nor will one become moral by learning any
propositions, principles, or concepts. However, the moral principle
is vital as a kind of reminder or back-up to aid agents in resisting the
non-moral dispositions which are also present in their characters:

although *principles* and abstract cognition generally are in no way the fountainhead or the prime basis of morality, they are nevertheless indispensable
for a moral course of life as the container, the *réservoir*, in which is
stored the disposition which has sprung from the source of all morality,
which disposition does not flow in every moment . . . Without firmly held
*principles* we should inevitably be vulnerable to anti-moral incentives when
they are aroused to affects by external impressions. (p. 218)

In other words, we are constantly liable to being provoked into seeking our own well-being or seeking to harm others, and cannot always
rely on a felt response to the suffering of others that motivates us to
act, even though we are the kind of person who is frequently disposed to do so. Being mindful of the moral principle can guide our

actions and keep them in line with what a person who felt compassion would do.

Returning to Schopenhauer's critique of Kant, we find him disapproving of the attempt to give an *a priori* foundation to ethics that looks away from any empirical or anthropological data, concluding that such an ethics can only rest in mid-air, on insubstantial, contentless concepts without application to the real lives of human beings. During a thorough analysis of Kant's *Groundwork of the Metaphysics of Morals* and *Critique of Practical Reason*, Schopenhauer produces criticisms of many other central Kantian concepts, such as 'highest good', 'end in itself', and 'the dignity of the human being'. On the other hand, Schopenhauer relies on certain elements of Kant's theoretical philosophy for his descriptive picture of human experience and action. He praises as Kant's greatest achievement the division between appearances and things in themselves, together with his claim that the world of objects in space and time, the objects of our cognition, can only be the world as it appears to us, while the world as it is in itself remains impossible for us to know. This position, referred to by Kant and Schopenhauer as *transcendental idealism*, provides the platform for the whole system of thought that is laid out in *The World as Will and Representation* and partially recapitulated in the two essays on ethics. Human cognition is of a world of objects, which must, for our cognition, be structured by certain *a priori* forms—space, time, and causality—that are not extrapolated from experience of objects but are the very conditions of its possibility. The empirical or experienced world is made up of matter, differentiated into objects by the necessary structure of space, time, and causal laws. This world of objects is what Schopenhauer calls 'the world as representation' (*die Welt als Vorstellung*), that is, the world as it necessarily presents itself to any subject of experience. But the world as representation does not exhaust reality, because we can conceive of the world's existing independently of the way it is structured for us by the conditions of our experience. The world also exists in itself (*an sich*). This dichotomy of representation and thing in itself runs right through *The World as Will and Representation* as a theme on which Schopenhauer plays many variations. The principal point we shall need to grasp is that, departing radically from Kant in a way that the latter would have found shocking, Schopenhauer claims that in itself the world is *will*.

The will, for Schopenhauer, is the single underlying reality beneath all appearances, and the true core of the human individual: each of us, in this sense, has the same essence, and we share it with all other beings in nature. The will is a force of sheer striving: it is not essentially rational, but 'blind', driving us constantly to act in pursuit of ends, the most basic of which are keeping ourselves alive and reproducing the species. Because it is the metaphysical essence of all of us, this striving never ceases in the life of an ordinary human being, and striving inevitably brings with it suffering. Schopenhauer's vision of human life in *The World as Will and Representation* is often seen as unremittingly pessimistic: we exist as manifestations of an insatiable urge to perpetuate life, and are always at its mercy. Whatever we achieve by willing never satisfies us: whenever a desire or need is satisfied, new desires rush in, and when a desire remains unsatisfied, we suffer. If we briefly satisfy all our current desires, we suffer again, through boredom. And there is no ultimate goal, or at any rate nothing attainable by willing, that gives an overall point to this existence.

Although little of this picture of human life or of the full metaphysical background to it makes an explicit appearance in the essays, some aspects of Schopenhauer's ethical system stand out more prominently when viewed in the light of *The World as Will and Representation*: for example, his notion that the very core of each human individual is will, not intellect or reason; his likening of human beings to hungry and vicious beasts kept in check only by the sanctions of law and state justice; his intolerance of the idea of moral progress or improvement of humanity; and his emphasis on the vulnerability of human beings to suffering. But the Norwegian and Danish essay competitions both required anonymous submissions, and although the Kantian division between thing in itself and representation would have been more than familiar to Schopenhauer's audience, expounding his own idiosyncratic version of it might have blown his cover—or more likely (given the relatively little attention his works had so far received) left him appearing to make novel and extravagant metaphysical pronouncements without the space to argue for them. Schopenhauer sometimes complains that any ethics is incomplete without a metaphysics; yet the discipline of dealing with the central questions of ethics in their own right and starting from more generally accessible assumptions undoubtedly led to a clearer presentation of his position on free will, the foundation of morals, and associated issues than he ever achieved elsewhere.

There are, however, two uses of the central metaphysical distinction between appearance and thing in itself that play important roles in the essays, one in application to the question of responsibility, the other in the explanation of the nature of compassion. In his earlier dissertation *On the Fourfold Root of the Principle of Sufficient Reason* Schopenhauer argued that the world as represented by a subject of experience necessarily consists of objects standing in a number of explanatory relations to one another. He had learned from Kant that space, time, and the connection between cause and effect pertain only to the world as representation, only to appearances, and not to the thing in itself. Space, time, and causality are, as it were, the rules for connecting objects together by which our faculty for cognition operates, and it operates in these ways because it must: space, time, and causality are '*a priori* forms of the understanding', ways of structuring cognition that are necessary because they are conditions of the possibility of experience. (Schopenhauer alters the layout of cognition found in Kant's *Critique of Pure Reason*: he retains Kant's distinction between intuition (*Anschauung*) and concept (*Begriff*), but does not assign the former to sensibility and the latter to the understanding in the way Kant does. For Schopenhauer, intuition, the perceptual awareness of particular things in space and time, involves the working of the understanding to create the distinction between a subjective sensation and the object taken to cause it, but this is not a case of conceptual judgement.) The account Schopenhauer gives of the *a priori* forms of intuition has the corollary that the world considered as existing beyond its appearance for our cognition, the world in itself, exists timelessly and cannot be regarded as causing anything. So Schopenhauer holds that representation and thing in itself are the obverse and reverse sides of the same reality. The world exists timelessly but also manifests itself in time as the individual objects and events that we experience—the one world 'objectifies itself' in time and space; in other words, it shows to us that aspect of itself that consists of a huge multiplicity of changing and interacting objects and events.

Now all of this impacts on the manner in which we view the human agent. Kant had proposed to resolve the difficulty of reconciling free will with the causal order of nature—a difficulty which he sets out as an antinomy, or pair of arguments for incompatible conclusions—by distinguishing two aspects of the agent, the *empirical character* and the *intelligible character*. My empirical character is best taken to consist of all the ways, discoverable through experience, in which I am disposed to behave as an object in space and time, producing my actions as the effects of natural causes. My intelligible character is supposed to be that aspect of myself that cannot be experienced, but which can be thought of as existing outside of the forms that govern experience. Under that aspect I can (and for Kant I must) regard myself as radically free to initiate my own actions. In both his essays on ethics Schopenhauer praises Kant effusively for the discovery of this distinction between empirical and intelligible characters, which, he says, 'belongs among the most beautiful and most profound ideas which this great mind, indeed, which humankind has ever produced' (p. 114), and goes on to appropriate the distinction for himself. Thus, the dramatic conclusion of the prize essay on freedom has it that:

> the empirical character, like the whole person, is as an object of experience, a mere appearance, hence bound by the forms of all appearance, time, space, and causality, and subject to their laws. By contrast, his *intelligible character*, which is the condition and basis of this whole appearance, is independent of these forms and, hence, subject to no time-distinction; consequently, it is constant and unalterable. For his will, as thing in itself, is of such quality, that to it certainly belongs absolute freedom, i.e., independence of the laws of causality (as a mere form of appearances). This freedom, however, is a transcendental one, i.e., not occurring in appearance, but only present insofar as we abstract from appearance and all its forms in order to arrive at that which, outside of all time, is to be thought of as the inner being of the person in himself. . . .
>
> As is easy to see, this path leads to the point that we must no longer seek the work of our *freedom*, as does the common view, in our individual actions, but in the whole being and essence (*existentia et essentia*) of the human being himself. This work must be thought of as the human being's free deed that merely presents itself to the cognitive faculty, linked to time, space, and causality as a plurality and diversity of actions. (p. 115)

What does this mean? First, note how much has changed in Schopenhauer's act of appropriating Kant's profound idea. For Kant, the idea of transcendental freedom attached to *reason*, or myself considered as rational, in which capacity I must be responsive to the force of the distinctive 'ought' of the moral law. To consider myself as responding purely rationally to a moral imperative, I have to disregard myself considered solely as part of nature, under the sway of natural, not to say earthy, inclinations and desires. That natural self is not a possible recipient of the 'ought' because it cannot act otherwise than nature prompts it to. But Schopenhauer will have none of this: when he speaks of people's 'will, as thing in itself', he means their nature, their deep inner essence, a pre-rational orientation to act that informs all their desires and inclinations and is of a kind with the essence of every other part of the natural world. At one point in *The World as Will and Representation* Schopenhauer refers to Kant's solution of the antinomy between freedom and causality as the point where his own philosophy springs from Kant's as from its parent stem. But it is vital for an understanding of both philosophers to see how misleading that metaphor is in one respect, for in this case the offspring and parent belong to quite different species of plant.

Can we make sense of Schopenhauer's attribution of freedom to the 'whole being and essence of the human being himself'? In what sense can my being be a deed? My coming into existence might at least be construed as an event. But my existence as such does not even seem to be an event, let alone something that is done by me or by anyone. And even my coming into existence does not seem to be something that I do. To make matters worse, the being and essence of me, if it does not belong to the empirical realm, is not party to space, time, and causality (though, as we hear, it presents itself in those forms, appearing as the many actions that express my essence): how are we to think of it as a 'deed' when it is not something that occurs in time? Had Schopenhauer had the benefit of an exposition of his metaphysics, he might perhaps have presented his conclusion a little differently. For in *The World as Will and Representation* it is not so much my individual will that is free, but rather *the will*, or the world as a whole, that, uncaused by anything outside itself, manifests itself in time and space as many things and events, including my essential character from which my actions follow. From this point of view my existence and my essence are contingent, and consciousness of myself as this contingent individual from whom necessarily flow acts of will that impinge on the wills of other beings burdens me with a sense of responsibility for my very existence. Schopenhauer has the idea that one rightly feels guilt about one's existing as an individual who expresses will, and sometimes links this notion with the Christian doctrine of original sin.

Nietzsche later described Schopenhauer as 'the first admitted and uncompromising atheist among us Germans' (*The Gay Science*, § 357), and there is indeed nothing remotely resembling a God, divine mind, or all-powerful being anywhere in Schopenhauer's system of thought. He is also scathing about theology and its detrimental influence on ethics. However, Schopenhauer's relations to religion are more complex than these observations might suggest. In the essays he is entirely dismissive of Islam and Judaism, adopting in the latter case the particularly offensive Latin term *foetor Judaicus* or 'Judaic stench'. But he allies himself strongly with certain carefully selected features of Christianity, Buddhism, and Hinduism, as he understands them. The differing dogmas of religions are really of little interest to him; rather, he is concerned with the kind of moral vision that underlies them. *The World as Will and Representation* has as its final message the need for salvation or redemption from an existence full of suffering, which it finds in the ideas of sainthood and denial of the individual will. Schopenhauer relies on his own philosophical resources to construct this position, but motivates it by drawing parallels with the mystical traditions of Christianity and the major Indian religions, areas of thought in which he was well read. While he was in the early stages of preparing for what would become *The World as Will and Representation* Schopenhauer had acquired a version of the ancient Indian *Upanishads*, translated into Latin by a scholar named Anquetil-Duperron under the title *Oupnek'hat*. It became one of his favourite books, from which he would quote throughout the remainder of his career, and it awakened in him an interest in collecting and studying other books and journals from the growing field of scholarship on Asiatic thought.

Schopenhauer was especially struck by Indian ideas about the illusoriness of the world of ordinary experience to which we are attached by desire, and the doctrine of the individual's identity with the rest of reality. In the essay *On the Basis of Morals* some of these ideas assist him, at least rhetorically, in presenting a final 'metaphysical basis' for his account of compassion. For Schopenhauer the phenomenon of compassion involves one person's feeling something towards another—but what exactly? He suggests that when I apprehend someone else as suffering, I can sometimes feel his or her suffering

(I suffer along with the other, as the German word for compassion, *Mitleid*, or 'suffering with', literally suggests). I do this, not by imagining the suffering, however fleetingly, to be mine, but by feeling it *'with* him, thus, *in* him: we feel his pain as *his* and do not imagine that it is ours' (p. 215). Suffering in sympathy with another can then turn my will towards alleviating or preventing the other's suffering, and this is compassionate, morally good, action. (If I prevented or assuaged someone's suffering solely egoistically, that is, out of a motivation to enhance my own well-being, perhaps through gaining reward or admiration, then my action would not be one of moral worth, for Schopenhauer.) So his question is, 'how is it possible that my will is immediately moved by *another's* well-being and woe, i.e., just as otherwise my will is only moved by my own well-being and woe' (p. 212)? He answers:

Obviously only through this: that another becomes *the ultimate end* of my will just as, otherwise, I am; and so through this: that I immediately will *his* well-being and do not will *his* woe, just as I otherwise immediately will only *that of my own*. This, however, necessarily presupposes that I suffer along with *his* woe, feel *his* woe, as otherwise I would only mine, and therefore, I immediately will his well-being as, otherwise, I would only my own. However this requires that I *be identified with him* in some way, i.e., that the complete *distinction* between me and the other, upon precisely which my egoism rests, to a certain degree be suspended. (p. 212)

We commonly speak of 'identifying' with someone else: Schopenhauer takes this in an uncommon sense and gives a radical metaphysical interpretation of what compassion involves.

The initial clue lies in his comment that the distinction between myself and the other is suspended. Recall the dichotomy of representation and thing in itself, and the claim that while the world as we represent it in cognition is subordinate to the forms of space and time, the world as it is in itself is not subordinate to those forms. Schopenhauer consistently takes the view that what distinguishes one individual thing from another is their different locations in space and time. Only two things that exhibit some difference in their trajectory through space and time can really be distinct things. Space and time together constitute the 'principle of individuation', or in the Latin that Schopenhauer likes to use, the *principium individuationis*. A human individual, empirically considered, is a being in space and time that is distinct from other individuals that also occupy space and time. But the world is not only there for our experience, it is not only a world as representation, but also a world that exists at the level of the 'in itself', and so we come once again to the idea that we can consider ourselves under two quite different aspects. Only now, rather than appealing to the idea that there is an 'in itself' or timeless character peculiar to me, Schopenhauer invokes the *principium individuationis*: in the world as it is in itself, with time and space removed, there are no distinctions and hence *no individuals* at all.

Hence, if plurality and separateness belong only to *appearance*, and if it is one and the same essence that presents itself in everything living, then that apprehension which suspends the distinction between I and Not-I is not in error. Rather it must be the opposite that is in error. We also find this latter indicated by Hindus with the name *Māyā*, i.e., illusion, deception, phantasm. (p. 267)

Which human outlook regards the distinction of I and Not-I as absolute and insurmountable? That of someone who pursues his or her own well-being and remains detached from the sufferings of all others—the egoist for whom everything that is not him- or herself is alien ('Not-I') and only instrumentally important. On the other hand, compassionate action, given that it depends on weakening the perceived distinctness of individuals, is an expression of the view of the world in itself beyond the principle of individuation:

This view, then, would be the metaphysical basis of ethics, and it would consist in the fact that *one* individual immediately recognizes in *another* himself, his own, true essence. Thus, as a result, practical wisdom, doing right and doing good, would coincide exactly with the most profound teaching of the most far-reaching theoretical wisdom, and the practical philosopher, i.e., the just, the benevolent, the generous person, would express through his deed the same knowledge that is just the outcome of the theoretical philosopher's greatest thoughtfulness and most laborious inquiry. Meanwhile moral excellence stands higher than all theoretical wisdom, which is always just a patchwork and reaches its goal through the slow path of inferences which the other reaches with a single stroke, and the one who is morally noble, even if he is so very lacking in intellectual excellence, reveals through his action the deepest knowledge, the highest wisdom, and shames the most gifted and learned if through their deeds they reveal that this great truth indeed remains foreign to their hearts. (pp. 267–8)

So, morally good people need not be metaphysicians. They do not even have to be especially educated, to have espoused any particular religious doctrine, or have learned any general principles prescriptive of the right way to act. What they are able to do, because of a disposition that resides in their essential character, is feel a sense of oneness with the whole, and attain an intuitive glimpse into the fundamental truth (the truth according to Schopenhauer and the various philosophical and religious traditions he invokes) that all is one, that separateness as such is not present at the most fundamental level of reality. Thus it is that, in Schopenhauer's view, metaphysics is required for ethics, not exactly in order to be compassionate, but rather to show theoretically how compassion is possible. But he needs this metaphysics also to show why acting out of the pure incentive of compassion is *better* than acting egoistically, and why morality has greater force in the end than egoism or malice. We have been told that only action arising out of the incentive of compassion has genuine moral worth. But there can be, for Schopenhauer, no absolute obligation to act morally. Rationality does not require it—indeed, he points out how morally evil characters can succeed on a greater scale by pursuing their ends rationally. The natural and expected way for human beings to act is egoistically': so much so, that their ever doing otherwise seems mysterious. So why is it better to act morally than not? It seems implicit for Schopenhauer that suffering is bad *per se*, and that a character oriented towards diminishing suffering is therefore good. But even more fundamental for him is the thought that what makes some people's character good, what orients them principally towards the lessening of suffering in others, is their intuitive insight into a deeper truth, their being cognitively attuned to the undifferentiated reality of the thing in itself. So it seems that Schopenhauer's final ground for morality, his justification of the claim that it is better to act morally than egoistically, lies in our having reason to seek the truth and act in accordance with it, and in morality's being the way, or a way, of taking us closer to the truth. To be morally bad or indifferent thus represents an error in understanding reality: our individuality itself is a kind of illusion for us, or at any rate a superficial and problematic condition that fails to be a trustworthy guide to what really is.

More recent ethical theorists have not tended to regard Schopenhauer's work as a prime historical reference-point. This means that the links and contrasts between Schopenhauer's ethics and contemporary ethics are much less explored than arguably they could or should be. Many of the issues around which Schopenhauer's essays revolve clearly remain central to ethics today. There has been no cessation to debates about free will, which contemporary philosophy tends to place where Schopenhauer places them, at the intersection between ethics and metaphysics. Such debates often continue to refer back to earlier treatments, and Schopenhauer may help here by giving us (in chapter 4 of the essay on freedom) an interesting history of the issue, from faint half-recognitions of the problem in Aristotle, through the Christian treatments of Augustine and Luther, to the early modern positions of Spinoza, Hume, Voltaire, and Priestley, and on to Kant and German Idealism. His own position combines a forthright and coherent determinism with the claim that the truth of determinism is powerless to convince us that we lack responsibility—in broad terms at least, a recognizable position in more recent thinking about the problem of free will. His very powerful naturalistic conviction of the continuity between human action and the behaviour of other organisms (though pre-Darwinian both chronologically and doctrinally) and his consequent problematizing of the nature of human self-consciousness and rationality give him a recognizable continuity with much of today's philosophy, as does his outrage at human cruelty to animals and his campaign to accord them the same kind of moral respect as we accord ourselves.

As regards the foundation of morals, Schopenhauer's critique of Kant, combined with the fact that he nonetheless remains within the Kantian ambience, gives him much in common with parts of contemporary ethical theory, Kantianism being still one of the most complete and influential accounts of ethics to date. The recent growth of virtue ethics, with its concentration on virtue and moral character rather than on rules, imperatives, or duties, is to some extent prefigured by Schopenhauer's insistence on purifying ethics of the notions of lawgiving and unconditionally authoritative obligations which he diagnoses as relics of an outmoded theological basis for morals, and his foregrounding of moral character-traits, feelings, and a compassionate way of responding to the world. A major point of reference for many of today's virtue ethicists is Aristotle's ethics, from which Schopenhauer explicitly distances himself on the grounds that 'eudaimonism' (the linking of virtue with *eudaimonia*, a term sometimes, if misleadingly, translated as 'happiness') is fundamentally wrong. Virtue, in Schopenhauer's view, is essentially non-egoistic, while to make 'happiness' the goal of life is to consign it ultimately to egoistic motivation—though recent work has suggested that this is a mistaken view about Aristotle and about ancient ethics more generally. An examination of Schopenhauer's ethics in the light of the lively current debates around virtue ethics and its divergences from Kantian ethics (and around Kant's own accounts of the virtues) has not yet occurred, but the time seems more ripe for this now than at any period since 1840. It would also be interesting to examine Schopenhauer's relationship with consequentialism, the other dominant trend in modern ethics: does he, or should we, see moral worth as residing primarily in enduring character-traits that make an agent compassionate, or rather in outcomes that prevent the most suffering and promote the most well-being?

Among figures that contemporary philosophy regards as important, by far the greatest influence of Schopenhauer's ethics was on Friedrich Nietzsche (1844–1900). At the beginning of his *On the Genealogy of Morals* (1887) Nietzsche refers to Schopenhauer as 'my great teacher', and simultaneously states that it was fighting his way out of Schopenhauer's conception of morality that taught him most. Nietzsche had been an ardent devotee of Schopenhauer's philosophy in his early period of the 1860s and 1870s. When he later calls for the value of moral values to be called into question, it is clear that Schopenhauer's ethics is a major factor in focusing him on his target. A system of philosophy for which God is dead, but that allies itself with Christian values and glorifies 'the instincts of compassion, self-abnegation, self-sacrifice', an ethics that explicitly courts alliance with what Nietzsche sees as the 'nihilism' of Buddhism—these specifically Schopenhauerian characteristics become for Nietzsche the key that opens up a critique of Western values on a wider scale. His central concerns of revealing the 'life-denying' qualities of morality and metaphysics, and undermining the value placed upon compassion, are essentially shaped by his reception of Schopenhauer's ethics, so that for anyone concerned with Nietzsche's critique of morality, as many philosophers increasingly are, Schopenhauer is required reading.

# NOTE ON THE TEXT AND TRANSLATION

*The Two Fundamental Problems of Ethics* contains Schopenhauer's two substantive essays on ethical subjects, 'Prize Essay on the Freedom of the Will' ('Preisschrift über die Freiheit des Willens') and 'Prize Essay on the Basis of Morals' ('Preisschrift über die Grundlage der Moral'). As given immediately above, the title of each essay is as it is found on a separate title-sheet placed at the beginning of the respective essay. However, on the title-page for the book Schopenhauer enumerates the two essays, giving the titles as submitted to the prize essay competitions. As submitted to the Royal Norwegian Society in 1838, the first essay was titled 'On the Freedom of the Human Will' ('Ueber die Freiheit des menschlichen Willens'). The second essay, submitted to the Royal Danish Society in 1839, was titled 'On the Foundation of Morals' (Ueber das Fundament der Moral').

Schopenhauer wrote both of these essays for prize competitions that required anonymous, self-contained monographs not presupposing knowledge of his philosophical work. Nonetheless, Schopenhauer held that the two essays, taken together, were an essential supplement to the fourth book of *The World as Will and Representation*, and he published the essays together. The two essays were first published in German by the Frankfurt publishing house of Johann Christian Hermann'sche Buchandlung, F. E. Suchsland, in September of 1840 (with an 1841 publication date). The second edition was published in September 1860, twenty years to the month after the first appearance, and just a few days before Schopenhauer's death. This second edition, from the Leipzig publisher F. A. Brockhaus, included both the preface from the first edition and Schopenhauer's shorter, but no less vitriolic, second preface.

Our translation is from the text of *The Two Fundamental Problems of Ethics* (*Die beiden Grundprobleme der Ethik*) in the fourth volume of Arthur Hübscher's edition of the collected works of Schopenhauer, long recognized as the standard German source in the field, serving Schopenhauer studies for decades. Although based on the first complete edition of Schopenhauer's works, edited by Schopenhauer's friend and literary executor Julius Frauenstädt (1873), Hübscher's *Arthur Schopenhauer: Sämtliche Werke* is the product of over 100 years of textual and philological criticism. We are indebted to the seventh volume of the 1988 edition of the *Sämtliche Werke* for completions and corrections of some of Schopenhauer's citations and for identifying authors and other figures now obscured by time. In completing this translation we have also consulted the earlier, scholarly edition of Schopenhauer's works edited by Paul Deussen, now available on CD-ROM. And although the present translation is our responsibility, we were greatly aided by consulting the work of earlier translators. English translators of the first essay, 'Preisschrift über die Freiheit des Willens', are Konstantin Kolenda (1960) and E. J. F. Payne, edited by Günther Zöller (1999). English translators of the second essay, 'Preisschrift über die Grundlage der Moral', are Arthur Broderick Bullock (1915) and E. J. F. Payne, edited by David E. Cartwright (1997). We have especially benefited by consulting Christopher Janaway's manuscript translation prepared for his *Cambridge Edition of the Works of Arthur Schopenhauer*.

## Textual Apparatus

Our translation includes marginal indications of the pagination of the 1860 edition, as provided by Hübscher, which generally also correspond to the pagination of the Hübscher edition. Footnotes, indicated by superscript figures, serve two purposes: the first is to provide Schopenhauer's own notes; the second is to provide foreign-language terms and quotations from Schopenhauer's text. In a few instances we preserve a Latin term of craft, such as *contradictio in adjecto*, giving a translation in the Explanatory Notes when the term first occurs.

Any brackets in the text or footnotes indicate material we have supplied. Other explanatory material is relegated to the Explanatory Notes, indicated by asterisks.

In the body of the translation we preserve Schopenhauer's citations, but in the Explanatory Notes or brackets in footnotes we frequently provide more information about the author and, in some cases, the citation, as, for example, to conform citations to classical text to contemporary practice. In the Explanatory Notes we also supply citations to Kant's works, indicating what is commonly called the 'Academy Edition', that is, *Kant's Gesammelte Schriften*, edited by the Royal Prussian (later German) Academy of Sciences (Berlin: Georg Reimer, later Walter de Gruyter, 1900–   ).

The German editions of the essays translated here use two forms of type for emphasis: *Sperrdruck*, s p a c e d   t y p e, and *Fettdruck*, **boldface**. We use *italic* type for the former and **boldface** for the latter. We have not, however, followed Schopenhauer's somewhat inconsistent practice of putting all personal names in *Sperrdruck*. We have used vernacular forms of Latinized names of modern figures, as, for example, using René Descartes for *Renatus Cartesius*.

## Translators' Principles

In keeping with the purpose of Oxford World's Classics, our translation aims to serve the student and general reader. In translating we have attempted to select words or syntactic structures so as not to favour interpretations, and although our text is primarily intended for students, we have tried to avoid notes which might determine or constrain readers' interpretations of Schopenhauer's text. Moreover, we have left it to the 'educated nose of the reader of the essay [to] catch the scent of the rotted spot'[(12)].

Because Schopenhauer himself was aware of the sometimes un-orthodox nature of his writing, having claimed that this was a function of his thinking (see e.g. *Gesammelte Briefe*, letter to F. A. Brockhaus of 7 Sept. 1843 and letter to Frauenstädt of 24 Nov. 1855), we have attempted to approximate the original, so as to allow our readers something of the experience of Schopenhauer's prose. To this end we have retained his paragraph structure. Where practicable, we have also sought not to sacrifice literalness for readability, and not unwar-rantedly to constrain reader's interpretive work. However, since readers of current English are generally more accustomed to syntax of more limited range than that of Schopenhauer's German, and since English is generally not inflected for gender but relies more on syntactic order, we have often had to approximate syntax and sometimes to supply the referent noun or noun-phrase where Schopenhauer used a pronoun. Nevertheless, in a few instances a passage is ambiguous in the German, so we have retained the ambiguity for our readers.

We have also followed Schopenhauer's use of abbreviations and in a few instances his non-standard punctuation, such as '?!'. In particular, we have preserved his use of dashes and added none of our own. Schopenhauer often uses the dash between sentences, in very few instances within sentences, rarely, for emphasis (the common practice today), and even to indicate omissions within quotations (a function nowadays of the ellipsis).

We provide the following glossary for those interested in key terms. It should be noted that while we generally translate the terms as listed below, there are instances in which alternate translations were warranted.

| | |
|---|---|
| acting | *Handeln* |
| action | *Handlung* |
| agent | *Handelnden* |
| apprehension | *Auffassung* |
| basis | *Grundlage* |
| cognition, recognition, or knowledge | *Erkenntnis, Kenntnis* |
| compassion | *Mitleid* |
| deed | *Tat* |
| doer | *Täter* |
| doing(s) | *Tun* |
| egoism | *Egoismus* |
| essence or being | *Wesen* |
| ethics | *Ethik* |
| ground(s), reason(s) | *Grund* |
| grounding, reason | *Begründung* |
| incentive | *Triebfeder* |
| injury | *Verletzung* |
| injustice | *Unrechtigkeit* |
| intuition | *Anschauung* |
| justice | *Gerechtigkeit* |
| loving kindness | *Menschenliebe* |
| malice | *Bosheit* |
| morality | *Moralität* |
| morals | *Moral* |
| participation | *Teilnehmung* |
| reason | *Vernunft* |
| reprehensible | *verwerflich* |
| representation | *Vorstellung* |
| right | *Recht* |
| to act | *handeln* |
| to do | *tun* |
| understanding | *Verstand* |

| | |
|---|---|
| urphenomenon | *Urphänomen* |
| voluntary | *willkürlich* |
| way of acting | *Handlungsweise* |
| will | *Wille* |
| willing | *Wollen* |
| wrong | *Unrecht* |

# SELECT BIBLIOGRAPHY

### German Editions of Schopenhauer's Works

*Gesammelte Briefe*, ed. Arthur Hübscher (Bonn: Bouvier, 1978).
*Der handschriftlicher Nachlaß*, ed. Arthur Hübscher, 5 vols. (Frankfurt-am-Main: Kramer, 1970).
*Faksimilenachdruck der 1. Auflage der Welt als Wille und Vorstellung*, ed. Rudolf Malter (Frankfurt-am-Main: Insel, 1987).
*Philosophische Vorlesungen, aus dem handschriftlichen Nachlaß*, 4 vols., ed. Volker Spierling (Munich: R. Piper, 1984–6).
*Die Reisetagbücher*, ed. Ludger Lütkehaus (Zurich: Haffmans, 1988).
*Sämtliche Werke*, 4th edn., ed. Arthur Hübscher, 7 vols. (Mannheim: F. A. Brockhaus, 1988).
*Schopenhauer im Kontext*, CD-ROM, ed. Paul Deussen [1911–23]; vols. I–V, and vol. VI (selections) (Berlin: Karsten Worm InfoSoftWare, 2001).
*Werke in fünf Bänden. Nach den Ausgaben letzter Hand*, ed. Ludger Lütkehaus, 5 vols. (Zurich: Haffmans, 1988).
*Werke in zehn Bänden (Zürcher Ausgabe)*, ed. Arthur Hübscher, 10 vols. (Zurich: Diogenes, 1977).

### English Translations of Schopenhauer's Works

*The Basis of Morality*, trans. Arthur Broderick Bullock (London: Swan Sonnenschein, 1903; 2nd edn., London: Allen & Unwin, 1915).
*On the Basis of Morality*, trans. E. F. J. Payne (Indianapolis: Bobbs-Merrill, 1965); revised edn., ed. David E. Cartwright (Oxford: Berghahn, 1995; repr. Indianapolis: Hackett, 1997).
*Essay on the Freedom of the Will*, trans. Konstantin Kolenda (Indianapolis: Bobbs-Merrill, 1960; repr. Oxford: Blackwell, 1985).
*On the Fourfold Root of the Principle of Sufficient Reason*, trans. E. F. J. Payne (La Salle, Ill.: Open Court, 1974).
*On the Fourfold Root of the Principle of Sufficient Reason and On the Will in Nature*, trans. Mme. Karl Hillebrand (London: George Bell & Sons, 1891).
*Manuscript Remains*, trans. E. F. J. Payne, 4 vols. (Oxford: Berg, 1988).
*Parerga and Paralipomena*, trans. E. F. J. Payne, 2 vols. (Oxford: Clarendon Press, 1974).
*Prize Essay on the Freedom of the Will*, ed. Günter Zöller, trans. E. F. J. Payne (Cambridge: Cambridge University Press, 1999).

*Schopenhauer's Early 'Fourfold Root': Translation and Commentary*, F. C. White (Aldershot: Avebury, 1997).

*The Two Fundamental Problems of Ethics*, trans. Christopher Janaway (Cambridge: Cambridge University Press, 2009): vol. 3 of Christopher Janaway (gen. ed.), *The Cambridge Edition of the Works of Schopenhauer*, 6 vols. (2009– ).

*On Vision and Colors*, ed. David E. Cartwright, trans. E. F. J. Payne (Oxford: Berg, 1994).

*On the Will in Nature*, ed. David E. Cartwright, trans. E. F. J. Payne (New York: Berg, 1992).

*The World as Will and Idea*, trans. R. B. Haldane and J. Kemp, 3 vols. (London: Routledge & Kegan Paul, 1883).

*The World as Will and Idea: Abridged in One Volume*, trans. J. Berman, ed. D. Berman (London: Everyman, 1995).

*The World as Will and Presentation*, vol. 1, trans. Richard E. Aquila in collaboration with David Carus (New York: Pearson/Longman, 2008).

*The World as Will and Representation*, trans. E. F. J. Payne, 2 vols. (New York: Dover, 1969).

### Books and Edited Collections in English

Atwell, John E., *Schopenhauer on the Character of the World: The Metaphysics of Will* (Berkeley: University of California Press, 1995).

Atwell, John E., *Schopenhauer: The Human Character* (Philadelphia: Temple University Press, 1990).

Ausmus, Harry J., *A Schopenhauer Critique of Nietzsche's Thought: Toward Restoration of Metaphysics* (Lewiston, NY: Edwin Mellen Press, 1996).

Barua, Arati, *The Philosophy of Arthur Schopenhauer* (New Dehli: Intellectual Publishing House, 1992).

—— (ed.), *Schopenhauer and Indian Philosophy: A Dialogue between India and Germany* (New Delhi: Northern Book Centre, 2008).

Bridgewater, Patrick, *Arthur Schopenhauer's English Schooling* (New York: Routledge, 1988).

Bykhovsky, Bernard, *Schopenhauer and the Ground of Existence*, trans. Philip Moran (Amsterdam: B. R. Grumer, 1984).

Cartwright, David E., *Historical Dictionary of Schopenhauer's Philosophy* (Lanham, Md.: Scarecrow Press, 2005).

—— *Schopenhauer: A Biography* (New York: Cambridge University Press, 2010).

Copleston, Frederick, *Arthur Schopenhauer: Philosopher of Pessimism* (1947; repr. London: Search Press, 1975).

Dauer, Dorothea W., *Schopenhauer as Transmitter of Buddhist Ideas* (Berne: Herbert Lang, 1969).

Fox, Michael (ed.), *Schopenhauer: His Philosophical Achievement* (Totowa, NJ: Barnes & Noble, 1980).

Gardiner, Patrick, *Schopenhauer* (Harmondsworth: Penguin Books, 1963; repr. Bristol: Thoemmes Press, 1997).

Gonzales, Robert A., *An Approach to the Sacred in the Thought of Schopenhauer* (Lewiston, NY: Edwin Mellen Press, 1992).

Hamlyn, D. W., *Schopenhauer* (London: Routledge & Kegan Paul, 1980).

Hannen, Barbara, *The Riddle of the World: A Reconsideration of Schopenhauer's Philosophy* (Oxford: Oxford University Press, 2009).

Hübscher, Arthur, *The Philosophy of Schopenhauer in its Intellectual Context*, trans. Joachim Baer and David E. Cartwright (Lewiston, NY: Edwin Mellen Press, 1989).

Jacquette, Dale (ed.), *Schopenhauer, Philosophy, and the Arts* (Cambridge: Cambridge University Press, 1996).

—— *The Philosophy of Schopenhauer* (London: Acumen, 2005).

Janaway, Christopher, *Schopenhauer: A Very Short Introduction* (Oxford: Oxford University Press, 2002).

—— *Self and World in Schopenhauer's Philosophy* (Oxford: Clarendon Press, 1989).

—— (ed.), *The Cambridge Companion to Schopenhauer* (Cambridge: Cambridge University Press, 1999).

—— (ed.), *Willing and Nothingness: Schopenhauer as Nietzsche's Educator* (Oxford: Clarendon Press, 1998).

Knox, Israel, *The Aesthetic Theories of Kant, Hegel, and Schopenhauer* (1936; repr. New York: Humanities Press, 1958).

Krukowski, Lucian, *Aesthetic Legacies* (Philadelphia: Temple University Press, 1993).

Lauxtermann, P. F. H., *Schopenhauer's Broken World-View: Colours and Ethics Between Kant and Goethe* (Dordrecht: Kluwer Academic Publishers, 2000).

von der Luft, Eric (ed.), *Schopenhauer: New Essays in Honor of His 200th Birthday* (Lewiston, NY: Edwin Mellen Press, 1988).

McGill, V. J., *Schopenhauer: Pessimist and Pagan* (New York: Haskell House, 1971).

Magee, Bryan, *The Philosophy of Schopenhauer* (Oxford: Clarendon Press, 1997).

Mannion, Gerard, *Schopenhauer, Religion and Morality: The Humble Path to Ethics* (London: Ashgate, 2003).

Marcin, Raymond B., *In Search of Schopenhauer's Cat: Arthur Schopenhauer's Quantum-Mystical Theory of Justice* (Washington, DC: Catholic University of America Press, 2006).

Neeley, G. Steven, *Schopenhauer: A Consistent Reading* (Lewiston, NY: Edwin Mellen Press, 2003).

Safranksi, Rüdiger, *Schopenhauer and the Wild Years of Philosophy*, trans. Ewald Osers (London: Weidenfeld & Nicolson, 1989).

Simmel, Georg, *Schopenhauer and Nietzsche*, trans. Helmut Loikandl, Deena Weinstein, and Michael Weinstein (Amherst: University of Massachusetts Press, 1986).

Singh, R. Raj, *Death, Contemplation and Schopenhauer* (Burlington, Vt.: Ashgate, 2007).

Tanner, Michael, *Schopenhauer: Metaphysics and Art* (London: Phoenix, 1998).

Weiner, David Abraham, *Genius and Talent: Schopenhauer's Influence on Wittgenstein's Early Philosophy* (Rutherford: Fairleigh Dickinson University, 1992).

White, F. C., *On Schopenhauer's Fourfold Root of the Principle of Sufficient Reason* (Leiden: E. J. Brill, 1992).

Wicks, Robert, *Schopenhauer* (Oxford: Blackwell, 2008).

Young, Julian, *Schopenhauer* (London: Routledge, 2005).

—— *Willing and Unwilling: A Study in the Philosophy of Arthur Schopenhauer* (Dordrecht: Martinus Nijhoff, 1987).

## Further Reading in Oxford World's Classics

Hegel, G. W. F., *Outlines of the Philosophy of Right*, trans. T. M. Knox, ed. Stephen Houlgate.

Kant, Immanuel, *Critique of Judgement*, trans. J. C. Meredith, ed. Nicholas Walker.

Nietzsche, Friedrich, *On the Genealogy of Morals*, trans. Douglas Smith.

*Upaniṣads,* trans. Patrick Olivelle.

# A CHRONOLOGY OF
# ARTHUR SCHOPENHAUER

1788 (22 Feb.) Arthur Schopenhauer born in Danzig to the patrician merchant Heinrich Floris Schopenhauer and Johanna Schopenhauer (born Trosiener), later a popular writer and novelist.

1793 (Mar.) the Schopenhauers move to Hamburg to avoid the Prussian annexation of Danzig.

1797 (12 June) Schopenhauer's only sibling, Louise Adelaide (Adele) born. (July) travels to France with his father, remaining in Le Havre for two years with the family of a business associate of his father.

1799 (Aug.) returns from France and is enrolled in Dr Runge's private school, an institution designed to educate future merchants.

1803 (May) the Schopenhauers, minus Adele, begin a tour of Holland, England, France, Switzerland, Austria, Silesia, and Prussia; the tour is Arthur Schopenhauer's reward for agreeing to continue his training as a merchant and for forgoing preparation for attending a university.

1805 (Jan.) begins apprenticeship with a Hamburg merchant. (20 Apr.) Henrich Floris dies; his wife and son believe that his death is suicide.

1807 (May) through his mother's encouragement, Schopenhauer ends his apprenticeship. (June) he attends a *Gymnasium* at Gotha. (Dec.) terminates his studies at Gotha, after being rebuked for writing a lampoon on an instructor; relocates to Weimar, but lives separately from his family.

1809 (Feb.) upon reaching the age of majority, Schopenhauer receives his inheritance, one-third of his father's estate. (Oct.) matriculates as a medical student at the University of Göttingen.

1810 In the winter semester he studies philosophy with Gottlob Ernst Schulze, who recommends reading Plato and Kant, thus introducing Schopenhauer to his two favourite philosophers.

1811 (Sept.) enrols in the University of Berlin to study philosophy. In the winter semester he attends Johann Gottlieb Fichte's lectures, becoming increasingly disenchanted with Fichte's philosophy.

1812 (Summer semester) attends Friedrich Ernst Schleiermacher's lectures. (Winter) regularly observes psychiatric patients at the Berlin Charité.

1813  (May) fearing military conscription and an attack by Napoleon, leaves Berlin for a short stay at Weimar. (June) retires to Rudolstadt to write his dissertation. (Oct.) *On the Fourfold Root of the Principle of Sufficient Reason* earns Schopenhauer a doctorate in philosophy, *in absentia*, from the University of Jena; his dissertation is published. (Nov.) returns to Weimar; Goethe, who received a dedicated copy of Schopenhauer's dissertation, interests the young philosopher in colour theory, a subject they would discuss periodically for the next few months. (Dec.) begins to borrow volumes of the *Asiatisches Magazin*, acquainting himself with Eastern thought.

1814  (Mar.) Schopenhauer borrows a Latin translation of the *Upanishads*; these Indian scriptures would become his 'Bible'. (May) after a series of vicious quarrels with his mother, Schopenhauer moves to Dresden; the philosopher will never see her again.

1816  (May) the fruit of Schopenhauer's work with Goethe on colour theory, *On Vision and Colours*, is published.

1818  (Dec.) Schopenhauer's principal work, *The World as Will and Representation*, appears, bearing a publication date of 1819. (Dec.) applies to the University of Berlin to qualify as a *Privatdozent*, an unsalaried lecturer; in his application Schopenhauer expressed his desire to teach at the same time as Hegel's principal lectures.

1820  (Mar.) Schopenhauer receives a passing grade on his test lecture, during which he and Hegel engage in a minor dispute. (Summer semester) offers and convenes lectures for the first and only time; does not complete the course; Schopenhauer's lectures are listed in Berlin's prospectus of lectures in 1820–2 and in 1826–31.

1826  Discovers the first edition of Kant's *Critique of Pure Reason*.

1830  (June) Schopenhauer's Latin revision of his colour theory, *Commentatio undecima exponens Theoriam Colorum Physiologcam eandemque primariam*, is published in *Scriptores Ophthalmologici minores*.

1831  (Aug.) flees from Berlin to Frankfurt-am-Main, due to a cholera epidemic.

1833  (July) permanently locates in Frankfurt, where he will live for the remainder of his life.

1836  (Mar.) *On the Will in Nature* published.

1838  (17 Apr.) Johanna Schopenhauer dies in Bonn; Schopenhauer does not attend his mother's funeral.

1839  (Jan.) Schopenhauer's prize-essay 'On the Freedom of the Human Will' receives the gold medal from the Royal Norwegian Society of

Sciences in Trondheim; a Norwegian translation is published the following year.

1840 (Jan.) despite being the only entry, the prize-essay 'On the Foundation of Morals' is refused the crown by the Royal Danish Society of Sciences in Copenhagen. (Sept.) Schopenhauer's two prize-essays are published as *The Two Fundamental Problems of Ethics* (bearing a publication date 1841); he includes a lengthy preface in which he berates the Royal Danish Society and Hegel.

1844 (Mar.) the second edition of *The World as Will and Representation* appears in two volumes.

1845 (Summer) begins work on *Parerga and Paralipomena*.

1847 (Dec.) a significantly revised second edition of *The Fourfold Root of the Principle of Sufficient Reason* appears.

1849 (25 Apr.) death of Adele Schopenhauer in Bonn; Schopenhauer does not attend the funeral. (Dec.) laments the loss of his white poodle Atma; soon thereafter acquires a brown poodle, also called Atma.

1851 (Nov.) *Parerga and Paralipomena* appears.

1853 (Apr.) an anonymous review (by John Oxenford), 'Iconoclasm in German Philosophy', appears in the English journal, the *Westminster Review*, launching Schopenhauer's fame. (May) the *Vossische Zeitung* publishes a German translation of Oxenford's review.

1854 (Sept.) second edition of *On the Will in Nature*. (Dec.) second edition of *On Vision and Colours*.

1855 (Oct.) the philosophy faculty at the University of Leipzig sponsor an essay contest for the exposition and criticism of the Schopenhauerian philosophy.

1857 First lectures on Schopenhauer are delivered at the universities in Bonn and Breslau.

1859 (Nov.) the third edition of *The World as Will and Representation* appears.

1860 (Sept.) the second edition of *The Two Fundamental Problems of Ethics* appears. (21 Sept.) Arthur Schopenhauer dies in Frankfurt-am-Main.

# THE TWO FUNDAMENTAL PROBLEMS OF ETHICS

treated in two academic prize essays

BY

## DR ARTHUR SCHOPENHAUER

Member of the Royal Norwegian Society of Sciences

I. **On the Freedom of the Human Will,** awarded the prize by the Royal Norwegian Society of Sciences, at Trondheim on 26 January 1839.

II. **On the Foundation of Morals,** not awarded the prize by the Royal Danish Society of Sciences, at Copenhagen on 30 January 1840.

Μεγάλη ἡ ἀλήθεια καὶ ὑπερισχύει.*

# CONTENTS

# PREFACE TO THE FIRST EDITION

THESE two essays originated independently of each other due to external circumstances; nevertheless, they mutually contribute to the completion of a system of the fundamental truths of ethics, in which system, it is hoped, one will not fail to recognize a progress of this science, which has stopped for an hiatus of a half-century. However, neither essay could be referred to the other, and it was likewise impossible to refer to my earlier writings, because each was written for a different academy for which a strict incognito is a well-known condition. Hence, it was unavoidable that some points were touched upon in both essays, since nothing could be assumed and everything had to begin from the very outset. These essays are really specialized expositions of two theories whose essential features are found in the fourth book of *The World as Will and Representation*, but there they were derived from my metaphysics, thus synthetically and *a priori*; here, however, where the nature of the case permitted no assumptions, these statements appear on an analytic and *a posteriori* basis;* hence what there was first, here is last. But because of their departure from a common point of view, and also because of the specialized exposition, both theories have here gained greatly in comprehensibility, persuasiveness, and development of their significance. Therefore, these two essays are to be seen as supplements to the fourth book of my principal work* in precisely the same way as my text *On the Will in Nature** is a very essential and important supplement to the second book. Incidentally, however much the subject of the last-named text appears to be different from the present one, there is an actual connection between them; indeed, that text is, to a certain extent, the key to the present, and an insight into this connection helps one completely understand both. When once the time comes for me to be read, it will be found that my philosophy is like Thebes with a hundred gates: one can enter from all sides and through each gate arrive at the direct path to the centre.

I have still to remark that the first of these two essays has already found its place in the most recent volume published at Trondheim by the Royal Norwegian Society of Sciences. In consideration of the great distance between Trondheim and Germany, this academy* has most willingly and generously granted my request to have this prize essay published in Germany. I here publicly express to them my sincere gratitude for their permission.

The second essay was *not* crowned with success by the Royal Danish Society of Sciences, although there was no other essay to compete with it. Since this society has published its judgement of my work, I am justified in examining and replying to the judgement. The reader will find the judgement at the end of the relevant essay, and it will be evident that the Royal Society has found in my work absolutely nothing to praise, but only something to censure, and that this censure consists in three different strictures, which I will now go through separately.

The first and main censure, to which the other two are only accessory, is that I misunderstood the question, as I had erroneously thought what was demanded was the establishment of the principle of ethics; whereas, the question was actually and mainly concerned with the *nexus of metaphysics with ethics. At its beginning*, the judgement states that I had completely neglected to explain this nexus ('for omitting what had been asked first and foremost');[1] however, three lines down this was forgotten, and it says the opposite; namely, that I had explained this ('the nexus between the ethical principle proposed by him and his metaphysics'[2]), but had supplied this as an appendix, and I had produced more than was required.

I will entirely ignore this self-contradictory judgement. I regard it as the child of the embarrassment in which it was written. Instead, I ask the impartial and learned reader to study attentively the *prize question* set by the Danish Academy together with the *introduction* preceding it (both are printed along with my German translation in the front of the essay) and, then, to decide *what this question really asks*, whether it is about the ultimate ground, the principle, the foundation of the true and actual source of ethics—or about the nexus between ethics and metaphysics.—In order to make this task easier for the reader, I will now thoroughly analyse the introduction and the question and expound their meaning as clearly as possible.

---

[1] *omisso enim eo, quad potissimum postulabatur.*
[2] *principii ethicae et metaphysicae suae nexum exponit.*

The *introduction* to the question tells us 'there is a necessary idea of morality, or a primary concept of the moral law, that emerges in two ways: that is, on the one hand, in morals as a science and, on the other hand, *in actual life*. In the latter, the same idea appears again in two ways: that is, partly in the judgement of our own actions, partly in that of the actions of others. Other concepts were connected to this original concept of morality, concepts which were derived from it. The society now bases its question on this introduction; namely, where is *the source and foundation of morals* to be sought — whether, perhaps, for example, in an original idea of morality that actually and immediately lies in consciousness or conscience? This, then, would have to be analysed along with the concepts arising from it. Or does morals have another ground of cognition?' When stripped of the inessential and presented in a completely clear form, the question in Latin reads as follows: Where are the *source and foundation of moral philosophy* to be sought? Are they to be sought in the explanation of the idea of morality that consists in an immediate consciousness, or are they to be sought in a different grounds of cognition?[1] This last interrogative sentence indicates in the most clear way that the question is concerned in general with the *ground of cognition of morals*. To cap this, I will now also add a paraphrased exegesis of the question. The introduction begins with two entirely *empirical* observations. It states that there is, in fact, a moral science, and likewise it is a fact that *in actual life* moral concepts become apparent, partly as we ourselves judge our own actions by our conscience and partly as we also judge the actions of others from a moral point of view. Similarly, there are many different moral concepts, e.g., duty, accountability, and so forth, which are universally valid. In all of this, an original idea of morality emerges, a fundamental thought of a moral law, whose necessity, however, is peculiar to it and is not purely *logical*, i.e., which cannot be demonstrated by the mere principle of contradiction, from the actions to be judged, or from the maxims laying as the basis of the actions. From this basic moral concept other main moral concepts have subsequently proceeded and have been dependent on it and inseparable from it. — Now on what does all this rest? — That would

x

xi

---

[1] *Ubinam sunt quaerenda* fons et fundamentum philosophiae moralis? *Suntne quaerenda in explicatione ideae moralitatis, quae conscientia immediate contineatur? An in alio cognoscendi principio?*

indeed be an important research subject. — Therefore, the society set the following task: *The source, i.e., the origin of morality, the foundation itself* should be sought (*quaerenda sunt*). Where is it to be sought; i.e., where is it to be found? Is it to be found in some innate *idea of morality* residing in our consciousness or conscience? This idea, together with those concepts dependent on it, then needs to be simply analysed (*explicandis*). Or is it to be found elsewhere; i.e., perhaps morals has a completely different ground of cognition for our duties, whose source is entirely different from those cited by way of suggestion and example? — This is the content of the introduction and question, reproduced here in more detail and with greater clarity, but faithfully and accurately.

Now who here can remain with even the faintest doubt that the Royal Society is asking about the *source*, the origin, the basis, the ultimate ground of cognition of *morals*? — But now the source and basis of *morals* can be simply no other than that of *morality* itself, since that which is theoretically and abstractly *morals* itself is practically and substantially *morality*. But the source of *morality* must necessarily be the ultimate ground for all morally good conduct, just as *morals*, therefore, must for its part also lay down the ground upon which to support everything that it prescribes to humans, unless it wants to either seize these precepts out of the air or to base them on false grounds. It must, therefore, establish the ultimate ground of all morality, since as a scientific structure, morals has this ground as its foundation-stone, just as morality in practice has this as its origin. It is thus undeniably the basis of moral philosophy[1] about which the problem asks. Consequently, it is as clear as day that the problem actually requires that a *principle of ethics* be sought and laid down, '*ut principium aliquod ethicae conderetur*', but not in the sense of a mere supreme prescription or fundamental rule, rather in that of a *real ground of all morality, and therefore of a ground of knowledge of morals*. — But now the judgement denies this in stating that my essay could not be honoured because I had presumed it. But anyone who reads this problem will and must presume this, since it is there in black and white, in clear and unambiguous words, and it is not to be denied as long as the Latin words retain their sense.

---

[1] *fundamentum philosophiae moralis.*

I have been prolix, but the matter is important and noteworthy. For it is clear and certain from all of this that *what this academy denies having asked, it had obviously and incontestably asked.* — On the contrary, it maintains that it asked something different; namely, that the *nexus between metaphysics and morals* was the main subject of the prize essay (this alone can be understood by 'the theme itself'[1]). Now let the reader see whether *one word* of this is to be found in the prize question or in the introduction. There is not one syllable or even a suggestion. Whoever asks about the connection between two sciences, nevertheless, must name them both, but neither in the question nor in the introduction is there any mention of metaphysics. Moreover, the whole of this main sentence will become clear if one brings it from its topsy-turvy to its natural position, where, in exactly the same words, it reads as follows:

The theme itself had asked for just such an investigation in which first and foremost the nexus between metaphysics and ethics would be clearly discussed. However, the writer, by omitting what had been asked first and foremost, thought it was a question of laying down some ethical principle. Therefore that part of the essay in which he discusses the nexus between the ethical principle laid down by him and his metaphysics, has been expounded by him only in an appendix.[2]

The question about the nexus between metaphysics and ethics simply is not included in the perspective from which the *introduction* to the question proceeds, since this draws on *empirical* observations, refers to moral judgements, etc., that appear *in everyday life*; then it asks on what all of this ultimately rests, and it finally proposes an innate idea of morality lying in consciousness as an example of a possible solution. Thus in its example it assumes as a solution, tentatively and problematically, a mere *psychological fact* and not a metaphysical theorem. But in doing so, it makes it easy to recognize that it requires the grounding of morals through some sort of fact, be it of consciousness or of the external world, but it does not expect to see this derived

---

[1] *ipsum thema.*

[2] *Ipsum thema ejusmodi disputation flagitabat, in qua vel praecipuo loco metaphysicae et ethicae nexus consideraretur: sed scriptor, omisso eo, quod potissimun postulabatur, hoc expeti putavit, ut principium aliquod ethicae conderetur: itaque eam partem commentationis suae, in qua principii ethicae a se propositi et metaphysicae suae nexum exponit appendicis loco habuit, in qua plus, quam postulatum esset, praestaret.*

from some sort of metaphysics. Therefore the academy would have been quite correct in having rejected a prize essay that solved the problem in this way.—But one should consider this carefully. Now in addition to all of this, the question about the *nexus of metaphysics with morals*, which is allegedly stated, but nowhere to be found, would be completely unanswerable and, consequently, *impossible*, if we attribute any insight to the academy. It is *unanswerable*, because there is no *metaphysics per se*, but only different (and, indeed highly different) metaphysics, i.e., all sorts of attempts at metaphysics, in con-

<sub>xiv</sub> siderable numbers; to wit, as many as there have been philosophers, all of whom sing completely different tunes and differ and dissent fundamentally with each other. Consequently, you might as well ask about the nexus between the metaphysics of Aristotle, Epicurus, Spinoza, Leibniz, Locke, or any other specified metaphysics and ethics, but never at any time about *metaphysics per se* and ethics because this question would not even have a definite sense since it asks about the relationship between a given and a completely indefinite, indeed, perhaps impossible, thing. For as long as no metaphysics is recognized as objectively true and indisputable, thus one given as a *metaphysics per se*, we do not know even once whether such a one is at all possible or what it will be and can be. Meanwhile, if one wanted to urge that we nevertheless had an entirely generic and thus, of course, undetermined concept of *metaphysics in general*, in view of which the question about the nexus in general between metaphysics *in abstracto* and ethics could be asked, then that is granted. However, the answer to the question taken in this sense would be so easy and simple that to offer a prize for it would be ridiculous. Of course, nothing further could be said than that a true and complete metaphysics also offers ethics its firm support and ultimate grounds. Moreover, one finds this thought already worked out in the first paragraph of my essay, where I especially indicate the difficulties of the present question, which, by its nature, precludes grounding ethics through any given metaphysics from which one could start and on which one could depend.

Thus I have incontestably shown in the above that the Royal Danish Society actually asked what it denied having asked, that, on the

<sub>xv</sub> contrary, what it claimed having asked, it did *not* ask, could not have asked, even once. According to the moral principle laid down by me, this proceeding of the Royal Danish Society, to be sure, would not be

correct, but since it does not accept my moral principle, it will have another for which it is correct.

But now I have exactly answered what the academy *actually* had asked. To begin with, I have proven in the *negative* part that the principle of ethics does not lie where, for the last sixty years, it has been accepted as safely established.* Then in the *positive* part, I uncovered the genuine source of morally praiseworthy actions, have *actually proven* that this is it and that it could be no other. Finally, I have shown the connection of this real ethical basis—not with *my* metaphysics, as the judgement falsely states, and also not with any specific metaphysics—but with a universal, fundamental idea common to many metaphysical systems, perhaps to most, undoubtedly to the oldest, and in my opinion, to the truest. I have not given this metaphysical presentation as an appendix, as the judgement says, but as the last chapter of the essay. It is the keystone of the whole thing, an observation of a more profound sort with which the essay ends. Here I said that I produced more than what was really required by the problem, and this comes from the fact that the problem does not in the least hint at a metaphysical explanation, much less would it lead to such, as the judgement maintains. Moreover, now whether this metaphysical discussion is a supplement, i.e., something in which I produced more than was required or not, is a matter of secondary importance, even of indifference. It is enough that it is there. But that the judgement chooses to make use of *this* against me is evidence of its embarrassment; it grasps at anything in order to raise some objection xvi to my work. Besides, given the nature of the case, that metaphysical observation had to be made at the end of the essay. Since, if it had come at the beginning, the principle of ethics would have to have been derived *synthetically*, which would have been possible only if the academy had said from which of the many very different metaphysics it wished to see an ethical principle derived. But the truth of such a principle would then be entirely dependent here on the presupposed metaphysics, and thus it would remain problematic. Accordingly, the nature of the question would make necessary an *analytic* foundation for the basic moral principle, i.e., a foundation drawn from the reality of things without the assumption of any metaphysics.* Precisely because in recent times this path was generally recognized as the only certain one, Kant, as well as English moralists who came before him, troubled himself to establish the moral principle in an analytic way, independent of any metaphysical assumption. To depart again from this would be an obvious step backwards. However, had the Academy required this, it should at least have expressed it in the most certain terms, but not once is there a hint of this in its question.

Moreover, since the Danish Academy has magnanimously passed over in silence the fundamental defect of my work, I will take care not to disclose it. I only fear this will not help us,* for I foresee that the educated nose of the reader of the essay will catch the scent of the rotted spot. In any event, it could lead the reader to mistakenly think that my Norwegian essay is just as greatly afflicted with the same fundamental defect. Of course, the Royal Norwegian Society was not thereby prevented from crowning my work. But to belong to this academy is also an honour the value of which each passing day I see more clearly and learn to estimate more fully. For as an academy they recognize no other interest than that of the truth, the light, the advance of human insight and knowledge. An academy is no tribunal of faith. Indeed, any academy, before it poses such high, serious, and critical questions as the two prize questions before us, must decide beforehand and determine for itself whether it is actually prepared to assent to the truth, no matter how it sounds (for an academy cannot know ahead of time). For afterward, after receiving a serious answer for a serious question, it is past the time to take it back. And if once the stony guest, having been invited, is there, upon his entrance even Don Juan is too much the Gentleman* to deny his invitation. This earnestness is without a doubt the reason why the European academies, as a rule, take care to guard against posing questions of this type: actually the two before us are the first which I remember having experienced, and just because of the rarity of the matter,[1] I undertook to answer them. Although it has for a considerable time been clear to me that I take philosophy seriously, so that I could not have become a professor of the same, I have certainly not believed that I could encounter this same failing in an academy.

The Royal Danish Society's second censure reads: 'The writer has also not satisfied us with the form of his essay'.[2] There is nothing to say

---

[1] *pour la rareté du fait.*
[2] *scriptor neque ipsa disserendi forma nobis satisfecit.*

xvii

against this: it is the Royal Danish Society's subjective judgement,[1] for the elucidation of which I publish my work along with the judge-  xviii ment of it, so that it will not be lost, but preserved:

> So long as the water flows and the mighty trees grow,
> So long as the sun rises and shines; so long as the moon glows,
> And the rivers retain their water, the ocean remembers its roar,
> I will announce to the traveller, that here lies Midas entombed.[2]

I remark at this point that I provide this essay here just as I had submitted it; i.e., I have neither struck out nor altered anything. But the few, brief, and inessential additions which I have written after the submission, I indicated with a cross at the beginning and end of each, to forestall all objections and excuses.[3]

The judgement adds to the above: 'nor has he sufficiently demonstrated this foundation.'[4] Against that I maintain that I have actually and seriously *demonstrated* my foundation of morals, with a rigour which approaches the mathematical. This is without precedent in

---

[1] 'They say: that does not please me!
And mean, they have killed it.'

(Goethe)

Addition to the second edition.

[Schopenhauer's note. He here cites Goethe, *Sprichwörterlich*. In the second edition Schopenhauer alters the first edition's preface by adding the lines from Goethe. He notes the 'addition to the second edition' so as to mark this alteration clearly.]

[2] ἔστ' ἄν ὕδωρ τε ῥέῃ, καὶ δένδρεα μακρὰ τεθήλῃ,
ἠελιός τ' ἀνιὼν φαίνῃ, λαμπρή τε σελήνη,
καὶ ποταμοὶ πλήθωσιν, ἀνακλύζῃ δὲ θάλασσα,—
ἀγγελέω παριοῦσι, Μίδας ὅτι τῇδε τέθαπται.

*Dum fluit unda levis, sublimis nascitur arbor,*
*Dum sol exoriens et splendida luna relucet,*
*Dum fluvii labuntur, inundant littora fluctus,*
*Usque Midam viatori narro hic esse sepultum.*

The last line was omitted in the first edition on the assumption that the reader would complete the verse. [Schopenhauer's note. He provides a Greek paraphrase of Plato, *Phaedrus* 264d as well as a Latin translation.]

[3] This applies only to the first edition: in the present the crosses are omitted because they are somewhat disruptive, particularly since countless new additions have been inserted. Therefore, whoever wants to be acquainted with the essay exactly in the form in which it had been submitted to the Academy must have the first edition at hand. [Schopenhauer's note.]

[4] *neque reapse hoc fundamentum sufficere evicit.*

*morals* and was only possible because I have penetrated more deeply than ever before into the nature of the human will and brought to the xix light of day, have laid out clearly, the three ultimate incentives out of which spring all actions of the human will.*

However, what follows in the judgement is: 'moreover, he has seen it necessary to admit the opposite himself.'[1] If that is supposed to mean that I myself had declared my foundation of morals to be insufficient, the reader will see that no trace of this is to be found and no such thing has occurred to me. But if, perhaps, they should be suggesting with that phrase, that I have said at one point—the reprehensibility of unnatural lust is not derived from the same principle from which the virtues of justice and philanthropy are derived—this shows that much is made out of little and would be yet another proof of how they have seized every opportunity to condemn my work. In conclusion and as a parting shot, the Royal Danish Society then gave me still another coarse reprimand, for which, even if its substance were well founded, I cannot understand their justification. I would, therefore, help them with it. It reads: 'several *supreme philosophers* of recent times were so rudely mentioned, that it caused just and grave offence.'[2] These supreme philosophers* are namely— Fichte and Hegel!* For concerning these two alone I have used such strong and coarse expressions that the phrase which the Danish Academy employed could perhaps warrant application; indeed, the outspoken censure would, in itself, even be fair if these people really were supreme philosophers. This is just the point at issue.

Concerning Fichte, what one finds in the essay merely repeats and elaborates on the judgement which I had already given in my principal work twenty-two years ago. So far as it arises here, I have provided compelling reason in a few detailed paragraphs devoted to xx Fichte himself, from which it sufficiently follows how remote he is from being a supreme philosopher. Still I have placed him as 'man of talent' high above Hegel. Upon the latter alone have I, without commentary, let loose my unqualified judgement of damnation in the most decided terms. For according to my opinion, he not only lacks all philosophical merit, but he has had upon philosophy, and thereby

---

[1] *quin ipse contra esse confiteri coactus est.*

[2] *Plures recentioris aetatis* summos philosophos *tam indecenter commemorari, ut justam et gravem offensionem habeat.*

on German literature generally, a most pernicious, even actually stupefying, one could even say pestilential influence, against which influence, therefore, at every opportunity, it is the duty of every capable person to think, to judge, even most emphatically to oppose. For if we are silent, who, then, will speak? The reprimand at the close of the judgement, therefore, concerns Hegel as well as Fichte. When the Royal Danish Society speaks of 'several supreme philosophers of recent times,[1] they speak principally of Hegel, to whom I have improperly failed to pay due respect. Indeed, he comes off the worst. Thus down from the judgement seat from which they reject with unqualified censure works like mine, they publicly pronounce this Hegel to be a supreme philosopher.

When a league of academic writers pledged to the glorification of the bad, when paid Professors of Hegelry, when languishing unpaid lecturers who aspire to professorships tirelessly and with unparalleled shamelessness extol to the four winds that such an ordinary mind, but such an extraordinary charlatan, is the greatest philosopher the world has ever possessed, it is worth no serious consideration, all the less since the clumsy deliberateness of this wretched effort must in time become evident, even to those of little experience. When it goes so far that a foreign academy will defend that philosophaster as a supreme philoso- xxi pher, indeed, permits itself to abuse the man who honestly, fearlessly, and forcefully stands up against false, vile, deceitful, purchased, and wholly fabricated fame, a man who alone appropriately estimates impertinent praise of the false, the bad, and the mind-rotting, then the matter becomes serious: for such an authoritative judgement could lead the ignorant to great and pernicious error. It must, therefore, be *neutralized*, and since I do not have the authority of the academy, this must be done through reasons and proofs. Therefore, such will I now present clearly and comprehensibly, in hopes that it will serve to recommend to the Danish Academy as Horatian advice for the future.

> Whom you will commend, consider again and again, so that
>    you do not
> Need to blush at the sins which others committed.[2]

---

[1] *recentioris aetatis summis philosophis.*

[2] *Qualem commendes, etiam atque etiam a[d]spice, ne mox Incutiant aliena tibi peccata pudorem.*
   [Horace, *Epistles* I. 18. 76–7].

If I were now to say to this purpose, the so-called philosophy of this Hegel is a colossal mystification that will certainly supply posterity with an inexhaustible theme of scorn for our time, a mystification crippling all intellectual powers, stifling all actual thought, and, by means of the most wicked misuse of language, putting in place the most hollow, most senseless, most thoughtless and (as its success confirms) most stupefying verbiage of a pseudo-philosophy which, with an absurd notion at its core, a notion grasped out of thin air, deprived of reasons as well as consequences, i.e., proven through nothing, not even itself explaining or proving anything, thereby even lacking originality, a mere parody of scholastic realism and at the same time of Spinozism, which monster is also supposed to represent Christianity turned backwards, so

xxii
> The front of a lion, the behind of a serpent, the
> middle of a she-goat[1] —

If I were now to say all this, I would be right. If I were to go on to say this supreme philosopher of the Danish Academy has smeared nonsense like no other mortal before him, so that whoever could read his prize work, the so-called *Phenomenology of Spirit*,[2] without thereby feeling as if he were in a madhouse — he would belong there; in saying so, I would not merely be correct. But then I would allow the Danish Academy the evasion of saying that the highest teaching of such wisdom is not accessible to a lowly intelligence like mine, and that what to me appears to be nonsense, is profound, unfathomable sense. So, I must then seek a secure grip which cannot slip loose and, therefore, drives the opponent into a corner from which no escape is at hand. To this end I will now irrefutably prove that this supreme philosopher of the Danish Academy is even missing common sense, however common it be. That one could be a supreme philosopher without this common sense is a thesis which the academy will not advance.

---

[1] πρόσθε λέων, ὄπιθεν δὲ δράκων, μέσση δὲ χίμαιρα,

ora leonis erant, venter capra, cauda draconis,

[Homer, *Iliad* VI. 181; Schopenhauer provides the Latin translation.]

[2] Actually called 'System of Science', Bamberg 1807. One must read it in this original edition, since in the *operibus omnibus* [collected works] *assecla* [partisan] editing is supposed to have licked it somewhat clean. [Schopenhauer's note.]

I will confirm this deficiency through *three* different examples. And I will take these from the book in which by far he should have been the most sensible, the most circumspect, and the most reflective, the book he wrote as his student compendium, titled *Encyclopedia of the Philosophical Sciences*, a book which a Hegelian has called the Bible of the Hegelians.

Thus, in the section called 'Physics', § 293 (second edition of 1827), he deals with specific gravity, which he calls specific weight, and questions the assumption that specific weight depends on difference of porosity through the following argument: 'An instance of the *existing* specifying of weight is the appearance that when an iron bar, balanced on its fulcrum, is *magnetized*, it loses its equilibrium and now appears to be heavier at one pole than at the other. Here one part is so infected, that, without altering volume, it becomes heavier. The matter, whose mass has not been increased, has therefore become *specifically* heavier.' Here the supreme philosopher of the Danish Academy draws the following conclusion: 'If a bar supported at its centre of gravity thereafter becomes heavier on one end, it sinks to that end: now, however, an iron bar sinks to one side after it is magnetized; thus, it has become heavier on that end.' A worthy analogy to this conclusion: 'All geese have two legs; you have two legs; thus, you are a goose.' For put into categorical form, Hegel's syllogism goes: 'All things which become heavier on one end sink toward that end; this magnetized bar sinks to one end; therefore, it has become heavier on that end.' That is the syllogistic reasoning of this supreme philosopher and reformer of logic, to whom unfortunately, no one has explained, that from the mere affirmative no conclusion can be drawn in the second figure.[1] In all seriousness, however, for anyone with healthy, common sense, it is *innate* logic which makes such a conclusion impossible, and the absence of such logic is denoted by the word *stupidity*. It requires no explanation to see how a textbook which contains argumentation of this kind and talks of increasing weight of bodies without increase of their mass is well suited to warp and distort the common sense of young people.—This is the first example.

---

[1] *e meris affirmativis in secunda figura nihil sequitur.*

The second example of the dearth of common sense in this supreme
philosopher of the Danish Academy is found in § 269 of the same
textbook, in the sentence: 'First, gravitation immediately contradicts
the law of inertia, for by the capacity of gravitation, matter *by itself*
is attracted toward other matter.'—How so?! not to grasp that it as
little counteracts the law of inertia that one body is more *attracted* by
another, than it is *repulsed* by it?! In the one case, as in the other, it is
the approach of an external cause which negates or alters the previous
state of rest or motion; and indeed, so with attraction as with repulsion, action and reaction are equal to one another.—And, so impu-
dently to write down such foolishness! And this in a textbook for
students, who, in their first rudimentary conception of the theory of
nature, which should not remain foreign to any scholar, will thereby
completely and, perhaps, forever be led into error. Of course, the
more unwarranted the fame, the more audacious he becomes.—To
one who can think (which was not the case with our supreme philosophers, who always were merely talking about 'the thought' just as
the signs of inns are about the princes who never stay there), it is no
easier to explain why one body repels the other than why it attracts it,
for unexplained natural forces serve as the ground for the one as well
as the other, as any causal explanation presupposes. So if one would
say that a body attracted to another by gravitation strives toward
the other 'by itself', then one must also say that a repelled body, 'by
itself' flees the repelling body; so in one case as in the other, the law
of inertia is abolished. The law of inertia follows immediately from
that of causality; indeed, it is actually only its reverse: 'Each alteration is brought about by a cause', says the law of causality: 'Where no
cause is present, no alteration occurs', says the law of inertia. Therefore, a fact that would contradict the law of inertia would just as well
contradict that of causality; that is, contradict *a priori* certainty and
show us an effect without a cause: to accept this is the essence of all
*stupidity.* —This is the second example.

The third proof of the innate quality to which I just referred is
found in § 298 of the same masterpiece of the supreme philosopher
of the Danish Academy, in which he, in a polemic against the
explanation of elasticity through pores, said: 'Moreover, if it is granted
in the abstract that matter is perishable, not absolute, there will be
objection to this in practice— — — — — — —; so that in fact,

matter is assumed to be *absolutely independent and eternal*. This error is introduced by the general error of the understanding that etc.' — Indeed, what simpleton has ever asserted that *matter is perishable*? And who calls the contrary an error? — It is *a priori* knowledge, as firm and certain as any mathematical knowledge, that matter *persists*, that is, that it does not arise and perish like all other things, but is indestructible and without origin, and remains through all time; therefore, its quantum can neither be increased nor diminished. It is simply impossible for us to imagine matter arising or perishing because the form of our understanding does not permit it. To deny this, to explain this as an error, is therefore at once to deny all understanding — which, therefore, is the third example. — Even the predicate *absolute* can be attributed to matter with full authority for it states that its existence lies completely outside the providence of causality and does not enter into the endless chain of causes and effects. The law of causality concerns only the accidents, conditions, and forms of matter and xxvi unites them with one another. This law extends only to the arising and passing of accidents, conditions, and forms of matter, only to the *alterations* occurring in matter, not to matter itself. Indeed, this predicate, *absolute*, has its only example in matter, in which it obtains reality and is permissible. Otherwise it is a predicate for which there is absolutely no subject to be found, whereby it would be a concept grasped out of thin air and realized through nothing, nothing more than a puffed-up plaything of comic philosophers. — Incidentally, the pronouncement above from this quite naive Hegel sheds light on the old women's spinning-wheel philosophy,* the laws of which this sublime, hyper-transcendent, high-wire walking, and unfathomably deep philosopher clutches childishly to his heart, never allowing them to be questioned.

Therefore, the supreme philosopher of the Danish Academy teaches expressly that without increasing their mass, bodies can become heavier, and that this is specifically the case with a magnetized iron bar; likewise that the law of gravitation contradicts the law of inertia; and finally also that matter is perishable. These three examples will suffice well to show what has long been obvious as soon as there is an opening in the dense covering of senseless gobbledegook which scorns all human reason, wrapped in which the supreme philosopher proceeds to stalk about impressing the intellectual rabble.

As the saying goes, the lion is known by its claws; but I must, decently or indecently,[1] say, the ass is known by its ears. —After all, from the three specimens of Hegelian philosophy[2] presented here, the just and impartial reader may now judge who actually should be mentioned as indecent: he who without formalities calls such a teacher of absurd-
xxvii  ities a charlatan, or he who decreed from the throne of academic infallibility[3] that he is a supreme philosopher?

I have still to add that from among such a rich selection of absurd-ities of all sorts which the works of this supreme philosopher offer, I have given precedence to the three above because, given their sub-jects, they do not on the one hand concern difficult, perhaps unsolv-able, philosophical problems which accordingly allow of a variety of different views, and on the other hand, do not concern specific phys-ical truths which presuppose precise empirical knowledge. Rather, the matter here concerns insights *a priori*, that is, problems, which anyone can solve through mere reflection; therefore, a wrong-headed judge-ment in things of this sort is certainly a decided and undeniable sign of a very uncommon lack of understanding. However, the audacious assertion of such nonsensical teachings in a textbook for students shows us what insolence seizes a common mind when it is proclaimed to be a great intellect. Therefore, to do this is a means which can serve no justifiable end. One should compare the three examples from physics[4] herein depicted with the passage in § 98 of the same master-piece which commences, 'and further the force of repulsion'—and see with what an air of infinite superiority this sinner looks down upon Newton's universal law of attraction and Kant's metaphysical foundations of natural science.* Whoever has the patience should now read §§ 40 to 62, in which this supreme philosopher gives a dis-torted presentation of Kantian philosophy while by his lowly nature he is incapable of enjoying the greatness of Kant's merits and the inexpressibly rare presence of a truly great intellect. Instead, he looks
xxviii  down upon this great, great man from the heights of self-assured, infinite superiority, as upon one whom he has indulged a hundred

---

[1] *decenter . . . indecenter.*

[2] *speciminibus philosophiae Hegelianae.*

[3] *ex cathedra academica.* [In Roman Catholic tradition, a papal pronouncement indicated as *ex cathedra*, 'from the throne', is considered to be infallible.]

[4] *speciminibus in physicis.*

times, as upon one in whose weak, sophomoric attempts, with cold estimation, half ironically, half pityingly, he identifies the errors and misconceptions for the instruction of his students. The same goes for § 254. This superciliousness toward genuine merit is actually a well-known trick of charlatans of all sorts; however, its effect does not readily fail with imbeciles. Therefore, in addition to this outpouring of nonsense, the great subterfuge of this charlatan was superciliousness; so that, at every opportunity, he looked down from the heights of his castle of verbiage with disdain, with fastidiousness, with contempt, with derision, upon not simply others' philosophemes, but also upon every science and its methods, upon everything which in the course of the centuries the human mind had achieved through sagacity, effort, and diligence. Thereby he garnered the esteem of the German public for the kind of wisdom obfuscated by his Abracadabra. This public even thinks:

> They seem to be of noble ancestry,
> For they look proud and act disdainfully.*

To judge of one's own device is the privilege of the few; authority and example lead the rest. They see with others' eyes, hear with others' ears. It is quite easy to think, as all the whole world now thinks; but not everyone is able to think as all the world will think thirty years hence. Therefore a person who is now accustomed to honour upon hearsay,[1] to assume the respectability of an author on *credit*, and who subsequently also wants to urge such upon others, may readily find himself in the position of the person who, having signed over a bad promissory note, expecting it to be honoured, gets it back with bitter protest. Such a person must then learn better means to scrutinize the firm of the one who draws such a check and that of the endorser.   xxix
I would have to deny my genuine conviction, if I did not accept that the contrived shouts of praise, in addition to the great number of his German partisans, has had a preponderant influence on the honorary title of a supreme philosopher which the Danish Academy uses in regard to this spoiler of paper, time, and minds. For this reason, it seems to me appropriate to remind the Royal Danish Society of the beautiful passage with which Locke (whom, to Locke's credit, Fichte

---

[1] *estime sur parole.*

considers to be the worst of all philosophers) closes the penultimate chapter of his famous masterpiece, and which I will repeat here:

But, notwithstanding the great Noise is made in the World about Errours and Opinions, I must do Mankind that Right, as to say, *There are not so many Men in Errours, and wrong Opinions, as is commonly supposed.* Not that I think they embrace the Truth; but indeed, because, concerning those Doctrines they keep such a stir about, they have no Thought, no Opinion at all. For if any one should a little catechise the greatest part of the Partisans of most of the Sects in the World, he would not find, concerning those Matters they are so zealous for, that they have any Opinions of their own: much less would he have Reason to think, that they took them upon the Examination of Arguments and Appearance of Probability. They are resolved to stick to a Party, that Education or Interest has engaged them in; and there, like the common Soldiers of an Army, show their Courage and Warmth, as their Leaders direct, without ever examining, or so much as knowing the Cause they contend for. If a Man's Life shows that he has no serious Regard to Religion; for what Reason should we think, that he beats his Head about the Opinions of his Church, and troubles himself to examine the grounds of this or that Doctrine? 'Tis enough for him to obey his Leaders, to have his Hand and his Tongue ready for the support of the common Cause, and thereby approve himself to those, who can give him Credit, Preferment, or Protection in that Society. Thus Men become Professors of, and Combatants for those Opinions they were never convinced of, nor proselytes to; no, nor ever had so much as floating in their Heads: And though one cannot say, there are fewer improbable or erroneous Opinions in the World than there are; yet this is certain, there are fewer, that actually assent to them, and mistake them for truths, than is imagined.*

Locke was quite right: whoever pays good wages can find any army at any time, even if the cause be the worst in the world. Through clever subsidies, a bad philosopher as well as a bad heir-apparent can be kept on top for a while. However, Locke here has overlooked a whole class of adherents of erroneous opinion and proponents of false fame, and, indeed, those who are the true adherents, the main body of the army,[1] are of just that sort: I mean the many who, without such pretensions, (e.g., as to become professors of Hegelry or to enjoy other benefices), but like genuine simpletons, conscious of the complete impotence of their power of judgement, repeat those who impress

---

[1] *gros de l'armée.*

them, and joining and trotting along with the crowd, when they hear xxxi an outcry, cry out, too. In order now to supplement Locke's explanation of a phenomenon which recurs in all times, I will give a passage from my favourite Spanish author, a passage which the reader will welcome, since it is thoroughly amusing and furnishes a specimen from a magnificent book, but one unknown in Germany. This passage should especially serve as a model for the many young and old *poseurs* in Germany, who in quiet, but deep consciousness of their intellectual incapacity, sing *the praise of Hegel* in refrain with scoundrels and who pretend to find wonderfully profound wisdom in the meaningless or wholly nonsensical proclamations of this philosophical charlatan. Examples are odious:[1] therefore, I dedicate to them the lesson, taken just in the abstract, that one never degrades oneself so profoundly as when one admires and prizes the bad. For Helvetius says correctly, 'the degree of intellect necessary to please us is a fairly accurate measure of the degree of our own intellect'.[2] It is much easier to excuse a brief misunderstanding of excellence. For on account of its originality, excellence in every field strikes us as so new and so strange, that to recognize it at first glance will require not only understanding, but also education in the same discipline. As a rule, excellence achieves late recognition, all the later as the discipline is loftier, and those who truly enlighten humankind share the fate of the fixed stars, the light from which requires many years before it descends to the horizon. In contrast, veneration of the bad, the false, the senseless, or the completely absurd, indeed, the nonsensical, permits no excuse, but one thereby proves that one is irredeemable, that one is a moron and consequently will remain so to the end xxxii of one's days, since understanding cannot be acquired. — However, I am certain of the gratitude of the honest and insightful who may still be found, insofar as, once again, upon provocation, I treat Hegelry, this pest of German literature, as it deserves. For they will be entirely of the opinion which Voltaire and Goethe express in such surprising agreement: 'The favour which one lavishes on bad works hinders the progress of the intellect as much as vigorous attack on good works'.[3]

---

[1] *Exempla sunt odiosa.*

[2] '*le degré d'esprit nécessaire pour nous plaire, est une mesure assez exacte du degré d'esprit que nous avons*' (Helvetius, *De l'esprit*, Discourse II, chap. 10, note).

[3] '*La faveur prodiguée aux mauvais ouvrages est aussi contraire aux progrès de l'esprit que le déchainement contre les bons*' (*Lettre à la Duchesse du Maine*, prefatory letter to *Oreste*).

'The real obscurantism is not that one hinders the dissemination of the true, the clear and the useful, but that one introduces the false.'*

But what other time has experienced such systematic and forceful introduction of the bad as the past twenty years in Germany? What other has produced a similar apotheosis of nonsense and craziness? For what other has Schiller's verse,

> I saw fame's sacred Laurel
> Profaned on the common brow*

been so exactly prophetic? Therefore, in fact, the Spanish rhapsody, which I will give as a cheerful closing of this preface, is so wonderfully timely that the suspicion could arise that it was written in 1840 and not 1640; thus, as a matter of information, I am providing a faithful translation from the *Criticón* of Baltazar Gracián, part III, *crisi* 4, p. 285 of the first volume of the first Antwerp quarto edition of Lorenzo Gracián of 1702.

xxxiii   . . . But the leader and interpreter of our two travellers[1] found only the rope-makers, among them all, to be worthy of praise, because they go in the opposite direction to all the rest.

When they had arrived, their attention was roused by what they heard. After looking everywhere, they caught sight of a clever windbag standing on an ordinary platform, surrounded by a crowd of people milling about, who had been worked up. He held them as his prisoners, chained by the ears, though not with the golden chain of the Theban,[2] but with an iron bridle. With a gift of the gab indispensable on such occasions, this fellow offered to display wonderful things.

'Now gentlemen,' he said, 'I will show you a winged wonder which is also a marvel of intelligence. I am pleased to be dealing with persons of real insight, genuine people; but I must observe that if any among you should not be endowed with a very extraordinary intellect, he can leave immediately, for the lofty and subtle things that will now occur cannot be intelligible to him. Therefore pay attention, gentlemen of insight and understanding!

---

[1] They are Critilo, the father, and Adrenio, the son. The interpreter is *desengaño*, that is, disillusionment: he is the second son of truth, whose first-born is hate: *veritas odium parit* [truth brings forth hate]. [Schopenhauer's note.]

[2] [Gracián] means Hercules, of whom he says in Part II, Crisis 2, p. 133 (as also in the *Agudeza y arte* [*de ingenio*] Discourse 19; and likewise in *Discreto* [*oráculo manual, y arte de prudencia*], p. 398), that little chains came from his tongue, which fettered the others by their ears. However, misled by an emblem of Alciatus, Gracián confused Hercules with Mercury, who, as god of eloquence, was so depicted. [Schopenhauer's note.]

Now the eagle of Jupiter will step forth, who talks and argues as befits such a one, who jests like a Zoilus and taunts like an Aristarchus.* Not a word will come from his mouth that does not imply a mystery and contain an ingenious idea with a hundred allusions to a hundred things. All that he says will be maxims of the *most sublime profundity*.'[1]        xxxiv

'Undoubtedly this will be somebody wealthy or powerful,' said Critilo, 'for if he were poor, everything he said would be worthless. With a silvery voice one sings well, and with a golden beak one talks even more beautifully.'

'Well, then!' continued the charlatan, 'Let those gentlemen who are themselves not intellectual eagles take their leave, for they can get nothing from here.'

What? No one going away? No one moving? The fact was that no one professed to have the insight that he was devoid of insight; on the contrary, all considered themselves to be men of great insight, estimated their intelligence to be uncommon, and had a high opinion of themselves. He now tugged at a thick rein, and it appeared—the dumbest of animals; for even to mention its name is offensive.

'Here you see', cried the impostor, 'an eagle, an eagle in all his brilliant qualities, in thought and in speech. Let not a one say the contrary, for he would then discredit his intelligence.'

'By heavens!' cried one, 'I can see his wings: oh, how magnificent they are!'

'And I', said another, 'can count the feathers: ah, how fine they are!'

'Really, don't you see it?' said another to his neighbour.

'I? Of course I can, and how distinctly!' exclaimed the latter.

But an honest and intelligent man said to his neighbour, 'As true as I am an honourable man, I can't see that there is an eagle there, nor that it has feathers, but only four feeble legs and quite a respectable schwanz.'*

'Hush!' retorted his friend, 'Don't say that; you will be ruined! They will think you are a big *et cetera*. Listen to what we others say and do, and        xxxv
thus go with the flow.'

'I swear by all the saints,' said another honourable man, 'that is not only no eagle, but its very antipode; I say that it is a great big *et cetera*.'

'Quiet! Be quiet!' said his friend, nudging him with his elbow, 'Do you want to be laughed at by everybody? You dare not say that it is anything but an eagle, even if you were to think the very opposite; we shall still say yes.'

---

[1] Hegel's expression from the Hegelian periodical *vulgo* [commonly called] *Jahrbücher der wissenschaftlichen Litteratur*, 1827, No. 7. The original [i.e. Gracián's wording] is merely *profundidades y sentencias* [profound thoughts and maxims]. [Schopenhauer's note.]

'Do you not perceive the fine points he advances?' exclaimed the charlatan. 'Whoever does not grasp and feel these must be devoid of genius.'

A baccalaureus immediately jumped up and shouted: 'How splendid! What great ideas! The most eminent in the world! What aphorisms! Let me write them down! It would be an eternal shame if even an iota of them were lost (and after his departure, I shall edit my notebooks).'[1]

At this moment the wondrous beast let out his ear-splitting cry, enough to upset a whole council meeting, and this was accompanied by such a torrent of indecencies that all stood aghast, looking at one another.

'Look! Look! My timid people,'[2] promptly exclaimed the crafty impostor. 'Look and stand up on tip-toe! Now that's what I call speaking! Is there another such Apollo? What do you think of the delicacy and subtlety of his thoughts and of the eloquence of his speech? Is there in all the world a greater intellect?'

The bystanders looked at one another, but no one dared to mutter nor to express just what he thought the truth was, for fear of being taken for a simpleton. Moreover, all broke out in a single voice of praise and applause. 'Ah! that beak! I am completely carried away by it!' exclaimed a ridiculous babbling woman. 'I could listen to it all day long.'

'And the devil take me, if it is not an ass that is to be found everywhere,' a timid man said quite softly; 'however, I will take care not to say so.'

'Upon my honour,' said another, 'that was indeed no speech, but the braying of an ass; but woe to the one who would say such a thing! Such is the way of the world; a mole passes for a lynx, a frog for a canary, a hen for a lion, a cricket for a goldfinch, an ass for an eagle. What does the opposite course matter to me? I keep my thoughts to myself, but talk like the others, and let us live in peace! It all amounts to just that.'

Critilo was reduced to extremities at having to see such vulgarity on the one hand and such cunning on the other. 'Can foolishness so possess people's minds?' he thought. But the braggardly rascal laughed at them all beneath the shadow of his large nose, and said to himself in triumph, as in a comic aside: '*Haven't* I bested them all for you? Could your procuress

---

[1] *Lectio spuria, uncis inclusa* [spurious addition put in parentheses.] [Schopenhauer's note.]

[2] One should write 'gescheut' [timid] and not 'gescheidt' [clever]; in the etymology of the word lies the foundation of its meaning, so artfully expressed by Chamfort: *l'écriture a dit que le commencement de la sagesse était la crainte de Dieu; moi, je crois que c'est la crainte des hommes* [*Maximes et Pensées*, chap. 2: 'The holy scriptures say the fear of God is the beginning of wisdom; I, however, believe it to be the fear of humankind.' Schopenhauer's note; he offers the quote from Chamfort in support of his rather free translation of the Spanish *entendidos*.]

do more?' And once more he gave them a hundred absurdities to digest, whereupon he again exclaimed: 'Let no one say it is not so, for otherwise he will be marked as a simpleton.'

At this the vile applause now rose even higher, and Andrenio joined in with all the rest.

But Critilo, who could stand it no longer, was ready to burst. He turned to his dumbfounded interpreter with these words: 'How long will this person abuse our patience, and how long will you keep silent? Insolence and vulgarity exceed all bounds!' xxxvii

To this, the other replied: 'Just have patience until time makes a statement; it will retrieve the truth, as it always does. Just wait till the monster turns its hindquarters to us, and you will then hear those who now admire it, deplore it.'

And this is precisely what happened, as the impostor again dragged in his dimorphous eagle-ass (the former as false as the latter is correct). At that very moment, first one and then another began to speak freely.

'On my honour,' said one, 'that was no genius, but an ass.'

'What fools we have been!' exclaimed another.

And so they inspired one another's courage, until all said: 'Has anyone ever seen such a deception? He has really not said a single word containing anything, and we have applauded him. In short, it was an ass, and we deserve to be pack-saddled.'

But the charlatan again stepped forward, promising another and greater marvel. 'Now,' he said, 'I will actually present to you nothing less than a world-famous giant, with whom neither Enceladus nor Typhoeus* compare in any way. At the same time, however, I must mention that whoever calls out to him "giant!" thereby earns good fortune; for he will help him to great honours, will heap riches upon him—thousands, indeed, tens of thousands, of piastres income—as well as honours, offices, and posts. Whereas, woe to the one who does not recognize him as a giant. Not only will he gain no favours, but he will get curses and punishment. Look out, everyone! Here he comes and shows himself; see how he towers above all!'

A curtain was raised and there appeared a tiny man who, if had he been hitched up to a hoist, would have been no more visible, no larger than xxxviii a man's forearm, a nonentity, a pygmy in every respect, in essence and in deed.

'Now, what are you doing? Why do you not shout? Why do you not applaud? Raise your voices, you orators! Sing, you poets! Write, you geniuses! Let your refrain be: the famous, the extraordinary, the great man!'

All stood aghast and looked at one another as if asking: 'What kind of giant is this? What heroic trait do you see in him?'

But soon the crowd of flatterers began to cry ever louder, 'Yes! Yes! the giant, the giant! The biggest man in the world! What a mighty prince is he! What a valiant marshal! What an eminent minister is so-and-so!'

At once, doubloons showered on them. Then the authors wrote, no longer stories, but panegyrics. The poets, even Pedro Mateo himself,[1] chewed their nails, fearing for their livelihood. And no one there dared say the opposite. Rather, they all tried to outdo one another, shouting: 'The giant! the great, the almighty giant!' For everyone hoped for a post, a benefice. Secretly and at heart, of course, they said: 'How boldly I lie! He has not even grown up, but is still a dwarf. But what can I do? Carry on and say what you think; then you will see where that will get you. On the other hand, acting as *I* do, I have clothing and food and drink, and can shine and become a great man. Therefore, he may be what he likes, but in spite of the whole world, he shall be a giant.'

Andrenio began to go with the flow, and he, too, shouted: 'The giant, the giant, the colossal giant!' And instantly gifts and doubloons were showered on him; so he exclaimed: 'That, that is the wisdom of life!'

xxxix But Critilo stood there, about to fly into a passion. 'I shall burst if I do not speak,' he said.

'Don't speak,' said the interpreter: 'and do not rush to your ruin. Wait until the giant turns his back on us, and then you will see how things go.'

And so it came about: for as soon as the fellow had finished playing his part as a giant, and now retreated into the shrouding room, everyone began to shout: 'What simpletons we have been! That was no giant, but a pygmy in whom there was nothing and who came to nought.' And they asked one another how it had been possible.

But Critilo said: 'What a difference there is between our talking about a person during his lifetime or after his death! How absence alters speech! How great is the distance between something over our heads and something under our feet!'

Yet this modern Sinon's trickery was not yet at an end.* He now rushed to the other side and fetched eminent men, true giants, whom he presented as dwarfs, good-for-nothings, indeed less than nothing. To this all agreed, and so these eminent men would have had to pass for dwarfs, but for people of judgement and critical faculty daring to grumble. In fact, he even produced the Phoenix and said it was a beetle. All agreed that it was so, and so it had to pass for a beetle.

So much for Gracián, and so much for the supreme philosophers, whom the Danish Academy quite earnestly believe may demand

---

[1] He had celebrated Henry IV [of France, 1553–1610, assassinated French Protestant Huguenot leader]: see *Criticón*, part III, Crisis 12, p. 376. [Schopenhauer's note.]

respect: whereby they have put me in the position of having to serve them with a lesson to counter their lesson.

I have still to remark that the public would have received the present two prize essays a half-year sooner if I had not expected that the Royal Danish Society, as is right and as all academies do, would make known their decision in the same journal in which they published their prize question abroad (in this instance in the *Halle'sche* xl *Litteraturzeitung*). This, however, they have not done, but one must obtain the decision from Copenhagen, which is all the more difficult, as not once in the prize question is the time of their decision given. For this reason, I have had to adopt this means six months too late.[1]

Frankfurt-am-Main
September 1840

---

[1] Indeed, they have subsequently publicized their judgement, that is, after the appearance of the present ethics and this censure. Specifically, their judgement was published in the *Intelligenzblatt der Halle'schen Litteraturzeitung*, November 1840, No. 59, and they have also printed their judgement in the *Jena'schen Litteraturzeitung* of the same month.—What was published in November had been decided the previous January. [Schopenhauer's note.]

# PREFACE TO THE SECOND EDITION

xli BOTH prize essays in this second edition have received rather important additions, which mostly are not long, but are inserted in many passages to assist with a thorough understanding of the whole. One cannot estimate them by number of pages because of the larger format of the present edition. Moreover, they would be even more numerous if not for the uncertainty of whether I would live to see this second edition. In the meanwhile, this uncertainty had necessitated that the thoughts relevant here be put down in turn wherever I could; namely, in part in the second volume of my principal work,* chap. 47, and in part in *Parerga and Paralipomena*, vol. 2, chap. 8—

The essay on the foundation of morals, which the Danish Academy had rejected and rewarded only with a public rebuke, appears again here after twenty years in this second edition. In the first edition I have already given the necessary refutation of the academy's judgement and have primarily proven in the same that the academy denied having asked what it had asked; on the contrary, what it claimed to have asked xlii was that which it absolutely had not asked. And, indeed, I have done so there (pp. 6–10) so clearly, fully, and thoroughly, that no shyster in the world could refute it. What relevance it has here, I need not begin to say. Concerning the conduct of the academy in general, after twenty years of coolest reflection I now have the following still to add.

If the goal of academies were to suppress the truth as much as possible, to stifle intellect and talent by any means, and boldly to preserve the repute of windbags and charlatans, then this time our Danish Academy would have served the purpose splendidly. However, because I cannot show the requisite respect for windbags and charlatans whom paid flatterers and deluded dunces proclaim to be great thinkers, I will, instead, offer the gentlemen of the Danish Academy some useful advice. When the gentlemen issue prize questions to the world, they must first reserve for themselves a modicum of the power of judgement, at least as much as serves to get by, just enough as is needed to be able to distinguish the oats from the chaff. For otherwise, if it is put too badly in Ramus' *Dialectics* one can run into trouble.[1]

---

[1] *Dialectices Petri Rami pars secund, quae est 'De judicio'.* [The Dialectic of Peter Ramus, part two, which is 'On judgment'.] [Schopenhauer's note.]

Namely from Midas' judgement Midas' fate follows, without exception. Nothing can prevent it; no grave faces nor noble airs can help. It will surely come to light. However great a wig one puts on, there is no lack of indiscreet barbers, of indiscreet reeds; indeed, nowadays one does not take the trouble first to bore a hole in the earth.*—But now, in addition to all of this, comes the childish confidence to deal me a public rebuke and to have it published in the German literary journals because I have not been such a simpleton as to let myself xliii be imposed upon by the continuous flattery of submissive ministerial creatures and brainless literary rabble who, along with the Danish Academy, regard as supreme philosophers mere buffoons who have never sought the truth, but rather their own interests. Has it not at all occurred to these academicians first to ask themselves whether they had even a shadow of justification for dealing me a public rebuke for my views? Are they so completely forsaken by all the gods that this does not occur to them?—Now come the consequences: the nemesis is here: the reeds already rustle! I have finally prevailed, in defiance of the long-standing, united opposition of all the professors of philosophy, and the eyes of the learned public are more and more opened about the supreme philosophers of our academicians. If these supreme philosophers are feebly supported by the despicable professors of philosophy who have long compromised themselves and who, for a little while, need them as material for their lectures, then these supreme philosophers have, indeed, sunk very low in public estimation, and Hegel in particular fast approaches the contempt that awaits him in posterity. For twenty years, opinion about him has come three-quarters of the way to outcome with which Gracián's allegory closes, as given in the preface to the first edition, and in a few years it will entirely coincide with the judgement that gave 'just and grave offence'[1] to the Danish Academy some twenty years ago. Therefore, as a gift in return for the Danish Academy's rebuke, I will grace their album with this verse from Goethe:

> You can always praise the waste,
> And thereby reap a quick reward. xliv
> You'll swim with the scum,
> The patron saint of muckers.

---

[1] *tam justam et gravem offensionem.*

> Abuse the best? — Just try it!
> Here's how it will go if you dare to be impudent:
> When people track you down,
> You will end up in the sludge, just as you deserve.*

That our German professors of philosophy considered the contents of these prize essays not to be worth consideration, let alone to take to heart, I have already befittingly acknowledged in the essay *On the Principle of Sufficient Reason*, second edition, pp. 47–9, and this goes without saying.* Why would elevated minds of this kind attend to that which is said by little people like me, little people upon whom, at the most, in their writings, they look down with a contemptuous glance and hurl their censure! No, what I present, they do not dispute: they stick by their freedom of the will and their moral law, even if reasons to the contrary be so numerous as blackberries. For they all adhere to the articles of faith, and they know the purpose for which they exist: they exist for the greater glory of God[1] and collectively deserve to be members of the Royal Danish Academy.

Frankfurt-am-Main
August 1860

---

[1] *in majorem Dei gloriam.*

# Prize Essay
# on the Freedom of the Will*

awarded the prize by the
Royal Norwegian Society of Sciences,
at Trondheim on 26 January 1839

Motto:
*La liberté est un mystère.**

*Num liberum hominum arbitrium e sui ipsius conscientia demonstrari potest?*
**Translated: 'Can the freedom of the human will be demonstrated from self-consciousness?'**

I

# DEFINITIONS OF CONCEPTS

GIVEN such a significant, serious, and difficult question, which essentially coincides with one of the main problems of all medieval and modern philosophy, great exactitude, and therefore, an analysis of the principal concepts that occur in the question, is certainly appropriate.

## (1) What does freedom mean?

Precisely considered, this concept is a *negative*. By this term, we mean only the absence of all hindering and restraining which, expressed as force, must then be positive. In keeping with the possible nature of this restraint, the concept has three very distinct varieties: physical, intellectual, and moral freedom.

(a) *Physical freedom* is the absence of all *material* hindrances of all sorts. So we say: free skies, free view, free air, free field, a free place, free heat (that is not chemically bound), free electricity, free course 4 of a stream where it is no longer restrained by mountains or sluices, etc. Even free room, free board, free press, postage-free mail indicate the absence of burdensome conditions, which, as hindrances to enjoyment, usually attach to such things.* Most often in our thinking, however, the concept of freedom is attributed to animate beings, the characteristic of which is that their movements proceed from *their will*, are voluntary, and, consequently, are called *free* when no material hindrance makes them impossible. Now since these hindrances can be of very different sorts, but that which they hinder is always *the will*, for the sake of simplicity it is preferable to understand the concept of freedom from the positive side, and, hence, to think of everything that moves only through its own will or acts only from its own will, which reversal of the concept actually alters nothing. As a result, in this *physical* meaning of the concept of freedom, animals and humans can be called *free* when neither chains, nor prison, nor paralysis, and, thus, in general no *physical, material* hindrance, impedes their action, but they proceed in accord with their *will*.

This *physical meaning* of the concept of freedom, especially as attributed to animate beings, is the original, immediate, and, thus the most common, in which it is cast with certainty, without doubt or controversy; instead, its reality can always be verified through experience. For as soon as an animate being acts only from its *will*, it is, in this meaning, *free*: whereby no account is taken of anything which might have influence on the will itself. For in its original, immediate and, therefore, popular meaning, the concept of freedom refers only to the ability to act, i.e., exactly to the absence of *physical* hindrance to its action. Hence one says, the bird in the sky, the wild beast in the forest are free; the human is by nature free; only the free are happy. One also calls a people free, thereby understanding that they are regulated only by laws that they themselves have created, for in that case the people follow only their own will. Political freedom is, therefore, to be counted among the physical.

5    Yet as soon as we turn away from this *physical* freedom and consider the two other kinds of the same, we no longer deal with a popular sense of the concept, but with the *philosophical*, which, as we all know, opens up the way to many difficulties. This sense divides into two completely different kinds: intellectual and moral freedom.

(b) *Intellectual freedom* ('the voluntary and involuntary with respect to thought'[1] in Aristotle's terms) is considered here merely for the sake of complete classification of concepts: therefore I take the liberty to set aside discussion of it until the very end of this essay, so that concepts necessary to understanding it will already have been explained, so that it can be handled concisely. In the classification, however, it must take its place next to physical freedom to which it is closely related.

(c) I turn therefore immediately to the third kind, to *moral freedom*, as that which actually is the free choice of the will* to which the question of the Royal Society refers.

On one hand, this concept is connected to that of physical freedom in a way which also makes one understand its necessarily much

---

[1] τὸ ἑκούσιον καὶ ἀκούσιον κατα διάνοιαν [Hübscher cites *Ethica Eudemia* II. 7: 1223a. 23–5.]

later origin. As I said before, physical freedom refers only to material hindrances, with the absence of which it coincides. In many cases, however, one observes, that, unrestrained by material hindrances, a person is kept from acting as would certainly have been consistent with his will by mere motives, such as threats, promises, perils, and the like. One must ask, then, whether such a person had still been *free?* or whether a stronger counter-motive could, like a physical hindrance, actually restrain and even render impossible the action that is consistent with his intrinsic will? The answer to this question should not be hard for one with common sense: that, of course, a motive could never be as effective as a physical hindrance, for this can generally completely overcome human physical powers; whereas, a motive could never be so overpowering, never have absolute power, but it might always be overcome by a *stronger counter-motive*, if only such a motive were present, and the particular person in this specific case were determined by it. Then, too, as we frequently see, even the typically strongest of all motives, the preservation of life, will indeed be overpowered by other motives, e.g.: in suicide and in sacrifice for the lives of others, for beliefs, and for all sorts of causes. Conversely, all degrees of the most excruciating torture on the rack have sometimes been overcome by the mere thought that otherwise life would be lost. If, however, this also made it evident that motives possess no purely objective and absolute compulsion, a subjective and relative compulsion could still obtain, that is, for the person concerned, which in the end was the same. Therefore the question remained, is the will itself free?—Here, then, the concept of freedom, which one previously had considered only in connection with *ability*, was set in relation to the *willing*, and the problem arose, of whether the willing itself was free. But, on closer consideration, the purely empirical and hence popular concept of freedom proves incapable of entering into this connection with *willing*. For following the ordinary conception, 'free' means—'*in conformity with one's own will*': if one then asks whether the will itself is free, one then asks if the will is in accord with itself: which, indeed, is self-evident, whereby nothing is said. According to the empirical concept of freedom, one says, 'I am free, when I can *do what I will*'. And by this 'what I will' freedom is already decided. But now, however, since we inquire about the freedom of *willing* itself, this question must be put accordingly: 'Can you also *will* what you will!'—which turns out to be as if willing were to depend on another willing which lies behind it. And put in this way, the question would be affirmed; so the second would immediately arise: 'Can you also will what you will to will?' And so, it would be driven into an infinity, since we always would think *one* willing to be dependent upon a prior or deeper willing, and futilely strive in this way ultimately to reach one which we think to be dependent upon nothing and must accept. But if we wanted to accept such, we could just as well take the first as the arbitrary final one, whereby the question would indeed be led back to the simple 'can you will?' But what one wanted to know is whether the mere affirmation of this question decides the freedom of the willing, and this question remains unresolved. The original, empirical concept of freedom, taken from doing, then refuses to enter into a direct connection with the willing. Therefore, to be able to apply this concept of freedom to the will, one must modify the concept, conceiving it more abstractly. This occurs when one in general thinks of the concept of *freedom* as the absence of all *necessity*. The concept thereby takes on a *negative* character, which I had recognized in it right from the outset. Next, therefore, one must discuss the concept of *necessity*, as the *positive* concept which lends *negative* meaning to the concept of freedom.

Thus we ask: what does *necessity* mean? The usual explanation, 'necessity is that whose opposite is impossible or what cannot be otherwise' — is a mere verbal explanation, a paraphrase of the concept, which does not increase our understanding. As a real explanation, however, I offer this: *necessity is that which follows from a given sufficient ground*, which proposition, like any correct definition, also allows conversion. Indeed, when this sufficient ground is logical, or mathematical, or physical (called a cause), the *necessity* will be logical (as in the conclusion when the premises are given), mathematical (e.g. the equality of the sides of the triangle when the angles are equal), or physical, real (as in the occurrence of the effect as soon as the cause is present); however, necessity always adheres to the consequent with equal strictness when the ground is given. Only insofar as we conceive of something as a consequent from a given ground, do we recognize it as necessary, and conversely, as soon as we recognize something as the consequent of a sufficient ground, we understand that it is necessary: for all grounds are compelling. This real explanation is so adequate and comprehensive that necessity and consequent from a given sufficient ground are actually convertible concepts;

i.e., generally the one can be put in the place of the other.[1]— 8
Consequently, the absence of necessity would be identical with absence
of a determinate sufficient ground. The *contingent* will be considered
to be the opposite of *necessity*; but herein there is no contradiction.
That is to say, anything contingent is so only *relatively*. Since in the
real world, where alone the contingent is to be encountered, every
event is *necessary* in relation to its cause: while in relation to all else,
with which it may coincide in space and time, it is contingent. Now,
however, the free, the distinguishing mark of which is absence of
necessity, must simply be independent of any cause, whereby the
*absolutely contingent* will be defined: a most problematic concept, the
conceivability of which I do not guarantee, but which, nevertheless,
in an even more curious way coincides with the concept of *freedom*.
In any case, the *free* remains that which is in no way necessary, that
is, dependent upon no ground. This concept, then, applied to the
human will, would mean that an individual will in its manifestations
(acts of will) would not be determined through causes or sufficient
grounds in general; for otherwise, since the result of a given ground
(of whatever type this might be) is always *necessary*, its acts would
not be free, but would be necessary. Kant's definition rests on this
point, according to which freedom is the ability to initiate a series
of alterations *by oneself*.\* For this 'by oneself' means, restored to its
true significance, 'without preceding causes', but this is identical
to 'without necessity'. Thus, although just such a definition of the
concept of freedom creates the appearance of being positive, upon
closer examination, its negative nature again becomes evident.— A
free will, therefore, would be one which would not be determined
by grounds — and since everything determining something else must
be a ground, with real things a real ground, i.e., a cause — a free will
would be one which would be determined by absolutely nothing.
Therefore, the particular manifestations (acts of will) of a free will
simply and completely originate from the will itself, without being 9
necessarily caused by previous conditions, and hence, without being
determined by anything according to rule. With this concept, therefore, clear thinking fails us, since the principle of grounds in all of

---

[1] One finds the discussion of the concept of necessity in my essay on the principle of
ground [*On the Fourfold Root of the Principle of Sufficient Reason*], second edition, § 49.
[Schopenhauer's note.]

its meanings, the essential form of our entire cognitive faculty, must be relinquished. In the meanwhile, we do not lack a technical term[1] for this concept: it is *liberum arbitrium indifferentiae*.[2] Moreover, this is the only clear, certain, firm, and determinate concept of that which is called freedom of the will; therefore one cannot depart from it, except in vague, hazy explanations, behind which hides hesitant half-wittedness, as when one speaks of grounds the consequences of which do not necessarily follow. Every consequence from a ground is necessary, and every necessity is the consequence of a ground. From the assumption of such a *liberi arbitrii indifferentiae*, the immediate inference and, therefore, the identifying mark which characterizes this concept, is that for a human individual thus endowed, under given, completely individual, and thoroughly determined external circumstances, two diametrically opposed actions are equally possible.

## (2) What does self-consciousness mean?

Answer: the consciousness of *one's own self*, in contrast to the consciousness of *other things*, which ultimately is the cognitive faculty. Now, indeed, even before any other things appear in this cognitive faculty, it contains certain forms of the manner of this appearance, which forms, therefore, are the conditions of the possibility of their objective existence, viz., their existence as objects for us: familiarly, these forms are time, space, causality. Now although these forms of cognition reside in ourselves, this is only to the end that we are able to be conscious of *other things* as such and always with reference to these forms; therefore, even though these forms reside in us, we must regard them as belonging not to *self-consciousness*, but rather to *the consciousness of other things*, i.e., that which makes objective cognition possible.

10    Further, I will not be tempted by the two meanings of the word *conscientia** as used in the question, to mislead me so as to drag into self-consciousness the familiar moral impulses of humans under the name of conscience, as well as practical reason, with its categorical imperatives, as Kant maintained; in part because such impulses arise first as a consequence of experience and reflection, and thus

---

[1] *terminus technicus.*

[2] [Customarily the Latin *liberum arbitrium indifferentiae* translates as 'free choice of indifference'.]

as a consequence of the consciousness of other things; and in part because the dividing-line between that which is innately and solely in human nature and that which proceeds from moral and religious education is still not sharply and indisputably drawn. Moreover, it cannot likely be the Royal Society's intention to drag conscience into self-consciousness, to play out again the question of the foundation of morals, and now to see repeated Kant's moral proof, or more precisely postulate, of freedom, known from moral laws *a priori*, on the strength of the inference 'you can because you ought'.

From what has just been said, it becomes clear that of our whole consciousness in general, the greatest part by far is not the *self-consciousness*, but the *consciousness of other things*, or the cognitive faculty. With all its powers, this faculty is directed outward and is the theatre (indeed, from the standpoint of a more profound investigation, the condition) of the real, external world, against which it initially reacts by intuitively apprehending, and, afterward works up into concepts what it has gained in this way, by, as it were, ruminating. *Thinking* consists of this endless combination of concepts, accomplished through the help of words. — Therefore, what we have remaining after subtracting the far greater part of our whole consciousness would only be *self-consciousness*. From here we already see that the wealth of the same cannot be great; therefore, if the data sought for the proof of the freedom of the will should actually lie in the same, then we may hope that they will not escape us. As the organ of the self-consciousness, an *inner sense*[1] has been advanced, but this is to be taken more in a figurative than in a literal sense, since self-consciousness is immediate. However this might be, our next question is: what, then, does self-consciousness contain? or: how will a human become immediately conscious of his own self? Answer: altogether as a *willing being*. Anyone will soon become aware, through observation of his own self-consciousness, that at all times its object is his own willing. By this, however, one must certainly understand not merely definite acts of will which immediately become deeds and

11

---

[1] This occurs already in [Marcus Tullius] Cicero as *tactus interior*: *Acad[emica] quaest[ionae]*, [*Academic Questions*] IV. 7; more significantly in Augustine, *De lib[ero] arb[itrio]* [*On the Freedom of the Will*] II. 3 ff.; then in Descartes: *Princ[ipia] phil[osophiae]* [*Principles of Philosophy*] IV. 190; and worked out in detail by Locke. [Schopenhauer's note.]

formal decisions together with the actions which proceed from them; rather, whoever is able to grasp in any way that which is essential, in spite of different modifications of degree and kind, will not hesitate also to count among the manifestations of willing all desiring, striving, wishing, craving, yearning, hoping, loving, delighting, exulting and the like, no less than unwillingness or repugnance, than abhorring, fleeing, fearing, scorning, hating, grieving, suffering, in short, all affects and passions. Since these affects and passions, more or less weak or strong, now violent and stormy or again tender and soft, are movements of our own will, checked or unrestrained, satisfied or unsatisfied; and since in many ways all refer to the accomplishment or lack of what is desired, to the enduring or overcoming of the abhorrent, they are thus definite affections of the same will that is active in decisions and actions.[1] But the above includes even that which one calls feelings of pleasure and displeasure; indeed, these are present in great variety of degree and kind, but each still reduces to affections of desiring or abhorring, and thus to the will becoming conscious of itself as satisfied or unsatisfied, checked or unrestrained. Of course, this extends even to bodily sensations, pleasurable or painful, and to all the countless sensations which lie between these two extremes, since in essence all these affections enter immediately in self-consciousness as something agreeable with the will or disagreeable to it. Precisely considered, one is only immediately conscious even of one's own body as the externally acting agency of the will and the seat of responsiveness to pleasurable or painful sensations, but which sensations themselves, as has just been said, reduce to quite immediate affections of the will that are either agreeable or disagreeable to it. Moreover, whether or not we include these mere feelings of pleasure or displeasure, we find that all movements of the will, all

---

[1] It is certainly noteworthy that the Church Father Augustine had fully recognized this, while many moderns, with their supposed 'faculty of feeling', do not see it. Namely, in *De civit[ate] Dei* [*The City of God*], Bk. XIV, ch. 6, he speaks of the *affectionibus animi* [affections of the mind] which he in the preceding book had subsumed under the four categories, *cupiditas, timor, laetitia, tristitia* [desire, fear, joy, sadness], saying: *voluntas est quippe in omnibus, im[m]o omnes nihil aliud, quam voluntates sunt: nam quid est cupiditas et laetitia, nisi voluntas in eorum consensionem, quae volumus? et quid est metus atque tristitia, nisi voluntas in dissensionem ab his, quae nolumus?* [The will is indeed involved in them all, or, rather, they are all nothing other than acts of will. For what is desire or joy but an act of will in sympathy with those things that we wish, and what is fear or grief but an act of will in disagreement with the things that we do not wish?] [Schopenhauer's note.]

alternating willing and not-willing, which, in constant ebb and flow, constitute the exclusive object of self-consciousness, or, if one wants, the inner sense, stand in thoroughgoing and universally acknowledged relation to that which is perceived and cognized in the external world. However, the latter, as was said, no longer lies in the province of immediate *self-consciousness*, for as soon as we touch the external world, we have reached the region where self-consciousness presses on *consciousness of other things*. But the objects perceived in the external world are the material and occasion of all movements and acts of will. One need not interpret this as begging the question:[1] for no one can dispute that our will always takes external things as its objects, toward which it is directed, around which it turns, and which at least give rise to motives, for otherwise one would be left with the will completely closed off from the external world, imprisoned in the dark inner recesses of self-consciousness. Just the necessity with which each act of will is determined by objects lying in the external world is for us now still problematic.

Thus we find self-consciousness very intensely, actually even exclusively, occupied with *will*. But now, whether such self-consciousness finds in this, its exclusive material, the data from which the *freedom* of that very will issues, as expounded above in its only clear and determinate sense of the word, is our aim, toward which we want now exactly to steer, toward which we so far have manoeuvred, and indeed already have noticeably come near.

---

[1] *petitio principii.*

## II

# THE WILL BEFORE SELF-CONSCIOUSNESS

IF a person *wills*, then he must will something: his act of will is always directed toward an object and can only be thought of in reference to such. What, then, does it mean to will something? It means: the act of will, which above all is itself only an object of self-consciousness, arises on the occasion of something belonging to the consciousness *of other things*, thus of something that is an object of the cognitive faculty, an object that in this reference is called a *motive* and at the same time is the material of the act of will, to which this act of will is directed; i.e., this act of will aims at some kind of alteration in the object, thus reacts to it: in this *reaction* consists its whole essence. At this point, it is already clear that this act of will cannot occur without an object, that it would lack both occasion and material. But the question is: if this object exists for the cognitive faculty, whether the act of will *must* also occur, or might not occur, or could not act, or a completely different, or even an opposite act could occur; so, whether that reaction may not take place or, under entirely the same circumstances, a different or even opposite one may occur. In short, this means: is the act of will necessarily called forth by the motive? Or, rather, with the motive's entrance into consciousness, does the will possess complete freedom to will or not to will? Thus, here the concept of freedom is taken, as discussed above, in the sense here alone proven to be applicable, as mere negation of necessity, and with this our problem is defined. But we have to seek data for the solution to the problem in immediate self-consciousness, and to this end we will carefully examine the evidence of self-consciousness, not, however, by cutting the knot with a summary decision, like *Descartes*, who made the assertion without anything further: 'On the contrary, we are so conscious of the freedom and indifference which is in us that we can conceive of nothing so clear and perfect' (Descartes: *Princ[ipia] phil[osophiae]* I, § 41.)[1] The inadmissibility of this assertion has already been censured by

---

[1] *Libertatis autem et indifferentiae, quae in nobis est, nos ita conscios esse, ut nihil sit, quod evidentius et perfectius comprehendamus.*

*Leibniz* (Leibniz, *Theodicy* I, § 50 and III, § 292), who himself on this point was certainly only a reed wavering in the wind, and who, after the most contradictory remarks, finally arrived at the result that the will would be inclined by the motive, but not necessitated. Specifically, he said: 'All actions are determined and never without influence because there is always a reason which inclines us, even if it is unnoticed, so that we act thus and in no other way' (Leibniz, *De libertate*: *Opera*, ed. Erdmann, p. 669).[1] This gives me occasion to remark that such a compromise between the alternatives posed above is not tenable, and one cannot say with a certain favourite measure of indecision that motives determine the will only to a certain extent, that the will would suffer their influence, but only to a certain degree, and then it could evade it. For as soon as we have attributed causality to a given force, thus having recognized that it is effective, then in the event of resistance, it may match that resistance by intensifying its power, and achieve its effect. He who is not to be bribed by ten ducats, but wavers, can be for 100, etc.

We turn, thus, to our problem of the immediate *self-consciousness*, in the sense which we have established above. Now indeed what information does this self-consciousness give us about the abstract question, namely, about the applicability or inapplicability of the concept of *necessity* to the occurrence of an act of will after a given motive, i.e., the motive presented to the intellect? or about the possibility or impossibility of an act of will's not taking place in such a case? We would find ourselves quite deceived, if we were to expect from self-consciousness profound and thorough explanations about causality generally and motivation in particular, and also about any necessity both bring with them; for self-consciousness as inherent in all humans is much too simple and limited a thing to have anything to say about such matters: these concepts are much better drawn from pure understanding, which is directed outward, and these concepts can always be raised in the forum of reflective reason. On the contrary, that natural, simple, yes, even silly self-consciousness cannot even comprehend the question, not to mention answer it. Its assertion concerning acts of will that each may hear introspectively, stripped

---

[1] *Omnes actiones sunt determinatae et nunquam indifferentes, quia semper datur ratio inclinans quidem non tamen necessitans, ut sic potius, quam aliter fiat.*

of all which is extraneous and inessential and reduced to its naked content, would be expressed something like this: 'I can will, and when I want to will an action, the moving members of my body will immediately carry out my will, as soon as I just will, without fail.' That means in short, '*I can do what I will*'. Immediate self-consciousness goes no farther than this assertion, no matter how one turns the question and in whatever form one may pose it. Its assertion, therefore, always refers to that which *can be done in conformity to the will*: this, however, is the same empirical, original, and popular concept of freedom established right at the beginning, by which *free* signifies '*in conformity to the will*'. Self-consciousness certainly would assert such freedom. But this is not that about which we inquire. Self-consciousness asserts the freedom of the *deed*—on the presupposition of willing: but the freedom of willing is that about which we inquire. Namely, we investigate the relationship of the will itself to the motive: concerning this point such an assertion of 'I can do what I will' offers nothing. The dependence of our deeds, i.e., our bodily actions, on our will, which self-consciousness indeed asserts, is something quite different from the independence of our acts of will from external circumstances, which would constitute freedom of will and about which self-consciousness can assert nothing because these lie outside of its sphere, for these concern the causal relation of the external world (which is given to us as consciousness of other things) to our decisions; self-consciousness, however, can judge nothing of the relation of that which lies completely outside its domain to that which is within. For no power of cognition can establish a relation, one of the members of which can in no way be given to it. Obviously, however, the very *objects* of willing that determine an act of the will lie outside the boundaries of *self-consciousness*, in the consciousness *of other things*; only the act of will itself lies *in* self-consciousness, and we are inquiring after the causal relation of those objects to the act of will. The act of will is just the concern of self-consciousness, besides its absolute mastery over the members of the body, which is actually what is meant by 'what I will'. And it is only the exercise of this mastery, i.e., *the deed*, that stamps such an act, only for self-consciousness, as an act of will. For so long as the act of will is grasped as coming-to-be, it is called a *wish*; when finished, a *decision*; but that this be so, the *deed* first proves to self-consciousness itself: for until it is a deed, the act of will is alterable. And here we already stand exactly at the main source of that certainly undeniable illusion, by which means the naive (that is, the philosophically untrained) opines that for him, in a given case, opposing acts of will would be possible, and thereby boasts about his self-consciousness, which, he opines, asserts thus. Namely, he confuses wishing with willing. He can *wish* opposing things;[1] but can *will* only one of them: and which of these it be, is first revealed to the self-consciousness by *the deed*. But about the law-like necessity, by virtue of which, through opposing wishes, one and not the other becomes will and deed, self-consciousness can even on this contain nothing, for it experiences the result so wholly *a posteriori*, but does not know it *a priori*. Opposing wishes with their motives arise and fall before self-consciousness, in alternation and repeatedly: about each of these it declares that either could become a deed if it becomes an act of will. For this latter, purely *subjective* possibility is, indeed, present in each, and is that very 'I can do what I will'. But this *subjective* possibility is completely hypothetical: it merely says, '*If* I will this, I can *do* it'. But the determination necessary for willing is not present in it, for self-consciousness contains merely the willing and not the determining ground of the willing, which lies in the consciousness of other things, i.e., in the cognitive faculty. On the other hand, it is the *objective* possibility which settles the matter: this, however, lies outside self-consciousness in the world of objects, to which the motive and the human belong as objects, and is, therefore, alien to self-consciousness and belongs to the consciousness of other things. This *subjective* possibility is of the same type as that which lies within the stone to give off sparks, which, however, are caused by the steel, in which the *objective* possibility lies. I will return to this from another direction in the next chapter, where we will consider the will no longer, as here, from within, but from the outside, and where, therefore, we will investigate the *objective* possibility of the act of will; then, after it has been illuminated from two different directions and illustrated through examples, the matter shall obtain its full clarity.

Thus the feeling which lies in our self-consciousness, 'I can do what I will', accompanies us constantly, but merely proves that the decisions or the decisive acts of our will, although springing from the

---

[1] Concerning this, see *Parerga [and Paralipomena]*, vol. II, § 327 of the first edition. [Schopenhauer's note.]

dark depths of our inner being, will always pass over into the intuitive world, to which our body, as all else, belongs. This consciousness builds the bridge between the inner world and outer world, which otherwise would remain divided by a bottomless cleft, since in the latter would be mere intuitions, independent of us in every sense, as objects—in the former, nothing but inconsequential and merely felt acts of will.—If one were to ask a completely naive person, he would then express this immediate consciousness, which is so frequently taken for that of a supposed freedom of will, something like this: 'I can do what I will: if I will to go left, then I go left: if I will go right, then I go right. It all depends on my will: thus, I am free.' This assertion is indeed perfectly true and correct: only with it the will is certainly a presupposition: namely, it takes for granted that the will has already decided; thus, nothing can thereby be settled about the will itself being free. For it says nothing about the dependence or independence of the *occurrence* of the act of will itself, but only about the *results* of this act, as soon as it occurs, or, to speak more precisely, of its inevitable appearance as an action of the body. But it is solely the consciousness underlying any assertion by which the naive person, i.e., the philosophically untrained person who nonetheless in other subjects can still be a great scholar, considers the freedom of the will to be something so very immediately certain that he pronounces it as an indubitable truth and actually cannot even believe that philosophers doubt it in earnest, but in his heart thinks that all the talk about it is mere sparring in schoolroom dialectic and fundamentally a joke. However, precisely because the inherent and surely important certainty stemming from this consciousness is always at hand, and, moreover, because a human is primarily and essentially a practical, not a theoretical, being, the active side of his act of will, i.e., its agency, is much more clearly recognized than the *passive side*, i.e., that of its dependence; hence, it is difficult to make the philosophically untrained person comprehend the actual meaning of our problem and to bring him to the point that he can grasp that the question is not now about the *consequences* but about the *grounds* of his willing in each case; his *doing* certainly depends entirely on his *willing*, but now one demands to know upon what *his willing itself* depends, whether on nothing at all or on something. He could certainly *do* the one, if he will, and just as well *do* the other, if he will; but he should now consider if he then would also be capable of *willing* the one as the other.

If in this respect one were now to pose the question to the person something like this: 'Can you actually comply with one as well as the other of opposing wishes which arise before you?—e.g. given a choice between two mutually exclusive items of property, give preference to the one just as well as the other?' To that he would say: 'Perhaps the choice would be difficult for me: nonetheless, it will always depend just on me if I *will* choose the one or the other, and on no other power: for I have complete freedom of which I *will* to choose, and I will always follow only my *will*.'—If one now says, 'But your willing itself, upon what does that depend?' so the person would answer from self-consciousness: 'On nothing but me! I can will what I want: what I want, that I will.'—And this latter he says without intending the tautology or, even in his innermost consciousness, relying on the principle of identity, only through which it is true. But here, pushed to the extreme, he speaks of a willing of his willing, which is the same as if he were to speak of an I of his I. One has driven him back to the core of the self-consciousness, where he hits upon his I and his will as indistinguishable, but nothing remains to judge them both. Whether, in this choice, where his person and the objects of choice are taken here as given, his *willing itself* could have turned out differently than it finally turns out, or whether by the data just given, the outcome is as necessarily determined as that, in a triangle, the greatest angle lies opposite the longest sides, that is a question which lies so far from natural *self-consciousness* that it cannot once be brought to comprehension, much less that it would have a ready answer or would as well carry within itself the undeveloped germ of the answer which it only need simply reveal.—In the way just given, therefore, the naive but philosophically untrained person, when faced with the perplexity which the question, if actually understood, must give rise to, will always seek to escape behind that immediate certainty, 'what I will, I can do, and I will what I will', as said above. He will attempt this anew, countless times, so that it will be hard to make him face the actual question which he has always sought to elude. And this is not to blame him, for the question is actually a most serious one. It pries with a searching hand in the innermost being of the person; it will know whether, like all the rest in the world, he, too, by his very nature, is a being determined once and for all, a being that, like everything else in nature, has his determined, unvarying qualities from which his reactions to any external occasion necessarily spring, which reactions accordingly, from this point of view, bear an unalterable character and, consequently, whatever may be somewhat modifiable in them, is completely abandoned to determination by external occasion; or whether he alone is an exception to all of nature. If we should finally succeed in making him face this very serious question and make it clear to him that here we inquire into the origin of his acts of will themselves, into what may be the ruled nature or wholly ruleless nature of their origin, then one might discover that immediate self-consciousness has nothing to offer regarding this; for here the naive person himself turns away from immediate self-consciousness and reveals his helplessness through reflection and all sorts of attempts to explain, the grounds of which he first tries to deduce from such experience as he himself and others have had, and next from universal laws of understanding, whereby, however, through the uncertainty and the vacillation of his explanations he suffices to prove that his immediate self-consciousness furnishes no information about the question when it is correctly understood, just as it previously furnished none when the question was erroneously understood. Ultimately this is so because the will is the actual self of the human, the true core of the human being; hence, the will constitutes the ground of his consciousness, as something simply given and present, beyond which he cannot go. For he himself is as he wills, and wills as he is. So to ask him whether he could also will other than he wills, is to ask him whether he could as well be another person than himself: and that he does not know. For the same reason the philosopher, who distinguishes himself from that person through mere practice, if he wants to achieve clarity in this difficult matter, must turn to his understanding, which produces cognitions *a priori*, to reason, which contemplates such matters, and to experience, which presents to him his own and others' doings, for the interpretation and examination of such cognition of the understanding as the only competent court of last resort, whose verdicts are never so easy, so immediate and simple 22 as those of self-consciousness, but which will be sufficient for the matter. It is the head which has raised the question, and it, too, must provide the answer.

Furthermore, it might not surprise us that immediate self-consciousness has no answer to show for this abstruse, speculative, difficult, and serious question. For this is a very limited part of our whole consciousness, dark in its interior, with all of its objective cognitive powers completely externally directed. All of its completely sure, i.e., *a priori* certain, cognitions concern just the external world, and, through the certainty of universal laws rooted within itself, it can determine with certainty what on the outside is possible, what impossible, what necessary, and in this way it brings about *a priori* pure mathematics, pure logic, even pure, fundamental natural science. At first the application of its forms, known to it *a priori*, to data given by sensory experience produces the intuitive, real, external world and, thereby, experience; furthermore, by applying logic and this fundamental faculty of thought to this outer world, it will produce concepts, the world of thoughts, and thereby the sciences, their achievement, etc. *The outside*, then, lies before its eyes with great brightness and clarity. But inside it is as obscure as a well-blackened telescope: no *a priori* principle illuminates the night of its own interior; these lighthouses only shine to the outside. As explained before, nothing is present to the so-called inner sense but one's own will, to the movements of which all so-called inner feelings, too, are traced back. But everything which this inner perception of the will produces goes back to willing and not-willing, along with the acclaimed certainty that 'What I will, that I can do', which actually says: 'I see immediately each act of my will (in a way to me entirely incomprehensible) present itself as an action of my body' — and put precisely, for the cognizing subject it is an empirical proposition. Concerning this there is nothing more to find here. For the question as posed, the tainted tribunal is incompetent; indeed, the question in its true sense cannot be brought before this tribunal, for it cannot understand the question.

I will now summarize in a shorter and easier way the answer we 23 received to our question of the self-consciousness. Every person's *self-consciousness* clearly says that he can do what he wills. Since even completely opposing actions could be thought of as *willed* by him, then it surely follows that he can also do that which is opposing, *if he wills*. This the untrained understanding confuses with the claim that in a given case opposing actions could be *willed*, and he calls this *the freedom of the will*. However, that in a given case he could *will* opposing actions is simply not supported by the assertion above, but merely this: that of two opposing actions, if he *wills this*, he can do it, and if he *wills that*, likewise he can do it; however, whether in a given case, he *could will* the one as well as the other remains undetermined by the assertion, and is the object of a more profound investigation than can be decided through mere self-consciousness. The shortest, if almost scholastic, form of this result would read: the assertion of the self-consciousness concerns the will merely as to the consequent;[1] the question about freedom, on the contrary, as to the antecedent.[2] — Therefore that undeniable assertion of the self-consciousness, 'I can do what I will', contains and determines absolutely nothing more about the freedom of the will than that in a single, individual case, and thus in a given individual character, every act of will itself would not be necessarily determined by the external circumstances in which this person here finds himself, but would now be one way, and perhaps again turn out otherwise. Concerning this, however, the self-consciousness remains completely mute: for the matter lies completely outside of its scope, since it depends on the causal relation between the external world and the human being. If one were to ask a person of common sense, but without a philosophical education, in what the freedom of the will would consist, a freedom he so steadfastly maintains on the assertion of his self-consciousness, then he will answer: 'in that I can do what I will, as long as I am not physically constrained.' Therefore it is always the relation of his *doing* to his *willing* of which he speaks. Yet as was indicated in the first chapter, this is mere *physical* freedom. If one were further to ask him, whether he thus in a given case could *will* one thing as well as its opposite, then he would hasten so to affirm; however, as soon as he begins to grasp the sense of the question, he will also begin to become doubtful, finally succumbing to uncertainty and confusion, and from this prefer to take refuge again behind his theme, 'I can do what I will', and with the same to entrench himself against all reasons and rationality. However, the corrected answer to his theme, as I hope to establish without a doubt in the next chapter, would read: 'You can *do* what you *will*: but in any given moment of your life, you can only *will* one definite thing and absolutely nothing other than this one.'

The Royal Society's question would already really be answered by the argument in this chapter, and, indeed, in the negative, although only in the main, as this statement of the facts in the case of self-consciousness will be more completely presented in what is to follow.

---

[1] *a parte post.*    [2] *a parte ante.*

Now, however, in *one* instance, even for this, our negative answer, there is still one check. Namely, if we were now to turn with this question to that authority to which we were referred in the preceding as the only competent one, namely, to pure understanding, to the faculty of reason reflecting on the data of the latter, and to the experience which is a consequence of both, and if the verdict of this might come out that a free choice of the will generally does not exist, but that the behaviour of a human being, like all else in nature, in any given case follows as a necessarily occurring effect, then this would still give us the certainty that the data, from which free choice of the will with which we are concerned would prove itself, *could not once be present* in immediate self-consciousness; that is, by means of the conclusion from the impossible to the non-existent,[1] which is the only possible way to establish *negative* truths *a priori*, our decision, which to this point was demonstrated empirically, would also have a rational ground and as a result be set as doubly certain. For a decided contradiction between the immediate assertions of the self-consciousness and the results of the fundamental principles of pure understanding, along with their application to experience, may not be taken as possible: such a mendacious self-consciousness cannot possibly be ours. In this connection, it is to be noted, that even the supposed antinomy* that Kant advanced on this theme should not even for him ever arise from thesis and antithesis of different sources of cognition, the one perhaps, proceeding from the assertion of self-consciousness, the other from reason and experience; rather, thesis and antithesis both rationalize from allegedly objective grounds, whereby, however, the thesis rests on nothing at all but indolent reason, i.e., on the need at some point to stand still in the regress; on the contrary, the antithesis has all actual objective grounds on its side.

Consequently, this *indirect* investigation, now to be carried out in the field of the cognitive faculty and the external world which lies before it, will at the same time cast much light on the prior *direct* investigation and so serve to enlarge and complete it, uncovering the natural misconceptions that arise from false interpretations of this really simple assertion of self-consciousness when this assertion comes into conflict with the consciousness of other things, which is the cognitive faculty, rooted in one and the same subject with self-consciousness.

---

[1] *a non posse ad non esse.*

Indeed, for the first time with the conclusion of this indirect investigation some light will dawn on us about the true meaning and content of that 'I will' which accompanies all of our actions and about the consciousness of originality and spontaneity by which they are *our* actions; in this way, the direct investigation carried out so far will finally achieve its completion.

# THE WILL BEFORE CONSCIOUSNESS
# OF OTHER THINGS

IF we now turn with our problem to the cognitive faculty, then we know from the outset that since this faculty is essentially directed to the external, the will cannot be an object of immediate perception for it as the will is for the self-consciousness, which nonetheless was found to be incompetent on the subject; but we know that here, only *beings* endowed with a will can be considered, for such beings are present for the cognitive faculty as objective and external appearances, i.e., as objects of experience, and furthermore as such can be examined and judged, partly according to universal, *a priori* certain rules fixed for the possibility of experience in general, partly according to the facts that complete and actual experience provides. Thus, here we have nothing more, as previously, to do with the *will* itself as it only lies revealed to the inner sense, but here we are concerned with the willing, *beings moved by will*, which are objects for the external sense. If we are now also thereby placed at a disadvantage in considering the actual object of our investigation only in a mediated way and from a great distance, then this disadvantage will be outweighed by the advantage that we now can employ for our investigation a much more perfect instrument[1] than was the dark, dumb, and one-sided, direct self-consciousness, the so-called inner sense; namely, the more per- 27 fect instrument is the *understanding*, furnished with all its external senses and all its powers of *objective* apprehension.

As the most universal and fundamentally essential form of understanding we find the *law of causality*, by which means alone intuition of the real, external world comes into being, as we instantly and immediately perceive the affections and alterations of our sense organs as '*effects*' and (without guidance, instruction, and experience) in a moment make the transition to their '*causes*' which, by this time, through this very process of understanding, present themselves as *objects in space*.[2] From this it becomes incontestably clear that the *law of causality* is

---

[1] *organon.*

[2] One may find the fundamental exposition of this doctrine in the essay on [*On the Fourfold Root of the*] *Principle of Sufficient Reason*, § 21 of the second edition. [Schopenhauer's note.]

known to us *a priori*, hence as a law *necessary* with regard to the possibility of any experience, without our needing the indirect, difficult, even unsatisfactory proof which Kant had given for this important truth. The law of causality is firmly established *a priori* as the universal rule to which all real objects of the external world, without exception, are subject. That this is so without exception is due to its apriority. The same law of causality essentially and conclusively applies to *alterations*, and it says that wherever and whenever, in the objective, real, material world, anything, great or small, much or little, *alters*, just *previously* something else must necessarily have altered, too, and for *this to have altered* yet another *before it*, and so on into infinity, without anyone's ever seeing, or even just to being able to think, let alone to presuppose any beginning-point to this regressive line of alterations that fills time as matter fills space. For the tireless, self-renewing question, 'What gives rise to this alteration?' never allows the understanding a final resting-point, however much it may tire, on account of which, a first cause is just as unthinkable as a beginning of time or a boundary to space. — The law of causality says

28 nothing less: if the earlier alteration—the cause—has occurred, the later alteration which arises therefrom—the effect—must occur inevitably, hence it follows *necessarily*. Through this character of *necessity*, the law of causality proves itself to be a form of the *principle of grounds*, which is the most universal form of our whole cognitive faculty and which appears in the real world as causality, in the world of thoughts as the logical law of the ground of knowledge, and even in empty, but *a priori* intuited space as the law of the position of all parts of space being strictly, reciprocally, and necessarily dependent on one another—which necessary dependence is the sole theme for geometry specially and fully to demonstrate. For just this reason, as I have already explained at the outset, *to be necessary* and *to be the consequence of a given ground* are interchangeable concepts.

All of the objective *alterations* which take place among objects existing in the real, external world are subject to the law of *causality* and occur, therefore, when and where they occur, always as *necessary* and inevitable. — There can be no exception to this, for the rule holds *a priori* for all possibility of experience. However, with regard to the rule's *application* in a given case, one need merely ask whether there is an *alteration* of a real object given in external experience: as soon as this is so, an application of the law of causality underlies its alterations; i.e., these must be brought about through some cause and for that very reason *necessarily*.

Given this rule, known *a priori* and, hence, valid without exception for all possible experience, if we now approach this experience itself more closely and we consider the real objects given by experience, to whose occasional alterations our rule refers, we then soon notice among these objects some profound and striking main distinctions by which these have long been classified: namely some are inorganic, i.e., lifeless; some organic, i.e., living, and, again, some of these are plants and others animals. Although these last are similar to one another in essence and corresponding in their concept, we find them in an extremely diverse and finely nuanced gradual scale of perfec- 29 tion, from those quite closely related to the plants, from which they are difficult to distinguish, up to the most perfected, corresponding to the concept of the animal in its most perfect form, at the pinnacle of which gradual scale we see humankind—ourselves.

Without letting ourselves be led into error by this diversity, if we now just consider all of these beings collectively as the objective, real objects of our experience, and if we accordingly proceed to apply to the alterations occurring in such beings the firmly established, *a priori* law of causality for the possibility of all experience, then we would indeed find that experience always turns out to follow the *a priori* known law; however, the great *diversity* which we recall among the nature of all those objects of experience corresponds also to a proportionate modification in the manner in which causality imposes its rule on them. Put more precisely, it appears that corresponding to the threefold distinction among inorganic bodies, plants, and animals, the causality which directs all their alterations likewise is of three forms, namely as *cause*, in the narrowest sense of the word, or as *stimulus*, or as *motivation*—except that this modification would not in the least undermine the established, *a priori* validity of the law of the necessity of the consequence.

The *cause* in the narrowest sense of the word is that by means of which all mechanical, physical, and chemical alterations of the objects of experience occur. At all times, it is characterized by two marks: first, through it Newton's third law, 'action and reaction are equal to one another', finds its application: i.e., the preceding state, that is to say, the cause, undergoes an equal alteration to that of the following, which is called an effect.—Second, that, in accordance with the second Newtonian law, the degree of the effect is always exactly proportional to the degree of the cause; consequently, an intensification of the latter brings about a like intensification of the former; so that, if once the type of effect is known, thereafter, from the degree of intensity of the cause, the degree of the effect can also be known, measured, and calculated, and vice versa. However, in empirical application of this second distinguishing mark, one must not confuse the actual effect with its superficial appearance. E.g., one must not expect that with the compression of a body, its volume would constantly decrease in proportion as the compressive force increases. For the space in which one forces a body constantly decreases; consequently, resistance increases; and although the real effect here, which is compression, actually increases in proportion to the cause, as Mariotte's Law says, this is certainly not to be understood from just any visible appearance. Furthermore, in many cases in which the degree of the influence is certain and determinate, suddenly the entire type of the effect will alter, actually because the type of reaction alters, because it was exhausted in a body of finite size; so, e.g., the warmth conducted to water will raise its temperature to a certain degree; however, above this degree only quick evaporation results. With this, however, the same relation occurs between the degree of the cause and that of the effect, and this is so in many cases. Such *causes in the narrowest sense* are those which affect the alterations of all *lifeless*, i.e., *inorganic*, bodies. Observation of all alterations, which are the object of mechanics, hydrodynamics, physics, and chemistry, guides the knowledge and hypotheses about causes of this type. Being exclusively determined by causes of this type alone is, therefore, the sole and essential mark of an inorganic or lifeless body.

The second type of cause is the *stimulus*, i.e., that cause which, first, itself suffers *no* counter-effect corresponding to its influence and, second, in which no proportionality obtains between its intensity and the intensity of the effect. Consequently, here the degree of the effect cannot be measured and determined ahead of time from the degree of the cause; rather, a slight increase in the stimulus can cause a very great increase in the effect, or even, conversely, a slight increase can completely cancel the aforementioned effect, indeed, even bring about an opposing effect. E.g., as is known, plants can be driven to an extraordinarily rapid spurt of growth by warmth or even by lime mixed in the soil, since each cause affects plants' life force as a stimulus;

however, if in this way the suitable degree of stimulus is exceeded
a bit, the result, instead of an enhanced and accelerated life, will be 31
the death of the plant. So, too, with wine or opium, we can stretch
and considerably heighten our mental powers; however, if the proper
measure of the stimulus is exceeded, the result will be just the
opposite. — Causes of this type, that is, *stimuli*, are those which determine all alterations of organisms *as such*. All alterations and development of plants and all purely organic and vegetative alterations or
functions of animal bodies proceed from *stimuli*. They are affected
in this way by light, warmth, air, nourishment, any drug, any touch,
fertilization, *etc.* — While at the same time, the life of animals has yet
a completely different sphere, of which I will soon speak; whereas,
the whole life of *plants* proceeds exclusively from *stimuli*. All their
assimilation, their growth, their striving with their crowns toward the
light, with their roots to better soil, their fructification, their germin-
ation, etc. is alteration from *stimuli*. In this way, in a few, particular
species, even a peculiarly quick movement happens, which nonetheless only follows from stimuli, on account of which they are in fact
called sensitive plants. As is known, these are mainly *Mimosa pudica*,
*Hedysarum gyrans*, and *Dionaea muscipula*.* Consequently, a *plant* is
any body whose characteristic movements and alterations, in accordance with its nature, always and exclusively follow from *stimuli*.

The third type among the moving causes is that which denotes the
character of *animals*: it is *motivation*, i.e., causality that occurs through
*cognition*. It enters in the gradual scale of natural beings at the point
at which a being is of more complicated and, therefore, manifold
needs which can no longer merely be satisfied with the occasion of a
stimulus that must be awaited; rather, this being must be in a position
to choose, to seize, indeed to seek out the means of satisfaction. For
this reason, there appears in beings of this sort, in place of mere
responsiveness to *stimuli* and the movement which result from such,
a responsiveness to *motives*, i.e., a faculty of representation, an intellect, in countless shades of perfection, presenting itself materially as 32
the nervous system and the brain, and even therewith, consciousness. It is known that plant life, which as such proceeds only upon
*stimuli*, serves as basis for animal life. But all movements that the animal as *animal* performs, which movements, therefore, depend exactly
on what physiology calls *animal functions*, occur in consequence of
a cognized object, thus, *on motives*. Consequently, an *animal* is any

body whose characteristic external movements and alterations, in accordance with its nature, always follow *from motives*, i.e., from certain *representations* which here are present to its already presupposed consciousness. Just as the capacity to represent, and, hence, consciousness, may have such infinite stages among the ranks of animals, so, too, in each animal just enough of such capacity is at hand that the motive presents itself to the animal and occasions its movement, whereby the inner, moving force, the particular expression of which is called forth by the motive, makes itself known to the self-consciousness at hand as that which we denote by the word *will*.

Now whether a given body is moved by *stimuli* or by *motives* can never remain in doubt, even from external observation, which is our standpoint here, for the type of effect of a stimulus is so obviously different from that of a motive. For a stimulus always works through immediate touch or even intussusception; then, too, when this is not visible, as when air, light, or warmth is the stimulus, the stimulus still reveals itself in that the effect bears an unmistakable relation to the duration and intensity of the stimulus, even though this relation does not remain the same for all degrees of a stimulus. When, in contrast, a *motive* causes a movement, all such distinctions completely disappear. For here the characteristic and closest medium of influence is not the atmosphere, but only *cognition*. The object affected by a motive needs nothing else whatsoever than to *be perceived*, *cognized*, whereby it is wholly indifferent to however long, or however near or far, and however clearly it is taken in apperception. Here all these differences alter the degree of the effect not at all: as soon as the object is simply perceived, it works in just the same way, presuming that it is at all a determining ground of the will that is to be excited here. For even physical and chemical causes, and likewise stimuli, work only insofar as the body to be affected is *responsive* to them. I just said 'of the will to be excited here', since, as already mentioned, what actually imparts to the motive the power to affect, the secret spring of the movement called forth by the motive, here makes itself known inwardly and immediately to the creature itself as that which the word *will* denotes. With bodies exclusively moved by stimuli (plants), we call this persistent, inner condition life force;—with bodies moved by mere causes in the narrowest sense, we call it natural force or quality: it is always presupposed in explanations to be the inexplicable because here in the interior of the being there is no self-consciousness to which it might be immediately accessible. Now if, departing from *appearance in general,* one wanted to inquire about that which Kant calls the thing in itself, whether in beings without cognition, even lifeless beings, this inner condition of its reaction to external causes might possibly be identical with that which we call in us *will,* as a recent philosopher actually has wanted to demonstrate to us—this I leave aside, yet without wanting exactly to contradict it.[1]

On the contrary, I should not leave unconsidered the difference within motivation that gives rise to the distinction of human above any animal consciousness. The former, which actually is denoted by the word *reason,* consists in that the human, unlike the animal, is not merely capable of *intuitive* apprehension of the external world, but is able to abstract from it universal concepts (*notiones universales*). In order to be able to fix and firmly hold these concepts in his sensible consciousness, he denotes them with words and makes of them countless combinations which always, like the concepts of which they consist, refer to the intuitively cognized world. These, however, actually constitute that which one calls *thinking* and by which the great advantages 34 of the human race over all else become possible, namely language, circumspection, retrospection, concern for the future, purpose, intention, methodical and cooperative action of the many, the state, sciences, arts, etc. All of these rest on the unique ability to have non-intuitive, abstract, universal representations which one calls *concepts* (i.e., comprehensions of things) because each subsumes many individuals under itself. All animals, even the most clever, are without this ability; hence, they have nothing but *intuitive* representations and as a result know only what is exactly of the present, live only in the present. The motives, by which their wills are moved, must, therefore, always be intuitive and in the present. From this, however, comes the result that extremely little *choice* is available to them, namely, merely among those things which lie before them intuitively in their narrow mental horizon and faculty of apprehension; that is, among those things which are present in time and space, whereby that which is more powerful as motive immediately determines their will. In this way, the causality of the motive here becomes quite obvious. An *apparent* exception is *training,* which is fear worked by means of habit.

---

[1] It goes without saying that here I mean myself and only on account of the required incognito could not speak in the first person. [Schopenhauer's note.]

To some extent an *actual* exception is instinct, insofar as, by means of instinct, in its way of acting *generally*, the animal is set in motion not really by motive, but by an inner urge and drive. However, in the detail of *particular* actions and in any moment, the animal receives its imminent determination through motives, and therefore reverts to the rule. A closer discussion of instinct would lead me here too far from my theme: the twenty-seventh chapter of the second volume of my principal work is dedicated to it.—In contrast, by virtue of his faculty for *non-intuitive* representations by means of which he *thinks and reflects*, the human has an infinitely wider mental horizon which grasps the absent, the past, the future; therefore, he has a much greater sphere of influence of motives and, consequently, also of choice, than that of the animal with its narrowly limited present. As a rule, what lies before his sensible intuition, present in space and time, is not that which determines his doing; rather, is it mere *thoughts* which he carries about everywhere with him in his head and which make him independent of the impression of the present. If, however, they fail to do this, one calls his action irrational: yet the same will be praised as rational, if it is carried out exclusively from very well-weighed thoughts and thus completely independent of the impression of the intuitive present. Just this, that the human is driven by a special class of representations (abstract concepts, thoughts), which the animal does not have, is itself externally visible as all of the human's doings, even the most insignificant; indeed, all of his movements and steps are impressed with the character of the *intentional and deliberate*. In this his drives are so obviously different from those of the animals, that one sees right away how fine, invisible strings (motives composed merely of thoughts) direct his movements while those of the animals are pulled by the thick, visible ropes of that which is intuitively present. The difference, however, does not go any further. Thought becomes *motive* just as intuition becomes *motive* as soon as it is able to have an effect on the will at hand. All motives are causes, and all causality entails necessity. Now when a human notices the influence of motives on his will, by means of his ability to think, he can present to himself the motives in whatever order he prefers, changed and repeated, in order to hold them before his will, which is called *reflecting*: he is capable of deliberation and has, by means of this capacity, a far greater *choice* than is possible for the animal. Hence he is, indeed, *relatively free*, namely, free of the immediate compulsion of *intuitively present* objects affecting his will as motives, to which the animal is absolutely subjected; in contrast, through thoughts, which are his motives, he determines himself independent of objects present. And it is fundamentally this *relative* freedom that the human obviously has over the animals which educated, but not profound, thinkers understand by freedom of will. However, this is merely relative, that is, in relation to the intuitive present, and merely *comparative*, that is, in comparison with animals. Only *the type* of motivation is altered by this relative freedom; in contrast, the *necessity* of the effect from the motive is not in the least cancelled or even just mitigated. An *abstract* motive, consisting of only a *thought*, is an external cause which determines the will just as does the intuitive motive, consisting of a real, present object; consequently, it is a cause just as any other, even, as the others, always real and material insofar as it is always finally based on an impression obtained *from the outside* at some time and in some place. It has just the advantage of a length of cable: by this I mean to say, that it is not, like mere *intuitive* motives, bound to a certain proximity of space in time, but can work its effect in a long concatenation, through the greatest distance, through the longest time, and through the intervention of concepts and thoughts. This is the result of the nature and eminent responsiveness of the organ that first of all experiences and registers the motive's influence, namely, of the human brain, or of *reason*. This certainly does not in the least nullify its *causality* and its attendant *necessity*. For this reason, only a very superficial view can take this relative and comparative freedom for absolute, for a *liberum arbitrium indifferentiae*. In fact, the capacity to deliberate originating from it produces nothing other than the often agonizing *conflict of motives* over which indecisiveness presides and the battleground of which is the whole mind and consciousness of the human being. For he lets motives repeatedly test their strength against one another on his will, whereby it is put into the same situation that a body is in when different forces work in different directions—until at last the decidedly strongest motive knocks the others from the field and determines the will, which outcome is called decision and, as a result of the battle, occurs with complete *necessity*.

If we now review the entire series of forms of causality, which separates into *causes* in the narrowest sense of the word, then *stimuli*, and finally *motives*, which again break down into the intuitive and the abstract, distinct from one another, then with this in mind we will

notice that when we go through the series of beings from the lowest
to the highest, the cause and its effect increasingly diverge from one-
another, becoming more clearly separate and heterogenous, whereby
the cause becomes less obvious and material, so that less and less seems
to lie with the cause and more and more with the effect, so that, all in
all, the connection between cause and effect loses its immediate comprehensibility and intelligibility. In fact, everything just said is least
the case with *mechanical* causality, which for this reason is the *most
comprehensible* of all. Since this is so, in the previous century a mis-
guided attempt arose, still enduring in France and recently also taken
up in Germany, to reduce all the other types of causes to this one
and to explain all physical and chemical processes by mechanical causes,
and from these the life process. One body, pushing, moves another body
at rest, and as much motion as the former imparts, just so much it loses:
here we see cause as if it were passing into the effect: both are completely homogeneous, exactly commensurable, and, besides, obvious.
And it actually is so with all purely mechanical effects. But one will
find that the higher we ascend, all of this is less and less the case and,
in contrast, what has been said above applies, if at each step we observe
the relation between cause and effect, e.g., between warmth as cause
and its various effects, such as expansion, glowing, melting, evaporation, combustion, thermoelectricity, etc.; or between vaporization as
cause and cooling or crystallization as effects; or between rubbing glass
as cause and free electricity, with its strange phenomena, as effect; or
between slow oxidization of plates as a cause and galvanism, with all
its electrical, chemical, and magnetic phenomena as effect. So as cause
and effect *distinguish* themselves more and more, become more *heterogenous*, their connection more *unintelligible*, the effect seems to contain
more than the cause could produce, for the cause appears less and less
material and obvious. All of this becomes clearer if we turn to *organic*
bodies, where the causes are mere *stimuli*, partly external, as light,
warmth, air, soil, nourishment; partly internal, as the fluids and parts
stimulating one another; and as their effect, life, presents itself in its
infinite complication and in the countless differences of kind, in the
manifold forms of the flora and fauna.[1]

---

[1] One may find a more thorough exposition of this divergence of cause and effect in
*The Will in Nature*, under the heading '[Physical] Astronomy', pp. 80 ff. of the second
edition. [Schopenhauer's note.]

But now with this ever-increasing heterogeneity, incommensurability, and unintelligibility of the relation between cause and effect, is the *necessity* of this relation in any way also reduced? In no way, not in the least. With just such necessity as a rolling ball sets one at rest into motion, so must the Leyden jar discharge when it is contacted by the other hand,—so must arsenic, too, kill every living thing,—so must the seed grain, which, kept dry, showing no alteration for millennia, as soon as it is put in the right soil and exposed to the influence of air, light, warmth, and moisture, germinate and develop into a plant. The cause is more complicated, the effect more heterogenous, but the necessity, with which these occur, is not a hair's breadth less.

In the life of plants and the vegetative life of animals, in every respect, the stimulus is very different from the organic function called forth by it, and both are clearly distinct; however, they are still not actually *separated*; rather, between them a contact, no matter how subtle and invisible, must exist. The complete separation appears first in the life of the animal, the actions of which are called forth by motives, since the cause, which to this point was always materially linked to the effect, now stands completely severed from it, of a completely different nature, primarily immaterial, a mere representation. Thus with a *motive*, which calls forth the movement of an animal, the heterogeneity between cause and effect, the separation of both from one another, their incommensurability, the immateriality of the cause and, hence, its apparent inadequacy compared to the effect, has reached the highest level, and the incomprehensibility of the relation 39 between the two would increase to the absolute level, if we were to know motives, too, as we know all other causal relations, merely *from the outside.* However, here a cognition of a completely different sort, an *inner* cognition, completes the external, and the result, which takes place here as effect from a given cause, is known to us intimately: we denote it by an *ad hoc* term,[1] will. However, that here, too, just as above with stimulus, the causal relation has not lost *necessity*, we declare as soon as we recognize it as a *causal relation* and think of it as the essential form of our understanding. Moreover, we find motivation completely analogous to the other two forms of causal relation discussed above, and only the highest level to which these rise up in

---

[1] *terminus ad hoc.*

gradual steps. At the lowest levels of animal life, the *motive* is still closely related to the *stimulus*: especially among zoophytes, radiata in general, and acephala among the molluscs, we have only a weak dawning of consciousness, just as much as is necessary to perceive their nourishment or prey and snatch it to themselves when it offers itself, and perhaps to change their place for a more favourable one; hence, among these low levels, the effect of a motive exhibits itself to us as clearly, immediately, decidedly, and unambiguously as that of a stimulus. Small insects are drawn to the flame by the shining light; flies land trustingly on the head of a lizard which has just devoured their kind right before their eyes. Who will dream here of freedom? Among the higher, more intelligent animals, effect and motive become increasingly mediated; that is, the motive is separated more clearly from the action which it calls forth, so that one could even use this difference of the distance between the motive and the act as a measure of the intelligence of animals. In the human being, this distance becomes immeasurable. In contrast, even among the most intelligent animals, the representation which will be the motive of their doing must still always be an *intuitive one*. Even when a choice becomes possible, it can only take place between things intuitively present. Between the call of his master and the sight of a bitch, a dog halts hesitatingly; the stronger motive will determine his movement, but then it follows as necessarily as with a mechanical effect. In the mechanical, we see the case of a body brought out of equilibrium oscillating for a long time between one and the other side until it is determined on which its centre of gravity lies and it falls toward that side. Now so long as motivation is limited to *intuitive* representations, its relatedness to the stimulus and the cause in general will be all the more obvious, in that the motive, as an effective cause, must be a real, a present one; indeed, even if very mediated through light, sound, odour, it must still work on the senses physically. Moreover, the effective cause lies as open to the observer as the effect: he sees the motive enter and the animal's doing follow without exception, so long as no other equally obvious motive, or training, counteracts it. It is impossible to doubt the connection between the two. So it will also occur to nobody to attribute to the animal a *liberum arbitrium indifferentiae*, i.e., a doing attributed to no cause.

Now where the consciousness is rational, that is, one of non-intuitive cognition, i.e., capable of concepts and thoughts, then motives become completely independent of the present and real surroundings and thereby remain hidden from the observer. For they are now mere thoughts, which the human carries about in his head, the origin of which, however, lies externally, often even quite far from it, sometimes in the individual's experience of years past, sometimes in strange tradition conveyed orally or in writing, even from the most distant time. Nonetheless, *there is always a real and objective source* of these thoughts, albeit among these motives, through frequent knotty combinations of complicated, external circumstances, there are many errors and, because of tradition, many deceptions and, as a result, also much folly. In addition, it is the case that the human often hides the motive of his doing from everyone else, sometimes even from himself, especially when he is afraid to acknowledge what it actually is that moves him to do this or that. In the meantime, one sees his doings result and by conjecture seeks to ascertain the motives, which one assumes as firmly and confidently as the cause of every movement of lifeless bodies that one might have seen take place, in the belief that 41 the one, as the other, is impossible without a cause. Accordingly and conversely, in one's own plans and undertakings one accounts for the effects of motives on humans with a confidence which would be just the same as that with which one calculates the mechanical workings of mechanical devices, if here one could know the individual character of the person to be dealt with as exactly as the length and thickness of the beams, the diameter of the wheels, the weight of the load, etc. Everyone follows this presupposition as long as he looks outward, is concerned with others, and pursues practical aims, since human understanding is determined for such aims. But if he tries to judge the matter theoretically and philosophically, to which human intelligence is actually not determined, and to make himself the object of judgement, then he allows himself to be misled by what we just described as the immaterial nature of abstract motives consisting of mere thoughts, because they are not bound to anything present and in their environs, and their hindrance itself, too, is only in mere thoughts as counter-motive. He is led so far into error, that he doubts their existence, or at least the necessity of their effect, and he thinks that what will be done could also just as well not take place, that the will determines itself, without causes, and each of his acts is itself the onset of a limitless succession of alterations brought about by it. Now as sufficiently proven in the first chapter, the false interpretation of the assertion of the self-consciousness, 'I can do what I will', most especially props up this error, particularly when this assertion, as always, is uttered about the influence of various present motives which merely solicit and would mutually exclude one another. All things considered, this is the source of the natural deception from which the error grows that in our self-consciousness lies the certainty of the freedom of our will in the sense, contrary to all laws of pure understanding and nature, that it is self-determining without sufficient grounds and its decisions, under given circumstances in one and the same person, could occur one way or the opposite.

42    Particularly to most clearly explain this error, so important to our theme, and thereby to complete the investigation of the self-consciousness engaged in the previous chapter, we will ourselves think of a person who, perhaps standing in the street, says to himself: 'It's 6 in the evening: the workday is ended. I can now take a walk, or I can go to the club; I climb the tower to watch the sun go down. I can also go to the theatre. I can also visit this, or maybe that friend. Indeed, I can run out of the city gate into the wide world and never return. It solely depends on me: in this I have complete freedom. What is more, I could now do none of these, but voluntarily go right home to my wife.' This is exactly the same, as if water were to say: 'I can break in high waves (sure! in the ocean in a storm, that is!); I can rush down rapidly (sure! in a streambed, that is); I can cascade down, foaming and gushing (sure! in a waterfall, that is); I can rise in the air as free as a spray (sure! in a fountain, that is); I can finally, completely evaporate and disappear (sure! at 80°C of heat). What is more, I could now do none of all these, but voluntarily stay, calm and clear, in a sparkling pool.' Just as the water can do any of these only when the determining causes for the one or for the other occur, so can this person do what he imagines, but subject to the same condition. Until the causes occur, it is impossible for him; then, however, he *must* do it just as well as the water, as soon as it is placed in the corresponding circumstances. Arising from a misinterpretation of self-consciousness, his error and in general the deception that he now could do any of these as well as the other, observed precisely, depends on the fact that for his imagination only *one* image at a time can be present and for the moment excludes all else. Now if he imagines the motive for one of these actions which he proposes as possible, then he will feel the effect of the same on his will, which is solicited by it: this

in technical terms is called an act of wishing.[1] But now he thinks that he could also raise this to an act of will,[2] i.e., leading to the proposed action: only this is a deception. Since circumspection would immediately occur and would remind him of the motives which pull the other way or stand in opposition, then he would see that this motive did not result in a deed. With every such successive imagining of different, mutually exclusive motives under constant accompaniment of the inner 'I can do what I will', the will immediately turns like a weather-vane on a well-greased pivot in a variable wind to each motive which the powers of imagination hold before it, to a succession of all motives which are possible and present, and with each, the person thinks he could *will* it, thus fixing the vane at a point, which is mere deception. For in truth, his 'I can do what I will' is hypothetical and carries with it the antecedent 'if I do not prefer to will something else'; this, however, suspends that ability to will.—Let us now return to that notional person, deliberating at 6 o'clock, and imagine that he might now notice that I stand behind him, philosophizing about him and disputing his freedom to do any of the actions possible for him. It could easily happen, then, that to refute me he could carry one out; however, then the necessary motive for him to do so would have been exactly my denial and its effect on his spirit of contradiction. Indeed, that spirit could only move him to one or the other among the *simpler* actions named above, e.g. to go to the theatre; but in no way would it move him to the last named, that is, to run out into the wide world. For such this motive is far too weak.—Many a man just as erroneously thinks, as he holds a loaded pistol in his hands, he could shoot himself with it. This mechanical instrument is the least important means for the act: the most important is an extremely strong and therefore rare motive which has the frightful power to overcome the lust for life or, more correctly, the fear of death. Only after such a motive has occurred, can he actually shoot himself, and then he must. If there then be a still stronger counter-motive, if one such is at all possible, the deed would be prevented.

I can do what I will: I can, if I will, give everything that I have to the poor and thereby become one myself—if I will!—But I am not able to *will* it because opposing motives have much too much power over me for me to be able to do it. Whereas, if I had a different character,

---

[1] *velleitas.*    [2] *voluntas.*

43

44

and indeed, to the extent that I were a saint, then I would be able to will it; however, then I would also have no choice but to will it: I would, thus, have to do it.—This all goes perfectly well with the 'I can do what I will' of the self-consciousness, in which even today some unthinking philosophasters suppose they see freedom of the will and accordingly assert it as a given fact of consciousness. Among these Mr Cousin distinguishes himself and, so, deserves here a *mention honorable*, as in his *Course in the History of Philosophy*, given in years 1819 and 1820 and published by Vacherot* in 1841, he teaches that the freedom of the will is an authentic fact of consciousness (vol. I, pp. 19–20), and criticizes Kant for having proved this merely from the moral law and put it forth as a postulate, since it is, indeed, a fact: 'why prove when a stipulation suffices'?[1] (p. 50) 'freedom is a fact and not a faith' (ibid.)[2]—In the meanwhile Germany, too, does not lack the ignorant, who, casting to the winds everything that great thinkers have said about the subject for two centuries and, bragging about the fact of the self-consciousness that was analysed in the previous chapter, as misconstrued by them as by the great masses, extol the freedom of the will as factually given. Perhaps I do them an injustice, for it could be that they are not so unknowing as they appear, but merely hungry, and, therefore, for a very dry piece of bread teach anything that would please a high ministry.

It is certainly neither metaphor nor hyperbole, but completely dry and literal truth, that as little as a ball on a billiard table can be set into movement before it receives a nudge, just so little can a man rise from his chair before a motive draws him away or compels him, but then his arising is as necessary and inevitable as the roll of a ball upon a nudge. And to expect that someone would do something to which absolutely no interest beckons him is like expecting that a piece of wood would move toward me without a cord which draws it. Should someone 45 who maintains just such a thing in the company of others experience obstinate opposition, he would get out of the matter quickly by having a third person suddenly in a loud and serious voice let out a cry, 'The beams are collapsing!' whereupon those in opposition would arrive at the insight that a motive is just as powerful to drive people out of the house as the strongest mechanical cause.

---

[1] 'pourquoi démontrer ce qu'il suffit de constater?'
[2] 'la liberté est un fait, et non une croyance'.

Because a human, like all objects of experience, is an appearance in time and space, and since the law of causality applies to all appearances *a priori* and so without exception, humans must also be subject to it. So it is said by pure understanding *a priori*; so it is confirmed by the analogy that runs through all of nature; so it is attested by the experience of every moment, so long as one does not let oneself be deceived by the illusion which is brought about by the fact that while natural beings, rising higher and higher, become more complicated and raise and refine their responsiveness to the merely mechanical, to the chemical, electrical, irritable, sensible, intellectual, and finally rational, likewise the nature of *effective causes* must also take the same steps and must correspond to each level of beings on which they would work. For this reason, then, the causes present themselves less and less palpably and materially so that they finally are no longer visible, but are well within the reach of the understanding, which in each case presupposes them with unshakeable confidence and discovers them with proper investigation. For here the effective causes have risen to the level of mere thoughts that struggle with other thoughts until the most powerful of them gives the other a knock-out blow and sets the person into motion, all of which happens with just such strictness of causal connection as when purely mechanical causes in complicated connection work against one another and the calculable result occurs unfailingly. Because of the invisibility of the cause, electrified cork pellets jumping around in the glass in all directions have the appearance of causelessness just as much as the movements of humans: the judgement is not up to the eyes, but to the understanding.

On the assumption of freedom of the will, each human action is an inexplicable miracle—an effect without a cause. And if one hazards the attempt to make the case to oneself for such a *liberum arbitrium indifferentiae*, one will soon become aware that, moreover, the understanding actually remains silent on the matter: it has no form of thinking for such a thing. For the principle of ground, the principle of universal determination and dependence of appearances on one another, is our cognitive faculty's most general form, which itself takes on different forms according to the differences among its objects. Here, however, we are supposed to think about something that determines without its being determined, that depends on nothing, but something else depends on it, that without compulsion, hence without ground, now produces A while B or C or D could be produced just as well, and, indeed, could be produced absolutely, could be produced under the same circumstances, i.e., without there now being anything about A which gives it preference over B, C, D (because this would be motivation, hence, causality). Here we will be led back to the same concept of *absolute chance* which was established as problematic at the very beginning. I repeat: about this, the understanding is silent, even if one is able to bring it to bear on the matter.

Now, however, let us remind ourselves, too, of what a *cause* primarily is: the preceding alteration which makes necessary the succeeding. No cause in the world can bring about its effect by itself or make it out of nothing. Rather, there is always something present on which it works, and only at this time, in this place, on this specific being, occasioning an alteration which is always in accordance with the nature of the being; therefore, the *force* for this alteration must already lie in this being. Every effect, then, arises from two factors, one inner and one outer; that is, from the inherent force of that upon which the effect is worked and the determining cause which compels the effect to manifest itself here and now. All causality and all explanations based upon it presuppose inherent force: for this reason, such explanations cannot explain everything; rather, there always remains something unexplained. We see this in the whole of physics and chemistry and in the reduction of which the whole explanation consists: their explanations everywhere presuppose natural forces that manifest themselves in phenomena. A natural force itself is subject to 47 no explanation; rather, it is the principle of all explanation. Likewise, it is itself also not subject to causality; rather, it is precisely that which gives to each cause its causality, i.e., its capacity to produce an effect. It alone is the common support for all effects of this sort and present in all of them. So the phenomena of magnetism are reduced to an inherent force, called electricity. With this the explanation falls silent: it merely provides the conditions under which such a force manifests itself, i.e., the causes which elicit its efficacy. The explanations of celestial mechanics presuppose gravitation as a force, by means of which here the particular causes work to determine the path of the heavenly bodies. The explanations of chemistry presuppose hidden forces which manifest themselves as elective affinities according to certain stoicheiometric relations. All effects finally depend on these forces and occur promptly when the specified causes call these forces forth. In the same way, all explanations of physiology presuppose the life force as that which reacts in determinate ways to specific internal and external stimuli. And so it is with everything. Even the causes, with which so comprehensible a science as mechanics concerns itself, such as impact and pressure, presuppose impenetrability, cohesion, rigidity, hardness, inertia, gravity, elasticity, which, no less than those just mentioned, are unfathomable natural forces. Thus, everywhere causes determine nothing more than the when and the where of the *manifestations* of original, inexplicable forces, and only on the presupposition of which forces can we consider them to be causes, i.e., necessarily bringing about certain effects.

Just as it is the case with causes in the narrowest sense and with stimuli, it is no less so with *motives*, for, indeed, motives are not different in essence from causality; rather, they are just a variety of the same, namely, causality acting through the medium of the cognition. Thus, here too, the cause calls forth only the manifestation of a force which is not to be further attributed to causes nor to be further explained, and which force is here called *will*, recognized not merely externally like other natural forces, but through self-consciousness, and so, internally and immediately. Only on the assumption that such 48 a will is present and, in any given case, of a determinate disposition, do the causes directed to it, here called motives, have an effect. This specially and individually determined nature of the will, by means of which nature the reaction to the same motives is in every person different, makes up that which is called *character*, and indeed, because it is not known *a priori*, but only through experience, it is called *empirical character*. First of all, the character determines the different motives' ways of working on a given person. For the character is just as much the basis of all effects which motives evoke as the universal natural forces are the basis of effects which causes in the narrowest sense evoke or as the life force is the basis of effects which stimuli evoke. And, like natural forces, it is also original, unalterable, and inexplicable. Among animals it differs with each species, as among humans with each individual. Only in the highest, cleverest animals does a noticeable, individual character first show itself, although with the quite dominant character of the species.

*The character of the human being* is, 1) *individual*: it is in each a different one. To be sure, the character of the species lies at the basis of everything; hence, its main traits repeat themselves in each.

However, here there is such a significant variation of degree, such a diversity of combinations and modifications of the traits by one another, that one can assume the moral difference of characters would match that of intellectual capacities, which is to say a great deal, and both would be incomparably greater than the bodily difference between a giant and a dwarf, between Apollo and Thersites.* Hence the effect of one and the same motive on different people is completely different, just as sunlight turns wax white, but colours silver chloride black; as heat softens wax, but hardens clay. For this reason, one cannot predict the deed from knowledge of the motive alone, but for this one must also know the character exactly.

2) The character of the human being is *empirical*. Only through experience can one become acquainted with it, not merely with that of others, but also with one's own. Therefore one will often be disappointed not only with others, but also with oneself, when one discovers that one does not possess the degree of this or that trait, e.g., justice, selflessness, courage, as one charitably supposed. Therefore, too, with a difficult choice before us, our own resolve, as well as that of another, remains a mystery to ourselves until the choice is made. As soon as we believe that the choice will be one way, it will go the other way; every time cognition puts this or that motive more closely before the will and tests the motive's power on the will, the sense that 'I can do what I will' produces the illusion of freedom of will. Finally the stronger motive asserts its power over the will and the choice often ends up other than we expected at the outset. Therefore, finally no one can know how another or he himself will act in any given circumstance until he has been in it: only after having stood the test is he certain of the other and then, and only then, of himself, too. Then, however, he is certain: tested friends, proven servants are trustworthy. In general we treat a person well known to us like anything else with whose traits we are already acquainted, and we predict with certainty what to expect from him and what not. Who has done something once will do it again, should the case arise, for better or worse. Therefore someone who requires great, extraordinary help will turn to the one who has passed the test of magnanimity, and he who would hire a murderer will look among those people who have already had blood on their hands. According to Herodotus'* tale (VII. 164), Gelon of Syracuse was compelled completely to entrust a very great sum of money to one man, for he had to give it to him to take abroad,

and it was wholly at the man's disposition. He chose Cadmus for this purpose as one proven to be of rare, indeed incredible, honesty and conscientiousness. His trust was perfectly justified.—Likewise, familiarity with ourselves, upon which self-confidence or distrust is founded, develops only from experience as the opportunity arises. Depending on whether we have shown in some cases circumspection, courage, honesty, discretion, refinement, or whatever else the case requires, or the lack of such virtues has come to light—as a result of this familiarity with ourselves, we are content with ourselves or the opposite. It is primarily someone's exact knowledge of his own empirical character that gives a person what is called *acquired character*: the one who possesses it recognizes exactly his own traits, good and bad, thereby surely knows what he may trust and expect of himself, but also what not. He now plays his own role artfully and methodically, with consistency and decorum, which previously was played out quite naturally by virtue of his empirical character, without once, as is said, acting out of character, which always indicates that in the particular case someone is mistaken about himself.

3) The character of the human being is *constant*: it remains the same throughout one's entire life. Under the alterable shell of his years, of his circumstances, even of his knowledge and views, the identical and essential man, like a crab in its shell, remains quite unalterable and always the same. Simply in direction and material, his character undergoes apparent modifications that are the results of the differences of stages of life and its needs. *The human being never alters*: as he has acted in a given case, so he will always act again under identical circumstances (which, however, also includes the correct knowledge of these circumstances). One can gain verification of this truth from daily experience; however, one finds it most striking, when one again encounters an acquaintance after twenty or thirty years and right away finds him up to exactly the same tricks as before.—Indeed, many a one will deny this truth with words: he himself, however, presupposes it by his acts, for he never again trusts another whom he once found dishonest; whereas, he relies on the one who earlier proved himself to be honest. For on this truth rests the possibility of all knowledge of humankind and of firm confidence in those tried, tested, proven. Even if such a trusted one has once deceived us, we never say, 'His character has altered' but, 'I was wrong about him'.— On this truth depends the fact that when we want to judge the moral

51  worth of an action, we above all seek to attain certainty about the
motive for it, but then our praise or censure concerns not the motive,
but the character that allows itself to be determined by such a motive,
this character being the second factor in this deed and the only factor inherent to the human being. — On the same truth depends the
fact that genuine honour (not knightly or fools' honour), once lost,
is never again to be restored, but the stigma of a single vile action
always adheres to a person, as one says, branding him. Hence the
proverb: 'Once a thief, always a thief.' — On it depends the fact that
in important affairs of state it can occur that treachery is needed, and
so a traitor is sought, used, and remunerated. Then, after the aim
is achieved, prudence demands that he be sent away because circumstances are alterable, but his character is unalterable. — On this
depends the fact that the greatest error of a dramatic poet is this:
that his characters are not sustained, i.e., not, as those portrayed by
the great poets, carried out with the constancy and strict consistency
of a natural force. I have pointed out this last in a detailed example
from Shakespeare in *Parerga* [*and Paralipomena*], vol. II, § 118, p. 196
of the first edition.* — Indeed, upon the same truth depends the
possibility of conscience, insofar as this often reproaches us in our
later years with the misdeeds of youth, as e.g., after forty years it
reproached J. J. Rousseau for having accused a maidservant, Marion,
of a theft which he himself committed.* This is only possible on the
presupposition that character, unaltered, remains constant, since, in
contrast, the most risible errors, the crudest ignorance, the most
incredible idiocy of our youth do not shame us in old age, for these
were matters of knowledge about which we have changed our minds,
having long put them aside like the clothing of our youth. — On the
same truth depends the fact that a person, even with clearest knowledge, indeed, with abhorrence of his moral faults and defects, indeed,
with the most sincere efforts of reform, actually does not reform himself, but, to his own surprise, despite earnest intentions and honest
52  promises, with renewed opportunity still travels the same path as
before. Only his *knowledge* can be corrected; hence, he can come to
the understanding that this or that means, which he had used earlier,
will not lead to his ends or will bring about more loss than gain: then
he alters the means, not the ends. On this the American penal system
depends: it does not undertake to improve the *character*, the *heart* of
the person, but to set his *head* straight and to show him that the ends

to which by virtue of his character he unwaveringly strives would be reached in a far more difficult way, with more troubles and dangers, by his previous path of dishonesty, than by that of uprightness, work, and contentedness. In general the sphere and realm of all correction and refinement lies only in *knowledge*. Character is unalterable; motives work of necessity, but they must work through *cognition* as that which is the medium of motives. Cognition, however, is capable of a manifold expansion, of constant correction, in countless degrees: toward this all education works. The cultivation of reason through cognition and insights of all sorts is morally important in that this cultivation opens the path to motives, from which path without cultivation the human being would remain barred. As long as he could not understand these motives, they did not exist for his will. Hence, under the same external circumstances, a person's situation can, in fact, the second time be completely different from the first, that is, only if in the meanwhile he has become capable of understanding this circumstance correctly and completely, whereby motives, of which he was previously incognizant, now work upon him. In this sense, the scholastics said quite correctly: 'the final cause (end, motive) works not through its actual, but through its cognized being.' Moreover, no moral influence extends further than the correction of knowledge, and to undertake to eliminate a person's character flaws through lectures and moralizing and, so, to want to transform his character, his actual morality, is just like a plan to change lead into gold through external influence or to bring an oak through careful cultivation to the point that it bears apricots.

In his *Discourse on Magic*, in which he defends himself against the charge of practising magic, Apuleius already expresses the belief in the unalterability of character as something indubitable. Apuleius appeals to his recognized character by saying: 'Certain evidence lies in the character of every person: by nature predisposed always in the same way to virtue or to malice, it offers firm proof to accept or reject an accusation of crime.'[1]

4) Individual character is *innate*: it is no work of art nor of circumstances subject to chance; rather, it is the work of nature itself.

---

[1] *Certum indicem cujusque animum esse, qui semper eodem ingenio ad virtutem vel ad malitiam moratus, firmum argumentum est accipiendi criminis, aut respuendi.* [Lucius Apuleius (c.123 CE), *Oratio de magia*.]

It reveals itself already in the child, indicating there on a small scale what it will be in the future on a large scale. For this reason, two children can as clear as day show the most profoundly different character given identical education and environment: it is the same as they will take into old age. Character is even inherited in its basic features, but only from the father; the intelligence, in contrast, is inherited from the mother, to which heredity I refer in chapter 43 of the second volume of my principal work.

From this explanation of the essence of the individual character, though, it follows that virtues and vice are innate. This truth may come as inconvenient to many a prejudice and many a spinning-wheel philosophy, with their so-called practical interests, i.e., their small, narrow concepts and limited, elementary-school views: this was, however, already the conviction of the father of morals, of Socrates, who, according to Aristotle's statement, maintained (*Great Ethics* I. 9) 'it is not up to us, whether we are good or evil'.[1] What Aristotle cites against this here is obviously corrupted: he also shares Socrates' opinion and expresses it most clearly in the *Nicomachean Ethics* VI. 13: 'For it seems that particular character traits are already somehow inherent to us all by nature, for a tendency to justice, and temperance, and courage, and the like, is already ours from birth.'[2] And if one reviews the virtues and vices assembled in Aristotle's *On Virtues and Vices*, in which they are gathered for brief survey, one will find that all of them can only be conceived of in real people as *innate* traits, and only as such would they be genuine. In contrast, if they were to result from reflection and were taken on arbitrarily, they would actually amount to a kind of *pretence*, and, hence, if they were continued and maintained under stressful circumstances, then they could not quite be counted on. And if one were also to add the Christian virtue of love, *caritas*, unknown to Aristotle and all of the

---

[1] *Ethica magna* I. 9 (or *Magna moralia* I. 9, 1187a 7): οὐκ ἐφ' ἡμῖν γενέσθαι τὸ σπουδαίους εἶναι ἢ φαύλους κτλ (*in arbitrio nostro positum non esse, nos probos, vel malos esse*). Schopenhauer provides the Latin translation. Many consider the *Great Ethics* to more likely be a later Peripatetic's compilation.

[2] Πᾶσι γὰρ δοκεῖ ἕκαστα τῶν ἠθῶν ὑπάρχειν φύσει πως· καὶ γὰρ δίκαιοι καὶ σωφρονικοὶ [καὶ ἀνδρεῖοι] καὶ τἆλλα ἔχομεν εὐθὺς ἐκ γενετῆς (*singuli enim mores in omnibus hominibus quodammodo videntur inesse natura: namque ad justitiam, temperantiam, fortitudinem, ceterasque virtutes apti atque habiles sumus, cum primum nascimur*). [*Nicomachean Ethics* 1144b 4; Schopenhauer omits καὶ ἀνδρεῖοι ('and courage') but offers for it in his Latin translation *fortitudinem*.]

ancients, it would be no different. How can the tireless goodness of *one* person and the incorrigible, deeply rooted malice of another, the character of the Antonines, of Hadrian, of Titus on one hand and that of Caligula, Nero, Domitian on the other, arising suddenly from the outside, be the work of accidental circumstance or mere knowledge and instruction!* Nero had none other than Seneca* as tutor. — Furthermore, in innate character, in the actual kernel of the whole person, lies the seed of all his virtues or vices. This conviction of the unprejudiced person also guided the hand of Velleius Paterculus* when he wrote down the following about Cato:* 'A man intimately connected to virtue, closer in all ways to the gods than to humans, who never did good to be seen as a do-gooder, but *because he could not act otherwise.*'[1]

On the other hand, on the assumption of free will, it is simply impossible to conceive that virtue and vice actually should arise or that at least the fact that two people of identical upbringing, under exactly the same circumstances and occasions, should act completely differently, even in opposite ways. The actual, original, fundamental difference of characters is incompatible with the assumption of such a free will, which means that for any person, in any situation, opposing actions should be equally possible. For then his character must from the very beginning be a *blank slate*,[2] as Locke says of the intellect, and can have no innate inclination to one or the other way because this would in fact already suspend the perfect equilibrium which one thinks of in *libero arbitrio indifferentiae*. Thus, given this assumption, the ground of the observed difference of different people's way of acting cannot lie in the *subjective*, but even less can it lie in the *objective*, since as soon as one assumes so, then it would be the objects which would determine the action, and the desired freedom would be completely lost. In any case, then, the only remaining expedient

55

---

[1] (*Homo virtuti consimillimus, et per omnia genio diis, quam hominibus propior: qui nunquam recte fecit, ut facere videretur, sed quia aliter facere non poterat.*) This passage was, of course, used as a regular weapon in the arsenal of the determinists, of which honour the good old historian, of 1,800 years ago, had not even dreamed. First Hobbes praised him, and Priestley after him. Then Schelling had done so in his essay on freedom, p. 478, repeated in a translation somewhat distorted for his purposes: wherefore he did not bring up Velleius Paterculus by name, but, in a way as crafty as it was genteel, said, 'an ancient'. Finally I, too, have not wanted to be deficient in citing this passage, for it is really to the point. [Schopenhauer's note.]

[2] *tabula rasa.*

would be to put the origin of this real and great difference of behaviours in the middle between subject and object, that is, to let it arise in a different way, as the objective is apprehended by the subjective, i.e., as it would be *cognized* by different people. But then everything traces back to correct or false *cognition* of the circumstances at hand, whereby the moral difference of ways of acting would be transformed into a mere difference of correctness of judgement and morals would be changed into logic. Now if the proponents of free will at last sought to save themselves from this nasty dilemma by saying that, indeed, there is no innate difference of character, but such difference would arise from external circumstances, impressions, experiences, examples, teaching, etc.; and if in this way a character has once come about, this explains the difference in behaviour; then, first, the reply to this is that in this way character would appear very late (while it actually is already recognizable in children) and most people would die before they have developed a character; second, however, that all these external circumstances, the product of which is supposed to be the character, lie completely beyond our power and one way or the other would be produced by chance (or, if one will, by providence); thus, if character and also the difference of behaviour would now spring from this, then all moral responsibility for the latter would completely fall away since obviously it ultimately would be the product of chance or providence. So we thus see that, given the assumption of free will, the origin of the difference of ways of acting, and therewith virtue or vice, even responsibility, are suspended in mid-air and can nowhere find a place in which to take root. From this, however, it becomes obvious that this assumption, as much as it appeals to the untrained understanding at first glance, actually stands in fundamental contradiction with both our moral convictions, and, as has been sufficiently shown, with the supreme principle of our understanding.

As I have proved in detail above, the necessity with which motives, like all causes in general, operate is not without presupposition. Now we have become acquainted with its presupposition, the ground and soil on which it stands: it is the innate, *individual character*. As each effect in inanimate nature is a necessary product of two factors, namely, the universal, *natural force* here expressing itself and the specific *cause* which here produces this expression, just so each person's deed is the necessary product of his *character* and of the *motive* which has occurred. If these both are present, then the deed follows inevitably. If another were to arise, either another motive or another character must be posited. Moreover, every deed could be predicted with assurance, indeed, calculated, were it not that, in part, character is very difficult to discover, and in part, too, that the motive is often obscured and always exposed to the countering effect of other motives that lie solely in the person's sphere of thought and are inaccessible to others. Given the innate character of the human being, in general, the aims to which he invariably strives are already essentially determined: the means that he uses for this purpose are determined partly by external circumstances and partly by his apprehension of these, the accuracy of which depends on his understanding and its education. Now as the end result of all this follow his specific deeds, hence, the whole role which he has to play in the world. — One finds 57 the result of the theory of individual character as presented here both correctly and poetically conceived in one of Goethe's most beautiful stanzas:

> As stood the sun to salute the planets
> Upon the day that gave you to the earth,
> You grew forthwith, and prospered, in your growing
> Heeded the law presiding at your birth.
> Sibyls and prophets told it: You must be
> None but yourself, from self you cannot flee.
> No time there is, no power, can decompose
> The minted form that lives and living grows.*

Hence this presupposition, on which the necessity of the effects of all causes depends, is the inner essence of each thing, whether it be now merely one of the universal natural forces made manifest in it, or it be a life force, or it be will: whichever being, of whatever kind it be, will always react according to its specific nature upon the occasion of an effective cause. This law, to which all things in the world are subject without exception, the scholastics expressed in the formula: 'doing follows essence.'[1] As a result of the same, chemists prove substances through reagents and one person others by the tests which he applies to them. In all cases, the external causes will necessarily

---

[1] *operari sequitur esse.*

evoke the fixed essence of the being since it can react in no other way than according to the way it is.

It is to be recalled here, that each *existentia* presupposes an *essentia*, i.e., every existing thing must also be *something*, have a determined essence. It cannot *exist* and at the same time be just *nothing*; namely, it cannot be something like the *Ens metaphysicum*, i.e., a thing which *is*, and only *is*, without all determinations and properties, and, consequently, without the decided manner of working that proceeds from these. Rather, just as little as an *essentia* without *existentia* produces a real thing, so little can an *existentia* without *essentia*. For every existing thing must have a nature essential and specific to it, by virtue of which it is what it is, which nature it always maintains, the expressions of which are necessarily evoked by causes; while on the contrary this nature itself in no way is the work of any causes, nor is modifiable by any causes. But all of this applies to a person and his will just as well as to all other beings in nature. He, too, has an *essentia* to his *existentia*, i.e., fundamental essential properties that make up his character and only require occasioning from without to come out. Consequently, to expect a person given the same occasion to act one way at one time and completely otherwise at another time would be the same as if one would expect that the same tree that bore cherries this summer would bear pears the next. Taken precisely, free will implies an *existentia* without *essentia*, which means that something *is* and at the same time *is nothing*, which again means that something *is not*, and, thus, is a contradiction.

It is to be ascribed to the insight herein, along with the law of causality which is known *a priori* and, hence, applicable without exception, that all really profound thinkers of all times, however differing their remaining views might also be, agree in that they maintain the necessity of the act of will with the appearance of motives and reject the *liberum arbitrium*. They have even gone to the extreme, to assert it through the most dogmatic, arrogant expressions, just because the incalculably great majority of the masses, who are incapable of thought and value only appearance and prejudice, constantly and stubbornly work against this truth. The best known of these is Buridan's ass, which for approximately a hundred years has been sought in vain in the extant writings of Buridan.* I myself possess an edition, apparently printed in the fifteenth century, but without place of publication, nor year of publication, nor pagination, in which I often sought in vain, even though on almost every page an ass appears as an example. Bayle,* whose article is the foundation of all which has been written about Buridan since, says quite incorrectly that only *one* Buridan Sophism is known. However, I have an entire quarto of *Sophismata* by him. Since he treated the topic so thoroughly, Bayle should also have known what, in fact, appears not to have been noticed even since, that this example, which to a certain extent has become a symbol or 59 type of the great truth for which I have advocated here, occurs much earlier than Buridan. It occurs in Dante, who possessed the whole knowledge of his time, lived before Buridan, and spoke nothing of an ass, but of humans, with the following words which open the fourth book of his *Paradise*:

> Between two foods, equally appetizing and distant,
> Would a free man die of hunger
> Before he would eat one.[1]

Indeed, it is found already in Aristotle, *On the Heavens* II. 13, with these words: 'just as in the example of the one who, though to the greatest degree hungering as much as thirsting, when put equidistant from food and drink, must necessarily stay where he is.'[2] Buridan, who had obtained the example from this source, substituted an ass for a human, merely because it was the custom of these sorry scholastics to use either Socrates and Plato, or an ass.[3]

The question of the free will is actually a touchstone by which one can differentiate the profound, thinking minds from the superfluous ones, or a boundary stone from which the two go their separate ways, while all of the former maintain that an action necessarily

---

[1] *Intra duo cibi, distanti e moventi*
*D'un modo, prima si morrìa di fame,*
*Che liber' uomo l'un recasse a' denti.*

[Schopenhauer gives a Latin translation:] *Inter duos cibos aeque remotos unoque modo motos constitutus, homo prius fame periret, quam ut, absoluta libertate usus, unum eorum dentibus admoveret.* [Dante Alighieri (1265–1321); the final book of his *Divine Comedy* is 'Paradise'.]

[2] *De caelo* [295b, 2]: καὶ ὁ λόγος τοῦ πεινῶντος καὶ διψῶντος σφόδρα μὲν, ὁμοίως δὲ, καὶ τῶν ἐδωδίμων καὶ ποτῶν ἴσον ἀπέχοντος, καὶ γὰρ τοῦτον ἠρεμεῖν ἀναγκαῖον [Schopenhauer provides a Latin translation:] *item ea, quae de sitiente vehementer esurienteque dicuntur, cum aeque ab his, quae eduntur atque bibuntur, distat: quiescat enim necesse est.*

[3] *asinum.*

results from a given character and motive, the latter, on the contrary, with the great masses, cling to the free will. So then, there are still those who strike a middle course, who, feeling themselves waylaid, tack back and forth, shifting the mark for themselves and others, taking refuge behind words and phrases, or so turning and twisting the question that one no longer knows where it leads. So has Leibniz already done, who was much more of a mathematician and polymath than a philosopher.[1] But to bring such wishy-washy speakers back to the topic, one must pose the questions as follows and not deviate from them.

1) Are two actions possible for a given person under given circumstances or only one? — All profound thinkers answer: only one.

2) After a given person's course of life is run, could something in it — recognizing that on the one hand his character is unalterably fixed and that on the other hand the circumstances, the influence of which he has experienced, are necessarily, completely, and in the smallest detail determined by external causes that always occur with strict necessity, made of a chain of entirely necessary links, running out to infinity — could even just the least little thing about some event, some scene, occur otherwise than it has occurred? — No! is the consistent and correct answer.

The conclusion of both propositions is: *Everything that occurs, from the greatest to the least, occurs necessarily.* Whatever occurs, necessarily occurs.[2]

Whoever is terrified by these propositions still has something to learn and something else to unlearn: thereupon, however, he will recognize that they are the most abundant source of comfort and peace of mind. — Our deeds are simply no first beginning, for in them nothing actually new attains existence: rather, *through that which we do, we simply experience what we are.*

Upon the conviction, if not clearly recognized, certainly felt, of the strict necessity of everything that occurs also depends the ancients' firmly held view of fate,[3] as well as the fatalism of the Muhammadan,

---

[1] Leibniz's lack of principle on this point shows itself most clearly in his letter to Coste, *Opera phil[osophica]*, ed. Erdmann, p. 447, and then, too, in *Theodicy* § 45–53. [Schopenhauer's note.]

[2] *quidquid fit, necessario fit.*

[3] *fatum,* εἱμαρμένη.

and even the universal, ineradicable faith in omens,[1] because even the most trivial accident occurs necessarily, and all events, so to say, keep tempo with one another; hence, everything resonates in everything. Finally this even connects to the fact that whoever without the least intention and quite accidentally maims or kills another will throughout his life deplore this misfortune[2] with a feeling which seems to be related to guilt, and will also suffer from others a peculiar type of discredit as *person piacularis* (a victim of misfortune). Indeed the felt conviction of the unalterability of character and the necessity of its manifestations has not been without influence even on the Christian doctrine of predestination.—If we do not accept the strict necessity of everything that occurs by means of a chain of causes linked to their predecessors without exception, but, rather, accept that the latter could be broken in countless pieces by an absolute freedom, then all *foresight of the future* in dreams, in clairvoyant somnambulism, and in second sight,* would be *objectively*, hence, absolutely *impossible*, therefore unthinkable. For then there would be absolutely no objective, actual future which could possibly be foreseen. Instead we now doubt only the *subjective* conditions for this, thus its *subjective* possibility. And today even this doubt can win no credibility among the well-educated, after countless testimonies of the most credible sort have established this anticipation of the future.

I further append a few observations as corollaries to the firmly established theory of the necessity of everything that occurs.

What would become of this world, if necessity were not to permeate and hold together all things, but especially were not to govern the procreation of individuals? A horror, a rubbish heap, a hideous visage without sense and meaning—namely, the work of true and real chance.

To wish that some sort of event had not happened is foolish self-torment, for this means to wish for something absolutely impossible and is as irrational as to wish that the sun would rise in the west. For everything that occurs, great or small, occurs with *strict* necessity, and it is completely futile to reflect on this event as if the causes that had led to it were trivial and accidental and could just as easily have

---

[1] *omina.*    [2] *piaculum.*

62  been otherwise. For this is illusory, because they all occur with just such strict necessity and have worked with just such complete power as those as a result of which the sun rises in the east. We should rather observe the events as they occur with the same eye as the print which we read, knowing well that it is there before we read it.

# PREDECESSORS

As evidence for the assertion above about the judgement of all profound thinkers with regard to our problem, I will call to mind some of the great men who have expressed similar ideas.

First of all, to reassure those who perhaps could believe that religious principles stand opposed to the truth for which I advocated, I call to mind that Jeremiah (10: 23) had already said: 'The doings of man lie not in his power, and it lies not in anyone's power how he walks or to direct his steps.' In particular, however, I refer to Luther, who in a book written specifically on the topic, *On the Bondage of the Will*,[1] fought with all his fierceness against free will. A few passages from this work suffice to characterize his opinion, which, naturally, he supports not with philosophical, but with theological grounds. I cite these from the edition of Seb. Schmidt, Strasburg, 1707.—In that work, p. 145 it reads: 'Concerning this we inscribed in all hearts that free will is nothing, although this conviction is obscured by so many opposing assertions and the authority of so many men.'[2]— p. 214: 'Here I would like to remind the advocates of free will that with this assertion of free will they deny Christ.'[3]—p. 220: 'All the testimony (of the Scriptures) concern Christ's battle against the freedom of the will. But these are innumerable, indeed, the entire 64 Scriptures. If, therefore, we were to make the scriptures the judge of our cause, then I will triumph in all ways, so that not one iota or one stitch remains that does not condemn the dogma of free will.'[4]

Now to the philosophers. The ancients are not to be taken seriously here, since their philosophy, still, as it were, in a state of

---

[1] *De servo arbitrio* [1525; Martin Luther (1483–1546)].

[2] *Quae simul in omnium cordibus scriptum invenitur, liberum arbitrium nihil esse; licet obscuretur tot disputationibus contrariis et tanta tot virorum auctoritate.*

[3] *Hoc loco admonitos velim liberi arbitrii tutores, ut sciant, sese esse abnegatores Christi, dum asserunt liberum arbitrium.*

[4] *Contra liberum arbitrium pugnabunt Scripturae testimonia, quotquot de Christo loquuntur. At ea sunt innumerabilia, imo tota Scriptura. Ideo, si Scriptura judice causam agimus, omnibus modis vicero, ut ne jota unum aut apex sit reliquus, qui non damnet dogma liberi arbitrii.*

innocence, had not yet brought the two most profound and thought-provoking problems of modern philosophy to clear consciousness, namely the question of the freedom of the will and that of the reality of the external world or the relationship of the ideal to the real. In any case, how far the problem of the freedom of the will had become clear to the ancients is fairly evident from Aristotle's *Nicomachean Ethics* III. 1–8, where one will find that in essence his thinking about this concerned merely physical and intellectual freedom; therefore, he always speaks only of the voluntary and involuntary,[1] taking voluntary and free as one and the same. The far more difficult problem of *moral freedom* had not yet presented itself to him, although in general to this point his thoughts extend almost to it, especially in *Nicomachean Ethics* II. 2, and III. 7, where, however, he falls into the error that the character derives from the deeds instead of the other way around. So he quite erroneously criticized Socrates' conviction that I brought up above.* In other places, however, he had made this his own, e.g. *Nicomachean Ethics* X. 10: 'Natural aptitude is obviously not under our power. It is given to those who are truly fortunate by some divine cause.'[2]—And soon thereafter: 'Therefore the character must have at the outset a natural affinity for virtue, loving what is noble and hating what is base,'[3] which agrees with the passage I have brought in above, as well as with *Great Ethics* I. 11. 'One cannot become the best by mere intention, unless there also exists the natural aptitude so to become: then one will become better.'[4] In the same sense, Aristotle considers the question about free will in *Great Ethics* I. 9–18 and *Eudemian Ethics* II. 6–10,* where he comes somewhat closer to the actual problem; still, everything is vacillating and superficial. In general his method is not to proceed directly to the topic, analytically, but synthetically, drawing conclusions from external marks. Instead of penetrating to reach the core of the thing,

---

[1] ἑκούσιον καὶ ἀκούσιον.

[2] τὸ μὲν οὖν τῆς φύσεως δῆλον ὡς οὐχ ἐφ' ἡμῖν ὑπάρχει, ἀλλὰ διά τινας θείας αἰτίας τοῖς ὡς ἀληθῶς εὐτυχέσιν ὑπάρχει (*quod igitur a natura tribuitur, id in nostra potestate non esse, sed ab aliqua divina causa profectum, isesse in iis, qui revera sunt fortunati, perspicuum est*).

[3] Δεῖ δὴ τὸ ἦθος προϋπάρχειν πως οἰκεῖον τῆς ἀρετῆς, στέργον τὸ καλὸν καὶ δυσχεραῖνον τὸ αἰσχρόν (*Mores igitur ante quodammodo insint oportet, ad virtutem accommodati, qui honestum amplectantur, turpitudineque offendantur*).

[4] Οὐκ ἔσται ὁ προαιρούμενος εἶναι σπουδαιότατος, ἂν μὴ καὶ ἡ φύσις ὑπάρξῃ βελτίων μέντοι ἔσται (*non enim ut quisque voluerit, erit omnium optimus, nisi etiam natura exstiterit: melior quidem recte erit*). *Ethica magna* [or *Magna moralia*] I. 11, [1187b, 28].

he stops at the external signs, even at words. This method readily leads to error and, among profound problems, never to the goal. Here now he stops before the supposed antithesis between the necessary and the voluntary, between ἀναγκαῖον καὶ ἑκούσιον, as if before a wall. Above and beyond this, however, lies first the insight that the voluntary is exactly *the same as the necessary* because of the motive, without which an act of will is as impossible as it is without a willing subject, and which motive is a cause just as much as a mechanical cause, from which it is differentiated only by inessentials. He himself even says (*Eudemian Ethics* II. 10), 'for the purpose is one of the types of causes'.[1] For just that reason this antithesis between the voluntary and the necessary is fundamentally false, even if it is the same today with many alleged philosophers as it was with Aristotle.

Cicero already sets out the problem of the free will in his book *On Fate*,* chapters 10 and 17. The subject of his essay, of course, quite readily and naturally leads to it. He himself adheres to free will, but we see that Chrysippus and Diodorus must have already brought the problem to consciousness more or less clearly.*—Lucian's thirtieth dialogue of the dead,* that between Minos and Sostratos, is also worth noting, for in it free will and, with it, responsibility is denied.

But to a certain degree the fourth book of the Maccabees in the *Septuagint** (lacking in the Luther translation) is an essay on free will insofar as it sets itself the task of making the argument that reason (λογισμός) possesses the power to overcome all passions and affects and covers this in its second book with the stories of the Jewish martyrs.

The oldest source with which I am familiar that appears to have a clear recognition of our problem is Clement of Alexandria, in that he (*Stromata* I, § 17) says: 'neither praise nor blame, nor honours nor punishments is justified if the soul does not possess the capacity of striving and resisting; rather, wickedness is involuntary:'[2]—then, after a sentence referring to something that he said earlier: 'so that 66

---

[1] ἡ γὰρ οὗ ἕνεκα μία τῶν αἰτιῶν ἐστίν (*nam id, cujus gratia, una e causarum numero est*). *Ethica Eudemia* II. 10, 1226b, 26.

[2] οὔτε δὲ οἱ ἔπαινοι, οὔτε οἱ ψόγοι, οὔθ' αἱ τιμαί, οὔθ' αἱ κολάσεις, δίκαιαι, μὴ τῆς ψυχῆς ἐχούσης τὴν ἐξουσίαν τῆς ὁρμῆς καὶ ἀφορμῆς, ἀλλ' ἀκουσίου τῆς κακίας οὔσης (*nec laudes, nec vituperationes, nec honores, nec supplicia justa sunt, si anima non habeat liberam potestatem et appetendi et abstinendi, sed sit vitium involuntarium*).

God is completely without guilt for our wickedness.'[1] This last, most remarkable sentence, indicates the sense in which the church at once grasped the problem and the decision, consistent with its interest, which it instantly anticipated.—Nearly 200 years later we find the doctrine of free will already treated thoroughly by Nemesius,* in his work *On the Nature of Man*[2] at the end of chapter 35, and chapters 39–41. Without any further explanation, the freedom of the will is here identified with voluntary choice or elective decision and accordingly is zealously asserted and demonstrated. Still it is already a venting of the subject.

However, fully developed consciousness of our problem, with all that it entails, we first find in the church father Augustine, who for that reason is considered here even though he is far more a theologian than a philosopher. In fact, because of this we immediately see him placed in noticeable difficulty and uncertain vacillation, which leads him to irrelevancies and contradictions in his three books composing *On the Free [Choice of] Will*.[3] On the one hand Augustine will not, like Pelagius,* concede so much to freedom of the will that in doing so original sin, the necessity of redemption, and free election by grace are suspended, such that a person could become righteous and worthy of eternal bliss through his own power. In the argument concerning the books *On the Free [Choice of] Will* in his *Retractions*, Book I, chapter 9,* he even intimates that he would have said still more on this side of the controversy (which Luther later so zealously defended) if these books had not been written before the appearance of Pelagius, against whose opinion he then composed the book *On Nature and Grace*.[4] In the meanwhile, he already said in *On the Free [Choice of]*
67 *Will* III. 18: 'Now, however, a human being is not good, nor does he have it in his power to be good, whether he does not see how he ought to be, or whether he does see, but does not wish to be the way he sees that he ought to be.'[5]—And soon thereafter: 'Now whether out of ignorance he does not possess free choice of will or whether he does

---

[1] ἵν᾽ ὅτι μάλιστα ὁ θεὸς μὲν ἡμῖν κακίας ἀναίτιοδ (*ut vel maxime quidem Deus nobis non sit causa vitii*).

[2] *De natura hominis.*

[3] *De libero arbitrio [voluntatis].* [Augustine's work, *On the Free [Choice of] Will*, of 388–95, is composed of a dialogue in three books.]

[4] *De natura et gratia*, from 413 or 415, is one of Augustine's pamphlets against Pelagius.

[5] *Nunc autem homo non est bonus, nec habet in potestate, ut bonus sit, sive non videndo qualis esse debeat, sive videndo et non volendo esse, qualem debere esse se videt.*

indeed see how he should correctly act and does wish to do so, but on account of his carnal habit, the effect of which has been naturally increased through the power of mortal original sin, he cannot carry it out;'[1] and in the aforementioned *Argument:*\* 'Therefore, if the will itself is not freed by divine grace from the servitude by which it has become a slave to sin and supported in overcoming depravity, then right and pious living are not possible for the mortal.'[2]

On the other hand, the following three reasons moved him to defend freedom of the will:

1) His opposition to the Manicheans,\* against whom the books *On the Free [Choice of] Will* are expressly directed because they deny free will and take up another primal source of evil as well as misfortune. He toys with them already in the last chapter of the book *On the Magnitude of the Soul:*[3] 'Free decision of will is given to the soul, and he who seeks to shake this through nugatory ratiocination is so blind that he . . . etc.'[4]

2) The natural delusion, which I uncovered, by which 'I can do what I will' is regarded as freedom of the will and 'voluntary' is immediately taken to be identical with 'free': *On the Free [Choice of] Will*: 'For what lies so much under the power of the will as the will itself?'[5]

3) The necessity to bring the moral responsibility of the human being into harmony with the justice of God. Namely, Augustine's acuity did not overlook a most serious difficulty, the removal of which is so difficult that, as far as I know, all later philosophers, with the exception of three whom we soon will consider more closely for this reason, would rather have quite quietly sneaked around it as if it were not there. However, Augustine states it with noble frankness, quite candidly, in the opening words to the books *On the Free [Choice of] Will*: 'Tell me, I beg you, whether God is not the author of evil?'[6] — And then in detail in the second chapter of the same: 'The following moves my soul: if sins come from the souls that God had

---

[1] *Mox: vel ignorando non habet liberum arbitrium voluntatis ad eligendum quid recte faciat; vel resistente carnali consuetudine, quae violentia mortalis successionis quodammodo naturaliter inolevit, videat quid recte faciendum sit, et velit, nec possit implere.*

[2] *Voluntas ergo ipsa, nisi gratia Dei liberatur a servitute, qua facta est serva peccati, et, ut vitia superet, adjuvetur, recte pieque vivi non potest a mortalibus.*

[3] *De animae quantitate.*

[4] *datum est animae liberum arbitrium, quod qui nugatoriis ratiocinationibus labefactare conantur, usque adeo coeci sunt, ut . . . caet[era].*

[5] *Quid enim tam in voluntate, quam ipsa voluntas, situm est?*

[6] *Dic mihi, quaeso, utrum Deus non sit auctor mali?*

68  created, but each soul comes from God; why, then, is it not the case
that, after a little interval, sins lead back to God?'[1] To which the
interlocutor replies: 'You have just now clearly said that which has
greatly tortured me in my thinking.'[2]—Luther has again taken up this
most thought-provoking observation and has emphasized it with all
the vehemence of his eloquence in *On the Bondage of the Will*, p. 144:
'But God must be of the sort who, by virtue of his *freedom* subjects
us to *necessity*, which natural reason must already confess. [...] If one
concedes omniscience and omnipotence, then it follows naturally and
incontestably that we are not made by ourselves, nor do we live, nor
do anything except through his omnipotence. [...] God's omniscience
and omnipotence stand in diametric contradiction to the freedom of
our will. [...] All humans will be compelled by inevitable consequence
to admit that not by our wills, but by necessity we become what we
are, that as a result we cannot do what we prefer by virtue of a freedom of will, but rather, as God has foreseen and *does* with infallible
and immutable resolution and virtue', etc.[3]

At the beginning of the seventeenth century we find Vanini*
completely imbued with this knowledge. It is the core and soul of
his persistent resistance against theism, concealed as cunningly as
possible because of the pressure of the time. At every opportunity
he returns to it, and he does not tire of expounding on it from the
most varied points of view. E.g. in his *Amphitheatre of Eternal Providence*, Exercise 16,[4] he says: 'If God wills sins, then he makes them:
for it is written, "all that he wills, he makes". If he does not will
them, but nevertheless they are committed, then we must say either
that he is improvident, or powerless, or cruel; for then he does not
carry out his resolution, whether through ignorance or powerless-
ness or negligence. [...] The philosophers inquire, if God did not

[1] *Movet autem animum, si peccata ex his animabus sunt, quas Deus creavit, illae autem
animae ex Deo; quomodo non, parvo intervallo, peccata referantur in Deum.*

[2] *Id nunc plane abs te dictum est, quod me cogitantem satis excruciat.*

[3] *At talem oportere esse Deum, qui libertate sua necessitatem imponat nobis, ipsa ratio
naturalis cogitur confiteri.—Concessa praescientia et omnipotentia, sequitur naturaliter, irre-
fragabili consequentia, nos per nos ipsos non esse factos, nec vivere, nec agere quidquam, sed
per illius omnipotentiam. — — Pugnat ex diametro praescientia et omnipotentia Dei cum
nostro libero arbitrio.—Omnes homines coguntur inevitabili consequentia admittere, nos non
fieri nostra voluntate, sed necessitate; ita nos non facere quod libet, pro jure liberi arbitrii, sed
prout Deus praescivit et agit consilio et virtute infallibili et immutabili.*

[4] *Amphitheatro aeternae providentiae, Exercitatio 16.*

will that shameful and base actions would occur in the world, then no doubt with a nod he would ban and exterminate all shameful acts from the world; for who among us is able to resist divine will? How can offences against God's will be perpetrated, if indeed, with every sinful act he provides the offender with the power to do so? Furthermore, if a person goes against God's will, then God is weaker than the person who opposes and prevails over him. From this they deduce that God desires the world to be as it is: if he willed a better one, he would have a better one'.[1]—And Exercise 44 reads: 'The instrument moves as directed by its principal; but our will in its operations behaves as an instrument, while God behaves as the actual agent; therefore, if the will operates badly, it is to be imputed to God. [...] Our will depends totally on God not only as to its movements, but also as to its substance: so nothing can truly be imputed to it, neither as to its substance, nor its operations, but everything must be imputed to God, who formed the will in this way and thus moves it. [...] Since the essence and the movement of the will are from God, the good and the bad operations of the will must be ascribed to him, if the will relates to him as an instrument.'[2] With Vanini, however, one must keep in mind that he generally used the stratagem of setting up his real opinion, convincingly and thoroughly demonstrated, in the person of an opponent, which opinion he abhors and will refute. Only afterward, in his own person, he will oppose it with shallow reasons and lame arguments and thereupon go off triumphant, just as if he had done well—relying on his readers' malignity. Through this cunning he had even deceived the most learned Sorbonne, which,

69

---

[1] *Si Deus vult peccata, igitur facit: scriptum est enim 'omnia quaecunque voluit fecit'. Si non vult, tamen committuntur: erit ergo dicendus improvidus, vel impotens, vel crudelis; cum voti sui compos fieri aut nesciat, aut nequeat, aut negligat. ———— Philosophi inquiunt: si nollet Deus pessimas ac nefarias in orbe vigere actiones, procul dubio uno nutu extra mundi limites omnia flagitia exterminaret, profligaretque: quis enim nostrum divinae potest resistere voluntati? Quomodo invito Deo patrantur scelera, si in actu quoque peccandi scelestis vires subministrat? Ad haec, si contra Dei voluntatem homo labitur, Deus erit inferior homine, qui ei adversatur, et praevalet. Hinc deducunt: Deus ita desiderat hunc mundum, qualis est: si meliorem vellet, meliorem haberet.—*

[2] *Instrumentum movetur prout a suo principali dirigitur: sed nostra voluntas in suis operationibus se habet tanquam instrumentum, Deus vero ut agens principale: ergo si haec male operatur, Deo imputandum est. ———— Voluntas nostra non solum quoad motum, sed quoad substantiam quoque tota a Deo dependet: quare nihil est, quod eidem imputari vere possit, neque ex parte substantiae, neque operationis, sed totum Deo, qui voluntatem sic formavit, et ita movet. ———— Cum essentia et motus voluntatis sit a Deo, adscribi eidem debent vel bonae, vel malae voluntatis operationes, si haec ad illum se habet velut instrumentum.*

having taken everything literally, had in sincerity set their imprimatur on his most ungodly writings. Three years later, with all the more heartfelt glee, they saw him burned alive after his blasphemous tongue had been cut out. Of course, such, indeed, is the real power of theologians' argument, and since it has been taken away from them, things have gone to hell in a handbasket.

Among the philosophers in the strict sense, if I am not in error, Hume* is the first who did not sneak around the serious difficulty which Augustine raised; rather, in his *Essay on Liberty and Necessity*, he laid it out openly without mentioning Augustine, nor Luther, much less Vanini. Toward the end of his essay, he says: '*The ultimate author of all our volitions is the creator of the world, who first bestowed motion on this immense machine, and placed all beings in that particular position, whence every subsequent event, by an unevitable [sic] necessity, must result. Human actions therefore either can have no turpitude at all, as proceeding from so good a cause, or, if they have any turpitude, they must involve our creator in the same guilt, while he is acknowledged to be their ultimate cause and author. For as a man, who fired a mine, is answerable for all the consequences, whether the train employed be long or short; so wherever a continued chain of necessary causes is fixed, that Being, either finite or infinite, who produces the first, is likewise the author of all the rest.*'[1] He makes an attempt to resolve this difficulty, but in the end it comes down to his finding it irresolvable.

Independent of his predecessors, Kant, too, trips on this stumbling-block in his *Critique of Practical Reason*, pp. 180 ff. of the fourth edition and p. 232 of the Rosenkranz: 'It seems, however, that as soon as one accepts God as the universal primordial being, one must also concede God to be the *cause of the existence of substance* and the actions of a human being to have in the same their determining ground which is completely outside of the human being's power, namely in the causality of a supreme being distinct from him, upon which the existence of the first and whole determination of his causality completely depends. [...] The human being would be a Vaucançonian automaton,* fabricated and wound up by the supreme master of all works of art, and his self-consciousness would even make him into a

---

[1] To many German readers a translation of this and the remaining English passages will be welcome. [Schopenhauer's note. Typically, Schopenhauer translated into German any English author whom he cites.]

thinking automaton in whom the consciousness of his spontaneity, if taken for freedom, would be mere deception in that it deserves only comparatively to be called such because the nearest determining causes of his movement and a long sequence of the same, drawn out to their determining causes, are still inner, but the final and highest would be found to be entirely in a strange hand.'* — He now tries to put an end to this great difficulty through the distinction between the thing in itself and appearance: in this way, however, the essence of the matter is so obviously not changed that I am convinced that he is not entirely serious in this. Even he himself admitted that his solution was uncertain, p. 184, where he adds: 'But, then, is any other of these that has been tried or may be tried, easier and more comprehensible? One would sooner say, the dogmatic teachers of metaphysics would thereby have proven more their *cunning* than their sincerity in that they removed this difficult point as far as possible from view in the hope that if they were to say absolutely nothing of it, no one would be likely to think of it.'*

After this quite noteworthy assemblage of highly diverse voices that all say the same thing, I return to our church father. The reasons for which he hopes to set aside the difficulty which he already felt in all its gravity, are theological, not philosophical, and thus not of unconditional validity. As I said, along with the two reasons introduced above, the support itself is the third reason why he sought to defend the *liberum arbitrium* granted to human beings by God. One such, which stands in the middle, between the creator and the sins of his creatures, separating them, would also actually suffice for the removal of the whole difficulty, as it is easily put into words and may suffice for thinking which does not go much further than these, if only it were to remain the least bit *conceivable* upon serious and deeper consideration. But how are we to imagine that a being, though in his whole *Existentia* and *Essentia* the work of another and yet able to determine himself primarily, originally, and fundamentally, could accordingly be responsible for his actions? The proposition 'doing follows being',[1] i.e., the effects of any being follow from its nature, invalidates that assumption and cannot itself be invalidated. If a person behaves badly, then it follows from this that he *is* bad. But to this proposition is attached its corollary: therefore, from whence the

72

---

[1] *operari sequitur esse.*

being, thence the doing.[1] What would one say of the watchmaker who is annoyed with his watch because it does not run well? Yet if one is eager to make the will into a *tabula rasa*, then one will scarcely have any choice but to grant that if, e.g., between two persons, one follows the exactly opposite way of acting from the other with respect to morality, this difference, which indeed must originate from somewhere, has its ground either in external circumstances, such that the guilt obviously does not concern the persons, or in an original difference of their wills themselves, such that guilt or merit once again cannot concern them, if their whole being and essence is the work of another. Since the aforementioned great men have futilely strained themselves to find an exit from this labyrinth, I freely admit that to think of the moral responsibility of the human will without its aseity* exceeds my power of comprehension, too. Without a doubt, the same incapacity has been that which has dictated the seventh of the eight definitions with which Spinoza opens his ethics:* 'that thing must be called free which exists only out of the necessity of its own nature and is determined to act only by itself alone, but that is necessary, or rather, compelled, which is determined by something else to exist and to act.'[2]

Namely, if bad action arises from the nature, i.e., from that which is innate to a person, the guilt obviously lies with the creator of this nature. For this reason, free will has been invented. Now, however, accepting this, from where it should arise is absolutely not to be comprehended because it is fundamentally a merely *negative* attribute and only signifies that nothing compels nor hinders the person from acting in one way or another. However, this never makes clear *from what*, then, the action arises, since it should not result from the innate or given nature of the person, as it then would fall to the charge of his creator; nor from external circumstances alone, as then, it would then be ascribed to chance, and thus, the person would in any case remain blameless—whereas he surely will be held responsible for it. The common image of a free will is an unweighted balance scale. It hangs at rest and will never move out of equilibrium if something is not laid on one of its pans. Just as it cannot produce movement of

73

---

[1] *corollarium: ergo unde esse, inde operari.*

[2] *ea res libera dicetur, quae ex sola naturae suae necessitate existit, et a se sola ad agendum determinatur; necessaria autem, vel potius coacta, quae ab alio determinatur ad existendum et operandum.*

itself, so the free will cannot produce an action out of itself simply because nothing can come of nothing. If the balance should sink to one side, so must a foreign body be laid upon it, which then is the source of the movement. Just so human action must be produced from something which *positively* effects it and is something more than a mere *negative* freedom. This, however, can only occur in two ways: either a motive, i.e., an external circumstance, does so to and for it, whence the person is obviously not responsible for the action, and then, so must all humans act in exactly the same way under exactly the same circumstances. Or it arises from a person's responsiveness to such motives, thus, out of his innate character, i.e., out of the inherent inclinations arising from the person, which inclinations can be different among individuals and by the power of which inclinations the motive can work. Then, however, the will is no longer free, for these inclinations are the weight which is laid on the balance scale's pan. The responsibility falls back on the one who has laid it there, i.e., whose work is the person with such inclinations. For this reason, the person is responsible for his doings only in the case that he himself is his own work, i.e., has aseity.

The whole point of view of the matter laid out here allows one to gauge how everything depends on freedom of the will as that which forms an impassable chasm between the creator and the sins of his creatures, from which it becomes understandable why the theologians so persistently cling to it and why their shield-bearers, the philosophy professors, most duty-bound, then so zealously support them that, deaf and blind to the most convincing counter-evidence of great thinkers, they cling to free will and fight for it as if for hearth and home.[1]

But finally to close my account of Augustine, interrupted above: on the whole his opinion is that the human being actually did have 74 completely free will only before the Fall, but after that, fallen to original sin, has to hope for his salvation through election by grace and redemption — which pronouncement sounds like a church father.

In the meanwhile, philosophy is awakened to a consciousness of our problem by Augustine and his quarrel with the Manicheans and Pelagians. From then on, through the scholastics, it became ever more clear to philosophy, to which Buridan's sophism and the aforementioned passage of Dante's bear witness. — But the first who got to the

---

[1] *pro ara et focis.*

bottom of the matter is, by all appearance, Thomas Hobbes, whose work specifically devoted to this subject, *Questions on Liberty and Necessity, Against Doctor Branhall*,[1] appeared in 1656. Nowadays it is rare. You may find it in the English language in *Thomas Hobbes's Moral and Political Works*, one volume in folio, London, 1750, pp. 469 ff., from which I quote the following main passage, p. 483:

6) Nothing takes a beginning from itself, but from the action of some other immediate agent, without itself. Therefore, when first a man has an appetite or will to something, to which immediately before he had no appetite nor will, the cause of his will is not the will itself, but something else not in his own disposing. So that, whereas it is out of controversy that of voluntary actions the will is the necessary cause, and by this which is said, the will is also necessarily *caused* by other things, whereof it disposes not, it follows that voluntary actions have all of them necessary causes, and therefore are *necessitated*.

7) I hold *that* to be a *sufficient* cause to which nothing is wanting that is needfull to the producing of the *effect*. The same is also a *necessary* cause: for if it be possible that a *sufficient* cause shall not bring forth the *effect*, then there wanteth somewhat, which was needfull to the producing of it; and so the cause was not *sufficient*. But if it be impossible that a *sufficient* cause should not produce the effect; then is a *sufficient* cause a *necessary* cause. Hence it is manifest, that whatever is produced, is produced [75] *necessarily*. For whatsoever is produced has had a *sufficient* cause to produce it, or else it had not been: and therefore also *voluntary* actions are *necessitated*.

8) That ordinary definition of a free agent (namely that a free agent is that, which, when all things are present which are needfull to produce the effect, can nevertheless not produce it) implies a contradiction and is Nonsense, being as much as to say, the cause may be *sufficient*, that is to say *necessary*, and yet the effect shall not follow. —

Page 485: 'Every accident, how contingent soever it seem, or how *voluntary* soever it be, is produced *necessarily*.'

In his famous book, *De cive*,\* chapter 1, section 7, he says: 'Everyone is urged to desire what is good for him and to flee from what is bad for him, but most of all from that which is the greatest of all natural evils, which is death; and this happens by a natural necessity no less than that by which a stone falls to the ground.'[2]

---

[1] *Quaestiones de libertate et necessitate, contra Doctorem Branhallum.*

[2] *Fertur unusquisque ad appetitionem ejus, quod sibi bonum, et ad fugam ejus, quod sibi malum est, maxime autem maximi malorum naturalium, quae est mors; idque necessitate quadam naturae non minore, quam qua fertur lapis deorsum.*

Immediately after Hobbes, we see Spinoza pervaded by the same conviction. To characterize his ideas on this point, a few passages will suffice:

*Ethics, Part I, proposition 32*: 'Will cannot be called a free cause, but only a necessary cause.' — *Corollary 2*: 'For will, like all the rest, needs a cause by which it is determined to act in a particular way.'[1]

*Ibid., Part II, last scholium*: 'As for the fourth objection (of Buridan's ass), I am quite ready to admit that a human being placed in such an equilibrium (namely, perceiving nothing but hunger and thirst, a certain food and a certain drink, each equally distant from him) would die of hunger and thirst.[2]

*Ibid., Part III, proposition 2, scholium*: 'These decisions of the mind arise in the mind with the same necessity as the ideas of things actually existing. Therefore whoever believes that he speaks or keeps silence or acts in any way from the free decision of his mind, does but dream with his eyes open.' — *Letter 62*: 'Everything is necessarily determined by external causes to exist and act in a given determinate manner. For instance, a stone receives from the impulsion of an external cause, a certain quantity of motion, by which it must necessarily continue to move. Now assume that a stone, while it continues to move, thinks and is itself conscious that it is endeavouring, as far as it can, to continue to move. Such a stone, being conscious merely of its own endeavour, and not at all indifferent, would believe itself to be completely free, and would think that it continued in motion solely because of its own will. This is that human freedom which all boast they possess, and which consists solely in the fact, that humans are conscious of their own willing, but are ignorant of the causes whereby that willing has been determined.— —I have thus sufficiently explained my opinion regarding free and constrained necessity, and also regarding so-called human freedom.'[3]

---

[1] *Voluntas non potest vocari causa libera, sed tantum necessaria.—Coroll. 2. Nam voluntas, ut reliqua omnia, causa indiget, a qua ad operandum certo modo determinatur.*

[2] *Quod denique ad quartam objectionem (de Buridani asina) attinet, dico, me omnino concedere, quod homo in tali aequilibrio positus (nempe qui nihil aliud percipit quam sitim et famem, talem cibum et talem potum, qui aeque ab eo distant) fame et siti peribit.*

[3] *Mentis decreta eadem necessitate in mente oriuntur, ac ideae rerum actu existentium. Qui igitur credunt, se ex libero mentis decreto loqui vel tacere, vel quidquam agere, oculis apertis somniant.—Epist. 62. Unaquaeque res necessario a causa externa aliqua determinatur ad existendum et operandum certa ac determinata ratione. Ex. gr. lapis a causa externa, ipsum impellente, certam motus quantitatem accipit, qua postea moveri necessario perget. Concipe jam*

77    A noteworthy circumstance, however, is that Spinoza only arrives at this insight in his last years (i.e. in his forties), after earlier, in the year 1665, when he was still a Cartesian, he had chosen the opposing opinion, decisively and energetically defending it in his *Thoughts on Metaphysics*,[1] chapter 12, and even having said in direct contradiction with the last scholium of Part II just quoted in reference to Buridan's Sophism: 'If we were to place a human being instead of an ass in such an equilibrium, we should have to regard the human being not as a thinking thing, but as the most shameful ass, if he were to die of hunger and thirst.'[2]

I will have more to say below about the same change of opinion and conversion in two other great men. This proves how difficult and profound is the correct insight into our problem.

In his *Essay on Liberty and Necessity*, from which I already had to quote a passage above, Hume writes with the clearest conviction of the necessity of the individual acts of will upon given motives and expresses it most clearly in his thoroughly comprehensible manner. He says: 'Thus it appears that the conjunction between motives and voluntary actions is as regular and uniform as that between the cause and effect in any part of nature.' And further: 'It seems almost impossible, therefore, to engage either in science or action of any kind, without acknowledging the doctrine of necessity and this inference from motives to voluntary actions, from character to conduct.'

But no author has so extensively and convincingly demonstrated the necessity of the act of will as Priestley in his conclusive work devoted to this subject, *The Doctrine of Philosophical Necessity.**

78    Anyone who is not convinced by this totally clear and comprehensibly written book must actually have an understanding paralysed by prejudice. As a characterization of his conclusions, I present here several passages which I cite from the second edition, Birmingham 1782.

---

*lapidem, dum moveri pergit, cogitare et scire, se, quantum potest, conari, ut moveri pergat. Hic sane lapis, quandoquidem sui tantummodo conatus est conscius et minime indifferens, se liberrimum esse et nulla alia de causa in motu perseverare credet, quam quia vult. Atque haec humana illa libertas est, quam omnes habere jactant, et quae in hoc solo consistit, quod homines sui appetitus sint conscii, et causarum, a quibus determinantur, ignari. —— His, quaenam mea de libera et coacta necessitate, deque ficta humana libertate sit sententia, satis explicui.*

[1]  *Cogitatis metaphysicis* [appended to *Renati des Cartes principiorum philosophiae* (*The Principles of René Descartes' Philosophy*), 1665].

[2]  *si enim hominem loco asinae ponamus in tali aequilibrio positum, homo, non pro re cogitante, sed pro turpissimo asino erit habendus, si fame et siti pereat.*

Foreword, p. xx: 'There is no absurdity more glaring to my understanding, than the notion of philosophical liberty.'—Page 26: 'Without a miracle, or the intervention of some foreign cause, no volition
or action of any man could have been otherwise, than it has been.'—
Page 37: 'Though an inclination or affection of mind be not gravity, it influences me and acts upon me as certainly and necessarily,
as this power does upon a stone.'—Page 43: 'Saying that the will
is self-determined, gives no idea at all, or rather implies an absurdity, viz: that a *determination*, which is an effect, takes place, without
any cause at all. For exclusive of every thing that comes under the
denomination of motive, there is really nothing at all left to produce the determination. Let a man use what words he pleases, he
can have no more conception how we can sometimes be determined
by motives, and sometimes without any motive, than he can have of
a scale being sometimes weighed down by weights, and sometimes
by a kind of substance that has no weight at all, which, whatever it
be in itself, must, with respect to the scale be *nothing*.'—Page 66:
'In proper philosophical language, the motive ought to be call'd the
*proper cause* of the action. It is as much so as any thing in nature is the
cause of any thing else.'—Page 84: 'It will never be in our power to
choose two things, when all the previous circumstances are the very
same.'—Page 90: 'A man indeed, when he reproaches himself for
any particular action in his passed [*sic*] conduct, may fancy that, if
he was in the same situation again, he would have acted differently.
But this is a mere deception; and if he examines himself strictly,
and takes in all circumstances, he may be satisfied that, with the
same inward disposition of mind, and with precisely the same view
of things, that he had then, and exclusive of all others, that he has
acquired by reflection *since*, he could not have acted otherwise than
he did.'—Page 287: 'In short, there is no choice in the case, but of the 79
doctrine of necessity or absolute nonsense.'

It is now to be noted that things went precisely the same way with
Priestley as with Spinoza and also with another very great man about
to be cited. Specifically, in the preface to the first edition, p. xxvii,
Priestley says: 'I was not however a ready convert to the doctrine of
necessity. Like Dr Hartley himself, I gave up my liberty with great
reluctance, and in a long correspondence, which I once had on the 80
subject, I maintained very strenuously the doctrine of liberty, and did
not at all yield to the arguments then proposed to me.'

The third great man, with whom things went the same way, is Voltaire,* who reports it with his own charm and naivety. Namely in his *Treatise on Metaphysics*, chapter 7, he had fully and vigorously defended so-called free will. But in his book written more than forty years later, *The Ignorant Philosopher*,[1] he taught the strict necessitation of acts of will, in the thirteenth chapter, which he closes thus: 'Archimedes is with equal necessity compelled to remain in his room when one shuts him in it, and when he is so steeped in a problem that the idea of going out does not occur to him:

'The fates lead the willing, the unwilling they drag.

'*The ignorant person who thinks thus has not always thought the same*, but in the end he was compelled to surrender.'[2] In the following book, *The Principle of Action*,[3] he says in chapter 13: 'a ball that strikes another, a dog that chases necessarily and wilfully after a stag, this stag that jumps a large ditch with no less necessity and will: all of this is no more irresistibly determined than we are to everything that we do.'[4]

Indeed this similar conversion of three most eminent minds to our insight must then stop short everyone who undertakes to dispute the well-founded truth with the wholly irrelevant 'but I can indeed do what I will' of his foolish self-consciousness.

81    After these, his close predecessors, we may not be surprised that Kant considered the necessity by which the empirical character was determined by motives to actions to be a matter already settled both for himself and for others, so that he did not hold himself up by proving it anew. In his 'Ideas for a Universal History' he begins with: 'Even for a metaphysical purpose, whatever one would like to make of a concept of *freedom of will*, the *appearances* of such freedom,

---

[1]  *Le Philosophe ignorant* [1766].

[2]  *Archimède est également nécessité de rester dans sa chambre, quand on l'y enferme, et quand il est si fortement occupé d'un problème, qu'il ne reçoit pas l'idée de sortir:*

   '*Ducunt volentem fata, nolentem trahunt.*' [Seneca, *Moral Letters* 107. 11].

   L'ignorant qui pense ainsi n'a pas toujours pensé de même, *mais il est enfin contraint de se rendre.*

[3]  Full title: *One Has to Choose Sides, or The Principle of Action* (*Il faut prendre un parti ou Le Principe d'action* [1772]).

[4]  *Une boule, qui en pousse une autre, un chien de chasse, qui court nécessairement et volontairement après un cerf, ce cerf, qui franchit un fossé immense avec non moins de nécessité et de volonté: tout cela n'est pas plus invinciblement déterminé que nous le sommes à tout ce que nous fesons.*

human actions, are just as determined by universal natural law as any other natural occurrence'.* In *Critique of Pure Reason*\* (p. 548 of the first or p. 577 of the fifth edition) he says: 'Because the empirical character itself must be drawn from appearances as effect, and from the rule which experience provides, all the actions of the human being in appearance are determined in accord with the order of nature by his empirical character and the other cooperating causes; and if we could investigate all the appearances of his power of choice down to their basis, then there would be no human action that we could not predict with certainty and recognize as necessary give its preceding conditions. Thus in regard to this empirical character there is no freedom, and according to this character we can consider the human being solely by *observing*, and, as happens in anthropology, by trying to investigate the moving causes of his actions physiologically.' Just the same is said on p. 798 of the first or p. 826 of the fifth edition: 'The will may well be free, yet this can concern only the intelligible cause of our willing. For in accordance with an inviolable fundamental maxim without which we could not exercise any reason in empirical use, we must explain the phenomena of its manifestations, i.e., actions, no differently from all other appearances of nature, namely in accordance with its inalterable laws.' Further, in *Critique of Practical Reason*,\* p. 177 in the fourth edition, or p. 230 in the Rosenkranz, 'One can therefore allow that were it possible for us to have such profound insight into a human being's way of thinking, as shown by inner as well as outer actions, that we would know every, even the least, incentive to actions as well as all the external occasions affecting them, then one could calculate a human being's conduct for the future with as much certainty as a lunar or solar eclipse.'

However, he connects to this his theory of the coexistence of freedom and necessity by means of a distinction between the intelligible character and the empirical, on which view, because I wholly support it, I will expand later. Kant has explained it twice, specifically in *Critique of Pure Reason*, pp. 532–554 of the first or pp. 560–582 of the fifth edition and even more clearly in *Critique of Practical Reason*, pp. 169–179 of the fourth edition or pp. 224–231\* of the Rosenkranz. Everyone who wishes to achieve a fundamental knowledge of the unity of human freedom and the necessity of actions must read these exceedingly well-thought-out passages.

To this point, the present discussion of the subject distinguishes itself among the works of all these noble and venerable predecessors mainly in two points: first in that, on the prompting of the prize question, I have strictly separated the inner perception of will in the self-consciousness from the outer and have considered each of them in itself, whereby the discovery of the source of the deception which affects most people irresistibly becomes first of all possible; second, in that I have considered the will in connection with all the rest of nature, which none has done before me, whereby for the first time the subject could be handled with as much profundity, methodical insight, and thoroughness as is possible.

Now for a few words more about some authors who wrote after Kant, whom I certainly do not consider to be my predecessors.

In his 'Investigation into Human Freedom', pp. 465–471, Schelling has provided an illustrative paraphrase of Kant's most important theory of intelligible and empirical character commended above. Through the liveliness of his colour, this paraphrase can serve to make the matter easier for many to grasp than Kant's thorough, but dry exposition would allow. In the meanwhile, in honour of truth and Kant, I may not mention this without finding fault with Schelling here, for where he explains one of the most important and most admirable, yes, in my judgement, the most profoundly significant of all Kantian theories, he does not clearly state that what he now expounds, in its content, belongs to Kant. What is more, he expresses himself so that most readers, to whom the content of the wide-ranging and difficult work of this great man is not exactly familiar, must suppose they read here Schelling's own thoughts. How much here the result has suited the design I will show by one example among many. Even today a young professor of philosophy in Halle, Mr Erdmann, says in his book of 1837 titled *Body and Soul*,* p. 101: 'although Leibniz, like Schelling in his essay on freedom, has the soul determine itself before all time . . .', etc. Schelling stands to Kant in the lucky position of Amerigo to Columbus: another's discovery was stamped with his name. However, he also has his cunning and not chance to thank. For he commences, p. 465: 'For first of all idealism had first brought up the doctrine of freedom in the area', etc., and then the Kantian thoughts follow immediately. Thus, instead of saying Kant here, as honesty would dictate, he cunningly says *idealism*: everyone will take this ambiguous expression to mean

Fichte's philosophy and Schelling's first, Fichtean philosophy and
not Kant's theory, since Kant protested against the naming of his
philosophy as idealism (e.g. *Prolegomena*, p. 51 and p. 155 in the
Rosenkranz edition) and even added to his second edition of *Critique
of Pure Reason*, p. 274, a 'refutation of idealism'. Then on the following page, Schelling quite cunningly mentions the 'Kantian concept'
in an aside, specifically to appease those who already know that it is
Kantian riches which the man here so pompously displays as his own
wares. Then, however, p. 472, in defiance of all truth and justice,
it is still said that Kant had *not* achieved this insight in his theory, 84
etc., while anyone can clearly see from the two gleanings I recommend above, immortal passages of Kant, that this insight owes its
origin exactly to him alone and which insight, but for him, no thousands of such minds the likes of Messrs Fichte and Schelling would
have been capable of grasping. Since I have to speak here of Schelling's essay, I may not be silent on this point; rather, I have just
fulfilled my duty toward this great teacher of humankind, who alone
with Goethe is the legitimate pride of the German nation, by vindi-
cating his right to that which incontestably belongs to him alone—
particularly at a time for which Goethe's words actually serve well:
'The boys are masters of the course.'*—Moreover, in the same essay,
with just as little propriety, Schelling has appropriated the thoughts,
even the words of Jakob Böhme,* without revealing his source.

Apart from this paraphrase of Kantian thinking, this 'Investigations
into Freedom' contains nothing which could serve to provide us with
a new or profound clarification of the very topic. This announces itself
right from the beginning through the definition: freedom is 'a capacity for good and evil'. Such a definition may be of use for a catechism:
in philosophy, however, nothing is thereby said and, consequently,
neither is anything to be done. For good and evil are anything but
simple concepts (*notiones simplices*) which are clear in themselves and
require neither elucidation, determination, nor proof. In general, this
essay concerns freedom only a little bit: most of its contents is a much
more detailed report on a god with whom Mr Writer pretends to be
intimately acquainted, such that he even describes for us this god's
genesis. It is just to be deplored that he mentions not a word of how he
came to have this acquaintance. The beginning of the essay makes up
a web of sophisms, the insipidity of which anyone will recognize who
has not allowed himself to be intimidated by the audacity of the tone.

Since then, and as a result of this and similar productions, in German
85 philosophy, 'intellectual intuition' and 'absolute thinking' have taken
the place of clear concepts and honest inquiry: to impress, to bewil-
der, to mystify the reader, to kick sand in the reader's eyes with all
sorts of artifices has become the method, and instead of judgement,
everywhere design rules discourse. Through all of this, philosophy, if
one will still call it such, was bound always to sink deeper and deeper
until at last it reached the deepest level of degradation in that ministerial creature, Hegel. Once again to stifle the freedom of thought
that Kant had won through great difficulty, Hegel made philosophy,
the daughter of reason and expectant mother of truth, into a tool of
state design, of obscurantism, and protestant Jesuitism. To disguise
this outrage and at the same time to accomplish the greatest possible
stultification of minds, he drew over it a cloak of hollow verbiage and
the most senseless gobbledegook that had ever been heard, at least
outside a madhouse.

Taken as a whole, in England and France philosophy still remains
about where Locke and Condillac* have left it. Maine de Biran,*
called by his publisher, Mr Cousin, 'the premier French metaphys-
ician of my time',[1] is, in his *New Considerations of the Physical and
Moral*,[2] which appeared in 1834, a fanatical adherent to *liberi arbitrii
indifferentiae* and takes it as a matter completely self-evident. Many of
the new German philosophical scribblers cannot see it any other way:
the *liberum arbitrium indifferentiae*, under the name 'moral freedom',
occurs in them as a settled matter, as if the great men cited above
had never existed. They explain freedom of will as given immediately in self-consciousness and, hence, so unshakeably proven that
all arguments against it could be nothing else than sophistry. This
excessive confidence arises out of just the idea that the good know
not what freedom of the will is and means; rather, in their innocence,
they understand nothing else by this than the mastery of the will over
the limbs of the body, as was analysed in the second chapter, which
mastery of course, no reasonable person has doubted and the expres-
86 sion of which is just 'I can do what I will'. They believe quite sincerely that this is freedom of the will and insist that it has exceeded
all doubt. This is just the sort of innocence to which, despite so many

---

[1] '*Le premier métaphysicien Français de mon tem[p]s*'.
[2] *Nouvelles considérations du physique et moral*.

great predecessors, Hegelian philosophy has retarded the thinking German spirit. To people of this stamp, one could readily exclaim:

> Are you not like women who consistently
> Return to just their first word,
> Even if one has reasoned with them for hours?*

Indeed, for many of them, the theological motives to which I alluded above are silently operant.

And then again, the medical, zoological, historical, political, and belletristic authors of our day: with what great pleasure they seize every opportunity to mention 'human freedom' and 'moral freedom'! With that, they imagine they are saying something. Of course, they will not get involved with an explanation of these concepts. Yet if one were allowed to examine these authors, one would find that by this they either mean absolutely nothing or just mean our old, venerable, well-known *liberum arbitrium indifferentiae*, in no matter what noble figures of speech they dress it up. Thus no one will ever succeed in convincing the great masses of the inadmissibility of this concept. However, scholars should indeed take care not to speak with such innocence. For this reason there are also even some faint-hearted ones among them who are quite amusing, in that while they are no longer bold enough to speak of freedom of the will, instead, to make it sound refined, say 'freedom of *spirit*' [*Geist*] and, in doing so, hope to slink through. For what they mean by this, I am fortunately able to offer the questioning, discerning reader this answer: nothing, just plain nothing—since it is even, in good German fashion and style, an indefinite and, indeed, actually vacuous expression, one which, in their inanity and cowardice, they hope to use as cover for their getaway. The word 'spirit', actually a figurative expression, always denotes *intellectual* abilities, in contrast to the will. These abilities, however, ought not at all to be free in their operation, but ought to accord, conform, and be subject first to the rules of logic and then to the given *object* of their cognition, so that they comprehend purely, i.e., *object-* 87 *ively*, and so that it may never be said that 'will replaces reason'.[1] In general this 'spirit', which prowls all around contemporary German literature, is a thoroughly suspicious fellow, of whom, when one encounters him, one should then enquire about his credentials.

---

[1] *stat pro ratione voluntas* [Juvenal, *Satires* VI. 223.]

To serve as a mask for a combination of cowardice and poverty of thought is his most frequent business. Moreover, the word *Geist* is known to be related to the word *gas*, which, stemming from Arabic and alchemy, means vapour or air, just as *spiritus* is related to πνεῦμα, *animus* to ἄνεμος.

As was said, with respect to our theme, in the philosophical and in the broader learned world things remain after all just as the afore-mentioned great spirits have taught. It is again confirmed that not only has nature at all times produced only the very fewest true think-ers as rare exceptions, but also that these few have themselves always existed for the very few. So delusion and error always assert their domain.

In a moral subject, the testimony of the great poets is of weight. They do not speak upon systematic investigation, but their keen insight reveals human nature. Hence their pronouncements imme-diately strike the truth.—In Shakespeare's *Measure for Measure*, Act II, Scene 2, Isabella begs the royal deputy Angelo for mercy for her condemned brother:

ANGELO: I will not do it.
ISABELLA: But can you if you would?
ANGELO: Look, what I will not, that I cannot do.

In *Twelfth Night*, Act I, it is said:

> Fate, show thy force: ourselves we do not owe;
> What is decreed must be; and be this so.*

88        That great judge and portrayer of the human heart and its most secret impulses, Sir Walter Scott, has brought to the light of day some deeply buried truths in his *St Ronan's Well*, volume 3, chapter 6. He presents a dying, repentant sinner, who on her deathbed seeks to lighten her most anxious conscience through confessions, and in the midst of these he has her say:

Go, and leave me to my fate; I am the most detestable wretch that ever liv'd,—detestable to myself, worst of all; because even in my penitence there is a secret whisper that tells me, that were I as I have been, I would again act over all the wickedness I have done, and much worse. Oh! for Heaven's assistance, to crush the wicked thought!

A proof of *this* poetic presentation is furnished by the following parallel fact which also strongly confirms the theory of the constancy of character. It was reprinted from the French newspaper *La Presse* in the [London] *Times* of 2 July 1845, from which I translate it. The headline read: 'Military Execution at Oran.' On the 24th of March a Spaniard named Aguil[era], *alias* Gomez was condemned to death. On the day before the execution he said in conversation with the gaoler:

'I am not as guilty as I have been represented,' [said he;] 'I am accused of having committed 30 murders, whilst I committed but 26. I had a thirst for blood from my infancy. At the age of 7 years and a half I stabbed a child. I murdered a pregnant woman, and at a later period I murdered a Spanish officer, in consequence of which I was compelled to fly from Spain. I took refuge in France, where I committed two crimes before I enlisted in the Foreign Legion. Of all my crimes, I regret the following more than all the others: — In 1841, I captured, at the head of my company, a deputy commissary-general, escorted by a sergeant, a corporal and 7 men, and I caused them all to be decapitated. Their death is a weight over me. I frequently see them in my dreams, and tomorrow I shall see them in the men appointed to shoot me; and, *nevertheless, were I to recover liberty, I would murder others.*'*

The following passage in Goethe's *Iphigenia* (Act IV, Scene 2) also belongs here:

ARKAS: For you have not heeded sincere advice.
IPHIGENIA: What I was able to do, I gladly did.
ARKAS: You can still change your mind in good time.
IPHIGENIA: *That never was in our power.*

A famous passage from Schiller's *Wallenstein** expresses our fundamental truth:

> Know that a human's deeds and thoughts
> Are not like the blind movement of the ocean's waves!
> The inner world is his microcosm,
> The deep shaft from which they spring eternally.
> They are as necessary as the fruit of the tree;
> Juggling chance cannot change them.
> When I have first investigated the human essence,
> I then know, too, his willing and his acting.

# V

## CONCLUSION AND HIGHER VIEW

As I have defended the truth here, I have gladly called to mind all these illustrious philosophical as well as poetic predecessors. Meanwhile, not authorities, but reasons are the weapons of philosophers; hence, I have pursued my case only with the latter, and I hope, indeed, having given you this sort of evidence, that I am now quite justified in drawing the inference from the impossible to the non-existent,[1] whereby the question posed by the Royal Society, first answered above in the negative by a direct and factual, hence, *a posteriori*, investigation of self-consciousness is now also answered indirectly and *a priori*, since what does not at all exist also cannot have in the self-consciousness data from which it can be demonstrated.

Now if the truth defended here may belong among those which go against the preconceived opinions of the short-sighted masses, which might even be offensive to the weak and ignorant, this could not restrain me from expressing it without circumlocution and without restraint, given that here I speak not to the people, but to an enlightened academy that had not posed its timely question to shore up prejudice, but with respect for the truth.—As long as it is a question of truth, the honest truth-seeker will ascertain and verify a truth, always looking to its grounds and not to its consequences, for there will then be time for consequences when the truth itself is established. Unconcerned about the consequences, only to test grounds and not first to ask whether or not a given truth harmonizes with the system of the rest of our beliefs—this is as Kant recommended, whose words I cannot restrain myself from repeating:

This confirms the maxim, already acknowledged and commended by others, that in any scientific investigation one should pursue its course undisturbed with all possible precision and openness, without concern for how it may offend anything outside its field, but as much as one can, truthfully and completely to carry it through for itself alone. Frequent observation has convinced me that, if one has brought this business to its end, that which, when half finished, appeared to me to be very dubious

---

[1] *a non posse ad non esse.*

considering external theories, if I did not concentrate so much on this reservation and just turned my attention to my business until it was completed, finally, in an unexpected way, completely accorded with the other matter, having come to the agreement by itself without the least consideration for those theories, without partiality and preference for them. Authors can spare themselves many an error, many a wasted effort (because it was spent on delusion) if they can only resolve to go to work with somewhat more openness. (*Critique of Practical Reason*, p. 190 in the fourth edition, or p. 239 in the Rosenkranz*)

In general, our metaphysical cognitions are infinitely far from having so much certainty that one should reject some well-founded truth because its consequences do not suit them. Moreover, any hard-fought and firmly held truth is an incursion on the domain of the problems of knowledge in general and a fixed point on which to apply levers that will move other loads, indeed, by which, in favourable circumstances, one rises at once to a higher view of the whole than one previously had. For the concatenation of truths in any domain of knowledge is so great that whoever has taken a single one into his secure possession may in any case hope from that to conquer the 92 whole. As, in a difficult algebraic problem, a single given positive value is of inestimable worth because it makes the solution possible, so in the most difficult of all human problems, which is metaphysics, the *a priori* certain and *a posteriori* proven knowledge of the strict necessity with which deeds follow from a given character and given motives is such an invaluable datum that, proceeding from it alone, one can arrive at the solution to the entire problem. Therefore, every-thing which does not point to a certain, scientific verification must yield when it stands in the way of well-grounded truth, but not the other way around, and by no means should it agree to accommoda-tions and limitation to accord with unproven, and perhaps erroneous, assertions.

I may still be permitted a general remark. A look back at our result gives rise to the observation that with regard to the two problems which in the previous chapter were already indicated to be the most profound in the modern philosophy, but of which the ancients were not clearly conscious—namely, the problem of free will and that of the relationship between the ideal and the real—the healthy, but untrained understanding is not only incompetent, but even has a decided natural tendency to error. To retrieve the untrained from

such error requires a philosophy which is already highly developed. That is, it is actually natural for the untrained to attribute too much to the *object* with respect to *cognition*. Therefore, Locke and Kant are needed to show how much of cognition arises from the *subject*. With respect to *willing*, on the contrary, the untrained understanding has reversed the tendency, attributing far too little to the *object* and far too much to the *subject*, because it allows everything to proceed from the *subject* without properly taking into account the factor which lies in the *object*, the motives, which actually determine the entirely individual nature of actions while only their universal and essential, namely their fundamental moral character, proceeds from the *subject*. In speculative inquiries, such a natural reversal of the understand-
93 ing should not surprise us since it is originally determined solely for practical and in no way for speculative purposes.

If, now, as a result of our previous presentation we have recognized all freedom of human action as suspended and human action as subject to the strictest necessity without exception, so we are thereby led to the point at which *true moral freedom*, which is of a higher sort, can be comprehended.

There is, of course, a fact of the consciousness which I have earlier completely overlooked in order not to disrupt the progress of the investigation. This is the perfectly clear and certain feeling of *responsibility* for that which we do, of *accountability* for our actions, resting on the unshakeable certainty that we ourselves are the *doers of our deeds*. Because of this consciousness, it never comes to anyone's mind, not even one who is completely convinced of the explanation, given in the previous chapters, of the necessity with which our actions occur, to excuse himself for a transgression by way of this necessity and to exonerate himself of the guilt by way of the motives since, yes, the deed was inevitable upon the motives' entry. For he certainly realized that this necessity has a *subjective* condition and that here *objectively*, i.e., under the existing circumstances, hence under the influence of the motives which have determined him, a completely different action, even one which is its exact opposite, was quite possible and could have occurred *if only he had been another*: on this alone it has depended. Because he is this, and no one else, because he has such and such a character, for *him*, to be sure, no other action was possible; however, in itself, hence *objectively*, it was possible. Therefore the *responsibility*, of which he is conscious first of all and ostensibly, concerns the deed, but fundamentally concerns *his character*: for *this* he feels responsible. And for *this* the others, too, make him responsible since their judgement immediately turns away from the deed to establish the qualities of the doer: 'he is a bad man, a scoundrel'—or 'he is a rascal'—or 'he is a petty, fake, vile soul'—so their judgement sounds, and their reproach redounds to his *character*. The deed, along 94 with the motive, is thereby taken into consideration as evidence of the character of the doer, serving as a sure symptom of his character, whereby it is forever irrevocably established. Aristotle put it just right: 'we speak an encomium for those who have achieved something. Deeds are signs of habitual character, since we would praise even one who had not achieved anything if we believe him to be one of the type who could'[1]—*Rhetoric* I. 9. Thus not on the fleeting deed, but on the enduring qualities of the doer, i.e., the character from which the deed issues, they cast their scorn, their loathing, and their contempt. For this reason, in all languages there are epithets about moral depravity, the insults which they express being more often predicated of the person than the actions. They are attached to character, for this must bear the guilt of which it has been plainly convicted merely on the occasion of the deeds.

Since where *guilt* lies, *responsibility* must also lie, and since this is the sole datum on which the inference of moral freedom is justified, so *freedom* must also lie in the same, thus in the *character* of the person, especially since we have sufficiently convinced ourselves that freedom is not to be encountered in individual actions, which, given character, occur with strict necessity. But as had been shown in the third chapter, the character is innate and unalterable.

So we will now somewhat more closely observe freedom in this sense, the only sense for which data are present, so that, having inferred moral freedom from a fact of consciousness and having found its place, we may also comprehend it philosophically as far as that may be possible.

In the third chapter it has been shown that any action of a human being is a product of two factors: his character along with the motive. This in no way means that an action is intermediate, as if it were a

---

[1] Ἐγκωμιάζομεν πράξαντας· τὰ δ' ἔργα σημεῖα τῆς ἕξεώς ἐστι, ἐπεὶ ἐπαινοῖμεν ἂν καὶ μὴ πεπραγότα, εἰ πιστεύοιμεν εἶναι τοιοῦτον.—*Rhetorica*, I, 9. (*Encomio celebramus eos, qui egerunt: opera autem signa habitus sunt; quoniam laudaremus etiam qui non egisset, si crederemus esse talem.*)

compromise between the motive and the character. Rather, the action requires both fully, since in its complete possibility it depends on
95   both at the same time, namely that the effective motive is suitable to this character and that by such a motive this character is determinable. The character is the empirically recognized, constant, unalterable nature of an individual will. Now since this character is just as much a necessary factor of every action as the motive, this explains the feeling that our deeds proceed from ourselves, or it explains each '*I will*' which accompanies all of our actions and by virtue of which everyone must recognize them as *his* deeds for which he then feels morally responsible.

Now just as was found above in the investigation of the self-consciousness, this is the 'I will, and I will always only what I will'—which misleads the untutored understanding into persistently asserting that there is an absolute freedom of commission and omission, a *liberum arbitrium indifferentiae*. But it is nothing more than the consciousness of the second factor of an action which in itself is wholly incapable of producing an action, just as, in contrast, with the entry of a motive it is incapable of refraining from it. But only when character is set into action does it give evidence of its inherent nature to the cognitive faculty as that which, essentially directed externally, not internally, first empirically recognized even the nature of its own will from its actions. It is actually this closer and ever more intimate acquaintance which one calls conscience, which for exactly this reason is first *directly* felt only *after* the deed; *prior* to the deed it is at most felt *indirectly* when it will be taken into account upon deliberation when something occurs in the future, perhaps by means of reflection and retrospection on similar instances through which it has already clarified itself.

Now here is the place to remember the account, mentioned in the previous chapter, that Kant had given of the relationship between empirical and intelligible character and thereby the compatibility between freedom and necessity, which belongs among the most beautiful and most profound ideas which this great mind, indeed, which humankind has ever produced. I need only refer to it, since it would be a superfluous prolixity to repeat it here. But only from it
96   can one understand, as far as human power is able, that our actions do indeed coexist with that freedom to which the feeling of responsibility attests, and by virtue of which we are the doers of our deeds

and are morally accountable for them.—This relationship between empirical and intelligible character, which Kant explained, depends entirely upon that which constitutes the main feature of his entire philosophy, specifically, on the distinction between appearance and thing in itself: and just as for him, the complete *empirical reality* of the world of experience coexists with its *transcendental ideality*, so, too, the strict empirical necessity of behaviour coexists with its transcendental freedom. Specifically, the empirical character, like the whole person, is as an object of experience, a mere appearance, hence bound by the forms of all appearance, time, space, and causality, and subject to their laws. By contrast, his *intelligible character*, which is the condition and basis of this whole appearance, is independent of these forms and, hence, subject to no time-distinction; consequently, it is constant and unalterable. For his will, as thing in itself, is of such quality, that to it certainly belongs absolute freedom, i.e., independence of the laws of causality (as a mere form of appearances). This freedom, however, is a transcendental one, i.e., not occurring in appearance, but only present insofar as we abstract from appearance and all its forms in order to arrive at that which, outside of all time, is to be thought of as the inner being of the person in himself. Because of this freedom, all of a person's deeds are his own work, however much they necessarily proceed from the empirical character upon its encounter with motives because this empirical character is merely the appearance of the intelligible character in our *cognitive faculty*, bound to time, space, and causality, i.e., is the way that our own being in itself presents itself. Consequently *will* is, indeed, free, but only in itself and outside of appearance; in this, by contrast, it already presents itself with a determined character to which all of its deeds conform and so, it necessarily occurs *as such* and in no other way because it is specifically determined by the supervening motives. 97

As is easy to see, this path leads to the point that we must no longer seek the work of our *freedom*, as does the common view, in our individual actions, but in the whole being and essence (*existentia et essentia*) of the human being himself. This work must be thought of as the human being's free deed that merely presents itself to the cognitive faculty, linked to time, space, and causality as a plurality and diversity of actions. However, because of the original unity of that which presents itself in these actions, they must convey exactly the same character and, hence, appear as strictly necessitated by the motives which in each case elicit them and individually determine them. For this reason, 'doing follows essence'[1] is certain and without exception for the world of experience. Every thing operates according to its nature, and its works, resulting from causes, proclaim this nature. Each person acts as he is, and the necessary action, always in accord with him, in the individual case, will be determined solely by motives. *Freedom*, which is not then to be met with in doing,[2] must *lie* in the being. At all times, it has been a fundamental error, putting the last first,[3] to attribute the necessity to the being and freedom to the doing. Conversely, in *being alone lies freedom*, but from being and motives, the doing follows of necessity: and *from that which we do, we know what we are*. On this, and not from the presumed *libero arbitrio indifferentiae*, rests consciousness of responsibility and the moral tendency of life. Everything depends on what someone *is*: from what he is, what he *does* will follow as a necessary corollary. The consciousness of self-determination and originality which undeniably accompanies all of our deeds, and by virtue of which they are our deeds despite their dependence on motives, is not deceptive: its true content, however, extends farther than deeds and originates higher up because our being and essence itself, from which all deeds proceed necessarily (on the occasion of motives), are in truth comprehended in it. In this

98   sense this consciousness of self-determination and originality as well as that of responsibility which accompanies our actions can be compared to a pointer which actually points to a more distant object than one in the same vicinity which it appears to indicate.

In a word: the human being always does what he wills, and, indeed, he does it necessarily. However, this depends on the fact that he already *is* what he wills: for from that which he *is* everything that he ever does follows of necessity. If one observes his deeds *objectively*, that is, externally, he would thus know apodictically that, like the works of every natural being, his deeds must be strictly subject to the law of causality; conversely, *subjectively*, everyone feels that he always does only that which he *wills*. This, however, merely indicates that his works are the pure externalization of his own being. Thus, every, even the lowest of natural beings, would feel the same, if it could feel.

---

[1] *operari sequitur esse.*
[2] *operari.*
[3] ὕστερον πρότερον [in rhetorical tradition, a figure of speech in which two temporally or logically sequenced actions are transposed].

Through my presentation, then, *freedom* is not suspended, but merely elevated, namely, from the realm of individual actions, where it is demonstrably not to be encountered, up to a higher region, but one not so readily accessible to our cognition; that is, it is transcendental. And so this is also the sense in which I would prefer Malebranche's dictum to be understood, 'freedom is a mystery',[1] under whose aegis the present essay has sought to solve the problem posed by the Royal Society.

---

[1] *la liberté est un mystère* [see epigraph on title-page].

# APPENDIX

## TO SUPPLEMENT THE FIRST CHAPTER

GIVEN the division of freedom into physical, intellectual, and moral which I offered at the very beginning, since the first and last have been dealt with, just for the sake of completeness I must now still discuss the second, so I shall be brief.

Intellect, or the cognitive faculty, is the *medium of motives*, that is, the medium by which motives work on the will, which is the true core of the human being. Only insofar as this medium of motives is in a normal state, fulfils its function properly, and, hence, presents the motives undistorted, just as they occur in the real, external world, to the will for its choice, can this will decide according to its nature, i.e., according to the individual character of the person. Thus *unconstrained* will externalizes itself according to its very own being: then the person is *intellectually free*, i.e., his actions are purely the result of the reaction of his will to motives, which occur for him in the external world just as they do for all others. As a result of this, his actions are morally and even juridically attributable to him.

This intellectual freedom will be *suspended* either when the medium of the motives, the cognitive faculty, is permanently or temporarily deranged or when external circumstances in a particular case distort the apprehension of the motives. The former occurs in the case of madness, delirium, paroxysms, and drowsiness; the latter in the case of decided and innocent error, e.g. if one dispenses poison instead of medicine or takes a servant who enters at night to be a robber and shoots him, etc. For in both cases, the motives are mistaken, on account of which the will cannot decide as it would be able to when the circumstances are such that the intellect correctly conveyed the motives to it. Hence crimes committed under such circumstances are also not legally punishable. For laws proceed on the correct assumption that the will is not morally free, in which case one cannot *direct* it, but that it is subject to compulsion by motives. Accordingly, laws will set more powerful counter-motives of menacing punishments against all possible motives to crime, and a criminal code is nothing else but a catalogue of counter-motives to criminal actions. However, if it were the case that the intellect through which these counter-motives had to work was incapable of apprehending them and presenting them to the will, then their effect would be impossible: they did not exist for it. It is as if one were to find that one of the cables that are to move a machine were snapped. In such a case, the guilt transfers from the will to the intellect, but the intellect is subject to no punishment. Rather, laws, like morals, concern only the will. It alone is the true human being: the intellect is merely its organ, its antennae to the outside, i.e., the medium of the motives' effect on it.

These kinds of deed are no more to be accounted for *morally*. For they are not a feature of the person's character: he would either have done something other than what he believed he was doing, or he was incapable of thinking of that which should have prevented him from doing so, i.e., incapable of admitting the counter-motives. It is the same as when one investigates a substance chemically, exposing it to the influence of several reagents to see to which reagent the substance has the strongest affinity, and on completing the experiment, one discovers that because of an acci-dental hindrance, one of the reagents could not have an effect at all, so that the experiment is invalid.

Intellectual freedom, which here we observe to be completely sus-pended, can furthermore also be merely *diminished* or partially suspended. This occurs especially through affect and intoxication. *Affect* is the sud-den, intense stimulation of the will through a representation which, in-truding from the outside, becomes a motive which has such vivacity that it obscures all others, not allowing them to enter clearly into consciousness so they could check it as counter-motives. While the affect is something intuitively present, these counter-motives, mere thoughts, usually of only an abstract nature, do not, then, as it were, get a chance to shoot and, thus, do not get what in English is called *fair play*: the deed has already occurred before they could counteract. It is as if in a duel, one party fires before the command. Here, too, depending on the nature of the circum-stances, juridical as well as moral responsibility is always more or less in part suspended. In England a murder committed in complete haste and without the least contemplation, in the most intense, sudden, rush of anger, is called *manslaughter* and mildly or, indeed, sometimes even not at all punished. — Intoxication is a state which disposes one to affects because it increases the vivacity of intuitive representations and, conversely, weak-ens thinking *in abstracto*, thus, even increasing the energy of the will. Here responsibility for the intoxication itself takes the place of responsibility for the deeds; therefore, one is not juridically culpable, although here intel-lectual freedom is partially suspended.

Aristotle has already spoken about this intellectual freedom, 'the voluntary and involuntary with respect to thought',[1] in the *Eudemian Ethics* II. 7 and 9, although very briefly and insufficiently, and somewhat more thoroughly

---

[1] τὸ ἐκούσιον καὶ ἀκούσιον κατα διάνοιον.

in the *Nicomachean Ethics* III. 2.*—This is what is meant when forensic medicine[1] and criminal justice asks whether the criminal was in a state of freedom and thus accountable.

In general, then, all crimes are regarded as committed in the absence of intellectual freedom when the person either did not know what he did, or, simply was not able to understand what should have deterred him from doing so, namely, the consequences of the deed. In such cases, for this reason, the criminal is not to be punished.

In contrast, those, who opine that no criminal should be punished because *moral* freedom is non-existent and, as a result, all actions of a given person are inevitable, proceed from the false view that punishment is the evil of the crimes themselves visited upon the criminal, a repayment of evil with evil on moral grounds. But such an opinion, even though Kant has taught it, would be absurd, pointless, and thoroughly unjustified. For how, indeed, would a person have the right to proclaim himself an absolute moral judge of another and as such, torment him because of his sins! Rather, law, i.e., the threat of punishment, has the purpose of being the counter-motive to crimes not yet committed. If the law fails in a particular case in this its effect, it must still be carried out, since otherwise it would also fail in this effect in all future cases. Actually on his part, the criminal in this case nevertheless suffers the punishment as a result of his moral nature, which nature, in conjunction with the circumstances that were the motives, and his intellect that deluded him with the hope of avoiding the punishment, had inevitably led to the deed. In this case, then, injustice could happen to him only if his moral character were not his own work, his intelligible deed, but were the work of another. The same relationship of the deed to its consequences obtains if the consequences of his vicious doings occur not as a result of human, but as a result of natural laws; e.g. when lewd debaucheries lead to horrible illness,* or also when a man attempting a burglary meets misfortune by chance, e.g., as in breaking into a pigsty at night to abduct its usual occupant, a man instead meets a bear, its master having stayed at this inn this evening, which bear comes to meet him with open arms.

---

[1] *Medicina forensis.*

# Prize Essay
# on the Basis of Morals*

not awarded the prize by the
Royal Danish Society of Sciences,
at Copenhagen on 30 January 1840

Motto:
Preaching morals is easy; grounding morals hard.
(Schopenhauer, *On the Will in Nature*, p. 128)*

The question posed by the Royal Society, including the introduction
put at the head of it, reads:

*Quum primitiva moralitatis idea, sive de summa lege morali principalis notio, sua quadam propria eaque minime logica necessitate, tum in ea disciplina appareat, cui propositum est cognitionem τοῦ ἠθικοῦ explicare, tum in vita, partim in conscientiae judicio de nostris actionibus, partim in censura morali de actionibus aliorum hominum; quumque complures, quae ab illa idea inseparabiles sunt, eamque tanquam originem respiciunt, notiones principales ad το ἠθικόν spectantes, velut officii notio et imputationis, eadem necessitate eodemque ambitu vim suam exserant, — et tamen inter eos cursus viasque, quas nostrae aetatis meditatio philosophica persequitur, magni momenti esse videatur, hoc argumentum ad disputationem revocare, — cupit Societas, ut accurate haec quaestio perpendatur et pertractetur:*

*Philosophiae moralis fons et fundamentum* utrum in idea moralitatis, quae immediate conscientia contineatur, et ceteris notionibus fundamentalibus, quae ex illa prodeant, explicandis **quaerenda sunt**, an in alio cognoscendi principio?

In translation:

Since the original idea of morality, or the principal notion of the supreme moral law, appears with a peculiar, but in no way logical necessity, both in that science the purpose of which is to demonstrate knowledge of the ethical, as well as in real life, where it shows itself partly in the judgement of our conscience about our own actions and partly in our moral judgement of the actions of others; and since several principal notions of morals, inseparable from this idea and having arisen out of it, as, for instance, the concept of obligation and that of accountability, assert themselves with equal necessity and to the same extent—and since it is indeed the method which philosophical inquiry of our time follows, it appears very important again to bring this subject under investigation;—thus, the Society wishes that the following question be carefully considered and treated:

**Are the source and basis of morals**[1] **to be sought** in an idea of morality which is immediately contained in conscience,* and in the analysis of the remaining fundamental moral notions originating from this, or in another cognitive principle?

---

[1] *philosophiae moralis* ['moral philosophy' or what Schopenhauer encompasses with the term *Moral*, morals].

# INTRODUCTION

## § 1

### *On the Problem*

A PRIZE question posed by the Royal Dutch Society at Harlem, 1810, and answered by J. C. F. Meister:* 'why do philosophers differ so much about the first principles of morals, but agree so much about the conclusions and duties which they derive from their principles?' — was a most easy task in comparison with that which lies before us. Since:

1) The present question of the Royal Society is directed to nothing less than the objectively true basis of morals and, hence, also of morality. It is an academy which raises the question: as such, it wants no admonition to righteousness and virtue directed to practical ends, supported by reasons the plausibility of which one extols and the weakness of which one veils, as occurs in lectures for the people. Rather, since as an academy it recognizes only theoretical and not practical ends, it wants the purely philosophical, objective, unveiled, and naked exposition of the ultimate ground for all morally good conduct, i.e., independent of all positive laws, all unproven presuppositions, and as a result of all metaphysical or even mythological hypostases. — This, however, is a problem, the overwhelming difficulty of which will 108 be evidenced by the fact that not only the philosophers of all times and lands have ground their teeth to stumps on it, but especially that all the gods of the Orient and Occident have it to thank for their existence. Thus if it is solved at this opportunity, then the Royal Society will truly not have invested their gold badly.

2) Moreover, theoretical investigation of the foundation of morals is at the altogether unique disadvantage in that this investigation could easily be taken for an undermining of the foundation of morals, which could entail the collapse of the structure itself. For here practical interest lies so close to the theoretical that it is hard to restrain well-meaning fervour from unreasonable entanglement.

Not everyone is able clearly to distinguish purely theoretical inquiry into objective truth, apart from all interest, even the moral-practical, from a sacrilegious attack on sacred, heartfelt conviction. Whoever, then, takes this task in hand, must for his encouragement at all times keep in mind that nothing is more remote from the activities of humankind, the bustle and noise of the market-place, than the deep stillness of the secluded sanctuary of the academy, where no sound from the outside may penetrate and where no other gods have a statue than solitary, exalted, naked truth.

The conclusion from these two premises is that, along with the right to question everything, a complete parrhesia* must be allowed me, and that if I *actually* accomplish anything in this matter, even so—much will have been accomplished.

But I still face other difficulties. What is more, the Royal Society demands the foundation of ethics in itself alone, isolated, presented in a short monograph, consequently apart from its connection with a whole system of a philosophy of some sort, i.e., of a metaphysics proper. This must not only make the accomplishment more difficult, but even necessarily incomplete. Christian Wolf[f]* has already said: 'the darkness in practical philosophy will not be dispelled unless it is illuminated by the light of metaphysics'[1] (*Practical Philosophy*, part II, § 28), and Kant: 'metaphysics must come first, and with-
109 out it there can be no moral philosophy at all' (*Groundwork of the Metaphysics of Morals*, Preface).* For just as any religion on earth, in prescribing morality, will not let the matter drop, but gives morality support in its dogma, the main purpose of which is exactly this, so in philosophy the ethical foundation, whatever it be, must even have its basis and its support in some kind of metaphysics, i.e., in a given explanation of the world and of existence in general; for the ultimate and true explanation of the inner essence of the totality of things must closely cohere with the explanation of the ethical significance of human behaviour and in any case with that which is laid down as the foundation of morality. If this foundation is not to be a mere abstract proposition, which, without contact with the real world, is suspended freely in the air, it must be some kind of given fact either in the objective world or in human consciousness, a fact which, as

---

[1] *Tenebrae in philosophia practica non dispelluntur, nisi luce metaphysica affulgente* (*Phil[osophia] Pract[icalis Universalis]*, Part II, § 28).

such, can be only a phenomenon and, hence, like all phenomena of the world, requires further explanation, which then would be demanded of metaphysics. Generally philosophy is such a coherent totality that it is impossible exhaustively to lay down some single part of it without also giving everything else. Therefore, Plato said quite correctly: 'Do you, then, think it to be possible to know well the nature of the soul without knowledge of the nature of the whole'?[1] — (*Phaedr.*, p. 371, Bip[ont]). A metaphysics of nature, a metaphysics of morals, and a metaphysics of the beautiful mutually presuppose one another and only in their coherence complete an explanation of the essence of things and of existence in general. Hence, whoever has carried out one of these three to its ultimate ground must at the same time have involved the others in his explanation; in the same way, whoever would have an exhaustive understanding of *any single thing* in the world, clearly understanding it to its ultimate ground, will also have completely understood all the rest of the world.

Proceeding from a given metaphysics, taken as true, one would in a *synthetic* way arrive at the foundation of ethics, whereby this ethics itself would be built from the ground up,* and, as a result, ethics would be found to be firmly supported. Conversely, given the isolation of ethics from all metaphysics made necessary by the task,   110 nothing remains but an *analytic* method which proceeds from either facts of external experience or facts of consciousness. These latter can trace it back to its ultimate root in the human mind, which then, however, must remain as basic fact, as urphenomenon,* without being traced further back to anything else; as a result, the whole explanation then remains one which is merely *psychological*. At best their connection with some kind of universal, metaphysical grounding view can be indicated as accessory. In contrast, this grounding fact, this ethical urphenomenon, could itself be grounded if one could first discuss metaphysics and, proceeding synthetically, an ethics could then be deduced from it. This, however, means to put forth a complete system of philosophy, which would be greatly to overstep the bounds of the stated question. Thus I am compelled to answer

---

[1] Ψυχῆς οὖν φύσιν ἀξίως λόγου κατανοῆσαι οἴει δυνατὸν εἶναι, ἄνευ τῆς τοῦ ὅλου φύσεως; (*Animae vero naturam absque totius natura sufficienter cognosci posse existimas?*) Plato, *Phaedrus* 270c [Schopenhauer cites the 12-volume (1781–7) Bipont edition of Plato's works].

the question within the bounds which the question itself lays down by its isolation.

And now finally the foundation on which I intend to place ethics will turn out to be very narrow; hence, among the many human actions which are legal and worthy of approval and praise, only the smaller part will prove to have sprung from purely moral grounds of movement; whereas, the greater part will be attributable to other sorts of motives. This is less satisfying and not so dazzling as something like a categorical imperative which always stands ready for us to command it to, in its turn, itself command what ought to be done and what not done, not to mention other material foundations of morals. So there is nothing left for me to do but to recall the saying of Qoheleth (4: 6): 'Better is one hand full of quietness than two fists full of trouble and vain striving.'* In all knowledge, there is always little of the genuine, the proven and imperishable, just as the layers of ore contain a tiny ounce of gold hidden in a hundredweight of rock. However, whether one now actually will prefer with me *trustworthy* possession to the *huge* possession, the little gold which remains in the pan to the extensive mass which was hauled up—or whether one, moreover, will accuse me of having taken away more of the foundation of morals than I have provided, insofar as I demonstrate that the lawful and praiseworthy actions of humans possess almost none, or at most but little pure moral content, yet in most cases these actions rest on the motives the effectiveness of which is ultimately traced back to the egoism of the actor;—I must set all of this aside, not without appehension, but with resignation. For I have long concurred with Ritter von Zimmermann,* when he said, 'Rest assured until you die, that nothing in the world is so rare as a good judge' (*On Solitude*, part I, chapter 3, p. 93). Indeed, in my mind I already see my presentation, which has provided such a narrow basis for all genuine, voluntary righteousness, for all loving kindness,* all magnanimity wherever these may be found, compared to that of competitors, who confidently put forth broad foundations of morals which grow to meet any load and are thrust upon any doubter's conscience, accompanied by a menacing sidelong glance at his own morality— I see it stand there, poor and meek as Cordelia stood before King Lear, with her meagrely worded assurance of her dutiful disposition compared to the effusive protestations of her more eloquent sisters. —So it indeed requires encouragement through a learned exhortation, such as: 'The force of truth is strong, and it will prevail'[1]—which still does little more to encourage one who has lived and laboured. In the meanwhile I will wager once with truth, for that with which *I* meet, will *also* be met with it.

## § 2

## *General Retrospect*

FOR the people, morals are grounded in theology as the expressed will of God. In contrast, we see philosophers, with few exceptions, taking great pains entirely to exclude this sort of foundation, indeed, preferring to take refuge in sophistic arguments in order to avoid it. Whence this opposition? Certainly no more effective grounding for morals can be imagined than the theological, for who would be so bold as to set himself in opposition to the will of the omnipotent and the omniscient? Surely no one, if only this will were proclaimed in a wholly authentic, so to speak, official way, leaving no room for doubt. But this is the condition that cannot be fulfilled. Rather the opposite is sought: to verify as such the law proclaimed to be the will of God by proving that there is an agreement between this will and our natural, moral insight established in a different way, hence appealing to these insights as the more immediate and more certain. Yet in addition there is the recognition that moral behaviour brought about by threats of punishment or promises of reward would be more an appearance of moral behaviour than true moral behaviour because it rests on the ground of egoism, and in the final account what would be decisive would be the greater or lesser ease with which one person rather than another believed on insufficient grounds. However, since Kant has now completely destroyed what passed for firm foundations of *speculative theology* and then wanted theology, which previously had been the prop for ethics, now, conversely, to be supported on ethics in order to secure for speculative theology some sort of existence, if only an ideal one, one now can no longer know which of the two should be the load and which the support, and to think at any time about a foundation of ethics through theology proves in the end to be a *vicious circle*.[2]

112

---

[1] *magna est vis veritatis, et praevalebit* [1 Esdras 3: 12; cf. the title-page motto].
[2] *circulus vitiosus.*

Certainly through the influence of Kantian philosophy and, at the same time, through the effect of unprecedented progress in all of the natural sciences with respect to which any earlier time appears to be a time of childhood compared to ours, and finally through familiarity with Sanskrit literature, with Brahmanism and Buddhism, in terms of time and scope, these most ancient and most widely disseminated, most distinguished among humankind's religions, indeed, the native, primordial religion of our own race, which is known to be Asiatic, and which now in its distant homeland is again getting belated information about them—through all of this, I say, in the course of the last fifty years the basic philosophical convictions of learned Europe have undergone a transformation, which, perhaps, many grant hesitantly, but which certainly is not to be denied. As a result of this, the old supports of ethics have decayed; however, confidence has remained that these supports will never collapse. From this comes the conviction that there must still be other supports for ethics than the former, supports which would suit the progressive insights of the times. Without a doubt, it is the recognition of this ever more palpable need which has led the Royal Society to the present, significant question.

At all times many respectable moral lessons have been preached, but the grounding of these has always been a troublesome matter. On the whole, in this matter there has been an evident attempt to find some sort of objective truth from which the ethical percepts can be logically deduced: these have been sought in the nature of things or in that of humans, but in vain. It has always followed that the human will is always directed to its own well-being, which in sum is comprehended under the concept *happiness*, the striving for which leads one in quite another way from that which might indicate morals. First there was the attempt to represent happiness as identical with virtue and then as a consequence and effect of the same: both have always proved unsuccessful, although no sophistry was spared in the attempt. Later there was the attempt to use purely objective, abstractly grounded principles, now *a posteriori*, again *a priori*, from which ethical good conduct could be inferred, but these lacked a point of reference in human nature by means of which they would have had the power to lead human efforts against human egoistic disposition. It seems to me superfluous to review all of these bases of morality through enumeration and criticism, not only because

I share Augustine's opinion, that 'it is not for the great to possess what men have known, but to possess that which be the truth of a thing',[1] but also because it would be 'to bring owls to Athens'[2] since earlier attempts to ground ethics are sufficiently familiar to the Royal Society, and the society makes clear through the prize question itself that the society is also convinced of the inadequacy of these. The less learned reader may find a summary of previous attempts in Garve's *Overview of the Foremost Principles of Ethics,*\* which is certainly not complete, but is sufficient for the main points. There is more in Stäudlin's *History of Moral Philosophy*\* and similar books.—Of course, it is disheartening to observe that ethics, this science which immediately concerns life, has not done better than abstruse metaphysics, and that since Socrates established the science, though continually pursued, it is still seeking even its first principle. However, in ethics, unlike in any other science, that which is essential is contained in the first principles while the derivatives are so simple as to be self-evident. For all can *conclude*; few can *judge*. Hence lengthy schoolbooks and lectures on morals are just as superfluous as they are boring. That I may now assume all earlier bases of ethics to be familiar simplifies matters for me. For anyone who surveys the ways philosophers of antiquity as well as those of recent times (the middle ages was satisfied with church creed) have seized the most varied and, at times, strange arguments in order to produce a demonstrable foundation for the universally recognized requirements of morality, and for all that with plainly bad results, will consider the difficulty of the problem and value my achievement accordingly. And anyone who has seen how all previously taken paths have not led to the goal will more willingly walk with me on one which is very different, one which either had not been seen earlier or which had been left behind in contempt, perhaps because it was the most natural. Indeed, my solution to the problem will remind many of Columbus's egg.\*

I will devote a critical investigation, and one all the more detailed, solely to the *most recent* attempt to ground ethics, the *Kantian* one, in part because Kant's great reform of morals gave this science a

---

[1] *non est pro magno habendum quid homines senserint, sed quae sit rei veritas* [*City of God*, Book XIX, 3].

[2] γλαῦκας εἰς 'Αθήνας κομίζειν. [To 'carry owls to Athens' is the Greek equivalent of the more modern English aphorism, to 'carry coals to Newcastle', used to indicate one's taking an item to an area where it is already in abundance.]

115  basis which had real advantages over the earlier attempts, and in part
because Kant's reform is the last significant event that has occurred in
ethics; hence, Kant's foundation of morals even today is universally
accepted and is taught everywhere, although it is cleaned up by others
in presentation and terminology. It is the ethics of the last sixty years
that must be cleared away before we can strike out in another direction. Moreover, an examination of Kant's ethics will give me occasion
to analyse and to discuss the most fundamental concepts of ethics so
I am able later to assume the result of this analysis and discussion.
However, because opposites illustrate each other, a critique of the
Kantian foundation of morals will especially be the best preparation
and introduction, indeed, the exact way, to my own, one which in its
essential points is diametrically opposed to the Kantian. For these reasons it would be a most wrong-headed beginning if one were to skip
the critique which is soon to follow in order to go to the positive part
of my presentation, for then it would be only half understandable.

On the whole, it is now really time that ethics be once seriously
examined. For more than half-a-century, ethics lay on a comfortable
cushion which Kant had laid under it: the categorical imperative of
practical reason. Yet in our times this categorical imperative is most
often introduced under the slightly pompous, but polished and current title, 'the moral law', under which, after a quick bow to reason
and experience, it slips through unnoticed. However, once it is in the
house, then there is no end of orders and commands, without its even
once being called into question.—It was right and necessary that as
inventor of the matter, and after having dispelled clumsier errors in
the process, Kant then set his mind at rest about it. But to have seen
how the cushion which Kant had laid out is now trampled wider and
wider as even jackasses waltz about on it—that is hard. I mean those
who write daily compendia, who, with the cool confidence of those
who lack intelligence, presume that they have founded ethics if they
just appeal to this '*moral law*' which is alleged to reside in our *reason*,
and then confidently pile up their long-winded and confused claptrap
116  by which they know how to make the clearest and simplest relations
of life unintelligible;—without ever in such an undertaking having
then asked themselves seriously whether such a '*moral law*' really also
stands written in our heads, breasts, and hearts as a suitable code
of morals. Therefore, I acknowledge the special pleasure with which
I now set out to pull the broad cushion out from under ethics, and

I frankly declare my intent to demonstrate that Kant's practical reason and categorical imperative are wholly unjustified, groundless, and fictitious assumptions, and to prove that Kant's ethics lacks a solid foundation, and thereby again to consign morals to its earlier state of complete helplessness, in which it must remain until I set about laying out the true, undoubtedly efficacious moral principle of human nature, based in our essence. For since this offers not so broad a foundation as that cushion, those who are accustomed to comfort in the matter will only relinquish their resting-place when they have clearly observed the deep hole in the ground on which it stands.

# CRITIQUE OF THE FOUNDATIONS OF ETHICS PROVIDED BY KANT

## § 3
### *Overview*

KANT has the great merit of having purged ethics of all *eudaimonism*. The ethics of the ancients was eudaimonic; that of the moderns is mostly a doctrine of salvation. The ancients wanted to prove virtue and happiness to be identical, but these were like two shapes that cannot be superimposed, no matter how one might arrange them. The moderns wanted to make them both correspond, not according to the *principle of identity*, but according to that *of grounds*, and thus, to make happiness a result of virtue, whereby they had to make use of either a world other than the one which it is possible to know or sophisms. Among the ancients, Plato alone is an exception: his ethics is not eudaimonistic; rather, he instead becomes mystical. In contrast, even the ethics of the Cynics and Stoics is but a special sort of eudaimonism: I do not lack grounds and evidence to prove that this is so, but to do so is outside of the scope of my present task.—Among the

118  ancients and moderns, then, Plato alone excepted, virtue was only a means to an end. Of course, if one wishes to consider it strictly, then even Kant banished eudaimonism from ethics more in appearance than in reality. For he still leaves a secret connection between virtue and happiness in his theory of the highest good, where they come together in an out-of-the-way and obscure chapter, while publicly virtue is estranged from happiness. This aside, with Kant, the ethical principle appears as one completely independent of experience and its instruction, as a transcendental or metaphysical one. He recognizes that the human way of acting has a significance that transcends all possibility of experience and, therefore, is the actual bridge to that which he calls the intelligible world, noumenal world,[1] the world of the thing in itself.

---

[1] *mundus noumenon.*

The fame which Kantian ethics has achieved, besides the merits referred to above, is due to the moral purity and sublimity of its results. Most people embraced these results without especially concerning themselves with the grounding of the same, which is presented in a very complex, abstract, and thoroughly artificial form, on which Kant had to use his complete acumen and powers of reasoning in order to give it an appearance of validity. Fortunately, he had devoted a separate work to the presentation of the foundation of his ethics, apart from the ethics itself, as the *Groundwork of the Metaphysics of Morals*, the theme of which is also exactly the same as the subject of our prize question. For he explains this very point at p. xiii of the preface: 'The present *groundwork* is nothing more than a search for and establishment of the supreme principle of morality, which alone constitutes an activity which in its purpose is complete and to be separated from all other moral investigation.'* In this book, as in no other, we find the basis, and, hence, the essentials of his ethics strictly systematically, concisely, and clearly presented. In addition, the book still has the significant advantage in that it is the oldest of his moral works, only four years younger than the *Critique of Pure Reason*, and hence from the time when, although he had already reached the age of 61, old age's corrupting influence on his mind was not yet noticeable. In contrast, one can already catch a clear whiff of this in the *Critique of Practical Reason*, in 1788, thus occurring a year later than the unfortunate revision of the *Critique of Pure Reason* in its *second edition* by which he has publicly despoiled this, his immortal, principal work. In the preface to the new edition prepared by Rosenkranz,* we have an explanation of this with which I can do nothing but agree after some examination of the matter.[1] The *Critique of Practical Reason* contains in essentials the same *Groundwork* as mentioned above, except that in this latter book it is in a more concise and rigorous form, while in the former book, in contrast, it is of great breadth of execution and interrupted by digressions, and is even propped up by some moralistic declamations to enhance the impression. As he wrote this, Kant had finally and belatedly achieved his well-deserved fame, because of which he was assured of boundless attentiveness, so he allowed the garrulity of age much more room to play in. In contrast, as to the *Critique of Practical*

119

---

[1] It originates with myself, but here I speak incognito. [Schopenhauer's note.]

*Reason* two things are to be regarded as peculiar: first the presentation of the relationship between freedom and necessity, which is elevated beyond all praise and which had certainly been composed earlier (pp. 169–179 of the fourth edition, and pp. 223–231* in the Rosenkranz), and which, moreover, concurs with that which he gives in the *Critique of* Pure *Reason* (pp. 560–586 of the fourth edition; R[osenkranz], pp. 438 ff.*); and second, the moral theology, which will increasingly be recognized as that which Kant actually had in mind by all this. Finally, in *Metaphysical First Principles of the Doctrine of Virtue*, that supplement to his deplorable *Doctrine of Right*, composed in the year 1797, the influence of senility is preponderant. For all of these reasons, in the present critique, I take the *Groundwork of the Metaphysics of Morals*, named first above, as my guide, and I ask the reader to note that all page numbers which I cite refer to this without further

120   addition. However, I will consider the two other works only as accessory and secondarily. In order to completely recall the book's contents, it will be extremely useful to an understanding of the present critique, which undermines the very ground of Kantian ethics, if the reader would beforehand read through with attentiveness this *Groundwork* of Kant's, to which this critique will above all refer, particularly since the book fills only 128 and xiv pages (and in all only 100 pages in the Rosenkranz). I cite it in the third edition of 1792 and add the page number of the new collected works of Rosenkranz by an R. preceding it.

§ 4

*On the Imperative Form of Kantian Ethics*

KANT'S first false statement[1] lies in his concept of ethics itself, a concept which we find articulated most clearly on p. 62 (R., p. 54*): 'In a practical philosophy it is not a concern to indicate reasons for what *happens*, but laws for what *ought to happen, even if it never happens.*' — This is already a decided *petitio principii.** Who told you* that there are laws to which we *ought* to subject our actions? Who told you that something *ought to happen, that never happens?* — What justifies your assuming this beforehand and thereupon immediately to press upon us an ethics in a legislative-imperative form as the only possible sort? I say, in opposition to Kant, that the student of ethics as well as the

---

[1] πρῶτον ψεῦδος.

philosopher in general must be content with an explanation and
interpretation of that which is given, hence, of that which actually
exists or happens in order to arrive at an *understanding* of these, and
that he has his hands full with much more than has been done previously, after millennia have run their course. As is consistent with
the above-mentioned Kantian *petitio principii*, right in the preface,
which is integral to the subject, it is immediately assumed *prior to* any
investigation that there are pure *moral laws*. This assumption remains
in what follows and is the very basis of the whole system. However,
we will first investigate the concept of a *law*. The actual and original meaning of this term has been restricted to civil *law*, *lex*, νόμος,
a human institution resting on human choice. A second, deriva-
tive, figurative, metaphorical meaning has the concept of *law* in its
application to nature, the constant, invariable processes of which we
partly *know a priori* and partly observe empirically, and which we
metaphorically call natural laws. Only a small part of this natural law
is that which can be known *a priori* and comprises that which Kant
has wisely and admirably singled out and grouped under the title
*Metaphysics of Nature*. Of course, there is also a *law* for the *human
will* insofar as the human belongs to nature. And, indeed, this law is
a strictly demonstrable, inviolable one, one without exception, rock-
steady, one which does not, like the categorical imperative, carry
along with it a 'so to say',[1] but a *real* necessity: it is the *law of motivation*, a form of the law of causality, specifically, causality mediated by
cognition. This is the single demonstrable law of the human will, to
which this will *as such* is subjected. The law says that any action can
occur only as a result of a sufficient motive. Like the law of causality
in general, it is a natural law. In contrast, *moral* laws, independent of
human ordinance, state institutions, or religious doctrine, may not
be taken to exist without proof; thus, by this assumption Kant committed a *petitio principii*. It appears all the more audaciously when he
immediately adds, on p. vi of the preface, that a moral law should
carry with it '*absolute necessity*'. However, such necessity always has as
its mark the inevitability of the result: how, then, can there be talk of
absolute necessity of these alleged moral laws? As an example of such,
he cites '*thou shalt (sic) not lie*'.* For as is well known, and as he himself
admits, these laws mostly, indeed, as a rule, remain without result.

---

[1] *vel quasi.*

In a scientific ethics, to assume still other, original laws for the will, independent of all human ordinance, except for the law of motivation, one has to prove and to derive their entire existence if one is intent in ethics not merely to recommend honesty, but also to practise it. Until this proof is provided, I recognize no other source for the introduction of the concept of law, precept, obligation in ethics than one foreign to philosophy, the Mosaic Decalogue.* In the above-mentioned example of a moral law which Kant first asserts, the orthography '*thou shalt*' even naively betrays this source. A concept which points to none other than such a source must not so readily press its way into philosophical ethics, but will be expelled until it is verified and established through legitimate proof. In it we have Kant's first *petitio principii*, and it is important.

Just as by means of a *petitio principii* in the preface, Kant had immediately taken the concept of *moral law* to be given and undoubtedly extant, so, too, he does it, p. 8 (R., p. 16),* with a closely related concept, that of *duty*, which is admitted into ethics as belonging without undergoing further scrutiny. But I am compelled here once more to lodge a protest. The concept, along with those related to it, such as those of *law, command, obligation*, etc., taken in this unconditional sense, has its origin in theological morals, and remains a stranger to the philosophical until it has produced valid credentials from the essence of human nature or from that of the objective world. Until then, for it and those related to it, I recognize no other source than the Decalogue. In general, in the centuries of Christianity, philosophical ethics has unconsciously taken its form from the theological. Since this ethics is now essentially dictatorial, the philosophical, too, has appeared in the form of prescription and doctrine of duty in all innocence and without suspecting that for this, first a further authority is necessary. Instead, it supposes that this is its own and natural form. Just as much as the ethical significance of human action is undeniably recognized by all peoples, times, and faiths, and also by all philosophers (with the exception of the true materialists), just as much as it is metaphysical, reaching beyond this apparent existence and touching upon eternity, just so little is this ethical significance to be understood in its essence in the form of command and obedience, of law and duty. Moreover, separated from the theological presuppositions from which they have proceeded, these concepts actually lose all meaning, and if one, like Kant, believes that one can replace these presuppositions by talking about *absolute* ought and *unconditional* duty, then one feeds the reader a line, indeed, actually gives him a *contradictio in adjecto*\* to swallow. Every *ought* simply has no sense and meaning except in relation to threatened punishment or promised reward. For this reason, Locke, too, long before Kant was thought of, said: 'For since it would be utterly in vain to suppose a rule set to the free actions of man without annexing to it some enforcement of good and evil to determine his will, we must, where-ever we suppose a law, suppose also some reward or punishment annexed to that law' (*On Understanding,*\* Bk. II, c. 33, § 6). Thus every ought is necessarily conditioned through punishment or reward, hence, to put it in Kant's terms, essentially and inevitably *hypothetical* and never, as he maintains *categorical*. But if these conditions did not exist, the concept of ought remains empty of sense. Therefore, an *absolute ought* is simply a *contradictio in adjecto*. It is simply impossible to think of a commanding voice, whether it comes from within or from without, in any way other than as threatening or promising. Then, however, obedience to it, clever or dumb, depending on the circumstances, is always self-interested, and hence, without moral worth. The complete inconceivability and absurdity of this concept of an unconditional ought, which lies at the foundation of Kant's ethics, itself enters his system late, specifically in the *Critique of Practical Reason*, like a concealed poison which cannot remain in an organism, but finally must break out and vent itself. That is, such an *unconditional ought* still postulates a condition after all, even more 124 than one, namely a reward, and at that the immortality of the one to be rewarded and the rewarder. Such is by all means necessary as soon as one makes duty and ought into the fundamental concept of ethics, since these concepts are essentially relative and only have any meaning through threatened punishment or promised reward. This recompense, afterward postulated for virtue, which seems only to work gratuitously, enters, however, respectably disguised under the name of the *highest good*, which is the union between virtue and happiness. At its basis, however, this is nothing other than morality stemming from happiness, or eudaimonism, and, as a result, is supported by self-interest, which Kant had solemnly ejected from the front door of his system as heteronomous, and which sneaks in again at the back door under the name of *highest good*. Thus the single assumption of an *unconditional, absolute ought* takes its revenge as a disguised contradiction. Otherwise the *conditional* ought certainly cannot be a fundamental ethical concept because everything which occurs with respect to reward or punishment necessarily is an egoistic doing and as such is without pure moral worth.—From all of these it is obvious that it requires a grand and more unbiased conception of ethics if one is serious about wanting to fathom the eternal significance of human action, significance which extends beyond appearance.

Just as all *ought* is at least bound to a condition, so, too, is all *duty*. For both concepts are closely related to one another and nearly identical. The single difference between them might be that *ought generally* can also rest upon mere compulsion; duty, in contrast, assumes commitment, i.e., the undertaking of a *duty*. Such a relationship takes place between master and servant, superior and subordinate, government and subjects. Just as no one takes on a duty without compensation, so every duty also confers a right. The slave has no duty because he has no right; but there is an *ought* for him, which rests on mere compulsion. In the following section, I will put forth the only significance which the concept of *duty* has in ethics.

125   Framing ethics in an *imperative* form as a *doctrine of duties* and thinking about the moral worth or worthlessness of human actions as fulfilment or violation of duties undeniably stems, along with the *ought*, only from theological morals and, hence, from the Decalogue. Accordingly, it essentially rests on and is inseparable from the presupposition of human dependence on another will that commands and decrees reward or punishment. As much as the presupposition of such a will is settled in theology, much less should one remain silent as it is drawn into philosophical morals without further scrutiny. Then, too, one must not assume that in philosophical morals *the imperative form*, the setting up of commands, laws, and duties, is self-evident and essential. It is a bad last resort to substitute the word 'absolute' or 'categorical' for external conditions upon which such concepts, by their very nature, essentially depend and through which, as was explained above, a *contradictio in adjecto* arises.

Now, however, Kant had silently and surreptitiously borrowed the *imperative form* of ethics from theological morals, the presuppositions of which (that is, theology) actually lie at the basis of his ethics, and in fact his ethics only has meaning and sense if it is not separated from theology, for indeed, these presuppositions are *implicite* in his ethics. Afterwards, then, at the end of his presentation, it was easy for him again to develop a theology from his morals, the familiar moral theology. For then, he needed only to draw forth expressly the concepts that had *implicite* been established by the *ought* and that lay hidden at the basis of his morals and then *explicite* to set them up as postulates of practical reason. So then there appeared, to the world's great edification, a theology which was merely supported by morals, indeed, which had proceeded from morals. But this came about because these morals themselves rested on hidden theological presumptions. I intend no sarcastic comparison, but in form the matter is analogous to the surprise which an artist in natural magic prepares for us when he lets us find a thing there where previously he had slyly slipped it.—Put *in abstracto*, Kant's procedure is this: that he 126 makes into a result that which should have been the principle or the presupposition (the theology), and he takes as a presupposition that which should have led to the result (the command). However, then after he had turned the thing on its head, no one, not even he himself, recognized it for that which it was, namely, the old, familiar theological morals. In the sixth and seventh sections,* we will consider the performance of this sleight of hand.

Certainly long before Kant, in philosophy the framing of morals in imperative form and as a doctrine of duties had also been in frequent use, but then morals themselves were grounded on the will of God which had already been proved by other means and thereby remained consistent. However, as soon as someone, like Kant, undertook to provide a foundation independent of such a will, wanting to establish ethics without metaphysical presuppositions, one was no longer justified in any imperative form, any 'you ought' and 'it is your duty', without laying as grounds some other derivation.

## § 5

### On the Assumption of Duties to Ourselves in Particular

KANT so welcomed this form of doctrine of duties however, that he allowed it into his discussion unquestioned, insofar as he, like his predecessors, laid down duties to ourselves along with duties to others. Since I completely reject this assumption, I will here interject my explanation where it is most appropriate.

Duties to ourselves, must, like all duties, be either duties of justice or duties of love. *Duties of justice* to ourselves are impossible, because of the self-evident principle, 'he who wills it suffers no injustice':[1] for

---

[1] *Volenti non fit injuria.*

namely, that which I do is always what I will; so, too, that which I do to myself is always just what I will, consequently never a wrong. But concerning duties of love to ourselves, here morals finds its work
127 already done and comes too late. That it is impossible to violate the duty of self-love is already presupposed by the highest commandment of Christian morals: 'love your neighbour as yourself,' by which the love everyone lavishes on himself is assumed to be the maximum and the condition of any other love. In no way, however, is 'love yourself as your neighbour' added, by which everyone would feel too little is demanded. Also, this would be the single duty by which a supererogatory act[1] would be the order of the day. Even Kant said, in the *Metaphysical First Principles of the Doctrine of Virtue*, p. 13 (R., p. 230*): 'What everyone inevitably wills of himself, that does not belong under the concept of duty.' This concept of duty to ourselves is always held in esteem and generally stands in special favour, at which one should not be surprised. But it has a comic effect in cases in which people begin to be concerned for their own person and in all seriousness speak of the duty of self-preservation, about which it is sufficient to note that fear gives people legs and it takes no command about duty to urge them on.

What is usually set forth as duties to ourselves is foremost a rationale against *suicide* based in prejudice, strong bias, and the shallowest reasons. To the human alone, who, unlike the animal, is not restricted to mere *bodily* suffering in the present, but also is given over to the incomparably greater pain of *intellectual* suffering, borrowed from the future and past, nature grants as compensation the privilege of ending his life when it is suitable, even before nature itself puts an end to it, and as a result, unlike the animal, which necessarily lives as long as it *can*, the human lives as long as he *will*. Now whether on ethical grounds he would have foregone this privilege is a difficult question, which at least cannot be decided by the usual, shallow arguments. Then, too, the grounds against suicide, which grounds Kant did not disdain to cite, p. 53 (R., p. 48) and p. 67 (R., p. 57*), I can conscientiously call nothing other than wretchedness, which
128 does not once deserve a reply. It is laughable to think that the same reflections would have wrestled the dagger out of the hands of Cato, Cleopatra, Cocceius Nerva (Tacitus, *Annals* VI. 26), or Arria,* wife

---

[1] *Opus supererogationis.*

of Paetus (Pliny, *Letters*, III. 16). If these are really genuine moral motives against suicide, in any case, they lie very deep and are not to be reached by the sounding-lead of ordinary ethics; rather they belong to a higher way of consideration than is suitable to the stand-point of the present essay.[1]

Besides this, what now still is customarily brought up under the rubric of duties to the self is in part rules of prudence and in part dietetic prescriptions, both of which do not belong under morals proper. Finally, one brings up here the command against unnatural sexual lust, onanism, pederasty, and bestiality. Among these, first onanism is primarily a vice of childhood, and countering it is much more a matter of dietetics than ethics. Hence even books against it are written by medical authorities (such as Tissot* and others), not by moralists. After dietetics and hygiene had done their part in this matter, having struck it down with irrefutable reasons, if now morals wants to take it in hand, she will find the work already done so well that little remains for her.—Now again, bestiality is a wholly abnormal offence, rarely committed, thus actually somewhat exceptional and so, to such a great degree shocking and contrary to human nature that it does more to condemn and deter itself than anything which rational arguments could do. Moreover, as a degradation of human nature, it is actually an offence against the species as such and *in abstracto*, not against an individual person.—Among the three sexual offences under discussion, only pederasty, then, falls under the aegis of ethics, and pederasty will naturally find its place in the discussion of justice. Specifically, pederasty offends against justice and as a result cannot be vindicated by 'he who wills it suffers no injustice'.[2] For the injustice consists in the seduction of the young and inexperienced who are thereby physically and morally perverted.            129

# § 6

## *On the* Foundation *of Kantian Ethics*

IMMEDIATELY connected with an *imperative form* of ethics, proven in § 4 to be a *petitio principii*, is a favourite idea of Kant's, certainly to

---

[1] There are ascetic grounds. One finds them in the fourth book of my principal work [*The World as Will and Representation*], vol. I, § 69. [Schopenhauer's note.]

[2] *Volenti non fit injuria.*

be excused, but not to be accepted.—Now and then we see a doctor who has employed a cure with brilliant success, one which henceforth he applies to nearly all illnesses: him I compare to Kant. Through the division between *a priori* and *a posteriori* in human cognition, he has made the most brilliant and far-reaching discovery of which metaphysics can boast. Is it any wonder that now he seeks to apply this method and division? *Ethics*, too, should then consist of a pure, i.e., *a priori* knowable part and an empirical part. He rejects the latter as inadmissible for the *grounding* of ethics. However, to find out the former and to present it separately is his task in the *Groundwork of the Metaphysics of Morals*, which accordingly should be a pure, *a priori*, science in the same sense as he laid down the *Metaphysical Principles of Natural Science*. Accordingly, that *moral law* is taken to exist entirely without justification and without derivation or proof, even as *a priori* knowable, independent of all *inner* as well as *outer experience*, '*solely resting on concepts of pure reason*, one which should be a *synthetic proposition a priori*' (*Critique of Practical Reason*, p. 56 of the fourth edition, R., p. 142\*). Closely connected to this is the fact that such a law must be merely *formal*, like everything known *a priori*, and so, must refer merely to the *form* and not to the *content* of the actions.— Just think what that means!—He expressly adds (p. vi of the preface to the *Groundwork*—R., p. 5\*) that it 'may not be sought in the nature of the human (the subjective) nor in the circumstances in the world (the objective)' and (in the same, p. vii; R., p. 6) that 'it must not borrow the slightest thing from acquaintance with the human, i.e., from anthropology'.\* He even repeats (p. 59—R., p. 52) 'that one may not for a moment even think of wanting to derive the reality of this moral principle from the special characteristics of human nature'; and in the same work (p. 60—R., p. 52) that 'whatever is derived from the special disposition of humankind, from certain feelings and propensities, and even, where possible, from a special inclination which is unique to human nature and not necessarily applying to the will of *every rational being*',\* could provide no basis for moral law. This irrefutably attests that he asserts the alleged moral law *not as a fact of consciousness*, as something empirically provable—which the philosophasters of recent times, one and all, would like to pass off as such.—Just as he does all inner experience, he quite decisively rejects all outer experience, as he discards any empirical bases of morals. Hence, as I bid you to note, he grounds his moral principle not upon any demonstrable *fact*

130

*of consciousness*, such as an inner disposition—no more than on any objective relation of things in the external world. No! That would be an empirical basis. Rather the basis of morals should be *pure concepts, a priori*, i.e., concepts that do not even have any content from outer or inner experience and, so, are mere shells without the kernels. Just consider what this means: human consciousness as well as the whole external world, including all experience and facts in them, are pulled out from under our feet. We have nothing on which to stand. But onto what should we hold? On a couple of completely abstract, wholly insubstantial concepts which, likewise, are entirely floating in the air. From these, yes, actually from the mere form of their connection to judgements, a *law* should result, a law which applies with so-called *absolute necessity* and should have the power to put bridle and bit on the impulse of lust, on the storm of passion, on the colossus of egoism. Well, we shall see about that.

Closely linked to this preconceived idea that the basis of morality should be of an absolutely necessary *a priori* nature and free from everything empirical is a second favourite idea of Kant's: specifically, the moral principle to be asserted, as it must be a *synthetic proposition, a priori, of merely formal content*, thus solely a matter for *pure reason*, should as such apply not only for *human beings alone*, but *for all possible rational beings* and 'only because of this'* should be valid incidentally and accidentally[1] for human beings, too. This is why it is based on *pure* reason (which recognizes nothing but itself and the law of contradiction) and is not based on some kind of feeling. Thus this *pure reason* is not here taken as a cognitive power of *the human being*, which is all that it really is, but rather, *as something hypostasized as existing by itself* without any warrant, and of this most pernicious example and model our current pitiful time in philosophy can serve as proof. Meanwhile this assertion of morals is not for humans as humans, but rather for *all rational beings* as such, which for Kant is such an important main point and favourite idea that he never tires of repeating it at every opportunity. Against this, I say that one is never warranted in setting up a *genus* which is given to us in only a single species. One could bring to the concept simply nothing other than what one would have inferred of this *single* species. Thus, what one predicated of the *genus*, one would always have to understand of the single species alone.

---

[1] *per accidens* ('by accident', i.e. 'not of necessity', 'not necessarily').

For in order for one to imagine the *genus*, one would have unwarrant-edly to consider as non-existent what belongs to this species. But then one would perhaps have eliminated the very condition which makes possible the remaining properties hypostasized as *genus*. Just as we recognize *intelligence generally* as simply a property of only animal beings and, as a result, are never justified to think of this property as existing outside of and independent of the animal nature, so, too, we recognize *reason* as a property of only the human race and are simply not warranted in thinking of it existing apart from this and setting up a genus 'rational being' which would be different from its single species, 'human', still less, however, in setting up laws for such an imaginary *rational being in abstracto*. To speak of rational beings apart from humans is nothing other than if one wanted to speak of heavy beings apart from bodies. One could not help but suspect that in this Kant thought a bit about the dear little angels or, indeed, had counted on their assistance in the conviction of the reader. In any case, herein lies a quiet assumption of the rational soul,[1] which is quite distinct from the sensitive soul and vegetative soul,[2] remains after death, and then would be nothing more than just rational.[3]* But in the *Critique of Pure Reason*, he himself has expressly and emphatically put an end to this completely transcendent hypostasis. Meanwhile, one sees in Kantian ethics, particularly in the *Critique of Practical Reason*, always hovering in the background, the thought that the inner and eternal essence of the human being consists in *reason*. Here, where the topic arises incidentally, I must be satisfied with the mere assertion of the contrary: namely, that reason, like the cognitive faculty in general, is something secondary, something belonging to appearance, indeed, something conditioned by the organism; whereas, the real core, that which alone is metaphysical and, therefore, indestructible in the human being, is *will*.

Thus the method that Kant had applied with so much success in theoretical philosophy, he also extended to practical philosophy, and, consequently, he also wanted here to separate pure cognition *a priori* from empirical cognition *a posteriori*. In so doing, he assumed that just as we know the laws of space, time, and causality *a priori*, so, too, or at least analogously, the moral rule of conduct for our doings is

---

[1] *anima rationalis.*        [2] *anima sensitiva and anima vegitiva.*
[3] *rationalis.*

given to us prior to all experience and expresses itself as categorical imperative, as absolute ought. But how infinitely great is the *difference* between these theoretical cognitions *a priori* and that alleged moral law *a priori*. The first, these theoretical cognitions *a priori*, depend on their expressing the mere forms, i.e., the functions, of our intellect, by means of which alone we are capable of apprehending an objective world and in which world they *must* therefore be presented. Hence this world, then, must present itself in these forms, since even for this world, these forms are absolutely given by law so that all experience *must* always exactly conform to them, just as everything which I see through a blue glass *must* present itself as blue.—The second, that alleged moral law *a priori*, experience defies at every step. Indeed, Kant himself leaves doubtful whether experience even one single time is governed by this law. What completely disparate things are here heaped together under the concept of *a priority*. Moreover, Kant overlooked the fact that in theoretical philosophy, as a consequence of his own theory, it is precisely because the above-mentioned cognitions are *a priori*, independent of experience, that they are restricted to mere *appearance*, i.e., to the representation of the world in our head, and completely invalid as regards the *essence* of the thing *in itself*, i.e., as regards that which exists independent of our apprehension. Accordingly, even in practical philosophy, his alleged moral law, if it originates *a priori* in our head, must likewise be only a form of *appearance* and leaves untouched the essence in itself of things. Except that this consequence would be a great contradiction with the fact itself as well as with Kant's views, since (e.g. *Critique of Practical Reason*, p. 175—R., p. 228*) he generally presents exactly *that which is moral in us* as in the strictest connection with the true *essence in itself of things*, indeed as immediately concerning this essence. Then, too, in the *Critique of Pure Reason* where the mysterious *thing in itself* generally appears somewhat more clearly, it shows itself as *that which is moral* in us, as *will*.—But he disregarded this.

In § 4 I have shown that Kant had unquestioningly taken over from theological morals the *imperative form* of ethics and, so, the concept of ought, of law, and of duty, while indeed he had to leave behind that which in theological morals lends these concepts force and meaning. Now in order to ground these concepts, he goes so far as to require that the *concept of duty* itself be also the *ground of its fulfilment*, hence of *that which obligates*. An action, he says (p. 11—R., p. 18*), first has

133

genuine moral worth when it occurs solely out of *duty* and merely for
the sake of *duty*, without any inclination to it. The worth of a character first occurs then when someone without sympathy in his heart,
134   cold and indifferent to the suffering of others, and *not actually born
a friend of humans*, still does good deeds solely for the sake of disagreeable *duty*. This assertion, shocking to genuine moral feeling, this
apotheosis of uncharitableness, directly opposed to Christian moral
teaching that above all else puts love, without which there is nothing
(1 Corinthians 13: 3), this tactless moral pedantry, Schiller has play-
fully satirized in two pointed epigrams* titled 'Scruple of Conscience
and Decision'. Some quite relevant passages of the *Critique of Practical Reason* seem to have given occasion for these epigrams, as e.g.
p. 150—R., p. 211:* 'The disposition that obliges a human being to
obey the moral law is to obey it from *duty*, not out of *voluntary inclination*, and in any event, not out of an effort undertaken by command,
nor one gladly undertaken'.—It must be ordered! What slavish morals! And in the same vein, p. 213—R., p. 257,* where it says 'that
feelings of compassion and of warm-hearted sympathy would be
burdensome to right-minded persons because these feelings would
throw their considered maxims into confusion and therefore would
cause them to desire to rid themselves of these feelings and just to be
subject to law-giving reason'. I confidently assert that what opens the
hands of the loveless benefactor, so indifferent to others' suffering
(described p. 11—R., p. 18*) (if he has no ulterior motives) can never
be anything else but slavish *fear of the gods*,* regardless of whether he
calls his fetish 'categorical imperative' or Fitzlipuzli.[1] What else could
move a hard heart, except fear?

In keeping with the views above, according to p. 13—R., p. 19,*
the moral worth of an action absolutely does not lie in the *intention*
with which it occurs, but in the maxim which one obeys.* Against
this, I offer for consideration that it is the *intention alone* which determines the moral worth or worthlessness of a deed, for which reason
the very same deed, depending on the intention, can be reprehensible
or praiseworthy. For this reason, too, as often as people discuss an
135   action of some moral importance, everyone inquires about the *intention*, and upon this alone the action is judged. So, too, conversely,
everyone justifies himself by *intention* alone if he sees that his action is

---

[1] More accurately, Huitzilopochtli, a Mexican deity. [Schopenhauer's note.]

misunderstood, or he excuses himself, if his action has a detrimental consequence. On p. 14—R., p. 20,* we finally receive the definition of the fundamental concept of the whole of Kantian ethics, duty: it is *'the necessity of an action out of respect for the law'.*—But that which is necessary occurs and is inevitable; whereas, actions out of pure duty not only most often do not occur, but even Kant himself admits, p. 25—R., p. 28,* 'there are *even no certain examples* of the disposition to act out of pure duty'; and p. 26—R., p. 29,* 'from experience it is absolutely impossible to make out *a single case* with certainty in which an action in accordance with duty rests solely on the representation of duty'; and more of the same on p. 28—R., p. 30 and p. 49—R., p. 50.* In what sense, then, can such an action be ascribed to *necessity?* Since it is fair always to present an author most favourably, we will say that his opinion is as follows: an action in accordance with duty is *objectively* necessary, but *subjectively* contingent. Except that is not exactly as easily thought as said. Where, then, is the *object* of this *objective* necessity, the consequence of which in objective reality mostly and, perhaps, always does not occur? In all fairness, about this interpretation I cannot help but say that the expression of the definition *'necessity of an action'* is nothing other than an artificially concealed, quite forced paraphrase of the word *ought*. This intention becomes still clearer to us, if we note that in the same definition the word *respect* [*Achtung*] is used where *obedient* [*Gehorsam*] was meant. Specifically the footnote on p. 16—R., p. 21,* reads: *'respect* signifies merely the subordination of my will to a law. The immediate determination through law and the consciousness of the same is called *respect.'*—In what language? What here is stated, in German, is called *obedience*. However, since the word *respect* cannot so inappropriately be put in the place of the word *obedience* without reason, so it must be well suited to some purpose, and this apparently is none other than to veil the descent of the imperative form and the concept of duty from *theological* morals. As we have previously seen, the expression *the necessity of an action*, which takes the place of *ought* in such a forced and awkward way, was only chosen for the purpose because *ought* is precisely the language of the *Decalogue*. The definition given above, 'duty is the necessity of an action out of respect for the law', would then read in an unforced and undisguised language, i.e., without a mask, *'duty* signifies an action that *ought* to happen out of obedience to a law'.—This is the 'core of the poodle.'*

136

Now, however, the *law*, this last foundation-stone of Kantian ethics! *What is its content? And where is it written?* This is the most important question. First I note that there are two questions: the one concerns the *principle*, the other the *foundation* of ethics, two quite different things, although they are usually mixed, and sometimes intentionally so.

The *principle*, or the highest *fundamental proposition* of ethics, is the shortest and most concise expression for the way of acting which an ethics prescribes, or, if it has no imperative form, the behaviour which it acknowledges to have genuine moral worth. It is therefore, in general, an instruction for virtue expressed through a proposition, hence, the 'what'[1] of virtue. — In contrast, the *foundation* of an ethics is the 'why'[2] of virtue, the *ground* of any obligation or recommendation or commendation, whether it be sought in the nature of the human being, or in circumstance of the external world, or wherever else. As in all sciences, in *ethics*, too, one should clearly distinguish the 'what' from the 'why'. In contrast, most moral philosophers obliterate this difference on purpose, probably because the 'what' is so easy to specify, while by contrast the 'why' is so terribly difficult to specify, so that one eagerly compensates for the poverty of the *one* with the plenty of the *other*, and one seeks to accomplish a fortuitous union of Poverty[3] and Plenty,*[4] embracing both in a single proposition. Most often this occurs when one does not express the well-known 'what' in its simplicity, but rather, one forces it into an artificial formula from which it must first be deduced as the conclusion of stated premises, whereby the reader then feels that he has not only come to know the matter, but also the ground of the matter. From this one can easily convince oneself of most of the commonly known moral principles. Since, however, in the part which follows, I do not intend the same tricks, but I intend to proceed honestly, not asserting the *principle* of ethics at the same time as its *foundation*, but rather being mindful clearly to separate them, so I will trace that 'what', that *principle*, that *fundamental proposition*, about the content of which all moral philosophers are actually in agreement no matter how many different forms in which they dress it, back to the expression which I hold to be the purest and simplest of all: 'Harm no one; rather, help everyone as much as

137

---

[1] ὅ, τι.     [2] διότι.     [3] πενία.     [4] πόρος.

you can.'[1] This is actually the proposition which all teachers of morality exert themselves to *ground*, the common result of their so many different deductions. It is the 'what' for which the 'why' is still always sought, the consequent for which the ground is sought, and hence is itself the given[2] for which the answer[3] is the problem of any ethics, as, too, it is for the prize question at hand. The solution to this problem will lead to the real *foundation* of ethics, which, like the philosophers' stone, has been sought for millennia. However, that the given, the 'what', the principle, actually has its purest expression in the formula given above is evident in that this has the relationship to every other moral principle as conclusion is to premises, hence as the conclusion at which one actually wants to arrive, so that every other moral principle is to be seen as a paraphrase, an indirect or veiled expression of this simple proposition. For example, this serves even for the fundamental proposition, taken to be simple and trivial. 'That which you do not want done to you, do not do to another.'[4] The flaw in this is that it merely expresses duties of justice and not duties of virtue, and it can be remedied by a restatement without the two negations.'[5] For then it, too, will actually say, 'harm no one; rather, help everyone as much as you can'. But this leads to it in a roundabout way, and thereby gains the appearance of having given a real ground, the 'why' for of every precept, which certainly is not the case since from my not wanting something done to me it in no way follows that I ought not to do something to others. The same serves for every *principle* or highest *fundamental proposition* that has been previously asserted.

Now to return to the question we posed above: according to Kant, what is the *law* in following which one's *duty* consists, and on what is this law grounded? We will find that Kant had in a rather artful manner closely connected the moral *principle* with the *foundation* of the same. At this time, I draw attention to Kant's demand, taken into consideration at the outset, that the moral principle should be purely *a priori*, purely formal, in fact a synthetic proposition *a priori*, and, hence, may neither have material content nor rest on anything

138

---

[1] *Neminem laede; imo omnes, quantum potes, juva.*

[2] *datum.*  [3] *quaesitum.*

[4] (*Quod tibi fieri non vis, alteri ne feceris.*) Hugo Grotius attributes this saying to the emperor Severus. [Schopenhauer's note.]

[5] *non* and *ne.*

empirical, i.e., on neither something objective in the external world nor on something subjective in consciousness, such as some sort of feeling, tendency, or drive. Kant himself was clearly aware of the difficulty of this problem, so he says on p. 60—R., p. 53:* 'here we see philosophy indeed placed in a precarious position which is supposed to be firm although neither in heaven nor on earth is there anything on which it depends or upon which it is based.' All the more, then, must we anxiously anticipate the solution to the problem which he had set himself, awaiting with curiosity how something is to come of nothing, i.e., how the law of material, human acting should become concrete from pure *a priori* concepts, without any empirical and material content—as a symbol of which we might consider that chemical process by which, in apparently empty space, solid ammonium chloride arises before our eyes out of three invisible gases (nitrogen, hydrogen, chlorine).—However, I will present this process, by which Kant solved this difficult problem, more clearly than he wanted or was able to do. This may be all the more necessary since the process seems seldom to be understood correctly. For almost all Kantians erroneously assume that Kant had directly set up the categorical imperative as a fact of consciousness; whereas, it was founded *anthropologically*, through *experience*, albeit inner experience, and so *empirically*, which runs counter to Kant's intent and was repeatedly rejected by him. Thus he says on p. 48—R., p. 44:* 'it is not to be settled empirically whether there is anywhere any such categorical imperative', and similarly on p. 49—R., p. 45,* 'the possibility of the categorical imperative is to be investigated wholly *a priori* since here it does not prove to be a useful advantage that the reality of it is given in experience'. But his first pupil, Reinhold,* is soon trapped in this error, as he said in his *Contributions to a Survey of Philosophy at the Beginning of the Nineteenth Century*, volume 2, p. 21: 'Kant takes moral law to be an immediately certain *factum*, to be an original fact of moral consciousness.' However, had Kant wanted to ground the categorical imperative as a fact of consciousness, hence, as empirically, then he would not have failed at least to demonstrate it as such. But nothing of the sort is to be found. To my knowledge, the first occurrence of the categorical imperative in the *Critique of Pure Reason* appears quite on the spur of the moment[1] (p. 802 of

---

[1] *ex nunc.*

the first and p. 830 of the fifth edition*), where it is unannounced and just connected to the preceding sentence with a wholly unwarranted 'therefore'. It is first formally introduced in the *Groundwork of the Metaphysics of Morals*, which we have particularly taken into consideration here, and indeed in a completely *a priori* way through a deduction from concepts. In contrast, in the 'Formula Concordiae of Criticism', in the fifth volume, p. 122, of Reinhold's above-mentioned journal, so important for Kant's critical philosophy, the following sentence stated: 'we distinguish moral self-consciousness from *experience*. As this moral self-consciousness is an original *fact*, no knowledge can surpass it. Moral self-consciousness is bound with experience in human consciousness, and we understand this moral self-consciousness to be the *immediate consciousness of duty; i.e. it is the necessity*, the conformity of the will to law, independent of pleasure and displeasure, to be taken as the incentive and the guiding principle of actions of the will.' So we would certainly have 'a sufficient proposition, indeed, that, too, which was assumed' (Schiller).* But in all seriousness: to what a shameless *petitio principii* we see Kant's moral law to have grown! If *it* were true, ethics would have a foundation of incomparable solidity and it would require no prize questions to encourage the search for it. But then, too, the great wonder would be that such a fact of consciousness would have been discovered so late, while for millennia a basis for morals has been sought eagerly and assiduously. I will further explain by what means Kant himself gave rise to the error just criticized. For all that, one should be astonished at the unchallenged prevalence of such fundamental error among the Kantians, but in the meanwhile, they have written countless books on Kant's philosophy, not once noticing the disfigurement which the *Critique of Pure Reason* suffered in the second edition through which it became an incoherent, self-contradictory book, as has first now come to light and, as I suspected, is laid out in Rosenkranz's preface to the second volume of the collected edition of Kant's works.* One must bear in mind that time spent at ceaseless lecturing *ex cathedra* and in writing books leaves many scholars little time for close study. That one learns by teaching[1] is not absolutely true; rather, one might sometimes parody it: by always teaching, I learn nothing,[2] and even

140

---

[1] *docendo disco* [Seneca, *Moral Letters* 7.].  [2] *semper docendo nihil disco.*

that which Diderot had Rameau's nephew say is not completely without reason:

'"And these teachers, do you really believe they will understand the sciences in which they give instruction? A farce, my dear sir, a farce. If they possessed these pieces of knowledge enough to teach them, then they wouldn't be teaching them."

'"And why?"

'"They would have wasted their lives in studying them."' (Goethe's translation, p. 104).*

Lichtenberg, too, says, 'I have frequently observed that professionals often do not know what is best'.* But (to return to Kantian morals) as far as the public is concerned, if the result agrees with their moral feelings, most people immediately assume that its derivation is already justified; if it appears difficult, they will not go into it deeply, but rather, will leave it to the 'experts'.

141    Kant's *grounding of his moral law* is thus in no way an empirical demonstration as a fact of consciousness, nor an appeal to moral feeling, nor a *petitio principii* through a distinguished modern name of an 'absolute postulate'; rather, it is a very subtle process of thought which he provides for us twice, pp. 17 and 51 — R., pp. 22 and 46, and of which the following is a clearer presentation.*

Since Kant rejected all empirical incentives of the will, he thereby removed in advance everything objective and everything subjective on which he could empirically ground a law for incentives, so there remained for him nothing as *substance* for this *law* than its own *form*. Now, this is only *conformity to law*. But this conformity to law is valid for all, thus, of *universal validity*. This, therefore, becomes the substance. As a result, the content of the law is nothing other than its universal validity itself. As a result, it will read: 'Act only according to the maxim of which you can at the same time will that it become a universal law for all rational beings.' — This, then, is the real *grounding of Kant's moral principle*, so generally known, and hence the *foundation* of his whole ethics. — See by comparison the *Critique of Practical Reason*, p. 61 — R., p. 147.* — To the great cleverness with which Kant had performed his trick, I pay my sincere admiration; however, in my earnest demonstration, I proceed in accordance with the standard of truth. Because I will be taking the matter up later, I only note that *reason*, because and insofar as it carries out the special argumentation previously discussed, is given the name of *practical reason*.

But the categorical imperative of practical reason is the law that results from the process of thought just explained. Thus practical reason is in no way, as most people, and even Fichte, see it: not as a special faculty which can be reduced no further, an occult quality,[1] a kind of moral instinct similar to the moral sense of Hutcheson;* rather, it is (as Kant, too, says in the preface, p. xii—R., p. 8,* and often enough elsewhere) one and the same with theoretical reason; specifically, it is *theoretical* reason itself, insofar as it completes the process of thought as just explained. Fichte called Kant's categorical imperative an *absolute postulate* (*Basis of the Entire Doctrine of Science*, Tübigen, 1802, p. 240 in the note). This is the modern, euphemistic expression for *petitio principii*, and so, too, he himself had completely accepted the categorical imperative and was thus drawn into the error criticized above.

The objection, then, to which that basis which Kant gave for morals is immediately and above all susceptible, is that this origin of a moral law within us is then impossible because it assumes that the human being of his own accord would come upon the idea to look around and inquire about a *law* for his will, one to which his will would be subordinated and to which it would be subject. It is impossible, however, for this to occur to him of its own accord; rather, at best such an inquiry would occur after another moral incentive had given the first impulse and inducement to it, an incentive which was positively effective, real, and, as such, presented itself unbidden and acted on him, even forced itself on him. But something like this would go against Kant's assumption according to which the process of thought explained above should *itself* be the origin of all moral concepts, the very fount[2] of morality. So long as this is *not* the case because, *ex hypothesi*, there is no other moral incentive than the process of thought presented above; so long as egoism alone remains the determining factor of human acting on the guiding thread of the law of motivation; i.e. so long as wholly empirical and egoistic motives, alone and undisturbed in every case, determine the acting of human beings, then on this assumption there is no demand and absolutely no reason at hand on account of which it would occur to him to inquire about a law which would constrain his willing, to which law he would have to subject his willing, let alone one about which he

----

[1] *qualitas occulta.*    [2] *punctum saliens.*

142

might investigate and ponder, whereby it would first be possible that he might come upon the strange train of thought of the reflection explained above. It makes no difference what degree of clarity one will give to the Kantian process of reflection, whether one would tone it down somewhat to just a dimly felt consideration. For no alteration in it challenges the fundamental truths that nothing comes from nothing and that an effect requires a cause. Like any motive that moves the will, a moral incentive must at least present itself, be positively effective, and consequently be *real*: and since for humans only the empirical, or at least that which is assumed to have the possibility of empirically existing, has reality, then a moral incentive must indeed be an *empirical* one, and, as such, must present itself to us unbidden, without waiting for our call for it, and must of its own accord force itself upon us and do so with such force that it has at least the possibility of overcoming enormously powerful opposing egoistic motives. For morals concern the *real* acting of human beings, and not *a priori* houses built of cards, to the results of which no person would turn in the seriousness and stress of life, the effect of which would be as great in the storm of passions as that of an enema syringe on a wildfire. I have already mentioned above that Kant considered it to be a great merit of his moral law that it is grounded simply on abstract, pure concepts, *a priori*, and so, on pure reason, whereby it is valid not merely for humans, but for all rational beings. We must all the more regret that pure, abstract concepts *a priori*, without real substance and without empirical basis of any sort, could never in the least set *humans* in motion: I can say nothing of other rational beings. Thus the second failing of the Kantian basis of morality is a lack of real substance. This has not previously been noticed because the actual *foundation* of Kantian morals, which was explained above, probably has been clear to only a few of those who celebrate and publicize it. The second failing, then, is the complete lack of reality and, hence, of all possible effectiveness. It floats in the air like a silken web of the most subtle concepts, most empty of content, based on nothing and, hence, able to support nothing and move nothing. And yet, Kant has burdened this with a load of infinite weight, namely, the assumption of the freedom of will. Despite his repeatedly expressing the conviction that freedom of human actions simply cannot occur, that theoretically the possibility of such freedom cannot once be comprehended (*Critique of Practical Reason*, p. 168 — R.,

p. 223*), that if there were exact knowledge of a human's character and all the motives affecting him, his actions could be calculated as precisely as a lunar eclipse (the same, p. 177—R., p. 230*), nevertheless, it is assumed merely on the credit of this foundation of morals, floating in thin air, that there can be freedom, if only as an idea and as a postulate, as in the famous conclusion: 'you can: for you ought.'* But if one has once clearly understood that a thing *is* not and *cannot be*, of what help, then, is any postulating? For rather, one should reject that upon which the postulate is grounded because it is an impossible presupposition, following the rule, 'from that which is not possible to that it is not is a sound conclusion',[1] and then by an apagogic* proof overturn the categorical imperative. Instead, here one false doctrine is built upon another.

Kant must at least have been secretly aware of the insufficiency of the foundation of morals consisting of a few wholly abstract concepts, empty of content. For in the *Critique of Practical Reason*, in which, as I have said, he generally goes to work less rigorously and methodically, and also because he was emboldened because by this time he had achieved fame, the foundation of his ethics gradually changes its nature, nearly forgetting that it is a mere web of combined, abstract concepts, and appears to want to become something more substantial. So, e.g., there is in that work, p. 81 — R., p. 163,* 'the moral law is, *as it were, a fact of pure reason*'. What should one think of this unusual expression? That which is factual is otherwise generally opposed to that which is known through pure reason.—Similarly, in the same book, p. 83 — R., p. 164,* there is talk of 'a reason which *immediately* determines the will', etc.—One should now recall that in the *Groundwork* he expressly and repeatedly rejects any anthropological grounding and proof of the categorical imperative as a fact of consciousness, as these proofs would be *empirical*.—Yet made bold by such incidental expressions, Kant's imitators went much farther on this path. Fichte (*System of Moral Philosophy*, p. 49*) expressly warns, 'that one not allow oneself to be misled, wanting further to explain the consciousness that we have duties and to derive grounds external to it, because doing so would undermine the dignity and absoluteness of the law'. Nice excuse!—And then in the same work, p. 66, he says, 'the principle of morality is a thought which grounds itself in the

145

---

[1] *a non posse ad non esse valet consequentia.*

*intellectual intuition* of the absolute activity of the intelligence and is the pure intelligence's immediate concept of itself'. Behind such flowery language such a windbag hides his perplexity!—Whoever wants to convince himself of how completely the Kantians always forgot or ignored Kant's original grounding and derivation of the moral law should check an essay worth reading in Reinhold's *Contributions to a Survey of Philosophy at the Beginning of the Nineteenth Century*, number 2, 1801. In that source, pp. 105 and 106, it is maintained 'that in the Kantian philosophy, autonomy (which is one with the categorical imperative) is a fact of consciousness, and can be traced back no farther since it presents itself through immediate consciousness'.—Then it would be anthropological and, thus, empirically grounded, which runs counter to Kant's expressed and repeated explanations.—Nevertheless in the same work it is said, p. 108, that: 'In the practical philosophy of criticism as well as in the collected pure or higher transcendental philosophy, autonomy is that which is self-grounded and self-grounding, and that which allows of and requires no further grounding, that which simply is original, true and certain through itself, that primordial truth, the primary, *par excellence*,[1] the absolute principle.—Therefore whoever imagines, demands, or seeks a ground for this autonomy outside of itself, of him the Kantian school must believe either that he lacks moral consciousness[2] or that he misunderstands it in speculating from false fundamental concepts. The Fichte–Schelling school declares him to be afflicted with the same sort of dullness which makes one incapable of philosophizing and constitutes of the character of the profane rabble and sluggish brutes, or as Schelling more tenderly expresses it, of the *profanum vulgus* and *ignavum pecus*.' Everyone senses how it stands with the truth of a doctrine which is asserted by such bluffs. But meanwhile, because of the respect which they inspired, we must explain the truly childish faith with which Kantians assumed the categorical imperative and from then on treated it as a settled matter. For since questioning a theoretical assertion could easily be confused with moral wickedness, anyone who does not become

146

---

[1] *prius* κατ' ἐξοχήν.

[2] Just as I thought! If they can no longer give a rational answer
They quickly shove it onto one's conscience. Schiller
[Schopenhauer's note.]
Schiller [From Schiller's *Xenien*, 'The Philosophers', lines 27–8.]

much aware of the categorical imperative in his own consciousness would prefer to refrain from saying anything about it aloud because he silently believed that for others the consciousness of the categorical imperative would likely have developed more strongly and appeared more clearly. For no one likes to turn his conscience inside-out.

Thus, more and more, in the Kantian school, practical reason with its categorical imperative appears as a hyper-physical fact, as a Delphic temple in the human soul out of the dark sanctuary of which oracular pronouncements, unfortunately not about what *will* happen, but, of course, about what *ought* to happen, are infallibly proclaimed. This *immediacy of practical reason*, once accepted, or, rather, slipped in surreptitiously, was unfortunately later carried over into the *theoretical*, especially since Kant himself had often said that both are, after all, just one and the same faculty (e.g., preface, p. xii—R., p. 8*). For once it had been established that with regard to the *practical*, reason makes pronouncements from the tripod,[1] it was easy to take the next step, to grant its sister, indeed, she who is actually consubstantial, to *theoretical reason*, the same privilege and to pronounce the one to have the imperial status of the other, the advantage of which was as immense as it was obvious. Now all the philosophasters and phantasts, the denouncers of atheism, F. H. Jacobi* at their head, streamed in the little gate that had unexpectedly been opened for them, to 147 bring their little satchels to market or to save at least the favourites among the old heirlooms which Kant's theory had threatened to pulverize.*—As in the life of an individual *one* false step of youth often spoils the whole career, so Kant's one false assumption of a faculty of practical reason, bestowed with wholly transcendent credentials, and, like the highest appellate courts, deciding 'without grounds', had the result that out of a strictly austere, critical philosophy arose teaching most heterogenous to it, teachings about a faculty of reason that was first a quiet '*presentiment*', then clearly '*apprehending*', and finally a lively '*intellectual intuition*' of the '*supersensible*', for this faculty of reason's 'absolute' proclamations and revelations, i.e., pronounced from the tripod, could serve each phantast's wildest dreams. This new privilege is blatantly being used to advantage. Here, then, lies the

---

[1] *ex tripode* [the Delphic oracle delivered its pronouncements to a priestess who sat on a tripod].

origin of any method that appeared immediately after Kant's teaching, any method that consists of mystifying, impressing, deceiving, kicking sand in the eyes, and blowing hot air, an era which in the history of philosophy will be denoted by the title 'Period of Dishonesty'. For the *characteristic of honesty*, of mutual inquiry with the reader, which the writings of all earlier philosophers exhibit, here has disappeared: the philosophaster of this time wants not to enlighten, but to delude his reader. Every page bears witness to this. As heroes of this period, Fichte and Schelling glitter. Finally, however, even unworthy of them, much lower than these men of talent, stands the gross, mindless charlatan Hegel. All sorts of philosophy professors make up the chorus, who with serious mien reiterate in public lectures about the infinite, about the absolute, and about so many other things of which they can know absolutely nothing.

Even a miserable pun must serve as a step toward *reason's status as a prophet*, which purports that because the word reason [*Vernunft*] derives from apprehension [*Vernehmen*], reason is a means to *apprehend* the so-called 'supersensible' (νεφελοκοκκυγία, Cloudcuckooland).*
The notion found boundless approval, and in Germany, throughout thirty years, was ceaselessly repeated with unspeakable pleas-
148  ure; indeed, it was made the foundation-stone of the structure of philosophical teaching;—yet it is as plain as day that *reason* [*Vernunft*] certainly derives from *apprehension* [*Vernehmen*], but only because reason gives the human being the advantage over the animal not merely to *hear*, but also to *apprehend* not that which takes place in Cloudcuckooland, but what one reasonable person says to another: the capacity to do so is called reason, and that is what is *apprehended* by this term. This is how all peoples, all times, all languages have grasped the concept of reason, namely as the faculty of universal, abstract, non-intuitive representations, called *concepts*, which are denoted and fixed through words. It is this faculty alone that actually gives the human being the advantage over the animal. For these abstract representations, concepts, i.e., *summations* of many individual things, condition *language*, and through *language* actual *thinking*, and through thinking the consciousness not merely of the present, which the animals also have, but of the past and the future as such, and then again, through this, clear memory, circumspection, precaution, purpose, methodical cooperation of the many, the state, commerce, arts, sciences, religions, and philosophy, in short, everything

that so strikingly differentiates the life of the human being from that of the animal. For the animal, there is mere intuitive representation and, hence, also only intuitive motives: for this reason, the dependence of its acts of will on motives is apparent. These have no less a place for the human being, and (on the presupposition of his individual character) motives, too, move him with strictest necessity, except that these motives are mostly not *intuitive*, but *abstract* representations, i.e., concepts, thoughts which nonetheless are the result of earlier intuitions and, thus, are external influences on him. These, however, give him a *relative* freedom, that is, in comparison to the animal. For the *intuitively* present environment does not determine him the way it does the animal, but he is determined by his thoughts, abstracted from earlier experiences or transmitted through instruction. Therefore, it is not apparent to the viewer at the same time as the deed what motive necessarily moves him; rather, he carries the motive around in his head. This gives not only all his doings and dealings, but even all his movements, a character apparently different from that of the animal: he is drawn, as it were, by finer, invisible threads; therefore, all of his movements carry the stamp of the intentional and deliberate, which gives them a look of independence apparently distinguishing them from those of the animal. All of these great differences, however, depend entirely on the capacity of *abstract representations*, of *concepts*. This capacity, then, is the essence of reason, i.e., that faculty which distinguishes the human being, called τὸ λόγισμον, τὸ λογιστικόν, *ratio, la ragione, il discorso, raison, reason, discourse of reason.* — If, however, one were to ask me what the difference is between this and *Verstand*, νοῦς, *intellectus, entendement, understanding*, I would say it is that cognitive faculty, which animals also have, except to a different degree, and that of which we have the most, namely the immediate consciousness, prior to all experience, of the *law of causality*, as that which constitutes the form of understanding itself and of which its whole essence consists. On it, first and foremost, intuition of the external world depends: for the senses in themselves are merely capable of sensation, which is far from intuition, but is just the material of it: 'the intellect sees and the intellect hears; the others are deaf and blind.'[1] *Intuition* arises when, through

149

---

[1] νοῦς ὁρᾷ καὶ νοῦς ἀκούει τἄλλα κωφὰ καὶ τυφλά (*mens videt, mens audit, cetera surda et coeca*) [Plutarch, *De sollertia animi* III. 961, attributes this saying to Epicharmus].

exactly this act of intelligence, we immediately connect the sensation from the sense organ with its *cause*, which presents itself as an *external object* in our intuitive form, *space*. In fact, this proves that the law of causality is known to us *a priori* and does not stem from experience, while experience itself, since it presumes intuition, first becomes possible through this law of causality. All excellence of understanding, all prudence, sagacity, penetration, acumen consists of the *perfection* of this quite immediate grasp of *causal relations*: for this lies at the basis of all knowledge of the *connection* of things in the broadest sense of the word. Its sharpness and correctness makes one person *more understanding*, more clever, more cunning than another. In contrast, through the ages, that person was called *rational* who did not let himself be guided by *intuitive* impressions, but by *thoughts and concepts* and who, as a result, always works reflectively, consistently, and with circumspection. Such acting is universally called *rational acting*. However, in no way does this imply righteousness and loving kindness. Rather, one can work most rationally, and thus, reflectively, circumspectly, consistently, intentionally, methodically, and in doing so yet follow the most self-interested, unjust, even the most wicked maxims. Therefore, it occurred to no one before Kant to identify acting justly, virtuously, and nobly with acting *rationally*; rather, the two were considered to be completely different and kept separate. The one rests on the *type of motivation*; the other on the *differences among basic maxims*. Only after Kant, since virtue was supposed to arise simply from pure reason, are virtuousness and rationality one and the same, in spite of the linguistic usage of all peoples, which is not accident, but the work of universal and, hence, unanimous human cognition. The rational and the vicious are quite compatible, and indeed only through their combination are great, far-reaching crimes possible. In the same way, irrationality and noble-mindedness coexist quite well: e.g., if today I were to give to a poor person that which tomorrow I should myself need as urgently as he, or if today I should allow myself to get carried away, sending a needy person a sum which my creditor awaits, and similarly in very many cases.

However, as I have said, resting on the assertion that as *practical reason*, purely *a priori*, oracular, it pronounces unconditional imperatives, and combined with the false explanation of *theoretical reason*, advanced in the *Critique of Pure Reason*, that it is a faculty essentially directed towards the *unconditioned* (the impossibility of which the understanding immediately cognizes *a priori*), giving form to three alleged ideas, this elevation of reason to the origin of all virtue, as a bad example which can be imitated,[1] led drivelling philosophers, with Jacobi at the head, to that *reason that immediately apprehends* the '*supersensible*' and to the absurd assertion that reason is a faculty essentially for things beyond all experience, and so related to *metaphysics*, a faculty immediately and intuitively cognizing the ultimate grounds of all things and everything existing, the supersensible, the absolute, the divine, etc.—If, instead of idolizing it, someone had wanted to use his reason, such assertions would have stood in opposition to the simple observation that if by virtue of a special organ for the solution to the riddle of the world, which organ his reason comprises, the human being carries within himself an innate metaphysics, only in need of development, then there must prevail among human beings just such complete agreement about the subject of metaphysics as about the truths of arithmetic and geometry. It would then be quite impossible that there should be found on earth a great number of fundamentally different religions and an equally great number of fundamentally different philosophical systems. Rather, then anyone who deviated from others in religious or philosophical views would at once have to be seen as one with whom something is not quite right in the head.—The following simple observation must press itself upon us no less forcefully. If we were to discover a species of ape which intentionally prepares tools for fighting, or building, or even some other use, we would immediately grant them *reason*. In contrast, if we find wild peoples without any metaphysics or religion, as such there are, it would not then occur to us to deny them *reason*. Through his critique, Kant has kept in bounds the reason that *proves* its so-called supersensible cognitions, but he must have found that Jacobian reason, which immediately apprehends the supersensible, truly to be beneath all critique. In the meanwhile, in the universities just this sort of immediate, imperial reason is still always imposed on innocent youth.

### Note

If we wanted thoroughly to investigate the assumption of practical reason, we must trace its family tree a little farther back. We will then find that it stems from a doctrine which Kant himself had thoroughly

---

[1] *exemplar vitiis imitabile* [Horace, *Epistles* I. 19. 17].

152  refuted, but of which Kant here is unconscious, a trace of an earlier way of thinking, which secretly underlies his assumption of practical reason with its imperatives and its autonomy. It is rational psychology, according to which the human is composed of two completely heterogenous substances, the material body and the immaterial soul. Plato is the first who formally asserted this dogma and had sought to prove it to be an objective truth. Descartes, however, raised it to the pinnacle of perfection, to the point of most precise statement and scientific rigour. But this is just what brought to light its falseness, which was successively demonstrated by Spinoza, Locke, and Kant. It was demonstrated by Spinoza (whose philosophy consists of a refutation of the twofold dualism of his teacher), who made it into his main proposition that precisely and expressly opposes Descartes's two substances: 'The thinking substance and the extended substance are one in the same substance, which is now comprehended under the one and now under the other attribute.'[1] It was demonstrated by Locke who rejected innate ideas, derived all knowledge from the sensible, and taught that it is not impossible that matter could think. It was demonstrated by Kant through the critique of rational psychology as it stands in the first edition.* In opposition, Leibniz and Wolf[f] championed the inferior party: this provided Leibniz with the undeserved honour of being compared with the great Plato, who is so unlike him. Here is not the place to elaborate on all this. Now according to this rational psychology, the soul was an original and essentially a *thinking being*, and as a foremost consequence, a willing being. Accordingly, depending on whether it set out in this, its fundamental activity, unalloyed with the body, or in conjunction with the body, it had a higher and lower cognitive faculty and, thus, a similar faculty of will. In its higher faculty, the immaterial soul was active solely by itself and without the cooperation of the body; hence, it was pure intellect[2] and was concerned with nothing but purely intellectual representations and similar acts of will that carried nothing with them of the sensible originating in the body.[3] Hence it cognized

153

---

[1] *Substantia cogitans et substantia extensa una eademque est substantia, quae jam sub hoc, jam sub illo attributo comprehenditur* [*Ethica* II, prop. 7, schol.].

[2] *intellectus purus.*

[3] *Intellectio pura est intellectio, quae circa nullas imagines corpereas versatur.* Descartes, *Meditations* [VI. 2], p. 188. ['Pure intellect is intellect which depends on no corporeal images.'] [Schopenhauer's note.]

nothing but pure abstractions, universals, innate concepts, eternal truths,[1] and the like. And accordingly its willing was also only under the influence of such purely intellectual representations. In contrast, the lower cognitive faculty and faculty of will were the effect of a soul which worked in unity with and was closely linked to the body and its organs and, hence, was impaired in its purely intellectual effectiveness. Now to this should belong any *intuitive* cognition, that which, as a result, would be unclear and confused; in contrast, that which is *abstract* cognition, originating from abstracted concepts, would be clear! Now the will that was determined by such cognition conditioned by the sensible was lower and mostly inferior, since its willing was produced through sensory stimulus; whereas, the other was willing unalloyed, produced by pure reason and belonged only to the immaterial soul. The most clear exposition of this doctrine was that of the Cartesian De la Forge;\* in his *Treatise on the Human Mind*, chap. 23, he says: 'It is nothing other than one and the same will, which is called sensible desire when it is stimulated by judgement formed in consequence of perceptions of the senses, and which is again designated rational desire when the mind forms judgements about its own proper ideas independently of the confused cognitions of the senses, which are the causes of its inclinations . . . What gave the occasion for regarding these two diverse propensities of the will as two diverse desires is that very often the one is opposed to the other because the intention which the mind builds up on its own proper perceptions does not always agree with cognitions which are suggested to the mind by the body's disposition, whereby it is often obliged to will something while its reason would make it choose something else.'—From the vaguely conscious trace of such views ultimately arises Kant's doctrine of the *autonomy* of the will, which as the voice of pure, practical reason, is law-giving for all rational beings as such and knows only *formal* determining grounds in contrast to the *material* determining grounds which alone determine the lower faculty of desire, against which the higher works. 154

Furthermore, this whole view, first presented quite systematically by Descartes, is already to be found in Aristotle, who expresses it clearly enough in *De anima* I. 1. Even Plato had already prepared

---

[1] *aeternae veritates.*

and indicated it in *Phaedo** (pp. 188 and 189, Bipont).—But as a
result of the Cartesian systematization and consolidation of the view,
a hundred years later we find it to have become completely emboldened, occupying the high ground, and, just because of this, meeting
its downfall. In fact, as a *résumé* of the dominant view of the time,
Muratori offers us *On the Power of the Imagination*,[1] chaps. 1–4 and
13.* In this work the imagination, the function of which is the entire
intuition of the external world on the data from the senses, is a purely
material, corporeal, cerebral organ (the lower cognitive faculty),
and only thinking, reflecting, and deciding remain for the immaterial soul.—However, in this way the whole matter becomes patently
doubtful, and this must have been sensed. For if matter is capable
of such intuitive, complicated apprehension of the world, then one
cannot conceive of why it should not also be capable of abstraction from this intuition and thereby of everything else. Obviously,
abstraction is nothing more than putting aside any differentiations
that are not necessary for a specific purpose, hence of individual and
species differences, e.g., if I overlook that which is specific to the
sheep, the oxen, the stag, camel, etc., and so arrive at the concept of
a ruminant. By this operation, representations forfeit intuitiveness,
and even as abstract, non-intuitive representations, concepts, they
are now in need of a word so they can become fixed in consciousness
and handled.—Despite all this, however, we see Kant still standing
under the influence of the after-effect of this old doctrine in the assertion of his practical reason with its imperatives.

§7

*On* the Supreme Principle *of Kantian Ethics*

AFTER I have tested the actual *basis* of Kantian ethics in the previ-
155  ous section, I turn now to the *supreme principle* of morals which rests
on this foundation, but is tightly bound to it, indeed, grows out of
it. Let us recall that it reads: 'Act only according to the maxim from
which you *can will* that it applies as a universal law for all rational
beings.'*—We will overlook that it is a strange way of proceeding
according to this assumption to instruct one who seeks a law for his

---

[1] *Della forza della fantasia.*

doing and abstaining first to seek a law for the doing and abstaining of all possible rational beings, and we remain with the fact that this ground-rule which Kant asserted is obviously still not itself the moral principle; rather, just a heuristic rule for it, i.e., a voucher for where it is to be sought, and, thus, as it were, still not cold cash, but a secure voucher. Who then, is it, really, who will convert it? To speak the truth straight out: it is a most unexpected paymaster—none other than *egoism*, as I will soon clearly show.

Thus the maxim, according to which I *can will* that everyone would act, would itself then be the actual moral principle. My *being able to will* is the pivot on which a given directive turns. But what *can* I then actually will, and what not? Given this view, to determine what I can will, I obviously again require a regulative, and in this I would first have the key to that directive which is given like a sealed order. Now where is this regulative to be sought?—It could not possibly be found anywhere else but in my egoism, this closest, ever-ready, original, and living norm of all acts of will that at least has the right of first occupancy[1] before any moral principle.—The instruction contained in Kant's supreme rule for finding out the actual moral principle rests specifically on the tacit presupposition that I can only will *that* by which I get what is best for me. Since in the stipulation of a maxim to be universally followed, I must now necessarily consider myself not merely as the active party, but also as the potential[2] and at times passive party, from this standpoint, my *egoism* decides for justice and loving kindness not because it wants to *practise* these, but because it wants to experience them, like a skinflint who, after hearing a sermon on beneficence, cries out: 156

> 'How magnificently put, how fine!—
> I almost want to go begging.'

Kant cannot avoid, and himself adds, this indispensable key to the directive of which his supreme principle of morality consists; however, he does not do so immediately upon his statement of the principle, as this would give offence; rather, he does so at a decent distance and deeper in the text, so that it is not obvious that here, despite the sublime, *a priori* machinations, egoism actually sits on the

---

[1] *jus primi occupantis.*     [2] *eventualiter.*

seat of judgement and renders the decision, and afterwards, from the point of view of the potentially[1] passive party, it has decided that this will be applicable to the active. Thus, p. 19—R., p. 24,* says: 'that I *cannot will* a universal law to lie because no one would then believe me anymore, or would pay me back in *like coin.'*—p. 55—R., p. 49:* 'The universality of a law, that anyone can make any promise he pleases with the intention not to keep it would make promising and the purpose of promising itself impossible, since *no one* would *believe.'*—p. 56—R., p. 50,* it is put in connection to the maxim of hard-heartedness: 'A will which would be decided in this way would contradict itself, since many cases could arise in which he would need others' love and sympathy, and through such a law of nature, arising from his own will, he would rob himself of all *hope of the help that he wishes for himself.'*—Similarly in the *Critique of Practical Reason*, pt. I, bk. 1, chap. 2, p. 123—R., p. 192:* 'If one were to look upon another's need with complete indifference, and *you were to belong* to such an order of things, would you belong to it with the assent of your will?'—'How rashly we enact a law which is unjust to ourselves!'[2] would be the answer. These passages sufficiently explain the sense in which the '*being able to will*' in Kant's moral principle is to be understood. However, that this is the case with the Kantian moral principle is most clearly expressed in the *Metaphysical First Principles of the Doctrine of Virtue*, § 30:* '*For* each wishes that he *would be helped*. If, however, he should make known his maxim of not wanting to help others, then everyone would *be entitled* to refuse him assistance. Thus the selfish maxim conflicts with itself.' *Be entitled*, it says, *be entitled!* Thus here it is as clearly as ever expressed that moral obligation completely depends on a presupposed *reciprocity*; as a result, it is simply egoistical and receives its interpretation from egoism, which, under the condition of *reciprocity*, cleverly consents to a compromise. It is suitable as a foundation of a confederation of states, but not as that of the moral principle. Therefore, when it is said in the *Groundwork*—p. 81—R., p. 67,* 'The principle, always act on the maxim, the universality of which as a law you can at the same time will . . . is the only condition on which a will can never be in conflict with itself';—so this is the true interpretation of the word *conflict*, that

---

[1] *eventualiter.*

[2] *Quam temere in nosmet legem sancimus iniquam!* [Horace, *Satires* I. 3. 67].

if a will had sanctioned the maxims of injustice and hard-heartedness, then, if it potentially became the *suffering party*, it would revoke them and thereby *contradict* itself.

From this explanation it is completely clear that this Kantian ground-rule is not, as he repeatedly maintains a *categorical* imperative; rather it is, in fact, a *hypothetical* imperative* because at its base lies the tacit *condition* that the law set up for my *acting*, as I elevate it to the universal, becomes a law for my *suffering*, and under this condition, as a potentially *passive* party I cannot at all will injustice and hard-heartedness. If, however, with some confidence in my superior intellectual and physical powers, I elevate this condition and consider myself always as an active and never as a passive party, then by the maxim chosen as universally valid, and presupposing that there is no other foundation of morals than the Kantian, I can quite easily will injustice and hard-heartedness as a universal maxim and thereby rule the world

158

upon the simple plan,
That they should take, who have the power,
And they should keep, who can.

Wordsworth.*

Thus, despite Kant's expressed assurances, with the defect of the real *grounding* of the supreme principle of Kantian morals, as explained in the previous paragraph, is associated the veiled *hypothetical* nature of the supreme principle, by which nature the principle is just based merely on *egoism* as the secret expositor of the directive provided by the principle. To this may be further added that the principle, considered merely as a formula, is only a paraphrase, a dressed-up, figurative expression of the well-known rule, 'that which you do not want done to you, do not do to another',[1] if one specifically repeats this without the two negations',[2] thereby freeing it of the blemish of containing only duties of justice and not the duties of love. For obviously this is the only maxim according to which I can will (with respect to my potential passive role, and hence, of course, to my egoism) that everyone act. This rule, 'that which you want done to you',[3] etc., is itself only a paraphrase, or, if you will, a premise for the proposition

---

[1] *quod tibi fieri non vis, alteri ne feceris.*
[2] *non* and *ne.*     [3] *quod tibi fieri.*

which I laid down as the simplest and purest expression of the way of acting about which all moral systems agree: 'Harm no one; rather, help everyone as much as you can.'[1] This is and remains the true, pure content of all morals. But on what is it grounded? What is it that gives this demand force? This is the ancient, difficult problem which lies before us today, too. For from the other side, egoism screams with a loud voice: 'Help no one; rather, harm everyone if it brings you advantage;' indeed, malice gives the variant: 'but harm everyone as much as you can.'[2] To put in opposition to this egoism and its attendant malice, a matching and even more than matching champion—that is the problem of all ethics. Here is Rhodes; jump here!'[3] —

159        Kant intends, p. 57—R., p. 60,* further to confirm the moral principle he asserted by undertaking to derive from it a division of duties which is long recognized and certainly grounded in the essence of morality, a division into duties of justice (also called perfect, stricter, rigorous, duties) and duties of virtue (also called imperfect, broader, meritorious, but best put as duties of love). Except that the attempt appears so forced and patently bad that it strongly testifies against the stated supreme principle. For specifically, the duties of justice are said to rest on a maxim, the opposite of which, taken as a universal law of nature, *cannot be thought* at all without contradiction; the duties of virtue, however, rest on a maxim, the opposite of which one can indeed think of as universal law, but which is impossible to will. —Now I beg the reader to consider that the maxim of injustice, the rule of force instead of right, which, accordingly, is said to be not only impossible *to think* as a natural law, but actually is the real and factual law ruling in nature, not simply just among animals, but also among humans. Civilized peoples have sought to obviate its injurious consequences through the institution of the state, but as soon as this, wherever and of whatever kind it be, is suspended or eluded this natural law immediately reappears. However, it rules perpetually between one people and another: the customary jargon of justice between peoples is, as you know, merely the language of diplomacy. Raw power decides. Conversely, genuine, i.e., uncoerced justice quite

---

[1] *Neminem laede; imo omnes, quantum potes, juva.*

[2] *Imo omnes, quantum potes, laede.*

[3] *Heic Rhodus, heic salta!* [This proverb is attributed to Aesop's fable of the braggart, 203 and 203b, suggesting that one must demonstrate that which one claims.]

certainly does occur, however, only as an exception from this law of
nature. Moreover, in the examples which Kant has put at the head of
this division,* he first (p. 53—R., p. 48*) illustrates the duties of justice with the so-called duty to onself not to end one's life voluntarily
when the pain outweighs the pleasures. This maxim, then, is said to
be impossible *to think* as a universal natural law. I say that, since here
the power of the state cannot intervene, unhindered, this very maxim
shows itself to be the *natural law that actually exists*. For certainly it
is the universal rule that a human actually resorts to suicide as soon
as the innate, enormously powerful drive for the preservation of life
is decidedly overpowered by great suffering: everyday experience 160
shows this. That there is generally some kind of thought that could
have deterred him from suicide after the powerful fear of death
intimately bound with the nature of every living thing has proven
here to be powerless, a thought that is even stronger—this is a daring
assumption, all the more so when one sees that this thought is so
difficult to discover that the moralists still do not know how to give
a determinate account of it. At least the kind of arguments that Kant
advanced against suicide in this context, p. 53—R., p. 49 and also
p. 67—R., p. 57,* certainly have not for even an instant restrained
the despondent. Thus a natural law that exists as an incontestable
fact and occurs daily is for the benefit of the division of duties from
the Kantian moral principle declared impossible to think without
contradiction!—I grant that, not without satisfaction, I now cast a
glance forward to the grounding of morals that I establish in the following part, from which foundation the division into virtues of justice and love (more correctly, into justice and loving kindness) results
quite naturally from the principle of separation which proceeds from
the nature of the case, and which of itself draws a sharp boundary so
that my grounding of morals indeed has produced that verification
about which Kant here makes his wholly groundless claim.

## § 8

### On the Derivative Forms of the Supreme
### Principle of Kantian Ethics

As is well known, Kant has again laid down the supreme principle
of his ethics in a second, quite different expression, in which he does
not, as in the first, express it merely indirectly, as a directive, as it is

to be sought, but directly. He prepares the way for this at p. 63—R., p. 55,* and indeed, through highly unusual, affected, even confused definitions of the concepts of *end* and *means* which admit of being much more simply and correctly defined: *end* is the direct motive of an act of will; *means* the indirect (the simple is the sign of truth[1]). However, he slinks through his strange definitions to the proposition: 'The human being, and generally every rational being, exists *as an end in itself*.'—Except I must immediately say that 'to exist as an end in itself' is unthinkable, a *contradictio in adjecto*. To be an end means to be willed. As I have said, any end is such only in relationship to a will, the end of which, i.e., the direct motive of which, it is. Only in this relation does the concept of *end* have a sense, and *end* loses this sense as soon as it is torn out of this relationship. However, this relation essential to it necessarily excludes any '*in itself*'. 'End in itself' is just like 'friend in itself'—'enemy in itself'—'uncle in itself'—'north or east in itself'—'over or under in itself', and so on. But 'end in itself' is essentially the same case as 'absolute ought'; secretly, even unconsciously, the same thought underlies both as a condition: the theological.—It is no better with '*absolute worth*', which is said to belong to such an alleged but unthinkable *end in itself*. For this, too, I must, without mercy, stamp as a *contradictio in adjecto*. Any *worth* is a comparative quantity, and it even necessarily stands in a double relation, since it is first *relative*, while it is *for* someone, and second it is *comparative*, while it is in comparison to something else against which it is valued. Apart from these two relations, the concept of *worth* loses all sense and meaning. This is too clear to require any further explanation.—Now just as these two definitions offend logic, so the proposition (p. 64—R., p. 56*) that non-rational beings (hence, animals) would be things and, therefore, also may be treated merely as means that are at the same time never ends offends genuine morals. In agreement with this, in the '*Metaphysical First Principles of the Doctrine of Virtue*', § 16,* it is explicitly said: 'The human can have no duty to any being other than just to humans', and then at § 17* he says: 'Cruel treatment of animals is opposed to the duty of humans *to themselves* because it dulls in humans the fellow-feeling for their suffering, whereby a natural tendency very serviceable to morality in relations *to other humans* will be weakened.'—Thus one should

---

[1] *simplex sigillum veri.*

have compassion with animals just for practice, and animals are, as it were, the pathological phantom for the practice of compassion toward humans. Along with all of non-Islamized (i.e., non-Judaized) Asia, I find such propositions disgraceful and detestable. At the same time, it again shows how thoroughly philosophical morals, as explained above, is only disguised theological morals, actually depending on the biblical. Because specifically (about which more later) Christian morals has no regard for animals, so in philosophical morals these are immediately fair game, just 'things', just *means* to favoured ends, thus something for vivisection, coursing, bullfighting, horse-racing, and whipping to death before an immoveable stone cart, etc. — Shame! on such morality of pariahs, chandalas, and mlechchas* — which theological morality fails to recognize the eternal essence which exists in every living being and which shines forth with inscrutable significance from all eyes which see the light of the sun. But this morality recognizes and has regard only for the singular worth of the species the distinguishing mark of which is *reason*, the condition on which a being can be the object of moral consideration.

By such a rough path, indeed, by hook or by crook,[1] Kant then arrives at the second statement of the fundamental principle of his ethics: 'Act in such a way that you always use humanity, in your own person as well as in the person of any other, always at once as an end, but never simply as a means.'* In this, through a very artificial and a very roundabout way, here is what is said: 'Consider not only yourself, but also others:' and this again is a paraphrase of the proposition: 'That which you do not want done to you, do not do to another,'[2] which, as was said, itself again contains only the premise for the conclusion that is the ultimate, true goal of all morals and all moralizing: 'Harm no one; rather, help everyone as much as you can,'[3] which proposition, as with anything beautiful, best appears naked. — Only in Kant's second moral formulation the alleged duties to the self are drawn in intentionally and clumsily enough. I have explained this above.

Another objection, which could be raised against this formulation, is that the condemned criminal, and indeed with justice and authority, is 163 treated only as a means and never as an end, that is, as an indispensable

---

[1] *per fas et nefas.*
[2] *quod tibi fieri non vis, alteri ne feceris.*
[3] *Neminem laede; imo omnes, quantum potes, juva.*

means to preserve, through its fulfilment, the law's power to deter, which is its end.

Now if this second of Kant's formulations neither accomplishes anything toward the *grounding* of morals nor can serve as adequate and immediate expression of its prescriptions—its supreme principle—then in another way it has the merit of containing a subtle psychological-moral insight,[1] as it indicates *egoism* through a highly characteristic mark that is well worth examining more closely here. Specifically, this *egoism*, with which we are all swelling and for which we have invented *modesty* to conceal our pudenda,[2] most often peeks out through all the veils that are cast over it, for in anything we encounter, as if instinctually, we first just seek any possible *means* for some sort of *ends* that are always countless for us. With each new acquaintance generally our first thought is whether the man could by some means be useful; now if he *cannot* be useful, then for most people as soon as they are convinced of this, he is just *nothing*. To seek in everyone else a possible means to our ends, to seek an instrument, almost runs in the very nature of the human glance, but whether this instrument will have to more or less *suffer* with this use is a thought that follows much later or even not at all. That we assume this disposition in others is shown in all sorts of ways, e.g., in that when we request of someone information or advice, we lose all trust in what he says as soon as we discover that he could have some *interest* in the matter, even one that is small or remote. For then we immediately assume he will make us into a means for his ends, and hence he will impart advice not in accord with his *insight*, but with his *intent*, even if the former should be ever so great and the latter so small. For we know only too well that an ounce of intent weighs more than a pound of insight. Conversely, in such cases, to our question: 'What should I do?' nothing will occur to another than what we could do to suit *his* ends; thus, he will immediately answer, as if mechanically, without also thinking of *our* ends because his will immediately dictates the answer before the question even gets to the forum of his own genuine judgement, and, thus, he seeks to direct us in accord with his ends without his even being conscious of it, but thinking himself to be speaking from insight while he only speaks from intent; indeed, even being able to go so far in this as to actually lie without even

---

[1] *apperçu.*    [2] *partie honteuse.*

noticing it himself. So overpowering is the influence of the will over that of cognition. As a result, whether one speaks from insight or intent is never admissible as testimony of one's own consciousness, but most often as that of one's interest. To consider another case: someone pursued by enemies, in mortal fear, who asks a travelling salesman he meets about an escape-route, could find that this salesman will answer his question with 'whether he could not use some of his wares?'—By this it should not be said that it *always* happens this way: more often many people will, of course, take a genuine interest in the well-being and woe of another, or, in *Kant's language*, view another as an end, and not as a means. But no matter how near or far the thought lies from each individual to observe others not as a means, as is usual, but at once as an end—this is the criterion of the great ethical difference of characters, and what it ultimately comes to in the final instance—that will indeed be the true foundation of ethics to which I will turn in the following chapter.

In his second formulation, Kant has distinguished egoism and its counterpart through a highly characteristic mark, the brilliance of which I have all the more emphasized and made clear through elucidation since I can value little else of the basis of his ethics.

The third and final form in which Kant presents his moral principle is the *autonomy* of the will: 'The will of any rational being is universally law-giving for all rational beings.' Of course, this follows from the first form. From the present form, however, it should (according to p. 71—R., p. 60*) result that the specific mark of distinction of the categorical imperative is this: that from willing out of duty the will *renounces all interest*. For this reason, all earlier moral principles failed, 'because they always lay an *interest* at the basis of actions, be it as compulsion or attraction, *whether this might be one's own or another's interest*' (p. 73—R., p. 62*) (even *another's*, which is to be well noted, please). 'In contrast, a universal law-giving will prescribes actions out of *duty* which *are founded on no interest at all*.' Now, however, I beg you to consider what this will really mean: indeed, nothing less than willing *without motive*, hence, an effect without a cause. Interest and motive are convertible concepts: does not interest mean *quod mea interest*, what is of concern to me? And is this not generally everything that incites and moves my will? Consequently, what is an interest other than the influence of a motive on my will? Thus, where a *motive* moves the will, there it has an *interest*; however, where no

165

motive moves it, there it can truly act no more than can a stone move from its place without a push or pull. This I will not even need to demonstrate to learned readers. From this, however, it follows that any action, since it necessarily must have a *motive*, also necessarily presupposes an *interest*. Kant, however, put forth a second, entirely new type of action that takes place without any interest, i.e., without any motive. And these are supposed to be actions of justice and loving kindness! To refute this monstrous assumption requires only reducing it to its actual sense, which was hidden by a play on the word *interest*.—Meanwhile, Kant celebrates (pp. 74 ff.—R., p. 62*) the triumph of the autonomy of the will by erecting a moral utopia under the name of a *kingdom of ends* that is populated by none other than *rational beings in abstracto* who, one and all, will without having *something* to will (i.e., without interest), except that they always will this one thing: that everyone always wills according to *one* maxim (i.e., autonomy). 'It is difficult not to write satire.'[1]

166     However, autonomy of will leads Kant to something else, something of more troublesome consequences than this innocent little kingdom of ends, which can be allowed to rest in peace as wholly harmless: namely to the concept of the *dignity of the human being*. Specifically, this dignity rests simply on human *autonomy* and depends on the fact that the law which the human being ought to follow is given by himself—hence he stands in the same relationship to this law as constitutional subjects stand to their constitution.—Nevertheless, this might stand as an embellishment of the Kantian moral system, except that this expression, '*dignity of human beings*', once Kant said it, afterward became the shibboleth of all confused and thoughtless moralists, who hid their lack of an actual basis of morals, or at least one that said something, behind this imposing expression, '*dignity of human beings*', cleverly reckoning that their readers, too, would prefer to see themselves invested with such *dignity* and, hence, would thereby be contented.[2] We will, however, also investigate this concept somewhat more closely and put it to the test

---

[1] *Difficile est, satiram non scribere* [Juvenal, *Satires* I. 30].
[2] The first who expressly and exclusively made the concept of the 'dignity of the human being' into the foundation-stone of ethics, and who afterward had developed an ethics on it, appears to have been G[eorg] W[ilhelm] Block in his *New Groundwork for the Philosophy of Morals* [*Neuen Grundlegung der Philosophie der Sitten*], 1802. [Schopenhauer's note.]

of reality.—Kant (p. 79—R., p. 66*) defines *dignity* as 'an unconditioned, incomparable worth'. This is the explanation, which, because
of its sublime sound, makes such an impression that it is not easy for
one to presume to approach in order to investigate it closely, where
one would then find that it is really just an empty hyperbole at the
heart of which nests, like a gnawing worm, a *contradictio in adjecto*.
Any *worth* is the evaluation of one thing in comparison with another;
thus, it is a comparative concept, and hence relative, and this relativ-
ity comprises the very essence of the concept of *worth*. The Stoics
already have correctly taught (according to Diog[enes] Laert[ius],
Book VII, c. 106) that 'the worth of a thing is the proven equivalent
interchange value, as assessed by someone experienced in the matter,
as for example, wheat for barley with a mule.'[1] An *incomparable,*   167
*unconditional, absolute worth*, to which *dignity* is supposed to be the
equivalent, is therefore, like so much in philosophy, a proposition put
in words for a thought that is as unthinkable as the highest number
or the greatest space.

> So right when concepts fail,
> A word shows up just in time.*

So then, here, too, the 'dignity of the human being', most welcome
words, showed up in time, through which words any moral system
spun out through all classes of duties and all instances of casuistry now
found a wide foundation from which it could preach in comfort.

At the close of his presentation (p. 124—R., p. 97*) Kant says: 'But
how *pure reason*, without other incentives that might be drawn from
somewhere else, can itself be *practical*, i.e., how the *mere principle of
universal validity of all its maxims* as laws, without any object of the will
in which one may take some preceding interest, in itself supplies an
incentive and an interest that could be called purely moral or, in other
words, how could pure reason be practical?—All human reason is
incapable of explaining this, and all efforts and work are lost.'—Now
one would think that if the existence of something is asserted, but
its possibility can never be conceived, it must indeed be identified as
actual fact: except that the categorical imperative of practical reason

---

[1] τὴν δὲ ἀξίαν εἶναι ἀμοιβὴν δοκιμαστοῦ, ἥν ἂν ὁ ἔμπειρος τῶν πραγμάτων τάξῃ· ὅμοιον
εἰπεῖν, ἀμείβεσθαι πυρούς πρὸς τὰς σὺν ἡμιόνῳ κριθάς (*existimationem esse probati remu-
nerationem, quamcunque statuerit peritus rerum; quod hujusmodi est, ac si dicas, commutare
cum hordeo, adjecto mulo, triticum*).

is expressly *not* asserted as a fact of consciousness or even grounded though experience. Moreover, we are often enough warned that it is *not* to be sought in such an anthropological-empirical way (e.g. p. vi of the preface—R., p. 5, and pp. 59–60—R., p. 52*). What is more, we are repeatedly assured (e.g. p. 48—R., p. 44*) 'that whether there is any imperative of this sort is not to be determined by example, and hence, not empirically'. And on p. 49—R., p. 45,* 'that the actuality of the categorical imperative is not given in experience'.—When one sums this up, one could actually suspect that Kant is putting one over on his reader. Even if, according to the present German philosophical public, this might be allowed and be correct, nonetheless, in Kant's time this had not been recognized as such, not to mention that ethics was exactly that theme that was least suited to joking. Thus we must maintain the conviction about whatever can neither be conceived *as possible* nor proven *as actual*, that its existence has no verification.—But now, too, if we only attempt to comprehend it by means of the fancy and imagine a person whose mind were possessed by an *absolute ought* that spoke in pure categorical imperatives, as if possessed by a demon that, contrary to the person's inclinations and wishes, constantly demanded to control the person's actions—then we see in this no correct image of the nature of human beings or the events of our inner selves; however, we do indeed recognize an artificial substitute for theological morals to which it is related as a wooden leg is to a living one.

Thus our result is that Kantian ethics, as well as all earlier ethics, lacks any secure foundation. As I have indicated with the examination of its *imperative form* provided right at the beginning, it is at its basis only an inversion of theological morals and a masquerade of the same in very abstract formulations apparently founded *a priori*. This masquerade must be all the more artful and unrecognizable, for through it Kant certainly even deceived himself, actually supposing that he could establish the concepts of the *command of duty* and the *law* independent of all theology and ground these concepts on pure cognition *a priori*, even though these obviously make sense only in theological morals. Opposed to this, I have sufficiently demonstrated that those concepts of his, lacking any real foundation, float freely in the air. Toward the end, through his own hands, the masked theological morals unveils itself in the doctrine *of the highest good*, in the *postulates of practical reason* and finally in *moral theology*. Indeed, all of this has disabused neither him nor the public about the true connection of the matter. Moreover, both were now delighted to see all these articles of faith grounded through ethics (if only ideally and for prac- 169 tical benefit). For they naively took the consequent for the ground and the ground for the consequent, because they did not see that all these alleged inferences from this ethics already lay at its basis as tacit and concealed, but unavoidably necessary, presuppositions.

If now, at the close of this rigorous and, for the reader, even tax- ing investigation, in the interest of levity a facetious, indeed frivolous, comparison might be permitted me, then I would compare Kant in his self-mystification to a man who at a masked ball flirts the whole even- ing with a masked beauty under the illusion of making a conquest, until at the end she unmasks and reveals herself—as his wife.

## § 9
### *Kant's Doctrine of Conscience*

THE alleged practical reason with its categorical imperative is obvi- ously most closely related to the *conscience*, although it is essentially different from conscience *first* in that the categorical imperative, in commanding, necessarily speaks *before* the deed; whereas, the con- science only speaks afterward. *Before* the deed, conscience can at best speak *indirectly*, specifically by means of reflection through which it holds up to itself the memory of earlier instances in which similar deeds afterward met its disapproval. It seems to me that even the etymology of the word *Gewissen* [conscience] rests on this, while only that which has already occurred is *gewiß* [certain]. Namely, in any, even in the best people, impure, base, wicked thoughts and wishes arise from external circumstances, aroused emotions, or from inner upset. For these, however, he is not morally responsible and need not burden his conscience. For these only indicate what *people in general* but not what *he* who thinks them, would be capable of doing. For other motives enter his consciousness both instantly and also simultaneously, opposing these wicked thoughts so that they can never become deeds; hence, they are like an outvoted minority in a legislative assembly. 170 From *deeds* alone anyone becomes acquainted with himself, as do others, empirically, and only *deeds* burden the *conscience* [*Gewissen*]. For deeds alone are not problematic, like thoughts, but in contrast to thoughts are *certain* [*gewiß*] and remain unchangeable, and are not merely thought but *known* [*gewußt*]. It is the same with the Latin, *conscientia*: it is Horace's 'to be conscious is to turn pale with guilt'. It is just the same with συνείδησις.* It is the person's *knowledge* [*wissen*] of that which he has done. *Second*, conscience always takes its material from experience, which the alleged categorical imperative cannot do since it is purely *a priori*.—For the moment we may assume that Kant's doctrine of conscience will also cast light back on that concept newly introduced by him. The main presentation of it is found in '*Metaphysical First Principles of the Doctrine of Virtue*', § 13, which few pages I will *assume to be at hand* for the critique of it now to follow.

The Kantian presentation of conscience makes a most imposing impression before which one stands with reverential awe, and against which one is all the less confident to turn in opposition. For one must fear to see one's theoretical objection misconstrued for a practical one, and if one denied the correctness of the Kantian presentation, to be regarded as having no conscience. I cannot be misled by this since here it concerns theory, not practice, and is not seen as concerning moral preaching, but concerns strict examination of the ultimate grounds of ethics.

First of all, throughout Kant makes use of *Latin, juridical expressions*, which appear to be ill-suited to render the most secret stirrings of the human heart. But he adheres to this language and the juridical presentation from beginning to end; thus, it appears to be essential and inherent to the subject. A complete court of law is presented to us in the inner chambers of the mind, with trial, judge, prosecutor, defence counsel, verdict. Now if the inner proceeding actually is the case, as Kant presents it, then one would be astonished that any person could be, I will not say so *bad*, but so *stupid* as to act against his conscience. For such a supernatural institution of a quite singular sort in our self-consciousness, such a masked Court of the Star Chamber* in the secretive darkness of our inner being, must instil in anyone terror and fear of the gods that truly prevent his taking brief, fleeting advantages against proscriptions proclaimed so clearly and closely under dreadful threats of terrible supernatural powers.—Whereas, in reality, we see the converse: the effectiveness of conscience is considered to be so weak that all peoples have been careful to come to its aid through positive religion or even thoroughly to replace it by such. Then, too, if there were such a quality of conscience, the present prize question of the Royal Society could never have come to mind.

On closer observation of the Kantian presentation we find, however, that its imposing effect is achieved primarily by Kant's actually attributing to moral self-judgement a form that is inherent and essential, which it really is not. Rather, this form can merely be adapted to moral self-judgement as it can be to any other rumination quite foreign to the genuinely moral, a rumination about what we have done and could have done differently. For in any case, not only will the obviously spurious, affected conscience founded on mere superstition, e.g., when a Hindu reproaches himself for having occasioned the murder of a cow, or a Jew recalls having smoked a pipe at home on the Sabbath—usually assume the same form of charge, defence, and judgement, but even the same self-examination which proceeds from absolutely no ethical viewpoint is, indeed, more a non-moral than moral sort and in any case will often proceed in such a form. So, e.g., if I have amicably but rashly vouched for a friend and now it becomes clear to me in the evening what a grave responsibility I have thereby taken on myself and how easily it could come about that thereby I could incur great misfortune, which the old voice of wisdom, 'give a pledge, and already there is trouble'[1] prophesies to me, then the prosecutor enters my inner being and also, opposing him, the advocate who seeks to explain away my rash voucher through the stress of the circumstances, of obligation, through the harmlessness of the matter, indeed, through praise for my amicability. Finally, too, the judge 172 enters, who pitilessly renders the judgement: 'Stupid move!' under which I collapse.

And as with Kant's favourite juridical form, so it is, too, with the greatest part of his remaining description. E.g., what he actually says at the very beginning of the section, about what is characteristic of conscience, also applies to any scruple of a completely different sort: it can be understood completely literally about the secret consciousness of one of independent means, who believes his expenses greatly exceed the interest, and that the capital will be exhausted and must gradually melt away: 'it follows him like a shadow when he thinks of escaping: he can even fool himself or lull himself to sleep through

---

[1] ἐγγύα, πάρα δ' ἄτα [Literally, 'pledge alongside Ate'. Ate was the goddess of mischief, troubles. See Plato, Charmides 165a.].

pleasures and distractions, but he cannot avoid now and then coming to himself, or awakening, whereupon he immediately hears its terrible voice', etc. — Now after Kant described this judicial form as essential to the subject and hence has continued it from beginning to end, he used it for the subsequent well-wrought sophism. He says that, 'but if through his conscience the accused is represented as *one and the same person with the judge*, which is a sort of representation absurd for a court of law, then indeed the accuser would lose every time',* which he explains through a very forced and unclear note. From this Kant now concludes that, in order not to fall into contradiction, we must think of the inner judge (in this judicial drama of the conscience) as distinct from ourselves, as *another*, and at that as knowing the secrets of the heart, omniscient, obliging all, and, as an executive power, an omnipotent one, so that Kant now leads his reader on a perfectly smooth path from conscience to fear of the gods as a wholly necessary consequence of the same, secretly trusting that the reader will follow him there all the more willingly since the earliest training had made such concepts familiar, indeed, second nature to him. So here Kant then finds it easy sport, which he should have disdained, and here he should be mindful not only to *preach* honesty but also to *practise* it. — I simply deny the proposition advanced above on which all these

173 consequences rest; indeed, I declare it to be a subterfuge. It *is not true* that the prosecutor must lose every time if the accused is the *same* person as the judge, at least not in an *inner* court: for in my example above of the voucher, has the prosecutor lost? — Or, in order not to fall into contradiction, must one all along assume here, too, such a personification[1] and necessarily objectively imagine *another* as the one whose verdict would have been these thunderous words: 'Stupid move'? Something of a living Mercury? Or a personification of cunning intelligence[2] recommended by Homer, and thereby here, too, strike a path to fear of the gods, albeit those of the pagans?

That in his presentation Kant resists attributing objective validity to his moral theology, which is here* already indicated in brief, but in essentials, but does put it forth in a necessarily subjective form, does not absolve him from the arbitrariness with which he constructs it, even if in only a necessarily subjective form, since such occurs by means of completely unfounded assumptions.

---

[1] *prosopopoeia.*    [2] Μῆτις.

So this much is certain, that the entire juridical-dramatic form, a form which Kant presents as one inherent to the subject itself and carries out thoroughly and to the end in order finally to draw consequences from it, is a form completely inessential and in no way inherent to conscience. Rather it is a much more general form, one which the consideration of any practical matter readily assumes, and which primarily arises out of the conflict of opposing motives that frequently occurs in such cases. Reflective reason examines in turn the weight of each opposing motive, whereby it makes no difference whether the motives are of the moral or the egoistical sort or whether the case concerns deliberation about that which is still to be done or rumination about that which is already completed. However, if we now strip Kant's presentation of this arbitrarily given dramatic-juridical form, then the nimbus cloud surrounding it disappears, too, along with its imposing effect, and merely this remains: that upon reflection on our own actions, we are occasionally overcome by a very special sort of dissatisfaction concerning not the consequence, but the action itself, and not resting on *egoistic* grounds, like any other 174 case in which we regret the imprudence of our doings, since in this case we are dissatisfied precisely because we have acted *too* egoistically, with *too* much regard for our own well-being and *too* little for that of others, or because we have indeed made into our ends the *woe* of another for its own sake without advantage to ourselves. That we are dissatisfied with ourselves and can grieve over the suffering, not which we have *suffered*, but which we have *caused*, this is the naked fact that nobody will deny. We will further investigate the connection of this to the only proven basis of ethics. However, like a clever legal adviser, Kant sought through its embellishment and exaggeration to make as much as possible of the original fact so as to have beforehand a quite broad basis for his morals and moral theology.

§ 10

*Kant's Doctrine of Intelligible and Empirical*
*Character. — Theory of Freedom.*

AFTER I, in the service of truth, have launched an attack on Kantian ethics, an attack which does not, like earlier ones, concern only the superficial, but which undermines it most profoundly, it seems to me that justice demands that I not continue without having brought to mind his greatest and most brilliant service to ethics. This consists in the doctrine of the coexistence of freedom with necessity, which he first advances in the *Critique of Pure Reason* (pp. 533–534 of the first and pp. 561–582 of the fifth edition*); however, an even clearer presentation of it is given in the *Critique of Practical Reason* (fourth edition, pp. 169–179 — R., pp. 224–231*).

First Hobbes, then Spinoza, then Hume, even Holbach* in *System of Nature*, and finally most thoroughly and most profoundly, Priestley, had all so clearly proven beyond a doubt the complete and strict necessity of acts of will on the occurrence of motives, that it is to be counted among the perfectly demonstrated proofs; hence, only ignorance and crudeness could continue to speak of freedom of the individual actions of human beings, a *libero arbitrio indifferentiae*. As a result of the irrefutable grounds of these predecessors, Kant, too, took the perfect necessity of the act of will as a settled matter about which no doubt could exist, as is proved in all these passages in which he only speaks of freedom from a *theoretical* viewpoint. Nevertheless, it remains true that our actions are accompanied by a consciousness of self-determination and originality by virtue of which we recognize them as our work and everyone feels unmistakably certain that he is the actual doer of his deeds and morally *responsible* for them. But now responsibility presupposes the possibility of having acted otherwise, hence of freedom in some sort of way. So in the consciousness of responsibility mediately lies that of freedom, too. A key which Kant finally found to the solution to this contradiction, stemming from the subject itself, became his profound distinction between appearance and thing in itself, which is the innermost core of his whole philosophy and is even its principal merit.

With his unchangeable, innate character, all the manifestations of which are strictly determined by the law of causality, here called motivation as mediated through the intellect, the individual is only *appearance*. Lying at the basis of this appearance, to be found outside space and time, free from all succession and plurality of acts, the *thing in itself* is one and unchangeable. Equally present in all the individual's deeds, stamped in all of them like the signet in a thousand seals, presenting itself in time and a succession of acts, his nature *in itself* is the *intelligible character* which determines the *empirical character* of this appearance, which, in turn, in all its manifestations, called forth by motives, must show the constancy of a natural law, for which reason all its acts follow with strict necessity. Now through this, that unalterability, that unyielding rigidity of every person's empirical character, which thoughtful persons at all times perceived ('while the rest believed a person's character capable of being reformed through rational remonstrations and moral exhortations'), was reduced to a 176 rational basis and consequently also established for philosophy, and, thereby, philosophy was brought into harmony with experience and was no longer shamed by the folk wisdom which had long before expressed that truth in the Spanish proverb: *Lo que entra con el capillo, sale con la mortaja* ('what comes in with the child's cap goes out again with the shroud') or *Lo que en la leche se mama, en la mortaja se derrama* ('what is imbibed with the milk is in turn poured out into the shroud').

I take this doctrine of Kant's of the coexistence of freedom with necessity as the greatest of all accomplishments of human profundity. It, along with the 'Transcendental Aesthetic', are the two great diamonds in the crown of Kantian fame that will never fade away.— It is well known that in his essay on freedom, Schelling has created a paraphrase of this theory of Kant's that through its lively colouring and clear presentation is more intelligible for many, a paraphrase which I would praise if Schelling would have had the honesty to say in it that he here expresses Kant's wisdom, not his own, which even today part of the philosophical public still considers it to be.

But now this Kantian doctrine and the essence of freedom in general can be made more intelligible by putting them in connection with a universal truth, the most concise expression of which I find often stated by the scholastics in the phrase: 'doing follows essence;' i.e., everything in the world does according to what it is, according to its nature, in which all its manifestations are, therefore, already potentially[1] contained, but actually[2] occur when external causes call them forth; whereby, then, this very nature appears. This is the *empirical character*; in contrast its inner, ultimate ground, not accessible to experience, is the *intelligible character*, i.e., the essence *in itself* of the thing.

In this the human being is no exception from the rest of nature: he, too, has his fixed nature, his unchangeable character, which is completely individual and differs with each person. This nature is

---

[1] *potentiâ.*    [2] *actu.*

177    *empirical* only for our comprehension, but for this reason only an *appearance*; on the other hand, what he may be in his essence in itself is called the *intelligible character*. All of his actions, consistent with his external nature as determined by motives, can occur in no other way than in accord with this unchangeable individual character: as one is, so must one act. Hence, for a given individual in any given case, only *one* action is possible: 'doing follows essence.' Freedom belongs not to the empirical, but only to the intelligible character. A given person's 'doing'[1] is necessarily determined externally through motives and internally through his character; hence, everything that he does occurs necessarily. But in his 'essence',[2] there lies freedom. He could have *been* another, and in that which he *is* lies blame and merit. For everything which he does follows from the self, as a simple corollary. — Through Kant's theory we are actually rescued from the fundamental error that misplaced necessity in 'essence' and freedom in 'doing' and we are led to the recognition that it is exactly the other way around. For this reason moral responsibility of the human indeed concerns primarily and ostensibly that which he does, but fundamentally that which he *is*, since this presupposes that when the motives appeared, his doings could never have resulted otherwise than they did result. Yet for a given character, however strict the necessity with which the deeds are called forth by the motives, it still will never occur to anyone, not even one who is convinced of this necessity, to try to exculpate himself and to turn the blame on the motives, since he clearly recognizes that here, considering the circumstances and the causes, thus *objectively*, a completely different, even a contrary action was quite possible, indeed would have occurred *if only he had been another*. However, as follows from the action, he is such and no other — and it is this for which he feels himself responsible: here in 'essence' lies the place where the sting of conscience strikes. For conscience is just the acquaintance with one's own self, arising from one's own way of acting and becoming ever more intimate.

178    Hence, certainly on the occasion of the 'doing', really the 'essence' is accused by conscience. Since we are conscious of *freedom* only through the means of *responsibility*, then where this lies, that, too, must lie: thus, in 'essence'. The 'doing' is subject to necessity. But as with others, so we come to know ourselves only *empirically*, and we have no cognition

---

[1] *operari*.    [2] *esse*.

*a priori* of our character. Moreover, we initially cherish a very high opinion of our own character, because the saying 'everyone is presumed to be good, until the contrary is proved'[1] applies in the inner forum,[2] too.

## Note

Whoever is able to recognize the essential in a thought, even if in completely different garb, will see with me that this Kantian doctrine of the intelligible and empirical character is an insight raised to abstract clarity that Plato already achieved and which, because he had not recognized the ideality of time, he could depict only in temporal form and, hence, merely mythically and in connection with metempsychosis. However, this recognition of the identity of both doctrines is now made quite clear by the elucidation and exposition of the Platonic myth which Porphyry* has provided with such great clarity and exactitude that the agreement with the abstract Kantian doctrine stands out unmistakeably. This description, from a work no longer extant, in which Porphyry comments precisely and specifically on the myth here under discussion, the myth Plato gives in the second half of the tenth book of the *Republic*, is completely[3] preserved by Stobaeus* in the second book of his *Eclogues*, chap. 8, §§ 37–40, which passage is, therefore, well worth reading. As a sample, I quote from it the short § 39, whereby the interested reader may be stimulated to take Stobaeus himself in hand. The reader will then recognize that this Platonic myth can be seen as an allegory of the great and profound knowledge which Kant had put forth in its abstract purity as the doctrine of intelligible and empirical character, and that consequently this had in its essentials already been accomplished by Plato millennia beforehand, indeed, reaches back much farther, since Porphyry is of the opinion that Plato had received it from the Egyptians. 179 However, now it is to be found already in the doctrine of metempsychosis of Brahmanism, from which, it is highly probably that the wisdom of the Egyptian priests originated.—the aforementiond § 39 reads:

For all that Plato means seems to be this. Souls have free power before entering into bodies and different modes of being to choose one or another

---

[1] *quisque praesumitur bonus, donec probetur contrarium.*
[2] *foro.*   [3] *in extenso.*

form of life, which they will pass through in a specific existence and in a body suited to it. (And a soul may choose a lion's mode of being as well as a man's.) However, this free power is removed at the same time as the soul enters one or the other form of life. For when they have once entered bodies and have become souls of living things instead of free souls, then they take that free power which is unique to the nature of the living thing. Sometimes this power is full of mind and full of motion, as in man; in some it is less moveable and is simple, as in almost all other living things. Moreover, the type of free power depends on the nature of the living thing because its motion is of the soul's own cause, but is according to the desires originating in the nature of the living thing.[1]

§ 11

## *Fichtean Ethics as Mirror for Magnifying the Mistakes of the Kantian*

180    As in anatomy and zoology many things about specimens and natural products are not so conspicuous to the pupil as when engravings portray these specimens and natural products with some exaggeration, so for anyone to whom, after the critique given in the preceding sections, the futility of the Kantian basis of ethics is not completely clear, I can recommend Fichte's *System of Moral Philosophy* as a means of clarification.

---

[1] Τὸ γὰρ ὅλον βούλημα τοιοῦτ' ἔοικεν εἶναι τὸ τοῦ Πλάτωνος ἔχειν μὲν τὸ αὐτεξούσιον τὰς ψυχὰς πρὶν εἰς σώματα καὶ βίους διαφόρους ἐμπεσεῖν, εἰς τὸ ἢ τοῦτον τὸν βίον ἐλέσθαι, ἢ ἄλλον, ὅν, μετὰ ποιᾶς ζωῆς καὶ σώματος οἰκείου τῇ ζωῇ, ἐκτελέσειν μέλλει (καὶ γὰρ λέοντος βίον ἐπ' αὐτῇ εἶναι ἐλέσθαι, καὶ ἀνδρός.) Κἀκεῖνο μέντοι τὸ αὐτεξούσιον, ἅμα τῇ πρός τινα τῶν τοιούτων βίων πτώσει, ἐμπεπόδισται. Κατελθοῦσαι γὰρ εἰς τὰ σώματα, καὶ ἀντὶ ψυχῶν ἀπολύτων γεγονυῖαι ψυχαὶ ζώων, τὸ αὐτεξούσιον φέρουσι οἰκεῖον τῇ τοῦ ζώου κατασκευῇ, καὶ ἐφ' ὧν μὲν εἶναι πολύνουν καὶ πολυκίνητον, ὡς ἐπ' ἀνθρώπου, ἐφ' ὧν δὲ ὀλιγοκίνητον καὶ μονότροπον, ὡς ἐπὶ τῶν ἄλλων σχεδὸν πάντων ζώων. Ἠρτῆσθαι δὲ τὸ αὐτεξούσιον τοῦτο ἀπὸ τῆς κατασκευῆς, κινούμενον μὲν ἐξ αὐτοῦ, φερόμενον δὲ κατὰ τὰς ἐκ τῆς κατασκευῆς γιγνομένας προθυμίας. (*Omnino enim Platonis sententia haec videtur esse: habere quidem animas, priusquam in corpora vitaeque certa genera incidant, vel ejus vel alterius vitae eligendae potestatem, quam in corpore, vitae conveniente, degant (nam et leonis vitam et hominis ipsis licere eligere); simul vero, cum vita aliqua adepta, libertatem illam tolli. Cum vero in corpora descenderint, et ex liberis animabus factae sint animalium animae, libertatem, animalis organismo convenientem, nanciscuntur; esse autem eam alibi valde intelligentem et mobilem, ut in homine; alibi vero simplicem et parum mobilem, ut fere in omnibus ceteris animalibus. Pendere autem hanc libertatem sic ab animalis organismo, ut per se quidem moveatur, juxta illius autem appetitiones feratur.*)

As in the old German puppet show, accompanying the Kaiser or some other hero was a buffoon who in his own manner and with exaggeration always repeated what the hero had said or done, so, too, behind the great Kant stands the originator of the doctrine of science, more correctly, the doctrine of empty science.* In order to secure his well-being and that of his family, this man effectively carried out his plan to provoke sensation by means of a philosophical mystification which was well suited to and sanctioned by the German philosophical public, a plan to *outdo* Kant in all points, to appear to be Kant's living superior and, by magnifying conspicuous points, to produce a perfect caricature of Kantian philosophy; he had also achieved this in ethics. In his *System of Moral Philosophy* we find the categorical imperative raised to a despotic imperative: the absolute ought, the law-giving reason, and the command of duty have developed into a *moral destiny*, an unfathomable necessity that the human race act strictly according to certain maxims (pp. 308–309), ones to which, judging by moral institutions, much must be attributed, although one never actually comes to know *what*; rather, one only sees simply that, as there dwells in bees a drive to build common cells and a hive, so a drive allegedly is supposed to dwell in the human to enact with others a strictly moral, great world-comedy in which we would be mere marionettes and nothing more, albeit with the significant distinction that the beehive actually comes to exist; whereas, instead of a moral world-comedy in fact a highly amoral one is enacted. So here we then see the imperative form of Kantian ethics, the moral law and absolute ought, further developed until it has become *a system of moral fatalism* 181 the exposition of which at times crosses over into the comic.[1]

---

[1] To prove what has been said, here I will provide space for just a few passages. p. 196: 'The ethical drive is absolute; it requires absolutely no end outside of itself.'— p. 232: 'Now as a consequence of the moral law, the empirical, temporal being, should be an exact expression of the original I.'—p. 308: 'The whole person is a vehicle for the moral law.'—p. 342: 'I am only a tool, merely a tool of the moral law, absolutely not an end.'—p. 343: 'Anyone is the means to the end of realizing reason: this is the ultimate final goal of his being: for this alone he exists, and if this should not happen, then he need not exist at all.'—p. 347: 'I am a tool of moral law in the sensible world!'—p. 360: 'It is a decree of the moral law to nourish the body, to care for the health of the same: it goes without saying that this may happen in no sense and to no other purpose than to be an *efficient tool* for the furthering of the *purpose of reason*.'—(Cf. p. 371) p. 376: 'Any human body is a tool for the furthering of the purpose of reason; therefore, the greatest possible usefulness of any tool must be for me a purpose: accordingly I must have concern for

If a certain moral pedantry is to be perceived in Kant's ethics, then in Fichte there is the most ridiculous moral pedantry, rich stuff for satire. One should read, e.g., pp. 407–409, the resolution of the well-known casuistic example in which one of two human lives must be lost. Similarly, we find all of Kant's errors raised to the superlative: e.g., p. 199: 'to act in accordance with the drives of sympathy, compassion, *loving kindness* is absolutely not moral, but to that extent is against morals'!—p. 402: 'the incentive for readiness for service must never be an unreflective good-heartedness, but the clearly thought-out purpose to serve the causality of reason as much as possible.'—But now among these pedantries, Fichte's philosophical crudeness obviously peers out—as is to be expected with a man whose teaching never allowed him time for learning—while he seriously advances the *liberum arbitrium indifferentiae* and establishes it with the most vulgar arguments (pp. 160, 173, 205, 208, 237, 259, 261).—Whoever is still not fully convinced that the motive, although operating through the medium of cognition, is a cause as any other, and hence carries the same necessity of consequence as any other, so that all human actions follow with strict necessity—he is still philosophically untrained and not instructed in elementary philosophical knowledge. Insight into the strict necessity of human actions is the boundary-line which separates philosophical minds from the rest, and having reached this line, Fichte clearly shows that he belongs among the rest. That he again, following Kant's trail (p. 303), says things in direct contradiction with the passages above proves, like so many other contradictions in his writings, just that he is one who was never serious in the search for truth and had absolutely no firm fundamental conviction, for in that case, too, such was completely unnecessary for his purposes. Nothing is more ridiculous than that this man has been posthumously praised for the strictest consistency, as his pedantic tone in broadly demonstrating trivial things was taken for such.

The most complete development of *Fichte's system of moral fatalism* is found in his last writing: *Science of Knowledge Presented in Its*

anyone.'—This is his derivation of loving kindness!—p. 377: 'I can and must only care for myself simply because and insofar as I am *a tool of the moral law*.'—p. 388: 'To defend a fugitive at the peril of one's own life is absolute obligation:—whenever human life is in danger you no longer have the right to think of the safety of your own.'—p. 420: 'In the sphere of the moral law, there is absolutely no view of my fellow man other than that he is a *tool* of reason.' [Schopenhauer's note.]

*General Outline*, Berlin 1810—which has the virtue of being only forty-six duodecimo pages thick and still contains his entire philosophy in a nutshell,[1] for which reason it is recommended to all those who consider their time too valuable to be squandered on the larger productions of this man which are composed in Christian-Wolf[f]ian prolixity and tedium and are actually aimed at the deception, not at the instruction, of the reader.

In this little book it states, p. 32: 'The intuition of the sensible world only exists so that in this world the I would be visible as *absolute ought.*'—On p. 33 even comes 'the ought of the visibility of the *ought*', and p. 36, 'an *ought* of the perception that I *ought*'. —This is the sort of thing to which we are led immediately after Kant, whose *imperative form* of ethics with its unproved *ought* secured for itself a quite comfortable place to stand[2] as a bad example which can be imitated.

Everything said here does not, after all, quash Fichte's merit, which consists in having obscured this late masterpiece of human profundity, indeed even in having crowded Kant's philosophy out of the nation in which it appeared, through windy, jabbering superlatives, through extravagances and nonsense appearing as masked profundity in his *Basis of the Entire Doctrine of Science*, and in this he has incontestably shown the world what passes for the competence of the German philosophical public since he had it play the role of a child from whose hand one coaxes a valuable gem by holding out to him a cheap toy. The fame that he achieved in this way lives still today on credit, and still today Fichte is always mentioned alongside Kant as his equal (Hercules and his ape![3]), indeed, is often placed above him.[4] For this reason his example had called forth every successor who was animated with the same spirit and crowned with the same success in the art of philosophical mystification of the German public. Everyone knows them, and here is not the place to speak of them at length, although their respective opinions are still always expounded from all

---

[1] *in nuce* [Latin: *nux*, stem: *nuc*, 'nut'].

[2] ποῦ στῶ.

[3] Ἡρακλῆς καὶ πίθηκος!—i.e. *Hercules et simia!*

[4] I support this with a passage from the most recent philosophical literature. Mr Feuerbach, a Hegelian (*c'est tout dire* [that says it all]), in his book *P[ierre] Bayle, A Contribution to the History of Philosophy*, 1838, p. 80 would thus have us understand: 'But even more sublime than Kant's are Fichte's ideas, which he expresses in his *Moral Philosophy* and scattered throughout his other writings. Christianity has in its sublimity nothing that could compare to Fichte's ideas.' [Schopenhauer's note.]

angles and seriously discussed by professors of philosophy as if they
184   actually were dealing with philosophers. Thus Fichte is to be thanked
that illuminating documents exist to be revised some day before the
tribunal of posterity, this court of appeal of the judgements of the
present. At almost all times this court of posterity has been for genuine
merit what the Last Judgement is for the saints.

# GROUNDING OF ETHICS

## § 12

### *Requirements*

THUS, too, Kant's grounding, taken for sixty years to be a firm foundation for ethics, sinks before our eyes into the deep abyss of philosophical errors, perhaps impossible to fill, because it turns out to be an inadmissible assumption and simply a cover for theological morals. — That earlier attempts to ground ethics can suffice even less, I may, as was said, presuppose to be understood. Mostly they are unproven assertions pulled out of thin air, and at the same time, just like Kant's grounding itself, rest on artificial subtleties, which demand the finest distinctions and the most abstract concepts, laboured combination, heuristic rules, propositions that balance on the point of a needle, and stilt-legged maxims from the heights of which one can no longer see down to real life with its tumult. Hence they are certainly well suited to echo in lecture halls and to furnish exercise in discernment. But it cannot be that which elicits the call, which nonetheless actually exists in every person, to do what is right and good, nor can it counterbalance the strong impulses to injustice and harshness, nor even form the basis of the reproaches of conscience, for in trying to 186 reduce these reproaches to a violation of such hair-splitting maxims can only serve to make them ridiculous. Thus artificial combinations of concepts of all sorts can, if we want to take the matter seriously, never contain the true impulse to justice and loving kindness. Rather, this must be something that requires little reflection and even less abstraction and combination, something that, independently of the cultivation of the intellect, speaks to anyone, even the most uneducated person, resting simply on an intuitive apprehension and immediately pressing itself on us out of the reality of things. As long as ethics does not produce a foundation of this sort, however much it is disputed and paraded in lecture halls, real life will mock it. So I must give ethicists the paradoxical advice to first look around a little in human life.

## § 13
### *Sceptical View*

OR perhaps upon retrospection on the attempts made in vain for more than two thousand years to find a secure basis for morals, might it result that there is simply no natural morals independent of human ordinance, but this is an artefact through and through, a means discovered the better to restrain the selfish and malicious human race, and that, consequently, without the support of positive religions, this would collapse because it had no inner verification and no natural basis? The courts and the police cannot reach everywhere: there are offences too difficult to detect, indeed, some for which the punishment is uncertain, in which case public protection fails us. Besides, civil law at most compels justice, but not loving kindness and beneficence, because everyone would want to take the passive and not the active role. This gives rise to the hypothesis that morals rest solely on religion and that both have as an end to be the complement for the necessary inadequacy of state institutions and legislation. A natural morals, i.e., one grounded simply on the nature
187 of things or of the human being, cannot, therefore, be given; hence, it becomes clear that philosophers are striving in vain to seek its foundation. This opinion is not without plausibility: the Pyrrhonists had already put it: 'There is neither good nor evil in nature;

but these things are judged in the human mind,

according to Timon',[1] Sextus Empiricus,* *Against the Mathematicians* XI. 140, and even in more recent times distinguished thinkers have acknowledged it as theirs. Therefore, it deserves careful examination even if it would be quite convenient to set it aside with an inquisitorial sideways glance at the conscience of those in whom such a thought could arise.

One would find oneself in a great and very childish error if one were to believe that all just and legal actions of human beings were of

---

[1] οὔτε ἀγαθόν τί ἐστι φύσει, οὔτε καλόν,

ἀλλὰ πρὸς ἀνθρώπων ταῦτε νόῳ κέκριται,

κατὰ τὸν Τίμωνα (*neque est aliquod bonum naturâ, neque malum, 'sed haec ex arbitrio hominum dijudicantur',—secundum Timonem*). [Timon of Phlius (c.320–230 BCE), Greek sceptic philosopher.]

moral origin. Moreover, between the justice which humans practise and genuine honesty of the heart there is at most an analogous relation, like between the expression of politeness and genuine love of neighbour, the latter of which is not, like the former, for appearance, but actually overcomes egoism. A righteousness of disposition, generally carried on for show, which wishes to be beyond all doubt, along with great indignation that will be aroused by the faintest indication of suspicion about it, and is ready to turn into the fieriest anger—only the inexperienced and the simple will take all of this at face value and as the effect of tender moral feeling or of conscience. In truth, rectitude generally exercised in human intercourse and asserted as rock-steady maxims rests primarily on two external necessities: first on legal order by means of which public force protects the rights of everyone, and second on the recognized need for a good name or civil honour necessary to progressing in the world. Yet anyone's steps come under the scrutiny of public opinion, which is mercilessly strict and never forgives a single misstep in this regard, but holds it as an indelible stain upon the guilty one to his death. In this, public opinion is actually wise, for it follows the principle *operari sequitur esse* and, thus, the conviction that character is unchangeable and, so, what one has done once, one will inevitably do again under precisely similar circumstances. Thus these two guards are the ones that watch over public rectitude, and without which, frankly, we would be in a bad way, especially with regard to possessions, this main point in human life, around which its dealings primarily turn. For purely ethical motives to probity, assuming that they are present, for the most part can find their application to civil possessions only after a wide detour. Specifically, these motives appeal above all and directly to *natural right*, but to the *positive* only indirectly, insofar as this natural right lies at the basis of the positive. Natural right, however, attaches to no other property than that which has been won through one's own labour, and when this property is seized, the powers the possessor used to acquire it are also seized, and thus robbed from him.—I unconditionally reject the theory of pre-occupation;* however, here I cannot go into its refutation.[1]—Now certainly, any possession grounded on positive right, however mediated, should ultimately rest on the natural right to property as its first source.

---

[1] See *The World as Will and Representation*, vol. I, § 62, p. 396 ff. [Hübscher, vol. II, pp. 396 ff.], and vol. II, chap. 47, p. 682 [Hübscher, vol. III, pp. 684 ff.]. [Schopenhauer's note.]

But in most cases, how far our civil possessions lie from this original source of the natural right of property. For the most part, it has a connection either very difficult or even impossible to demonstrate: our property is inherited, gained through marriage, won in the lottery, or if not that, certainly not won through our own work by the sweat of our brow, but through cunning and bright ideas; e.g., in speculative trade, indeed, also through stupid ideas, which, by means of chance, the god of success[1] has crowned and exalted. In very few cases is it actually the fruit of real labour and work, and even then this is often only intellectual work, as with the lawyer, doctor, official, teacher, work which, according to the view of the untrained person, appears to require little exertion. It requires significant education to recognize the ethical right to all such possessions, and as a result to respect it from purely moral impulses. — Consequently many secretly consider the property of others to be possessed solely by positive right. They therefore find means to snatch it away from them by means of use, or indeed, just by circumventing laws, and they think nothing of it: for it seems to them that the former lost it in the same way as they had gained it earlier, and so they believe their own claims to be as well grounded as those of the previous owner. From their point of view, in civil society, the right of the more cunning takes the place of that of the stronger. — Meanwhile, the *rich man* is often actually of steadfast rectitude because he is devoted to a rule with his whole heart and maintains a maxim on the observance of which depends all his possessions together with the great deal of advantage he has over others, so in all seriousness he embraces the principle 'to each his own',[2] and never departs from it. There is, indeed, such an *objective* attachment to loyalty and faith, such resolve to keep them sacred and such attachment rests simply on the fact that such loyalty and faith are the bases of all free intercourse among humans, of good order, and of secure possession, quite often doing *us* some good, and with this end in view, must even be maintained with sacrifice, just as one must *expend* something for good acreage. In fact, as a rule, one will find such well-founded honesty only among the well-to-do or at least among people devoted to profitable earnings, but most often among merchants who have the clearest conviction that commerce has mutual trust and credit as its indispensable support; hence, merchants' honour is of a quite special sort. — In

189

---

[1] *Deus Eventus.*     [2] *suum cuique.*

contrast, *the poor man*, who gets the short end of the stick and by virtue of the inequality of possession sees himself condemned to hard work and poverty while others live in abundance and idleness before his very eyes, will find it difficult to recognize that what lies at the basis of this inequality is a corresponding inequality of merit and honest earnings. 190 But if he does not recognize this, then from where should he receive the purely ethical impulse to probity which prevents him from stretching out his hand to others' abundance? Mostly it is legal order which restrains him. But if once the rare opportunity arises whereby he is assured of being beyond the effect of law and he could through a single deed throw off the oppressive burden of poverty which the sight of others' abundance makes all the more palpable and at the same time could come into possession of pleasure he so often envied, what would then restrain his hand? Religious dogma? Seldom is faith so firm. A pure moral motive to justice? Perhaps in a few cases, but in most cases for the man in humble circumstances it will be only the very important concern for his good name, for his civil honour, for the apparent risk of forever being expelled for such a deed from the great Masonic lodge of honourable people who follow the law of rectitude and so have divided up among themselves and manage property all over the world, for the risk that because of a single dishonest action, he would be for a lifetime a pariah of civil society, one whom no one trusts any more, from whose company everyone flees, and from whom all advancement is thus cut off, i.e., in a word, 'a villain who has stolen'—and to whom the proverb applies: 'whoever once steals is a lifelong thief.'

These, then, are the guardians of public rectitude, and whoever has lived and had his eyes open will grant that, by far, almost all probity in human intercourse is owed only to these guardians, indeed, that there is no lack of people who hope to elude *their* vigilance and who, thus, observe justice and honesty only as a pretence, as a banner, under the protection of which one conducts one's predations with all the more success. Thus we need not immediately fly into a sanctimonious fit and rage if a moralist once raises the problem of whether all honesty and justice might ultimately be merely conventional and, following this principle, then strives to reduce the rest of morals to more distant, mediated, but still ultimately quite egoistic grounds, 191 as Holbach, Helvetius, d'Alembert,* and others of their time have ingeniously sought to do. This is really true and correct, even of the greatest number of just actions, as I have shown above. There can be no doubt that it is also true of a considerable number of actions of loving kindness, since these often proceed from ostentation and more often from belief in a future retribution that may well be dealt out squared or even cubed, and they admit of still other egoistic grounds. Yet it is just as certain that there are actions of disinterested loving kindness and completely voluntary justice. I do not find proofs of these in facts of consciousness, but only in experience, the isolated, but indubitable cases in which not only the danger of legal prosecution, but also of detection and even of any suspicion are completely excluded, and then, too, cases in which a poor man gives that which is his to a rich man: e.g., a case in which something lost and found, or something deposited by a third party who then died, was returned to its owner, or one in which a fugitive secretly makes a deposit with a poor man by, who faithfully preserves it and gives it back. Without a doubt there are similar cases, but the surprise, the emotion, the esteem with which we receive these clearly indicates that these belong among unexpected things, the rare exceptions. Indeed, there are truly honest people—just as there really are four-leaved clovers, but Hamlet speaks without hyperbole when he says: *To be honest, as this world goes, is to be one man pick'd out of ten thousand.*\*—Cases in which the participants themselves adhere to no religious belief, which occurs more often than is publicly acknowledged, will suffice as proof against the objection that the actions mentioned above are based on religious dogma, and, hence, concern for punishment and reward in another world.

192    Regardless of the *sceptical view*, one appeals first of all to *conscience*. But doubt will arise, even about the natural origins of *conscience*. At least there is also a spurious conscience[1] which is often confused with it. Remorse and anxiety which many a one experiences about that which he has done is often based in nothing else but fear of that which could happen to him because of it. Violation of external, arbitrary, and distasteful rules torment many with inner reproaches, quite like a conscience. So, e.g., it lies very heavily on the heart of the sanctimonious Jew that, although in the second book of Moses, chap. 35, it says, 'you shall kindle no fire on the Sabbath day throughout your habitations',\* nonetheless, on Saturday he had smoked a pipe in his house. Many a noble or officer is gnawed by secret self-reproach

---

[1] *conscientia spuria.*

when, in some circumstance, he has not properly observed the laws of the fool's code which is called knightly honour. This goes so far that many of this station, when put in a situation in which it is impossible to keep the word of honour he has given, or even just to satisfy this code in disputes, will shoot himself dead. (I have witnessed both.) In contrast, the same man will break his word every day with a light heart as long as the shibboleth 'honour' is not attached.—In general, every inconsistent action, every thoughtless action, every action against our intentions, principles, convictions, no matter what sort they be, indeed, every indiscretion, every blunder, every boorishness, afterwards secretly vexes us and leaves behind a sting in our heart. Many a one would be amazed if he were to realize of what his conscience, which seems to him to be so imposing, is actually composed: approximately ⅕ fear of humans, ⅕ fear of the gods, ⅕ prejudice, ⅕ vanity, and ⅕ habit, so that he finally is no better than the Englishman who said, 'I cannot afford to keep a conscience'.—By *conscience* religious people of any faith frequently understand nothing other than the dogmas and precepts of their religion and the self-examination they undertake based on these, and the expressions *force of conscience* and *clear conscience* are also used in this sense. Theologians, scholastics, and casuists of the middle ages and more recent times take it in just this way. Everything which anyone knew of the regulations and precepts of the church made up his *conscience*, including the intention to believe it and follow it. Accordingly, there was a doubting, an opining, an erring conscience, etc., and for its correction, a council of conscience was held. How little the concept of conscience, like other concepts, is fixed by its own object, how differently it has been conceived by different authors, how wavering and uncertain it appears among authors one can see in summary from Stäudlin's *History of the Doctrine of Conscience*. All of this is not intended to confirm the reality of the concept and has thus raised the question whether there actually is, then, also a real, innate conscience. I have already in § 10 had occasion, with the doctrine of freedom, to briefly provide my concept of conscience, and I will return to this below.

    Taken together, these sceptical objections are certainly in no way sufficient to deny the existence of all genuine morality, but to moderate our expectation of a moral predisposition among humans and hence the natural foundation of ethics, since so much that is attributed to this demonstrably originates in other incentives and the observation of the moral depravity of the world sufficiently proves that the incentive to goodness cannot be very powerful, especially since it often does not work even when the opposing motives are not strong, although then the difference among individual characters fully asserts itself. Meanwhile the recognition of that moral depravity is made more difficult because it is checked and concealed by civil order, by the necessity for honour, indeed, even by politeness. Finally there is also the fact that through education the morality of the very young is supposed to be promoted, by presenting rectitude and virtue to them as the maxims everywhere followed in the world. Now when experience teaches them something else, often to their great harm, then the discovery that the teachers of their youth were the first who had betrayed them works more detrimentally on their own morality than if these teachers had even given the first example of frankness and honesty by candidly saying: 'The world is in a bad way, for humans are not as they should be; do not let this mislead you, but be better.'—All of this, as I have said, makes more difficult our recognition of the actual immorality of the human race. The state, this masterpiece of rational self-reflection, of the collective egoism of all, has put the protection of everyone's rights in the hands of a force infinitely superior to the power of any individual, compelling the individual to respect the rights of all others. So the boundless egoism of almost everyone, the malice of most, the cruelty of many do not come into prominence: compulsion has restrained them all. The deception springing from all of this is so great that if in individual cases in which the power of the state cannot protect or is eluded, we see come to the fore insatiable greed, vile greed for money, deeply disguised duplicity, insidious malice of humans, we often recoil in horror and let loose an outcry, imagining that we have met with a horror never before seen, except that without the compulsion of law and the necessity of civil honour such occurrences would be the whole order of the day. One must read histories of crime and descriptions of anarchistic conditions in order to recognize what, with respect to morality, the human actually is. The thousands who there before our very eyes throng in peaceful intercourse are to be viewed as just so many tigers and wolves whose jaws are powerfully muzzled. Hence, if one once thinks of the power of the state suspended, i.e., of this muzzle thrown off, any intelligent person recoils from the scene that then is to be expected, whereby he makes known how little he finally trusts the effect of religion, of conscience, or of the natural foundation of morals, whatever that may also be. But in the light of these immoral tendencies set free, the true moral incentive in humans would show its efficacy undisguised, and so would be recognized most readily, while at the same time the incredibly great differences of moral character would appear unveiled and would be found to be just as great as differences of intelligence, 195 which is certainly to say a lot.

Perhaps one might want to object that ethics has nothing to do with how humans actually act, but is the science that declares how they *ought* to act. This, however, is just the principle that I deny, as I have sufficiently demonstrated in the critical part of this essay that the concept of *ought*, the *imperative form* of ethics, applies only in theological morals, apart from which, however, it loses all sense and meaning. By contrast, I set for ethics the purpose of interpreting, expounding, explaining, and reducing to their ultimate ground humans' ways of acting, which from a moral view are extremely variable. Therefore there remains no other path to the discovery of the foundations of ethics than the empirical, specifically to investigate whether there are any actions at all to which we must grant *genuine moral worth*—which will be the actions of voluntary justness, pure loving kindness, and real noble-mindedness. These, then, are to be viewed as a given phenomenon that we have to explain correctly, i.e., to reduce to its true grounds, hence, to demonstrate the specific incentive which in any instance moves humans to actions of this sort, different from any other specific sort. This incentive, including the responsiveness to it, will be the ultimate ground of morality and knowledge of the same will be the foundation of morals. This is the unassuming path along which I direct ethics. As it contains no construction *a priori*, no absolute law-giving for all rational beings *in abstracto*, whoever would think it not sufficiently distinguished, infallible, and academic, he may return to categorical imperatives, to the shibboleth of the 'dignity of the human being', to the hollow expressions, the phantoms of the mind and soap bubbles of the schools, to principles of which experience speaks scornfully at every step and of which, outside the lecture halls, no one knows anything nor has ever experienced. In contrast, experience stands on the side of the foundation of morals which is reached on my path, daily and hourly bearing its quiet witness.

196

## § 14

### *Antimoral[1] Incentives*

THE principal and fundamental incentive for humans, as for animals, is *egoism*, i.e., the urge for existence and well-being.—The German word *Selbstsucht* [selfishness] carries with it a false connotation of sickness.\* The word *Eigennutz* [self-interest], however, denotes egoism insofar as egoism is under the direction of reason which enables it upon reflection to pursue its goals *methodically*; therefore, one could correctly call animals egoistic, but not self-interested. Thus, for the more general concept I will use the word *egoism*.—This *egoism* is in animals, as in humans, most precisely connected with their innermost core and essence, indeed, actually identical. Therefore as a rule all human actions spring from egoism, and from this we must first and foremost always attempt to explain any given action. Similarly, one generally bases in egoism one's calculations of all means by which one tries to direct a person to some sort of goal. *Egoism* by its nature is boundless: the human wills unconditionally to preserve his existence; wills it unconditionally free of pains, among which are included all want and privation; wills the greatest possible amount of well-being, and wills every pleasure of which he is capable, even seeks wherever possible to develop new capacities for pleasure. Everything which opposes the striving of his egoism provokes his animosity, anger, hate:

197  he will seek to annihilate it as his enemy. He wills to enjoy everything possible, have everything; since, however, this is impossible, at least to be master of everything: 'everything for me, and nothing for others' is his motto. Egoism is colossal: it towers over the world. For if any individual were given the choice between his own and the rest of the world's annihilation, then I need not say what the result

---

[1] I permit myself the unconventional compound ['anti-moral', *antimoralische*], since 'anti-ethical' [*antiethisch*] would not be meaningful here, 'Customary and non-customary' [*sittlich und unsittlich*], which are now in fashion, are but poor substitutes for 'moral and immoral' [*moralisch und unmoralisch*], first because 'moral' [*moralisch*] is a scientific concept that as such requires a Greek or Latin designation, for reasons which one may find in my principal work [*The World as Will and Representation*], vol. II, chap. 12, pp. 134 ff. [Hübscher, vol. III, pp. 143 ff.], and second because 'customary' [*sittlich*] is a weak and docile expression, difficult to distinguish from 'modest' [*sittsam*], for which the popular term is 'prudish' [*zimperlich*]. One must make no concessions to German jingoism. [Schopenhauer's note.]

would be for most. Accordingly everyone makes himself the centre of the world, refers everything to himself, and whatever simply occurs, e.g. the greatest changes in the fate of nations, he will first refer to *his* interests, no matter how trivial and incidental these may be, before thinking about anything else. There is no greater contrast than that between the great and exclusive interest that each takes in his own self and the indifference with which, as a rule, everyone else regards this self, just as he regards theirs. This even has a comical side, to see countless individuals, of whom each, at least from a practical point of view, considers only himself to be *real* and to some extent views others to be mere phantoms. This ultimately depends on each person's being *immediately* given to himself; whereas, others are given to him only *mediately* by the representation of them in his head: and the immediacy asserts its right. Namely, as a consequence of the subjectivity essential to any consciousness everyone himself is the whole world: for everything objective exists only mediately as mere representation of the subject so that everything always depends on self-consciousness. Each one carries in himself as his representation a single world which he cognizes and of which he knows, so therefore, he is the centre of it. For just this reason anyone is all in all to himself: he finds himself to be the holder of all reality, and nothing can be more important for him than he himself. Now although in his subjective view his self is presented in this colossal magnitude, it shrinks in the objective to nearly nothing, namely to approximately $\frac{1}{1000,000,000}$ of humankind currently living. He now knows with complete certainty that this self, this microcosm, more important than all else, of which the macrocosm appears as a mere modification or accident, this, his whole world, must perish in his death, which for him means the same as the end of the world. These, then, are the elements out of which, on the basis of the knowledge of life, grows egoism, 198 which always lies like a wide trench between one person and another. If one were once actually to jump over this trench to help another, then it is like a miracle which provokes wonder and earns applause. Above, § 8, in the explanation of the Kantian moral principle I have had the opportunity to discuss how egoism shows itself in everyday life, in which, in spite of the politeness one puts in front of it like a fig-leaf, it always peeps out from one corner or another. Politeness is the conventional and systematic denial of egoism in the trifles of daily intercourse and is readily recognized as hypocrisy, yet it is required and praised because what it conceals, egoism, is so obscene that one does not want to see it, although one knows that it is there, just as one wants to know that offensive objects are at least covered by a curtain.—Since egoism unconditionally pursues its ends when either it is not opposed by an external force, among which may be counted any fear, be it of earthly or supernatural powers, or by the genuine moral incentive, then, to the detriment of all, 'the war of all against all'[1] would be the order of the day among the countless mobs of egoistic individuals. Hence reflective reason quite soon invents the institution of the state, which, arising from mutual fear of mutual force obviates the detrimental consequences of universal egoism as much as possible by *negative* means. In contrast, where these two powers opposing egoism are not effective, egoism will immediately show itself in its most fearful magnitude, and the phenomenon will not be a pretty one. To express the strengths of this anti-moral power without prolixity, I thought to describe the magnitude of egoism with a single stroke of the pen, so I sought some sort of really emphatic hyperbole, and finally I hit upon this: many a person would be capable of beating another to death merely to grease his boots with his victim's fat. But with this there remained the doubt whether this actually were a hyperbole.—Thus *egoism* is the primary and most important, although not the only power against which *the moral incentive* will have to struggle. Here one already sees that this incentive, in order to prevail against such an opponent, must be something more real than a quibbling sophistry or an *a priori* soap bubble.—Meanwhile, in war, the first thing is that one reconnoitre the enemy. In the war at hand, as the main force on its side, egoism will above all set itself against the virtue of justice, which, according to my view, is the first and real cardinal virtue.

In contrast, the virtue of *loving kindness* will more often be opposed by *ill-will* or *spitefulness*. Therefore we next want to consider the origins and gradations of these. *Ill-will* is very abundant, indeed, almost commonplace in its lower degrees, and it easily approaches the higher. Goethe was quite right to say that in this world indifference and aversion are right at home (*Elective Affinities*, pt. I, chap. 3). It is very fortunate for us that prudence and politeness throw their mantle over these and do not allow us to see how universal is mutual ill-will and

---

[1] *bellum omnium contra omnes* [Hobbes, *Leviathan*, I. 13].

how 'the war of all against all'[1] is carried on, at least in thoughts. But occasionally it appears, e.g., in frequent and relentlessly evil gossip; however, it becomes quite visible in the outbreaks of anger, which often exceeds its cause many times over and would not prove to be so strong if it had not, like the gunpowder in a flintlock, been compressed as hate long-preserved through inner brooding. In large part ill-will arises from the inevitable collisions of egoism that appear each step of the way. Then, too, it is also provoked objectively by the sight of the vices, failings, weaknesses, foolishness, shortcomings, and imperfections of all sorts, which, everyone more or less, at least occasionally, displays to others. It can go so far in this that perhaps to many, particularly in moments of melancholy mood, the world appears from an aesthetic point of view as a cabinet of caricatures, from an intellectual point of view as a madhouse, and from a moral point of view as a den of thieves. If such a melancholy mood persists, then misanthropy arises. —Finally, a prime source of ill-will is *envy*; or, rather, this itself *is* already ill-will, provoked through another's luck, possessions, or advantages. No person is completely free of it, and Herodotus (III. 80) has said it: 'envy in the beginning is innate to the human.'[2] However, the degrees differ greatly. It is at its most implacable and most poisonous when directed at personal characteristics, because for the envious one there remains no hope, and at the same time it is at its most vile because he hates that which he should love and honour. But it is so:

> Those seem to be envied most of all
> Who soar aloft on their own strong wings
> And escape the common cage of all,[3]

as Petrarch complains. One may find more detailed observations on envy in the second volume of *Parerga [and Paralipomena]*, § 114. — In a certain respect, the opposite of envy is *Schadenfreude*.* Yet to feel envy is human; to enjoy *Schadenfreude* is devilish. There is no more unfailing sign of a thoroughly bad heart and profound moral baseness than an inclination to pure, heartfelt *Schadenfreude*. One should

---

[1] *bellum omnium contra omnes.*
[2] Φθόνος ἀρχῆδεν ἐμφύεται ἀνθρώπῳ (*Invidia ab origine homini insita est*).
[3] *Di lor par più, che d'altri, invidia s'abbia*
*Che per se stessi son levati a volo,*
*Uscendo fuor della commune gabbia*
[*Trionfo del Tempo (The Triumph of Time)*, V. 91–2].

forever avoid those in whom one perceives it: 'This man is black-hearted; of him, you Roman, beware.'[1] — Envy and *Schadenfreude* in themselves are merely theoretical; in practice they become malice and cruelty. Egoism can lead to crimes and misdeeds of all sorts, but the misfortune and pain it causes another is merely a means and not an end, and thus occurs only accidentally. In contrast, for malice and cruelty another's suffering and pains are an end in itself the attainment of which is a delight. For this reason these constitute a higher degree of moral depravity. The maxim of extreme egoism is: 'Help no one; rather, harm everyone if (thus always still conditioned) it brings you advantage.'[2] The maxim of malice is: 'Harm everyone as much as you can.'[3] — Just as *Schadenfreude* is only theoretical cruelty, so cruelty is only *Schadenfreude* in practice, and *Schadenfreude* will appear as cruelty as soon as the opportunity occurs.

To demonstrate the specific vices which spring from the two fundamental powers indicated above would be in place only in a fully developed ethics. Such an ethics would derive from *egoism* something like greed, gluttony, lust, self-interest, avarice, covetousness, injustice, hard-heartedness, pride, arrogance, etc. — but from *spitefulness*, jealousy, envy, ill-will, malice, *Schadenfreude*, fault-finding, calumny, insolence, petulance, hatred, anger, treachery, perfidy, vengefulness, cruelty, etc. — The first root is more bestial, the second more devilish. The prevalence of the one or the other, or even a moral incentive still to be demonstrated below, provides the principal line of the ethical classification of characters. No person is completely without something of all three.

With this I would certainly have ended the terrible military review of anti-moral powers, which reminds one of the princes of darkness in Milton's *Pandemonium*.* However, my plan required that I take into consideration this dark side of human nature, through which my path of course departs from all other moralists and becomes similar to that of Dante who first leads into hell.

It becomes clear from the overview of anti-moral powers given above how difficult is the problem of discovering an incentive that could move humans to a way of acting opposed to all those inclinations

---

[1] *hic niger est, hunc tu, Romane, caveto* [Horace, *Satires* I. 4. 85].
[2] *Neminem juva.; imo omnes, si forte conducit . . . laede.*
[3] *omnes, quantum potes, laede.*

rooted deep in human nature, or even if this way of acting were given in experience, to account for it sufficiently and unartificially. The problem is so difficult that for its solution, for humanity at large, one must everywhere take as help machinery from another world. Gods were indicated whose will and command were now the required ways of acting, and whose every command was reinforced through punishment and reward, either in this world or another to which we would go after death. Let us assume that belief in a doctrine of this sort takes root universally, as certainly is possible through incul- 202 cation at a very early age, and let us also assume something which is much more difficult and proves to be less verifiable in experience, that it would produce the intended effect. Then, indeed, legality of actions, even beyond the borders where courts and the police can reach, would be accomplished in this way, but everyone would feel that this in no way would be the same as what we actually under- stand by morality of disposition. For obviously all actions called forth by motives of *such a kind* always would be rooted simply in mere egoism. How could there be talk of disinterestedness when reward entices me or threat of punishment deters me? A firmly held belief in reward in another world is to be regarded as a promissory note which is completely secure, but payable at a very distant date. The ubiquitous promise of the satisfied beggar that the gift will be returned to the giver a thousandfold in the next world may move many a skinflint to generous alms-giving as a good investment, one he is pleased to dispense, firmly convinced that in the next world he will immediately rise again as an enormously rich man. — For the great masses of people, perhaps there must be the support of induce- ments of this sort: accordingly the various religions, which are just the metaphysics of the people, hold these out for them. With this, however, it is to be noted that we are sometimes just as much in error about the true motives of our own doings as we are about those of others. Hence many a reliable person, able to account to himself for his most noble actions only through motives mentioned above, nevertheless acts out of much nobler and purer incentives, but ones which are also much more difficult to make clear. So he actually acts out of immediate love of neighbour, but only knows how to explain his actions through the command of his god. In contrast, philoso- phy seeks here, as everywhere, the true, ultimate explanations for the problem at hand, grounded in the nature of the human being, independent of all mythical interpretations, religious dogmas, and transcendent hypotheses, and demands to see it demonstrated in outer or inner experience. The task at hand, however, is a philosophical one; hence, we have completely to disregard all solutions conditioned by religions, to which I have here called attention simply to

203 cast light on the great difficulty of the problem.

## § 15

### *Criterion of Actions of Moral Worth*

Now the first thing would be to settle the empirical questions of whether actions of voluntary justice and disinterested loving kindness, which may then rise to noble-mindedness and magnanimity, are to be found in experience. Unfortunately this question still does not admit of being decided absolutely empirically because the *deed* is always only given in experience, but the *impulses* are not obvious, so the possibility always remains that an egoistic motive had influence on a just or good action. In a theoretical investigation, I will not resort to the impermissible trick of shifting the matter onto the reader's conscience. But I believe that there will be very few who will doubt it and who do not from their own experience have the conviction that people often act justly, simply and only so that the other does not suffer a wrong; and indeed, that there are people in whom the principle is *innate* to give another his due, who therefore intentionally offend no one, who do not seek their own advantage unconditionally, but thereby also consider the rights of another, and who in undertaking mutual obligations are not simply vigilant that the other *contributes* what is his, but also *receives* what is his because they sincerely do not want those who deal with them to come up short. These are the *truly honourable people*, the few just[1] among the countless unjust.[2] But there are such people. Similarly, one will, I think, admit that many a person helps and gives, contributes and sacrifices, without having in his heart a further intention than that the other, whose need he sees, be helped. And that Arnold von Winkelried,* as he cried out: 'Comrades true and loyal, care for my wife and child,'[3] and embraced as many

---

[1] *Aequi.*    [2] *Iniqui.*
[3] '*Trüwen, lieben Eidgenossen, wullt's minem Wip und Kinde gedenken.*'

of the enemy spears as he could seize—therein had a self-interested intention; let him think so who can; I cannot do it.—In § 13 above, I have already called attention to cases of free justice, that are not 204 to be denied without chicanery and obstinacy.—But should anyone still insist upon denying me the existence of all such actions, then, according to him, morals would be a science without a real object, like astrology and alchemy, and it would be a waste of time further to dispute about its basis. With him, therefore, I am at an end, and I speak to those who will admit the reality of the matter.

Actions of the sort mentioned above are those alone to which genuine *moral worth* is attributed. As the special feature and characteristic of such actions, we find the exclusion of any sort of motives by which all human actions are otherwise called forth, namely the *self-interested* in the broadest sense of the word. Hence, even the discovery of a self-interested motive, if it is the only one, completely annuls the moral worth of an action, and when it operates as an accessory, diminishes it. The absence of all egoistical motivation is thus *the criterion for an action of moral worth.* Indeed there may be the objection that actions of pure malice and cruelty are also not self-interested; however, it is obvious that this cannot be meant, since they are actions opposite to those of which we speak. Whoever adheres to the definition strictly may expressly exclude all actions having as their essential characteristic that they aim at another's suffering.—It may be added that actions of moral worth leave with us, as a completely internal and therefore not so evident mark, a certain contentment that is called the approval of conscience; similarly actions opposed to these, actions of injustice and unkindness, and even more, actions of malice and cruelty, receive an opposing inner self-judgement; furthermore, as a secondary and accidental external mark, actions of the first sort call forth the approval and respect of impartial witnesses, and those of the second sort call forth the opposite.

We now have to observe actions of moral worth, established and given as factually existing, as a phenomenon that lies before us to be explained, and then we have to investigate *what it is* that can move 205 human beings to actions of this sort, which investigation, if we succeed, must necessarily bring to light the genuine moral incentive, and since on this incentive all ethics may be supported, our problem would be solved.

## § 16

*Statement and Proof of the Only Genuine Moral Incentive*

AFTER the previous, absolutely necessary preparations, I come to the proof of the true incentive that lies at the basis of all actions of genuine moral worth. This proof will result for us in such an incentive that by its seriousness and by its indubitable reality will be completely removed from all quibbles, sophistry, and sophisms, assertions snatched out of thin air, and *a priori* soap bubbles that the previous systems have tried to make the source of moral acting and the basis of ethics. Since I *propose* this moral incentive, not as something to be arbitrarily accepted, but as something I will actually *prove* to be the only one possible, and since this proof requires a combination of many thoughts, I put forth in advance some premises which are the presuppositions of the argument and indeed can be taken as *axioms*, except for the last two, which refer to the discussions provided above.

(1) No action can take place without a sufficient motive any more than a stone can move without a sufficient push or pull.

(2) No action can fail to take place when a sufficient motive for the character of the agent is present, unless a stronger counter-motive makes its omission necessary.

(3) What moves the will is simply well-being and woe in general and taken in the broadest sense of the word, just as conversely well-being and woe means 'in accord with or contrary to a will'. Thus, any 206 motive must have a reference to well-being and woe.

(4) Consequently any action refers to a being predisposed to well-being and woe, and has these as its ultimate end.

(5) This being is either the agent itself or another who then takes a passive role in the action since it is done to his detriment or to his advantage and benefit.

(6) Any action that has as its ultimate end the well-being and woe of the agent itself is an *egoistical* one.

(7) Everything said here about actions applies just as well to the omission of such actions, for which motive and counter-motive are present.

(8) As a result of the discussion given in the preceding sections, *egoism* and *the moral worth* of an action completely exclude one another.

If an action has an egoistic end as a motive, then it can have no moral worth; if an action should have moral worth, then its motive may not have an egoistic end, immediate or mediate, near or far.

(9) As a result of the elimination of the alleged duties to ourselves carried out in § 5, the moral significance of an action can only lie in its relation to others; only with respect to them can it have moral worth or reprehensibility, and consequently be an action of justice or loving kindness, as well as the opposite of the two.

———————

From these premises, the following is evident: the *well-being and woe*, which (according to premise (3)) must be the ultimate end lying at the basis of any action or omission, is either that of the agent himself or that of some other who takes a passive role in the action. In the *first case*, the action is necessarily *egoistic* because an interested motive lies at its basis. This is not merely the case with actions that one obviously undertakes for one's own advantage and benefit, which is most often so, but it occurs just as much when one expects from an action some sort of distant result *for oneself*, be it in this or another world, or when one has in view one's honour, one's reputation among people, anyone's esteem, the sympathy of witnesses, etc.; no less if one intends to uphold a maxim through the universal observance of which one potentially[1] expects a benefit *for oneself* such as one of justice or of universal, helpful support, etc.—likewise, when one considers it advisable to follow some absolute command that issues from an authority unknown, but apparently superior, since nothing other than *fear* of the detrimental consequences of *disobedience* can move us even if they are only thought of generally and vaguely;—the same is true if someone tries through some action or omission to maintain his own high opinion of himself, his clearly or unclearly conceived worth or dignity, which otherwise he would have to relinquish and thereby see his pride humbled;—and finally when one wants to work by Wolf[f]ian principles toward his own perfection. In short, whatever one wants to assert as the ultimate motivating ground for an action, the result will always be that, in a roundabout way, ultimately the *agent's own well-being and woe* is the actual incentive; hence, the

207

———————

[1] *eventualiter.*

action is *egoistic* and as a result is *without moral worth*. There is only a single case in which this does not take place: specifically when the ultimate motivating ground for an action or omission lies directly and exclusively in the *well-being and woe* of some *other person* who takes a passive role in it; thus, the one taking the active role in the action or omission has in view solely the well-being and woe of *another* and altogether intends nothing but that this other remain unharmed or even receive help, support, and relief. *This end alone* presses the stamp of *moral worth* on his action or omission, which thereafter exclusively depends on the action's occurring or not occurring simply for the advantage and benefit *of another*. That is, as soon as this is not the case, the *well-being and woe* which drives *any* action or restrains it can

208 only be that of the *agent himself*, but then the action or omission is always *egoistic* and, hence, *without moral worth*.

But now if my action should occur simply and solely *for another's sake*, then *his well-being and woe is immediately my motive*, just as *my own* is in all other actions. This expresses our problem narrowly, specifically as this: how is it possible that my will is immediately moved by *another's* well-being and woe, i.e., just as otherwise my will is only moved by my own well-being and woe, and thus, becomes my direct motive, and sometimes another's well-being and woe even becomes so to such a degree that I more or less disregard my own, which otherwise is the only source of my motives? — Obviously only through this: that another becomes *the ultimate end* of my will just as, otherwise, I am; and so through this: that I immediately will *his* well-being and do not will *his* woe, just as I otherwise immediately will only *that of my own*. This, however, necessarily presupposes that I suffer along with *his* woe, feel *his* woe, as otherwise I would only mine, and therefore, I immediately will his well-being as, otherwise, I would only my own. However, this requires that I *be identified with him* in some way, i.e., that the complete *distinction* between me and the other, upon precisely which my egoism rests, to a certain degree be suspended. Now, however, since I do not live *in another's skin*, it is only by means of the *cognition* that I have of him, i.e., the representation of him in my mind, that I identify with him so much that my deed proclaims the distinction to be suspended. However, the process analysed here is not one dreamed up or snatched out of thin air, but indeed quite real and in no way uncommon; it is the everyday phenomenon of *compassion*, i.e., the quite immediate *participation*, independent of considerations of any other sort, primarily in the *suffering* of another, and hence the prevention or removal of this suffering is that in which ultimately all satisfaction and all well-being and happiness consist. Only this compassion is the actual basis of all *free* justice and all *genuine* loving kindness. Only insofar as an action has originated from compassion does it have moral worth, and anything proceeding from any other motives has none. As soon as this compassion is aroused, the well-being and woe of another immediately lies in my heart, and in just the same way, if not always to the same degree, as otherwise only that of my own lies in my heart. Thus the distinction between him and me is now no longer absolute. 209

Certainly this process is astonishing, indeed, mysterious. In truth, it is the great mystery of ethics, its urphenomenon and the boundary-stone beyond which only metaphysical speculation can dare take a step. We see removed in this process the partition by which, in the light of nature (as the old theologians called reason), being became completely separated from being, and the Not-I to a certain extent becomes the I. However, we now want to leave untouched the metaphysical explanation of the phenomenon and first see whether all actions of free justice and genuine loving kindness actually result from this process. Then our problem will be solved, since we will have demonstrated the ultimate foundation of morality in human nature itself, which foundation can no longer be a problem for *ethics*, but, like every existing thing *as such*, for *metaphysics*. But a metaphysical explanation of the ethical urphenomenon already lies beyond the question posed by the Royal Society, which question is directed to the basis of ethics, and such an explanation, in any case, can only be appended as a supplement to be done optionally and to be considered optionally. — However, before I now turn from the fundamental incentive explained above to the derivation of the cardinal virtues, I still have two important remarks to add as supplementary.

(1) To aid easier comprehension I have simplified the derivation of compassion, given above as the only source of actions of moral worth, by intentionally not having attended to the incentive of *malice*, which, like compassion, is disinterested, but which makes another's *pain* its ultimate end. Now, however, including the same, we can resume the proof given above more completely and stringently.

210     In general, there are *three fundamental incentives*\* for human actions, and any possible motive works only through the stimulation of these incentives. They are:

(a) Egoism, which wills one's own well-being (is boundless).

(b) Malice, which wills another's woe (extends to the most extreme cruelty).

(c) Compassion, which wills the well-being of another (extends to noble-mindedness and magnanimity).

Every human action must trace back to one of these incentives, although two of these can also work in unity. Since we now have accepted actions of moral worth as factually given, then they must proceed from one of these fundamental incentives. However, according to premise 8, these actions cannot stem from the *first* incentive, and still less from the *second*, since all actions stemming from the second are morally reprehensible, while the first, in part, produces morally indifferent actions. Thus, these actions must proceed from the *third* incentive, and this will receive its verification *a posteriori* in what follows.

(2) Our immediate participation is limited to another's *suffering* and will not, at least not directly, be stimulated by his *well-being*; rather, in and of itself, this leaves us indifferent. Likewise, J. J. Rousseau says this in *Émile* (Book IV): 'First maxim: it is not in the human heart to put ourselves in the place of people who are more fortunate than ourselves, but only of those who are more pitiable,'[1] etc.

The reason for this is that pain, suffering, which includes all want, deprivation, need, indeed, every wish, is *that which is positive, which is immediately felt*. In contrast, the nature of satisfaction, of enjoyment, or pleasure, consists only in that a deprivation is ended, a pain is stilled. Thus these work *negatively*. Hence need or wish is even the condition of any pleasure. Plato\* already recognized this and exempted only good smells and the joys of the intellect (*Republic* IX, pp. 264 ff. Bip[ont]). Voltaire, too, says: 'There is no genuine pleasure without genuine need.'[1] Thus that which is *positive*, that which makes

211     itself known, is pain; satisfaction and pleasures are *negative*, the mere suspending of the former. On this it ultimately rests that only

---

[1] *Première maxime: il n'est pas dans le coeur humain, de se mettre à la place des gens, qui sont plus heureux que nous, mais seulement de ceux, qui sont plus à plaindre.*

suffering, want, peril, helplessness of others are direct and, as such, awaken our participation. One who is happy and content, *as such*, leaves us indifferent, because actually his condition is negative: the absence of pain, of want, and of need. Indeed, we can rejoice at others' happiness, well-being, pleasure: but then this is secondary and thoroughly mediated in that previously their suffering and deprivation saddened us; or, in contrast, we share another's happiness and pleasure, not *as such*, but insofar as he is our child, father, friend, relative, servant, subject, etc. But another's happiness and pleasure *purely as such* does not stimulate our immediate participation as does another's suffering, deprivation, unhappiness *purely as such*. Even *for ourselves*, only our suffering, which includes every want, need, wish, even boredom, actually stimulates our activity, while a state of satisfaction and happiness leaves us inactive and in idle rest. In view of this, how could it not be just the same with respect to others? since indeed, our participation depends on an identification with them. Even the sight of another's happiness and pleasure *purely as such* can readily stimulate our envy, for which the predisposition lies in every person and which has found its place among the anti-moral powers discussed above.

In consequence of the above presentation of compassion as a process of becoming motivated immediately by the suffering of another, I must still correct the often-repeated error of Cassina* (*Saggio analitico sulla compassione*, 1788; German by Pockels), who opines that compassion arises through an instantaneous deception of the fantasy because we place ourselves in the place of the sufferer, and now, in our imagination, we fancy that we suffer *his* pain in *our* person. It is in no way so; rather, it remains precisely clear and present to us at every moment that he is the one who suffers and not *we*, and it is precisely *in his* person, not in ours, that we feel suffering, to our sorrow. We suffer *with* him, thus, *in* him: we feel his pain as *his* and do not imagine that it is ours; indeed, the more happy our own circumstances, the more our consciousness contrasts its own happiness with the situation of the other, the more responsive we are for compassion. The explanation for the possibility of this highly significant phenomenon is not so simple that it can be attained in a

212

---

[1] *Il n'est de vrais plaisirs, qu'avec de vrais besoins* [*Précis de l'Ecclésiaste* (*Précis of Ecclesiastes*), line 30].

merely psychological way as Cassina attempted it. It can only be deduced metaphysically, and I shall attempt to give such an explanation in the last section.

Now, however, I turn to the derivation of actions of genuine moral worth from the demonstrated source of the same. As the universal maxim of such actions, and consequently, as the supreme principle of ethics, I have already put forth in the previous chapter the rule: 'Harm no one; rather, help everyone as much as you can.'[1] Since this maxim contains two clauses, the corresponding actions automatically fall into two classes.

## § 17
### *The Virtue of Justice*

ON closer observation of the process of compassion, demonstrated above to be the ethical urphenomenon, it is evident at first glance that there are two clearly separated degrees to which the suffering of another immediately becomes my motive, i.e., can determine me to do or not to do something: specifically, first only to the degree that, working against egoistic or malicious motives, it restrains me from causing another's suffering, from myself becoming the cause of another's pain, from giving rise to that which still does not exist; but second, to the higher degree, wherein compassion, working positively, impels me to help actively. The separation between the so-called duties of justice and virtue, more correctly between justice and loving kindness, which appeared in such a forced way in Kant, here yields the separation completely automatically and thus attests to the correctness of the principle: it is the natural, unmistakable, and sharp boundary between the negative and the positive, between not harming and helping. The denominations used up to now, duties of justice and duties of virtue, the latter called also duties of love or imperfect duties, first and foremost, erred in coordinating *genus* and *species*, since justice is also a virtue. Then the same error provides the basis for the much too broad extension of the concept of *duty* which I will trace back to its true limits below. So in place of the two duties given above, I therefore posit two virtues, that of justice and that of loving kindness, which I call cardinal virtues because from them, all

---

[1] *Neminem laede; imo omnes, quantum potes, juva.*

remaining virtues proceed practically and can be derived theoretically. Both are rooted in natural compassion. This compassion, however, is itself an undeniable fact of human consciousness, and is essential to it, resting not on presuppositions, concepts, religions, dogmas, myths, education, and cultivation; rather, it is original and immediate, lies in human nature itself, and for that very reason holds good in all circumstances and reveals itself in all countries and times; hence it is everywhere appealed to with confidence as something necessarily present in every human being, and it never belongs among the 'strange gods'. On the contrary, he who shows a deficiency of it is called inhuman, just as 'humanity' is often used as a synonym for compassion.

The first degree of the effectiveness of this genuine and natural moral incentive is thus only *negative*. Originally we are all inclined to injustice and violence because our need, our desire, our anger, and hate immediately enter into consciousness and, hence, have right of first occupancy;[1] in contrast, another's suffering caused by our injustice and violence thus enters consciousness merely in a secondary way through *representation* and only through experience, thus *mediately*. Therefore Seneca said: 'to no one does a good disposition come before a bad one' (*Ep.* 50).[2] Thus the first degree of the effect of compassion is that it steps before me, checking the inherent antimoral powers in me, as a result of which I cause others to suffer, calling to me 'stop!', and places itself around the other as a fortification that protects him from the harm to which otherwise my egoism or malice would drive me. In this way from the first degree of compassion arises the maxim 'harm no one';[3] i.e. the principle of *justice*, which virtue has in this first degree of compassion its only clear, 214 purely moral origin, free of all admixture, an origin it can never have apart from this because otherwise it would have to rest on egoism. If my temperament is responsive to this degree of compassion, then the same will restrain me wherever and whenever I would want to use another's suffering as means to achieve my ends, no matter whether this suffering be an instantaneous one, or occurring later, a direct one, or indirect, mediated through connecting links. Consequently, then, I will no more seize another's property than I will his person;

---

[1] *jus primi occupantis.*
[2] *ad neminem ante bona mens venit, quant mala* [Seneca, *Moral Letters* 50. 7].
[3] *neminem laede.*

I will no more cause him mental than bodily suffering; thus I will not only refrain from any physical injury, but no more cause him mental pain through insult, anguish, annoyance, or slander. The same compassion will restrain me when I seek the satisfaction of my lusts at the cost of a female individual's happiness in life, or to seduce another's wife, or even morally and physically to corrupt the youth by temptation to pederasty. However, it is in no way required that compassion actually be provoked in every single case, for it often would come too late; rather, from the knowledge achieved once and for all of the suffering which any unjust action necessarily brings to another, which is intensified by the feeling of the endurance of injustice, i.e., of another's superior power, in noble temperaments the maxim 'harm no one'[1] arises, and rational deliberation elevates it to the firm resolve, fixed once and for all, to respect the rights of anyone, not to allow oneself any infringement on these rights, to keep oneself free of self-reproach for being the cause of another's sufferings, and consequently not through violence or cunning to shift onto others the burdens and suffering of life to which circumstances could lead anyone, but oneself to bear one's allotted portion in order not to double that of another. For although *principles* and abstract cognition generally are in no way the fountainhead or the prime basis of morality, they are nevertheless indispensable for a moral course of life as the container, the *réservoir*, in which is stored the disposition which has sprung from the source of all morality, which disposition does not flow in every moment, but when the case for its application occurs, flows down through diversionary channels. Thus the same holds in the moral as in physiological, where, e.g., the gall-bladder is necessary as a *réservoir* for the products of the liver, and so in many similar cases. Without firmly held *principles* we should inevitably be vulnerable to anti-moral incentives when they are aroused to affects by external impressions. Steadfastness and adherence to principles, despite opposing motives working against them, is *self-control*. Here, too, lies the cause of why women, who because of the weakness of their reason, are far less capable than men of understanding universal principles, remaining steadfast, and adhering to rules of conduct, and as a rule are inferior to men in the virtue of justice, and thus also honesty and conscientiousness; therefore, injustice and deceit

215

---

[1] *neminem laede.*

are their most frequent vices and lies their real element; in contrast, they surpass men in the virtue of *loving kindness*, for the occasion for this is mostly *intuitive* and therefore speaks immediately to compassion to which women are decidedly more readily responsive. But only the intuitive, the present, the immediately real has true existence for them; that which is only knowable by means of concepts, the distant, the absent, the past, the future, is not readily grasped by them. Thus here, too, there is compensation: justice is more of a masculine, loving kindness more of a feminine virtue. To entertain the thought of women as occupying juridical office, arouses laughter, but the sisters of mercy readily surpass the brothers of mercy. However, now since the *animal* completely lacks abstract or rational cognition, it is not capable of any resolves, not to mention principles and, hence, *self-control*; rather, it is unarmed against impression and affect. For just this reason it has no conscious *morality*; however, species show great difference of malice and goodness of character, and among the highest genera, even individualities.—As a result of what has been said, in individual actions of the just, compassion works only indirectly by means of principles, and not so much actually[1] as potentially,[2] somewhat as in statics, the greater *velocity* produced by the greater length of the beam of a scale, by means of which a smaller mass holds a greater one in equilibrium, works at rest only poten- 216 tially, but just as if actually. However, compassion remains always ready actually to appear: hence, if sometimes in individual cases the chosen maxim of justice may perhaps stumble, then no motive (setting aside the egoistic ones) is more effective at supporting the maxim of justice and enlivening just resolves than that which is created out of the original source itself, compassion. This applies not merely when it concerns harm to persons, but also when it concerns property; e.g., if someone feels a desire to keep something of value that he found, then nothing—excluding all motives of prudence and religion against it—will so readily bring him back to the path of justice as the idea of the worry, of the heartbreak, of the woeful lamentation of the one who lost it. Recognizing this truth, it often happens that to the public appeal for the return of lost money will be added the assurance that the one who lost it is a poor man, a domestic servant, etc.

---

[1] *actu.*    [2] *potentiâ.*

It is to be hoped that these observations will make it clear that as little as it might appear at first glance, certainly justice, too, as a genuine free virtue, has its origin in compassion. Yet whoever believes this soil too barren to be one in which such a great, real cardinal virtue could be solely rooted, should recall from the above how small is the amount of genuine, voluntary, disinterested, and unvarnished justice that one finds among humans, how this always appears only as an astonishing exception, and how genuine justice bears the same relation of quality and quantity to its pretender, the sort of justice which rests on mere prudence and is everywhere loudly acclaimed, as gold bears to copper. I would like to call the latter 'common justice',[1] and the other 'heavenly',[2] since indeed she* is the one who, according to Hesiod, left the earth in the iron age to live with the heavenly gods. The demonstrated root is strong enough for this plant, which on earth is always rare and exotic.

Consequently, an *injustice* or a *wrong* always consists in an *injury* to another. Hence the concept of *wrong* is a *positive* one and precedes that of *right* as that which is *negative* and simply refers to actions that one can exercise without injuring others, i.e., without doing *wrong*. It is easy to see that all actions belong to this when they have the purpose of warding off an attempted wrong. For no participation in another's suffering, no compassion for him, can require of me, that I allow myself to be injured by him, i.e., to suffer wrong. That the concept of right is *negative* in contrast to *wrong*, as of the *positive*, is made known by the first explanation which the father of philosophical jurisprudence, Hugo Grotius,* presented about this concept in the preface to his work: 'Justice here signifies nothing but what is just, and indeed more in the negative sense than in the positive, insofar as justice is that which is not unjust'[3] (*On the Law of War and Peace*, Book I, chap. 1, § 3). The negativity of justice proves true, contrary to appearance, even in the trivial definition: 'Give to each his own.'* If it is his own, one need not give it to him: thus this means: 'Do not take from someone that which is his own.'—Because the demand for justice is simply negative, it can be compelled: for 'harm

---

[1] δικαιοσύνη πάνδημος.
[2] οὐρανία.
[3] *Jus hic nihil aliud, quam quod justum est significat, idque negante magis sensu, quam ajente, ut jus sit, quod injustum non est* (*De jure belli et pacis*, Book I, chap. 1, § 3).

no one'[1] can be practised by everyone at the same time. Here the institution that compels is the *state*, the only purpose of which is to protect individuals from one another and the whole from external enemies. Some German philosophasters of this mercenary age would like to twist it into an institution for education and edification in morality; in the background of this lurks the Jesuitical purpose of eliminating personal freedom and the individual's personal development in order to make him into a mere cog in a Chinese machine of state and religion. But this is the path by which in the past one has arrived at the inquisitions, burning of heretics,[2] and religious wars; Frederick the Great's pledge, 'In my country, each shall be able to tend to his salvation in his own fashion', indicated that he never wanted to tread that path. In contrast, nowadays we still everywhere see the state (with the more apparent than real exception of North America) also taking over the care for the metaphysical need of its citizens. Governments appear to have chosen as their principle the tenet of Quintus Curtius: 'Nothing is more effective at ruling the multitudes than superstition: otherwise unbridled, savage, fickle, as soon as they are captured by some delusion of religion, they rather obey their priests than their leaders.'[3]  218

The concepts of *wrong* and *right* as synonymous with injury and non-injury, to the latter of which also belongs warding off injury, are apparently independent of all positive legislation and are prior to these; thus, there is a pure ethical right, or a natural right, and a pure doctrine of right, i.e., one independent of all positive law. The principles of the same indeed have an empirical origin, insofar as they arise on the occasion of the concept of *injury*, but in themselves they rest on the pure understanding which provides the *a priori* principle, 'the cause of a cause is the cause of its effect',[4] which here indicates that regardless of whatever I must do in order to ward off another's injuring me, he himself is the cause, and not I; thus I can counter all encroachments from his side without doing him wrong. It is, as it were, a moral law of repercussion. Thus from the combination of the

---

[1] *neminem laede.*

[2] *autos-de-fé.*

[3] *Nulla res efficacius multitudinem regit, quam superstitio: alioquin impotens, saeva, mutabilis; ubi vana religione capta est, melius vatibus, quam ducibus suis paret* [Quintus Curtius Rufus, IV. 10. 7].

[4] *causa causae est causa effectus.*

empirical concept of injury with the rule which the pure understanding provides, arise the fundamental concepts of wrong and right, which everyone grasps *a priori* and immediately applies on the occasion of experience. For the dubious empiricist, since for him only experience is relevant, one may refer to savages who all quite correctly, often even precisely and exactly, distinguish wrong and right, which is quite apparent in their bartering and other transactions with the crews of European ships, and in their visits to them. They are emboldened and confident when they are right, and, in contrast, anxious when right is not on their side. In disputes they approve of a just settlement; whereas, unjust dealings provoke them to war. — The *doctrine of right* is a part of morals that determines the actions that one may not practise if one does not want to injure others, i.e., does not want to wrong others. Thus herein morals has the *active* part in view. But legislation turns this around, taking this chapter of morals to use it with concern for the *passive* role and considering the same actions as ones which no one need suffer since no wrong should befall him. Against these actions, the state now erects a bulwark of laws as positive right. Its intent is that no one *suffer* wrong: in contrast, the intention of moral doctrine of right is that no one *do* wrong.[1]

With any unjust action the wrong is of the same *quality*; that is, injury of another, whether it be a person, his freedom, his property, his honour. But the *quantity* can be very different. This difference of the *magnitude of the wrong* appears not yet to have been properly investigated by moralists; however, in actual life it is generally recognized because the magnitude of the censure which is issued is proportionate to the magnitude of the wrong. It is the same with the *justice* of actions. To explain this: e.g., one who, dying of hunger, steals bread, commits a wrong: but how small is his injustice compared to that of a rich person who in some way makes off with a poor person's last possession. The rich person who pays his day-labourer acts justly: but how small is this justice compared to that of a poor person who voluntarily returns a purse to the rich fellow who lost it. But the measure of this so significant difference in the *quantity* of justice and injustice (given the same quality) is no direct and absolute one as the one on a scale; rather, it is a mediated and relative one, like

---

[1] One may find a detailed doctrine of right in *The World as Will and Representation*, vol. I, § 62. [Schopenhauer's note.]

that of sine and tangents. Therefore, I propose the following formula: the magnitude of the injustice of my action is equal to the magnitude of the evil which I inflict on another, divided by the magnitude of the advantage which I thereby achieve—and the magnitude of the justice of my action is equal to the magnitude of the advantage which the injury of another would have brought me, divided by the magnitude of the detriment which he thereby would have suffered.—But besides, now there is a *double injustice* that is specifically distinct from any simple one, however great, made manifest through the magnitude of the uninvolved witness's indignation, which is always in proportion to the magnitude of the injustice, and which reaches the highest degree only in the case of the double injustice that is detested as something so revolting and so atrocious, as an outrage, an abomination[1] at which the gods, as it were, cover their faces. This *double injustice* takes place when someone has expressly assumed the obligation to protect another in a certain way: his failure to fulfil this obligation would lead subsequently to the other's injury and, hence, to a wrong; yet a double injustice would lie in his going beyond this wrong by himself attacking and injuring the other in just the way he should have protected the other. Such is the case, e.g., when an appointed guard or escort turns into a murderer, a trusted custodian turns into a thief, the trustee cheats the ward of her property, the advocate prevaricates, the judge takes a bribe, the one of whom advice is asked deliberately imparts ruinous advice to the asker—all of which may be subsumed under the concept of *treachery*, which is abhorred everywhere. For this reason, even Dante put traitors in the lowest circle of hell where Satan himself also dwells (*Inferno*, XI. 61–6).

Since now the concept of *obligation* has come up here, it is the place to determine the concept of *duty* which is so frequently applied in ethics as in life, but to which too great an extension is given. We have found that wrong always consists in the injury of another, be it to his person, his freedom, his property, or his honour. From this it appears to follow that any wrong must be a positive attack, a deed. But there are actions the mere *omission* of which is a wrong: such actions are called *duties*. This is the true philosophical definition of the concept of a *duty*, which, in contrast, loses all specificity and thereby gets lost if one as in previous morals wants to call any praiseworthy way

220

---

[1] ἄγος.

of acting a *duty* whereby one forgets that what is a *duty* must also be *indebtedness*. A duty, τοδέον, *le devoir, die Pflicht, is thus an action through the mere omission of which one injures another, i.e., commits a wrong.* Obviously this can only be the case if the one omitting to do so had pledged to do so, had specifically *pledged* to do so. For that reason all duties rest on an agreed-to obligation. As a rule, this is an explicit, mutual agreement, as, e.g., between a prince and his people, government and civil servants, master and servant, advocate and client, doctor and patients, generally between anyone who had undertaken some sort of task and his customer in the broadest sense of the word. Therefore every duty confers a right because no one can obligate oneself without a motive, i.e., without some personal advantage. I know of only *one* obligation which is *not* taken on by means of an agreement, but immediately through mere action, because those to whom one has this obligation were not present when it was undertaken: it is the obligation of parents to their children. Whoever brings a child into the world has the *duty* to support it until it is capable of supporting itself, and should this time *never* occur, as in the case of the blind, cripples, cretins, etc., the duty never ends. For by the mere failure to provide help, thus by an omission, he would injure his child, indeed, lead to its demise. The moral duty of children to their parents is not quite so immediate and definite. Since it depends on every duty's conferring a right, parents, too, must have a right in relation to their children, which in this case is grounded in the duty to obey; later, however, this duty also ceases, along with the right with which it had originated. What takes its place is gratitude for that which parents have done beyond that which was strictly their duty. However, even though ingratitude is odious, often even a disgraceful vice, gratitude is not to be called a *duty* because its absence is no injury to another, and, thus, is no *wrong.* Moreover, the benefactor must have presumed that he had tacitly settled a bargain.—In any case one could regard reparation for harm done as an obligation immediately arising through an action. Indeed, as a counterbalance to the consequences of an unjust action, this is merely an attempt to erase it, something purely negative resting on that fact that the action itself should not even have occurred.—Still it is to be remarked here that equity is the enemy of justice and is often grossly confused with it; thus, one should not concede too much to it. The German is a friend of equity; the British side with justice.

The law of motivation is just as strict as that of physical causality and thus carries with it a compulsion which is just as irresistible. Accordingly, there are two ways of practising wrong: that of *force* and that of *cunning*. Just as by force I can kill another, or rob him, or compel him to obey me, so I can also carry out all this through cunning by holding up false motives to his intellect, as a result of which he must do what he would otherwise not have done. This occurs by means of the *lie*, the reprehensibility of which rests solely on, and thus attaches to, its being a tool of cunning, i.e., of compulsion by means of motivation. However, this is so only as a rule. For first my lies themselves occur not without a motive, but this motive will, with rare exceptions, be an unjust one, specifically the intention to direct according to my will others over whom I have no power, i.e., to compel them by means of motivation. This intention even lies at the basis of a mere braggartly lie because whoever uses it seeks by this means to put himself in higher esteem than is his due. — The binding quality of a *promise* and of a *contract* rests on that fact that if not fulfilled, they are the most solemn lie, the intent of which is to exercise moral compulsion over others as is all the more evident here since the motive for the lies, the performance demanded of the other party, is expressly indicated. Fraud is of a contemptible nature because by double-dealing it disarms its man before it attacks him. *Treachery* is the pinnacle of fraud and is deeply abhorred because it belongs to the category of *double injustice*. But without wrong, thus with right, just as I can repel force with force, so when I lack the power or when it seems more convenient, I can repel force with cunning. Thus in those cases in which I have a right to use force, I also have the right *to lie*, as, e.g., to robbers and outlaws of any sort whom I thereby entrap through cunning. Therefore a promise compelled by force is not binding. — But *the right to lie* in fact extends even further: it applies in the case of any completely unwarranted question concerning my personal or business affairs, hence, one which is prying, when in answering even the mere retort, 'I do not want to say it', would endanger me by awakening suspicion. Here a lie is self-defence against unwarranted curiosity, the motive for which is usually not benevolent. For, just as I have the right beforehand to set up physical resistance against the assumed ill-will of others and, hence, their presumed physical force, even at the risk of the trespassers, and thus, as a preventive measure, to protect my garden wall with sharp spikes and at night let vicious hounds loose in my courtyard, indeed, depending on the circumstances, even to set man-traps and trip-guns, for the bad consequences of which the intruder has no one to blame but himself, so I also have the right to keep secret by all means anything which, if known, would expose me to others' attack, and I also have cause for this, because in this case, too, I assume others' ill-will to be quite possible and must take precautionary measures against it. Thus Ariosto said:

As much as pretence is censured and evidences bad intent, nonetheless, it has in very many things apparently brought about good while it prevented harm, disgrace, and death: for we do not always speak with friends in this much more gloomy than cheerful, mortal life which teems with envy. (*Orl*[*lando*]. *fur*[*ioso*]., IV. 1)[1]

Thus I may, without wrong, even beforehand, cunningly oppose a merely presumed encroachment through cunning, and, therefore, I need not give an account to anyone who unwarrantedly pries into my private relations, nor with the answer, 'This I will keep secret',
224  show the place where a secret lies which would be dangerous to me and perhaps advantageous to him, but in any case grants him power over me:

They want to know the secrets of the house, and thence to be feared.[2]

Rather, I am then authorized to dismiss him with a lie at his peril, even if it places him in detrimental error. For here the lie is the only means to counter prying and suspicious curiosity; for this reason I am in a situation of self-defence. 'Ask me no question, and I'll tell you no lies,'* is the correct maxim here. That is to say, the British, for whom the reproach of lying serves as the gravest insult and who for just that reason actually lie less than other nations, consider all unwarranted questions concerning relationships of others to be an impertinence to which the expression 'to ask questions' refers. — Also any prudent

---

[1]  *Quantunque il simular sia le più volte*
*Ripreso, e dia di mala mente indici,*
*Si trova pure in molte cose e molte*
*Avere fatti evidenti benefici,*
*E danni e biasmi e morti avere tolte:*
*Che non conversiam' sempre con gli amici,*
*In questa assai più oscura che serena*
*Vita mortal, tutta d'invidia piena.*
[Schopenhauer provides a German translation rendered in English above.]

[2]  *Scire volunt secreta domus, atque inde timeri.* [Juvenal, *Satires* III. 113].

person acts according to the principle given above, even if he is of the strictest rectitude; e.g., he returns from a distant place where he had raised some money, and an unknown traveller, accompanying him, asks, as usual, first *whereto* and then *wherefrom*, and by and by, what might have taken him to that place—so anyone would answer with a lie in order to prevent the danger of robbery. If a man is encountered in another's house, courting the daughter, and is asked about the reason for his unexpected presence, unless he is a fool, he will without reflection answer falsely. And so many instances occur in which any reasonable person would lie without any scruple of conscience. This view alone removes the glaring contradiction between morals as taught and morals as they are practised every day, even by the most honest and best. However, for this reason, the restriction, stated above, to cases of self-defence must be strictly observed since otherwise this doctrine would often be horribly abused, for in itself a lie is a very dangerous tool. But in spite of public peace, just as the law allows anyone to carry a weapon and to use it, specifically in the case of self-defence, so morals provide for the use of a lie in the same case, but *only* in this case. With the exception of cases of self-defence 225 against power or cunning, any lie is a tool for wrong; for this reason justice demands truthfulness to everyone. But against the lie's being in its very essence completely unconditional and reprehensible without exception, it may be said that there are cases in which it is even a *duty* to lie, especially for doctors; similarly, there are *magnanimous* lies, e.g., that of the Marquis Posa in *Don Carlos* or that in the *Gerusalemme liberata*, II. 22;* and generally in all cases in which someone wants to bear another's guilt; finally, even that of Jesus Christ, who once intentionally had said an untruth (John 7: 8). Accordingly, in his *Philosophical Poetry*, madr. 9, Campanella said exactly: 'It is fine to lie if it results in great good.'[1] But then the current doctrine of the white lie is a miserable patch on the garments of a shabby morals. At Kant's suggestion,* many compendia derive the unlawfulness of a lie from the human *capacity of speech*; these derivations are so inane, childish, and insipid, that, if only to ridicule them, one might seek to embrace the devil and say with Talleyrand: 'humans have received

---

[1] *Bello è il mentir, se a fare gran ben' si trova.* [From a madrigal by Tommaso Campanella (1568–1639) 'Delia bellezza. segnal del bene, oggetto d'amore'; in a footnote Schopenhauer translates line 149 into German from the 1834 edition published in Lugano by G. Ruggia.]

speech in order to conceal their thoughts.'[1]—Kant's unconditional and boundless abhorrence of lying, which he displays at every opportunity, rests either on affectation or on prejudice: in the chapter in his *Doctrine of Virtue*, 'Concerning Lying', he indeed inveighs against lying in all slanderous terms, but he does not even adduce an actual basis for their reprehensibility, which would have been still more effective. Declaiming is easier than proving, and moralizing is easier than being upright. Kant would have done better to let that special zeal loose against *Schadenfreude*: this, not lying, is the real devilish vice. For it is quite opposite to compassion and is nothing other than impotent cruelty which so gladly sees another suffering that which it 226 is incapable of bringing about itself, and it thanks chance for doing so in its place.—According to the principle of knightly honour, a reproach of lying is to be taken as so very grave that it actually must be washed out with the blood of the accuser. This is not based in a lie's being *wrong*, for then the accusation of a wrongdoing through force would be just as insulting, which obviously is not the case. Rather, according to the principle of knightly honour, right is actually based on might. Now whoever resorts to lies in order to carry out a wrong proves that he lacks the might or the necessary courage to use force. Every lie evidences fear: that condemns him.

## § 18

### *The Virtue of Loving Kindness*

THUS justice is the first and fundamentally essential cardinal virtue. Ancient philosophers, too, have also recognized it as such, although they coordinated it with three others selected unsuitably.* In contrast, they had not yet put forth loving kindness, *caritas*, ἀγάπη, as a virtue: even Plato, who in morals rises to the greatest heights, nevertheless gets only as far as voluntary, disinterested justice. Indeed, in practice and in fact, at all times loving kindness has existed, but the greatest service of Christianity consists in its first speaking of this virtue theoretically and formally, even advancing it as the greatest of all virtues and extending it even to enemies; however, this refers only

---

[1] *l'homme a reçu la parole pour pouvoir cacher sa pensée* [Charles Maurice de Talleyrand-Périgord (1754–1838), *Mémoires* (Paris, 1842), IV. 447; letter of Talleyrand to the Spanish diplomat Izquierdo].

to Europe, since in Asia for a thousand years boundless love of neighbour had already been as much a topic of teaching and precept as it had been in practice because the *Veda*, and *Dharmaśāstra*, *Itihāsa*, and *Purāna*,* and in his teaching, too, the Buddha Shakia-Muni never tired of preaching it. — And if we want to take it strictly, then in the ancients we can also find traces of the recommendation of loving kindness; e.g., in Cicero, *On Moral Ends* V. 23;[1] even already in Pythagoras, according to Iamblichus, *On the Life of Pythagoras* chap. 33.[2] Now it is incumbent upon me to provide the philosophical derivation of this virtue from my principle.

Above, I have factually demonstrated and indicated the origin of the mysterious process of *compassion*, by means of which another's suffering in itself and as such immediately becomes my motive. The second degree clearly differentiates itself from the first degree by the *positive character* of the actions arising from it, since compassion does not just restrain me from injuring another, but even impels me to help him. Now depending partly on how lively and deeply felt is this immediate participation and partly on how great and urgent is the other's distress, I will be moved by this purely moral motive to make for another's need or distress a greater or lesser sacrifice than could consist in the exertion of my physical or intellectual powers for him, or in the loss of my property, my health, freedom, even my life. Thus here in immediate participation, neither supported by nor requiring argumentation, lies the only clear origin of loving kindness, of *caritas*, ἀγάπη, that is, the same virtue for which the maxim is 'help everyone as much as you can'[3] and from which everything follows which ethics prescribes under the terms duties of virtue, duties of love, imperfect duties. This completely immediate, indeed, instinctive participation in another's suffering, that is, compassion, is the only source of such actions if they *have moral worth*, i.e., if they are free of all egoistical motives. For this very reason they should awaken in ourselves that inner contentment which is called good, satisfied, approving conscience, and they should call forth in the witness a characteristic assent, esteem, admiration, even a humbling reflection on himself, which is a fact not to be denied. If, in contrast, a benevolent action has some other sort of motive, then it can be nothing other than egoistical, if it

---

[1] *De finib[us]*.  [2] [Iamblichos, fl. 330 CE], *De vita Pythagorae*.
[3] *omnes, quantum potes, juva.*

is not downright malicious. For, as put forth above, corresponding to the primary incentives for all actions, namely egoism, malice, compassion, *motives* that can generally move humans can be brought under three rather universal and principal classes: (1) one's own well-being, (2) another's woe, (3) another's well-being. Now if the motive of a benevolent action is not of the *third* class, it simply must belong to the *first* or *second*. The *second* is sometimes actually the case: e.g., if I benefit one in order to offend another whom I do not benefit; or to make another's suffering all the more palpable to him; or also to shame a third who would not have benefited the other; or, finally, thereby to humble the one whom I benefit. The *first*, however, is more frequently the case, that is, whenever, in doing a good deed I have in view *my own well-being*, be it ever so distant or indirect, as when I act with concern for reward in this or in another world; or to achieve high esteem and the reputation of having a noble heart; or out of the conviction that he whom I help will at some time help me or could even be of use or service to me; finally even if I am urged on by the thought that the maxims of generosity or of charity must be strictly maintained since they could at some time also bring me good; in short, whenever my purpose is simply something other than a purely *objective* one by which I want to know that another is helped, is rescued from his distress and oppression, that he is freed of his suffering: and nothing but this and only this! Then and only then have I truly shown the loving kindness, *caritas*, ἀγάπη, the preaching of which is the great, distinguishing merit of Christianity. But just the instructions which the gospel adds to its behest to love, such as 'let not your left hand know, what your right hand does',[1] and the like, are grounded in the feeling of that which I have deduced here; namely, that only another's distress and no other consideration must be my motive if my action is to have moral worth. In the same place (Matthew 6: 2) it is correctly said that those who give with ostentation already have their reward therein. But even regarding this the *Vedas* impart to us, as it were, a higher dedication, in that they repeatedly assure us that he who desires some sort of reward for his work is still clinging to the way of darkness and will not be ripe for salvation. — If someone, in giving alms, were to ask me what he thereby gains, my

228

---

[1] μὴ γνώτω ἡ ἀριστερά σου, τί ποεί ἡ δεξιά σου (*sinistra tua manus haud cognoscat, quae dextra facit*) [Matthew 6: 3].

answer in good conscience would be: 'This, that a poor person's lot 229 will be just that much easier; apart from this absolutely nothing. Now if this serves no purpose for you and it actually does not matter to you, then you really have not wanted to give alms, but to make a bargain: so you are defrauded of your money. If, however, it does matter to you that someone oppressed by want suffer less, then you have just accomplished your purpose in that he suffers less, and you see exactly how much your gift is rewarded.'

But now how is it possible for a suffering that is not *mine* and that does not touch *me* to become for me a motive which could just as immediately move me to act as could my own suffering? As has been said, this is so only by the fact that although this suffering is given to me only as something external, merely by means of external intuition or cognizance, I nonetheless *experience it with him*, I *feel it as mine*, and not *in myself*, but *in another*, and thus there occurs what Calderón* has already expressed:

> that between seeing suffering and suffering there is no difference.
> 'The Worst Is Not Always Certain', Act II, [Scene 9][1]

This, however, presupposes that I have identified with the other to a certain extent, and as a result for the moment the barrier between I and Not-I has been suspended: only then will there be the opportunity immediately to take on as my own another's need, his distress, his suffering; then I no longer perceive him as he is given in empirical intuition, as completely distinct from me, as a stranger about whom I am indifferent; rather, I suffer *in him* even though his skin does not enclose my nerves. Only through this can *his* woe, *his* distress, become a motive *for me*; otherwise, it can only be my own. *This process* is, and I repeat it, *mysterious*: for it is something for which reason can give no immediate account, the grounds of which are not to be ascertained by the way of experience. And yet it is an everyday occurrence. Everyone has often experienced it himself; it has not remained foreign to even the most hard-hearted and selfish. It occurs daily before our 230 eyes in single acts on a small scale, generally when from immediate impulse without much reflection, one person helps another and

---

[1]      *que entre el ver*
*Padecer y el padecer*
*Ninguna distancia habia.*
'*No siempre el peor es cierto*', *Jorn.* II, p. 229

hastens to another's aid, indeed, sometimes even puts his life in the most obvious danger for one whom he has seen for the first time without thinking any more about it than just that he sees another's great distress and danger. It occurs on a large scale when, upon longer reflection and more intense debate, the high-minded British nation gave 20 million pounds sterling to purchase the freedom of Negro slaves in its colonies, to the approving jubilation of the whole world. Whoever wants to deny compassion as the incentive for this fine, large-scale action in order to ascribe it to Christianity, should recall that in the whole New Testament not one word is said against slavery, for the practice was universal at that time, too, and even in 1860 in North America, in debates over slavery, one man had taken as precedent that Abraham and Jacob also had kept slaves.

Now what in any particular case would be the practical results of this mysterious inner process, ethics might discuss in chapters and paragraphs on duties of virtue, or duties of love, or imperfect duties, or whatever else. The root, the basis of all this is what has been presented here, from which the principle arises: 'Help everyone as much as you can;'[1] and from this all that remains is quite simple to accomplish, just as from the first half of my principle, that is, from the 'harm no one',[2] all duties of justice arise. Ethics is in truth the simplest of all sciences, as is only to be expected, since everyone has the obligation to construct it for himself and even to derive the rule for any case that presents itself from the supreme principle which is rooted in his heart. For few have the free time and patience to learn a ready-made ethics. All virtues follow from justice and loving kindness; hence, these are the cardinal virtues upon the derivation of which the cornerstone of ethics is laid down. — Justice is the whole ethical content of the Old Testament, and loving kindness is that of the New: this is the 'new commandment'[3] (John 13: 34) in which, according to Paul (Romans 13: 8–10), all Christian virtues are contained.

# § 19

## *Confirmations of the Foundation of Morals as Presented*

THE truth now expressed, that compassion as the sole non-egoistic incentive, is also the only genuine moral incentive, is strangely, indeed,

---

[1] *omnes, quantum potes, juva.*     [2] *neminem laede.*     [3] καινὴ ἐντολή.

almost incomprehensibly, paradoxical. I will thus try to make it less strange to the convictions of the reader by demonstrating it to be confirmed through experience and the testimony of universal human feeling.

(1) To this end I will first take as an example an imaginary case which can serve in this investigation as a crucial test.[1] But in order not to make the matter too easy, I do not choose a case of loving kindness, rather a violation of a right and indeed, the gravest of violations.—— Suppose that there are two young people, Caius and Titus, both passionately in love, though each with a different girl. And because of external circumstances, a more highly favoured rival stands in the way of each one. Both have decided to dispose of their respective rivals, and both are completely secure from any detection, even from any suspicion. However, as each more closely contemplates his own plan for murder, after an inward struggle, each gives it up. Now suppose they are to give us an honest and clear account of the grounds of their giving up their decisions.—— Now the account which Caius gives may be put entirely at the choice of the reader. He might have been restrained on religious grounds, such as the will of God, retribution in the days to come, future judgement, etc. Or instead, he might say: 'I considered that in this case the maxim for my conduct would not have been suitable to provide a universally valid rule for all possible rational beings, since I would indeed have been treating my rival only as a means and at the same time not as an end.'——Or he might say with Fichte: 'Every human life is a means for the realization of the moral law; thus without being indifferent to the realization of the moral law, I cannot annihilate someone who is determined to contribute to the same' (*System of Moral Philosophy*, p. 373).——(Incidentally, he could overcome this scruple by hoping that when he comes into possession of his beloved, he could soon produce a new instrument of the moral law.)——Or he might say, following Wollastone:* 'I have determined that this action would be the expression of an untrue proposition.'——Or he might say, following Hutcheson:* 'the moral sense, the feelings of which, as with those of any other sense, are incapable of further explanation, had determined me not to do it.' Or he might have said, following Adam Smith:* 'I foresaw that my action would have aroused absolutely no sympathy for me among

232

---

[1] *experimentum crucis.*

the witnesses.' Or, after Christian Wolf[f]: 'I recognize that I thereby work against my own perfection and would also promote no other.'—Or he might say, following Spinoza: 'To the human, nothing is more useful than a human: therefore, I did not want to kill a human.'[1] In brief, he might say whatever one wants. But Titus, whose account I reserve for myself, might say: 'As it came to the arrangements, and therefore, for a moment, I had to concern myself not with my passion but with my rival, then for the first time what became quite clear was what would really happen to him. But now compassion and mercy seized me: I felt sorry for him; I did not have the heart for it; I could not do it.'—Now I ask any honest and unbiased reader: which of the two is the better person?—In the hands of which of the two would you prefer to place your fate?—Which of them has been restrained by pure motive?—Therefore, where does the foundation of morals lie?

(2) Nothing so shakes the deepest ground of our moral feeling as cruelty. We can pardon any other crime, only not cruelty. The reason for this is that cruelty is the exact opposite of compassion. If we received report of a very cruel deed, as, e.g., is that which the papers have just reported about a mother who had murdered her 5-year-old boy by pouring boiling oil down his throat and her younger child by burying it alive—or that which has just been reported from Algiers, that after a chance quarrel and struggle between a Spaniard and an Algerian, the Algerian, as the stronger one, completely ripped out the lower jawbone of the Spaniard and carried it off as a trophy, leaving the other still alive—then we are gripped by horror and cry out: 'How is it possible to do such a thing?'—What is the sense of this question? Is it, perhaps: How is it possible to so little fear punishment in a future life?—Hardly.—Or: How is it possible to act according to a maxim that is absolutely unsuitable to become a universal law for all rational beings?—Certainly not.—Or: How is it possible to so thoroughly neglect his own and the other's perfection?—Just as unlikely.—The sense of this question is quite certainly just this: How is it possible to be so completely without compassion?—Thus it is the greatest lack of compassion which impresses on a deed the stamp of the most profound moral reprehensibility and repulsiveness. Consequently, compassion is the real moral incentive.

---

[1] *homini nihil utilius homine: ergo hominem interimere nolui* [*Ethics*, IV, prop. 8 scholium].

(3) In general the basis of morals and incentive for morality which I have advanced is the only one that can be credited with real and extensive effectiveness. Of the remaining moral principles of the philosophers, almost no one would want to assert this, since these principles consist of abstract, sometimes hair-splitting propositions without any other foundation than an artificial combination of concepts so that even their application to a real action often would have a ridiculous aspect. A good deed accomplished simply with regard for the Kantian moral principle would fundamentally be the work of a philosophical pedantry or, instead, lead to a self-deception through which the agent's reason would interpret a deed, which would have had other, perhaps nobler incentives, as the product of the categorical imperative and a concept of duty that is unsupported. However, a definite effectiveness of *philosophical* moral principles accounted for by mere theories or even of *religious* moral principles laid down solely for a practical purpose can rarely be demonstrated. We see this first in that, despite the great differences among the world's religions, the degree of morality, or, perhaps, immorality, shows absolutely no corresponding difference; rather, in essence, it is generally about the same. Only one must not confuse coarseness and refinement with morality and immorality. The Greeks' religion had an extremely slight moral tendency, almost confined to the oath; no dogmas were taught and no morals were publicly preached. But we do not see because of this, all things considered, that the Greeks had been morally worse than the peoples of the Christian era. Christian morals are of a much loftier sort than those of all the other religions that have ever appeared in Europe, but anyone who for that reason would want to believe that European morality had even improved itself proportionally and now, at least, excels among current systems of morality, would soon be convinced that among Muhammadans, Guebres,* Hindus, and Buddhists there can at least be found just as much honesty, fidelity, tolerance, gentleness, benevolence, generosity, and self-denial as among Christian folk; rather, the long list of human cruelties which have accompanied Christianity, of its countless religious wars, its irresponsible crusades, of its extermination of most of the original inhabitants of the Americas and the populating of this part of the world with Negro slaves[1] dragged out of Africa, without right, without the semblance of right, torn from their families, their homeland, their part of the world, and condemned to a

life-sentence of servitude, of its tireless persecution of heretics and
outrageous Courts of the Inquisition, of its St Bartholomew's Night
Massacre, of its execution by the Duke of Alba* of 18,000 people in
the Netherlands, etc., etc.—would all the sooner assure a renuncia-
tion of the malignity of Christianity. But generally if one compares
the excellent morals which the Christian, and more or less any religion, preaches, with the practice of its adherents, and imagines what
this would come to if the secular arm did not hinder crimes, indeed,
what we would have to fear if all laws were suspended for just a day,
then one must recognize that the effect of all religions on morality
is actually very slight. Of course, weakness of faith is to blame for
this. Theoretically, and as long as it remains a matter of pious observation, everyone's faith seems firm to himself. But the deed is the
hard touchstone of all our convictions: if it comes to this test and
now faith were to be tried through great renunciations and severe
sacrifices, then the weakness of faith will be revealed. If a person seriously contemplates a crime, then he has already broken through the
barrier of genuine, pure morality. Then, however, the first thing that
restrains him is always the thought of the courts and the police. If he
dismisses this thought in the hope of getting away with it, then the
second barrier that opposes him is concern for his honour. But now
if he gets over this fence, then after overcoming these two powerful impediments, the odds are against some sort of religious dogma's
having sufficient power over him to restrain him from the deed.
For he whom near and certain dangers do not deter, distant ones,
resting merely on faith, will hardly keep in check. Moreover, it can be
objected that this good action, which proceeds completely from religious convictions, has not been disinterested, but has occurred with
a view to reward or punishment and, consequently, has no purely
moral worth. We find this view starkly expressed in a letter of the
famous Grand Duke of Weimar, Karl August, where it says: 'Baron
Weyhers himself found that one must be a bad fellow who is inclined
by religion, and not by nature, to do good. *In vino veritas*' (*Letters to
J. H. Merck*, Letter 229).—Now in contrast, note the moral incentive
I have advanced. Who for a moment would dare to deny that in both

---

[1] According to Buxton, *The African Slavetrade* (1839), even now their number is
*annually* increased by approximately 150,000 fresh Africans, in the capture and transport
of whom over 200,000 others perish miserably. [Schopenhauer's note].

great and small ways, every day and every hour, it expresses a decisive and truly wondrous effectiveness in all ages, among all peoples,
in all of life's situations, even in conditions of lawlessness, even in the
midst of the horrors of revolution and war; who would dare to deny
that it daily hinders much injustice, even often quite unexpectedly
calls into being many good deeds without any hope of reward; and
who would dare to deny that wherever it and only it has been solely
effective, with feeling and esteem we all unconditionally attribute to
the deed genuine moral worth?

(4) For boundless compassion for all living beings is the firmest and
most certain guarantee of moral good conduct and requires no casuistry. Whoever is filled with it will certainly injure no one, infringe on
no one, do no one harm, rather, forbear everyone, forgive everyone,
help everyone as much as he can, and all his actions will carry the
imprint of justice and loving kindness. In contrast, if one were once
to try to say: 'This person is virtuous, but knows no compassion;' or:
'There is an unjust and malicious person; however, he is very compassionate;' then the contradiction is palpable.—Tastes differ, but
I know of no finer prayer than that with which ancient Indian drama
ended (as in earlier times the English dramas ended with a prayer for
the king). It goes: 'May all living beings remain free of pain.'

(5) From particular instances, too, it can be inferred that the true
fundamental moral incentive is compassion. It is, e.g., equally unjust
to cheat a rich person as it is to cheat a poor one out of a hundred
Taler through legal devices which otherwise pose no risk, but in the
second case, the reproach of conscience and rebuke of uninvolved
witnesses will turn out to be much louder and more severe; hence
Aristotle already says 'it is more terrible to do injustice to one who is
unfortunate than to one who is fortunate' (*Probl[ems]* XXIX. 2).[1] In
contrast, the reproaches will be still milder than in the first instance
if advantage has been taken of the state treasury, for this cannot be
an object of compassion. One can see that the material for one's own
and others' rebuke is not given immediately in the violation of the
law, but in the suffering brought on another. Of course, mere violation of the law as such, e.g., that against the state treasury mentioned
above, will also be objected to by conscience and by others, but only

[1] δεινότερον δέ ἐστι τὸν ἀτυχοῦντα, ἢ τὸν εὐτυχοῦντα, ἀδικεῖν (*iniquius autem est, injuriam homini infortunato, quam fortunato, intulisse*) [950b 3].

insofar as the maxim of respecting *any* law, which makes for a truly honourable man, is thereby broken, and, so, indirectly and to a lesser degree. Indeed, were it a state treasury *in trust*, then the case is quite different because the concept of *double injustice* applies here, with its specific characteristics as established above. On this analysis here rests the fact that greedy extortionists and legal scoundrels are generally most severely rebuked for having snatched away the goods of widows and orphans, precisely because these, who are completely helpless, even more so than others, should have awakened compassion. Thus it is the complete lack of compassion which convicts a person of wickedness.

(6) Even more apparently than justice, compassion lies at the basis of loving kindness. No one will receive demonstrations of genuine loving kindness from others so long as things go well for him in every respect. Of course, the fortunate one can in many ways experience the good wishes of his relatives and friends, but expressions of any pure, selfless, objective participation in another's condition and fortune, which are the effect of loving kindness, are reserved for one who is in some respect suffering. For we do not sympathize with the fortunate one *as such*; rather, he remains *as such* a stranger to our hearts: 'let him have what is his.'[1] In fact, if he has many advantages over others, he will easily arouse envy, which at his first fall from the heights of good fortune threatens to turn into *Schadenfreude*. However, this threat most often remains unfulfilled and does not come to be the Sopho-clean 'his enemies laugh derisively'.[2] For as soon as the fortunate one falls, in the hearts of others a great transformation takes place, which for our consideration is instructive. That is, first, it shows what sort of interest it was that friends in the time of his good fortune took in him: 'when the casks are drained to the dregs, friends scatter.'[3] But in contrast, that which he feared more than misfortune itself, and that which was for him an unbearable thought, the rejoicing of those envious of his good fortune, the derisive laughter of *Schadenfreude*, does not occur. Envy is appeased: it disappears with its cause, and the compassion that enters in its place brings forth loving kindness. Often those who are envious of and enemies of a fortunate one, upon his fall, turn into considerate, comforting, and helpful friends.

[1] *habeat sibi sua.*
[2] γελῶσι δ' ἐχθροί (*rident inimici*) [*Electra* 1153].
[3] *diffugiunt cadis cum faece siccatis amici* [Horace, *Odes* I. 53. 35, 26].

Having experienced something of the sort, at least to a lesser degree, and having encountered some sort of misfortune, who has not seen with surprise that those who previously revealed greatest coldness, even ill-will toward him, now approach him with unfeigned partici- 238 pation in his misfortune? For misfortune is the condition of compassion, and compassion the source of loving kindness.—Related to this observation is the remark that nothing so quickly assuages our anger, even when it is just, as the statement about the object of our anger: 'he is an unfortunate one.' For what rain is to fire, compassion is to anger. Therefore, I advise anyone who would prefer not to have anything to regret, that, when burning with anger against another and thinking about inflicting great suffering on him—he might vividly imagine having already inflicted it on his intended victim, and now, seeing his victim struggle with psychological or physical pains, or distress and misery, he would then have to say to himself: that is my work. This, if anything, might dampen his anger. For compassion is the true antidote to anger, and by using this artifice on himself, he may anticipate while there is still time,

> compassion, whose voice
> makes her laws heard when we take revenge.[1]
> (Volt[aire], *Semiramis*, Act V, Scene 6)

Generally, nothing so readily sets aside our spiteful attitude toward others as when we take on a point of view from which they appeal to our compassion.—Even that, as a rule, parents always love the sickly child most, is due to the child's constantly evoking compassion.

(7) The moral incentive that I presented is further proved to be genuine in that it also takes under its protection *animals*, which are cared for in other European systems of morals in such an unjustifiably bad way. That animals are alleged to be without rights, the delusion that our actions toward them are without moral significance, or, as is said in the language of that morals, that there are no duties toward animals, is frankly a revolting crudity and barbarism of the Occident, at the source of which lies Judaism. In philosophy it rests on the absolute difference between human and animal, assumed despite all evidence, which difference, as is well known, was expressed most decisively and stridently by Descartes, as a necessary consequence of his errors. That is, since the Cartesian–Leibnizean–Wolf[f]ian 239

---

[1] *la pitié, dont la voix, | Alors qu'on est vengé, fait entendre ses lois.*

philosophy built up a rational psychology from abstract concepts and constructed an immortal rational soul,[1] then the natural claims of the animal world apparently ran counter to this exclusive privilege and patent of immortality for the human species, and nature, as on all such occasions, quietly submitted its protest. Anxious about their intellectual conscience, philosophers then had to try to support rational psychology through the empirical and, thus, made efforts to open an enormous chasm, an immeasurable gulf, between human and animal, in order, despite all evidence, to present them as fundamentally distinct. Boileau* has already mocked such efforts:

> Do animals also go to the university?
> And do we see among them the flourishing of the four faculties?[2]

Finally, animals were supposed not to know how to distinguish themselves from the external world and to have no consciousness of themselves, to have no I! Against such insipid assertions, one need only point out the inherent, boundless egoism in any animal, even the smallest and lowliest, to sufficiently show how animals are very conscious of their I, in contrast to the world or the Not-I. If such a Cartesian were to find himself in the claws of a tiger, he would become conscious of the sharp distinction such a one posits between the I and the Not-I. Corresponding to such sophistications of philosophers, in the popular way we find peculiarities of many languages, especially of German, in that they have completely separate words for eating, drinking, being pregnant, birthing, dying, and the corpses of animals, so as not to have to use that word which indicates the same act among humans, and so through diversity of words to be able to hide the complete identity of the matter. Since ancient languages knew no such duplicity of expressions, but rather naturally indicate the same thing with the same word, so without a doubt, this miserable artifice is the work of European clerics, who, in their profanity, did not believe that they could go far enough in denying and blaspheming the eternal essence that lives in all animals, whereby they had laid the basis for the customary hardness and cruelty to animals in Europe, which no noble Asian can view without righteous horror. In the English language we do not encounter this vile trick, doubtless because

240

---

[1] *anima rationalis.*
[2] *Les animaux ont-ils les universités?* | *Voit-on fleurir chez eux les quatre facultés?*

the Saxons, when they conquered England, were not yet Christians. But then an analogy to this trick is found in the peculiarity that in the English language all animals are of neuter gender[1] and they are represented by the pronoun *it* just like lifeless things, which especially for the primates, such as dogs, monkeys, etc., turns out to be completely outrageous and is unmistakeably a clerical device in order to reduce animals to things. The ancient Egyptians, whose entire lives were dedicated to religious purposes, placed in the same vaults with human mummies those of ibis and crocodiles, etc., but in Europe it is an abomination and a crime if a faithful dog is buried next to his master's resting-place, upon which, with a loyalty and attachment not found among the human race, he awaited his own death.— Nothing more decisively leads to knowledge of the identity of that which is essential in the animal's appearance and that of the human than the pursuit of zoology and anatomy. What should one, therefore, say when today (1839) a canting zootomist,* urging an absolute and radical difference between human and animal, presumes and goes so far as to impugn and calumniate honest zoologists, who, distanced from all clerical wiles, sycophancy, Tartuffianism, pursue their way by following the hand of nature and truth?

One must be truly blind in all senses or totally chloroformed by Judaic stench[2] not to recognize that the essential and primary thing is the same in the animal and in the human, and that what differentiates the two lies not in the primary, in the principal, in the primordial, in the inner essence, in the core of the appearances of both, which in the one as well as in the other is *the will* of the individual. But what differentiates the two lies only in that which is secondary, in the intellect, in the degree of cognitive power, which is incomparably higher in humans because of the additional faculty of *abstract* cognition, called *reason*; however, it is demonstrably higher only because of greater cerebral development, that is, because of a somatic difference of a particular part, the brain, and just because of quantity. In contrast, the psychic and somatic similarities between animal and human are incomparably greater. One must remind such an occidental, Judaicized despiser of animals and idolater of reason that just as he was suckled by *his* mother, so, too, the dog was suckled by *his*. That even Kant has fallen into this error of his contemporaries and

---

[1] *generis neutrius.*    [2] *foetor Judaicus.*

compatriots is a reproach I have made above. That the morals of Christianity do not consider animals is one of its defects which it is better to admit than to perpetuate, and at which one must be all the more astonished since these morals in other respects show the greatest agreement with those of Brahmanism and Buddhism, merely less strongly expressed and not carried out to extremes; therefore, one can hardly doubt that these morals, like the idea, too, of a human becoming a god (avatar), originated in India and might have come through Egypt to Judaea, so that Christianity would be a reflection of the original light of India off the ruins of Egypt, which, however, unfortunately fell on Jewish soil. It could be taken as a fitting *symbol* of the defect of Christian morals, which I just reproached, despite their otherwise greatly agreeing with Indian morals, that John the Baptist appears quite like an Indian Sanyassi,* but at the same time— clad in animal skins! which, as is known, would be an abomination to any Hindu, for even the Royal Society at Calcutta received its copy of the *Vedas* on the promise that they would not, in European fashion, have it bound in leather; hence, it is to be found in their library bound in silk. A similar, characteristic contrast is provided between the gospel story of Peter's fishing catch, which the saviour, by a miracle, blesses to such an extent that the boats were overfilled with fish almost to the point of sinking (Luke 5), and the story of Pythagoras, initiated in Egyptian wisdom, who purchased the fisherman's catch while the net still lay under the water, in order to bestow freedom on all the captured fish (Apul[ius], *On Magic*, p. 36. Bip[ont edition]).—Compassion for animals is so closely associated with goodness of character that one may confidently assert that whoever is cruel to animals could not be a good person. This compassion also appears to have originated from the same source as the virtue to be practised toward humans. So, e.g., people of refined feelings, recalling that in an evil mood, in anger, or heated by wine, they had undeservedly and unnecessarily or unduly mistreated their dog, their horse, their monkey, will experience the same remorse, the same dissatisfaction with themselves which is experienced on recollection of having done some injustice to a human, in which case it is called the voice of a reproachful conscience. I recall having read that an Englishman who, while hunting in India, had shot a monkey, could not forget the glance which this dying monkey cast upon him, and ever since could no longer shoot a monkey. Similarly, in the years 1836 and 1837, Wilhelm Harris, a true Nimrod, travelled deep into the interior of Africa to enjoy the pleasures of hunting. In his travelogue, which appeared in 1838 in Bombay, he explains that after he had killed his first elephant, which was a female, and on the following morning sought the fallen animal, all the other elephants had fled the region; except that the baby of the fallen one had remained all night by the dead mother, and now forgetting all fear, approached the hunters with the liveliest and clearest testimony to his inconsolable grief and embraced them with his little trunk to call for their help. Then, says Harris, a sincere remorse for the deed seized him, and he felt as if he had committed a murder. We see the English nation, one of refined feelings, pre-eminently distinguished by a conspicuous compassion for animals, a compassion which appears at every opportunity and which, despite the 'cold superstition'* which otherwise degrades the nation, has had the power to move it, through legislation, to fill in the void that religion has left in morality. For this void is just the reason why in Europe and America organizations for animal protection are needed which can only be effective through the means of the help of courts and the police. In Asia religions grant animals adequate protection; hence, no person there would think of such organizations. Nevertheless, in Europe a sense of the rights of animals is gradually awakening in proportion to the fading and vanishing of the strange idea that the animal world was brought into being merely for humans' use and amusement, as a result of which animals are treated just like things. For these are the sources of the crude and completely reckless treatment of animals in Europe, and in the second volume of *Parerga* [*and Paralipomena*], § 177, I have demonstrated the Old Testament origin of this treatment. Thus, to the renown of the English, let it be said that they were also the first among whom the law to protect animals from cruel treatment had been taken quite seriously, and the miscreant must actually make amends for having committed a crime against animals, even if they belong to him. Indeed, still not satisfied, there exists in London an organization voluntarily formed for the protection of animals, the Society for the Prevention of Cruelty to Animals, which by private means at significant expense does a great deal to work against the torture of animals. Their emissaries are secretly on the alert, in order later to appear as the ones who denounce those who torture speechless, sensate beings, and everywhere these emissaries' presence is feared.[1] At steep bridges in London the Society keeps a team of horses, which are hitched to any heavily laden wagon for free. Is that not great? Does it not compel our approval just as well as a good deed to humans? In the year 1837, the Philanthropic Society of London also offered a prize of £30 for the best exposition about the moral grounds against the torture of animals, which grounds, however, had to be taken primarily from Christianity, which, of course, made the task more difficult: in 1839 the prize was awarded to Mr Macnamara. In Philadelphia there is for similar purposes an Animal Friends Society. T. Forster

---

[1] How seriously the matter is taken is shown by the following very recent example, which I translate from the *Birmingham Journal* of December 1839: 'Arrest of a company of 84 dog-fighters.—Since it had been discovered that yesterday a dog-fight was to take place according to plan in Fox Street in Birmingham, the Society of the Friends of Animals took preventive measures to ensure the help of the police, of whom a strong detachment marched to the site of the fight and, as soon as they were admitted, arrested the entire company present. These participants were then bound together in pairs with handcuffs and all of them collected in the middle with a long rope: in this way they were led to the police station, where the mayor held a session with the magistrate. The two principals were each sentenced to a punishment of 1 pound sterling together with 8 ½ shillings costs, and in case of non-payment, 14 days' hard labour in prison. The rest were released.'—The dandies, who tend never to be missing from such noble pleasures, must have looked very embarrassed in the procession.—But we find an even harsher example from more recent time in *The Times* of 6 April 1855, p. 6, one the newspaper itself even uses to serve as an example. That is, the paper reports about a case, taken to court, of the daughter of a very wealthy Scottish baronet who had tortured her horse extremely cruelly, with club and knife, for which she had been sentenced to a punishment of 5 pounds sterling. But that is nothing to a girl of that kind, and she would actually have skipped away from there unpunished, had not *The Times* followed up with the correct, sharp reprimand, in that it twice set the girl's first and last name in large letters, and continued: 'We cannot but say that a few months' imprisonment, with a few private whippings, administered by the hand of the stoutest woman in Hampshire, would have constituted a much more fitting punishment for Miss *N. N.* Such a wretch is not entitled to the privileges and honour due to her sex; we cannot think of her as a woman at all.'— I dedicate these newspaper reports especially to the associations against the torture of animals now established in Germany, so that they see how one must attack the issue if anything is to come of it; though I pay my full acknowledgement to the praiseworthy zeal of Councillor Perner in Munich who has devoted himself entirely to this branch of beneficence and spread the initiative for it throughout the whole of Germany. [Schopenhauer's note. In the first (1841) edition of the essay, the first example given in this note appears to paraphrase the *Birmingham Journal* of 7 December 1839, p. 3; in the second example, given in the second edition (1860), Schopenhauer translated closely the *Times* article he cites. The original does give the miscreant's name all in capitals: EMILY FRANCES GORDON.]

(an Englishman) has dedicated to this Society his book *Philozoia, Moral Reflections on the Actual Condition of Animals and the Means of Improving the Same* (Brussels, 1839). The book is original and well written. Naturally, as an Englishman, the author also sought to base his admonitions to humane treatment of animals on the Bible; however, he slips about so that he finally grabs onto the argument that indeed Jesus Christ was born in a stall near little oxen and asses, which circumstance would symbolically signify that we would have to consider the animals to be our brothers and treat them accordingly. — Everything cited here testifies that the moral chord under consideration here is also gradually beginning to sound in the occidental world. Moreover, that compassion for animals must not go so far that, like the Brahmans, we would have to give up animals as food, rests on the fact that in nature the capacity for suffering keeps pace with intelligence, on account of which by abstaining from animals as food, humans, especially in the north, would suffer more than would the animal through a quick and even unforeseen death, which perhaps should be alleviated even more by means of chloroform. In contrast, without animals as food, the human race would never be able to exist in the north. By the same standard, humans have animals work for them, and only imposing an excess of strain becomes a cruelty.

(8) If we once completely disregard any possible metaphysical investigation of the ultimate ground of that compassion from which alone non-egoistical actions can proceed, and if we examine the same from an empirical standpoint merely as a natural arrangement, then it would be clear to anyone that compassion is the most likely alleviation of the countless and multifarious sufferings with which our life is beset and which no one completely escapes, and at the same time compassion is the counterbalance to the burning egoism that fills all beings and often develops into malice — nature could achieve nothing more effective than its having planted in the human heart this wondrous disposition by which the suffering of one will be experienced by the other as well and from which comes the voice that loudly and distinctly calls out to this one, 'Forbear'! to that one, 'Help!' depending on the circumstances. Certainly there is more hope for everyone's welfare from the resulting mutual aid than from a universal, abstract, strict command of duty, yielded by certain rational considerations and combinations of concepts. From this all the less success

246 is to be expected, since for the uneducated, universal propositions and abstract truths are completely unintelligible, as for them only the concrete has meaning—but all of humanity, with the exception of an extremely small part, is always ignorant and must remain so, because much physical work, inevitably necessary for most, does not allow the cultivation of the mind. By contrast, awakening compassion, which has been proved to be the *sole source of disinterested actions and consequently the true basis of morality*, requires no abstract cognition, but only intuitive cognition, the mere apprehension of the concrete instance, which speaks to compassion immediately, without further mediation of thought.

(9) We will find the following in complete agreement with this last observation. The grounding which I have given ethics leaves me without predecessor among schools of philosophers; indeed, in relation to these doctrinal opinions it is paradoxical, since many of them, e.g., the Stoics (Sen[eca], *On Clemency*, II. 5), Spinoza (*Ethics*, IV, *prop[osition]* 50), Kant (*Critique of Practical Reason*, p. 213—R., p. 257\*), flatly repudiate and censure compassion. In contrast, however, my grounding has on its side the authority of the greatest moralist of recent times: this is, without a doubt, J. J. Rousseau, the profound judge of the human heart, whose wisdom derives not from books, but from life, and whose theories are intended not for the ivory tower, but for humanity, for he is a foe of prejudice, a student of nature, which endowed him alone with the gift of being able to moralize without being boring because he came upon truth and touched the heart. I will allow myself to present a few passages from him in corroboration of my view, and because of this I have been as sparing of quotations as possible in the previous sections.

In the *Discourse on the Origin of Inequality* (Bip[ont] edition), p. 91, he says: 'There is another principle that has escaped Hobbes, which is that it has been given to man to moderate, on certain occasions, the ferocity of self-love or the desire of self-preservation prior to the appearance of that love, to temper the ardour with which he naturally pursues his private welfare, *through an innate repugnance to seeing the*
247 *suffering of beings that resemble him.* I shall surely not be contradicted in granting to man *the only natural virtue*, which even the most passionate detractor of human virtues could not deny. I mean that of

*compassion*', etc.—p. 92: 'Mandeville* was aware that men, in spite of all their morality, would never have been better than monsters if nature had not given them *compassion* to assist reason, but he did not perceive that *from this quality alone flowed all the social virtues* which he would deny humankind. In fact, what is generosity, what clemency, what humanity, but *compassion* applied to the weak, to the guilty, or to the human species in general? Even benevolence and friendship, if we judge right, are the effects of a constant compassion fixed upon a particular object, for what is it to wish that a person may not suffer, but to wish that he may be happy'?— —'In fact, commiseration must be all the more energetic, the more intimately *the animal that beholds any kind of distress identifies himself with the animal suffering*.'— p. 94: 'It is therefore certain that compassion is a natural sentiment, which, by moderating in every individual the activity of self-love, contributes to the mutual preservation of the whole species. It is this compassion, which in a state of nature, takes the place of laws, manners, virtues, but with this advantage: that no one is tempted to disobey her gentle voice; it is this compassion which will always hinder a robust savage from plundering a feeble child or an infirm old man of the subsistence he has acquired with pain and difficulty if the savage has but the least prospect of providing for himself by any other means; it is this compassion which, instead of the sublime maxim of rational justice, "do to others as you would have others do to you," inspires all men with that other maxim of natural goodness, a great deal less perfect, but perhaps more useful, "do good to yourself with as little harm as you can to others". It is, in a word, *to this natural sentiment, rather than in fine-spun arguments, that we must look for the cause of that repugnance which every man would experience* to do *evil*, even independently of the maxims of education.'—One should compare this with what he says in *Émile*, Book IV, pp. 115–120 (Bip[ont] edition), where it is said in other terms: 'Indeed, how can we let ourselves be stirred by compassion, unless we go *beyond* 248 *ourselves and identify ourselves with the suffering animal, by leaving, so to speak, our own nature and taking his?* We only suffer insofar as we suppose he suffers: *the suffering is not ours, but his.*— — —*present to the young man* objects on which the expansive force of his heart may take effect, objects which dilate it, which extend it to other creatures, which take him outside himself; should we not carefully remove everything that narrows, concentrates, and strengthens the power of *the human self*', etc.?[1]

Setting aside that, as I have said, I am without the authority of the schools, I state that the *Chinese* accept five cardinal virtues* (*chang*), among which compassion (*sin*) stands at the head. The remaining four are: justice, courtesy, wisdom, and righteousness.[2] Accordingly among the Hindus, on a memorial tablet erected in remembrance of a dead prince, we see compassion for humans and animals taking first place among the virtues with which the prince was credited. In Athens Compassion had an altar in the forum: 'The Athenians have in the

---

[1] *Il y a un autre principe, que Hobbes n'a point apperçu, et qui ayant été donné à l'homme pour adoucir, en certaines circonstances, la férocité de son amour-propre, tempère l'ardeur qu'il a pour son bien-être par une* répugnance innée à voir souffrir son semblable. *Je ne crois pas avoir aucune contradiction à craindre en accordant à l'homme* la seule vertu naturelle *qu'ait été forcé de reconnaître le détracteur le plus outré des vertus humaines. Je parle de la* pitié *etc.—* p. 92: *Mandeville a bien senti qu'avec toute leur morale les hommes n'eussent jamais été que des monstres, si la nature ne leur eut donné la pitié à l'appui de la raison: mais il n'a pas vu, que* de cette seule qualité découlent toutes les vertus sociales, *qu'il veut disputer aux hommes. En effet qu'est-ce que la générosité, la clémence, l'humanité, sinon la* pitié *appliquée aux faibles, aux coupables, ou à l'espèce humaine en général? La bienveillance et l'amitié même sont, à le bien prendre, des productions d'une pitié constante, fixée sur un objet particulier; car désirer que quelqu'un ne souffre point, qu'est-ce autre-chose, que désirer qu'il soit heureux? — — La commisération sera d'autant plus énergique, que* l'animal spectateur s'identifiera *plus intimément avec* l'animal souffrant.—p. 94: *Il est donc bien certain, que la pitié est un sentiment naturel, qui, modérant dans chaque individu l'amour de soi-même, concourt à la conservation mutuelle de toute l'espèce. C'est elle, qui dans l'état de nature, tient lieu de lois, de mœurs et de vertus, avec cet avantage, que nul ne sera tenté de désobéir à sa douce voix: c'est elle, qui détournera tout sauvage robuste d'enlever à un faible enfant, ou à un vieillard infirme sa subsistence acquise avec peine, si lui même espère pouvoir trouver la sienne ailleurs: c'est elle qui, au lieu de cette maxime sublime de justice raisonnée 'fais à autrui comme tu veux qu'on te fasse', inspire à tous les hommes cette autre maxime de bonté naturelle, bien moins parfaite, mais plus utile peut-être que la précédente 'fais ton bien avec le moindre mal d'autrui qu'il est possible'. C'est, en un mot,* dans ce sentiment naturel plutôt, que dans les argumens subtils, *qu'il faut chercher la cause de la répugnance qu'éprouverait tout homme à mal faire, même indépendamment des maximes de l'éducation.—Émile,* Book IV, pp. 115–120 (ed. *Bip*[ont]): *En effet, comment nous laissons-nous émouvoir à la pitié, si ce n'est en nous transportant hors de nous et en nous* identifiant avec l'animal souffrant; en quittant, pour ainsi dire, notre être, pour prendre le sien? *Nous ne souffrons qu'autant que nous jugeons qu'il souffre*: ce n'est pas dans nous, c'est dans lui, que nous souffrons. — — — offrir au jeune homme *des objets, sur lesquels puisse agir la force expansive de son cœur, qui le dilatent, qui l'étendent sur les autres êtres, qui le fassent partout se* retrouver hors de lui; *écarter avec soin ceux, qui le resserrent, le concentrent, et tendent le ressort* du moi humain *etc.—* [emphases are Schopenhauer's].

[2] *Journ*[*al*] *Asiatique*, vol. 9, p. 62, to be compared with *Meng-Tseu*, ed. Stan[islas] Julien, 1824, Book 1, § 45, and with *Meng-Tseu* in *Livres sacrés de l'Orient par Pauthier*, p. 281. [Schopenhauer's note.]

*Agora* an altar to Compassion. Alone among the Greeks the Athenians worship this divinity, which more than all the gods is most influential in human life and its ups and downs', Pausanias I. 17.[1] Lucian also mentions this altar in *Timon*, § 99. — A saying of Phocion* preserved by Stobaeus represents compassion as most sacred among humans: 'one must not tear the altar from the temple nor compassion from human nature.'[2] In the *Wisdom of India*, which is a Greek translation of the *Pañcatantra*,* it reads (Sect[ion] 3, p. 220): 'It is said that compassion is the first among the virtues.'[3] One sees that in all times and in all lands, the source of morality has been quite well known, except for in Europe; for this only the Judaic stench is guilty,[4] for it pervades everything here; then, it must simply be a command of duty, a moral law, an imperative, in short, an order and command that is obeyed: the Europeans will not depart from it and do not want to recognize that it always has only egoism as its basis. Certainly those who are individual and superior have given credence to this felt truth: so it is with Rousseau, as was cited above, and Lessing, too, said in a letter of 1756: 'The compassionate person is the best person, inclined to all social virtues, to all sorts of magnanimity.'*

## § 20

## *On the Ethical Difference of Characters*

THE last question requiring an answer for the completeness of my foundation of ethics is this: on what rests the very great difference in human moral behaviour? If compassion is the fundamental incentive for all genuine, i.e., disinterested justice and loving kindness, why would one person, but not another, be moved by it? — Since ethics has discovered the moral incentive, might it perhaps also be capable of putting this incentive into action? Can ethics transform a hard-hearted person into a compassionate person and thereby into a just and

---

[1] Ἀθηναίοις δὲ ἐν τῇ ἀγορᾷ ἐστι Ἐλέου βωμός, ᾧ μάλιστα θεῶν, ἐς ἀνθρώπινον βίον καὶ μεταβολὰς πραγμάτων ὅτι ὠφέλιμος, μόνοι τιμὰς Ἑλλήνων νέμουσιν Ἀθηναῖοι. Παυσ., Ι. 17. (*Atheniensibus in foro commiserationis ara est, quippe cui, inter omnes Deos, vitam humanam et mutationem rerum maxime adjuvanti, soli inter Graecos, honores tribuunt Athenienses.*)

[2] οὔτε ἐξ ἱεροῦ βωμὸν, οὔτε ἐκ τῆς ἀνθρωπίνης φύσεως ἀφαιρετέον τὸν ἔλεον (*nec aram e fano, nec commiserationem e vita humana tollendam esse*) [*Anthology* I. 31].

[3] Λέγεται γὰρ, ὡς πρώτη τῶν ἀρετῶν ἡ ἐλεημοσύνη (*princeps virtutum misericordia censetur*).

[4] *foetor Judaicus.*

philanthropic one?—Certainly not: the difference of characters is innate and ineradicable. Malice is as innate to the malicious man as poisonous fangs and poisonous glands are to the snake, and the man can no more change than can the snake. 'Willing cannot be taught',[1] said Nero's teacher. In the *Meno*, Plato thoroughly investigates whether or not virtue can be taught. He quotes a passage of Theognis:

> But teaching
> Never makes a bad man good[2]

and arrives at the result: 'virtue is neither from nature nor teaching, but the one endowed with it is so fated by the gods, without the mind';[3] here it seems to me that the difference between 'nature'[4] and 'fated by the gods'[5] appears to approximately indicate the difference between physical and metaphysical. In fact, the father of ethics, Socrates, maintains, according to Aristotle's statement: 'it is not up to us to be good or bad'[6] (*Great Ethics* I. 9). Aristotle himself expresses the same sense: 'For it seems that particular character traits are already somehow inherent to us all by nature, for a tendency to justice, and temperance, and courage, and the like, is already ours from birth' (*Nicomachean Ethics* VI. 13).[7] We find the same conviction quite decidedly asserted in the fragments of the Pythagorean Archytas, which, in any case, are very old, if perhaps not genuine, and which have been preserved by Stobaeus in the *Anthology*, chap. I, § 77. They are also reprinted in the *Short Sententious and Moral Works of the*

---

[1] *Velle non discitur* [Seneca, *Moral Letters* 84, 14].

[2] ἀλλὰ διδάσκων
Οὔποτε ποιήσεις τὸν κακὸν ἄνδρ' ἀγαθόν.
(*sed docendo nunquam ex malo bonum hominem facies*) [*Meno* 96a; Theognis (540–500 BCE), Greek elegist].

[3] ἀρετὴ ἂν εἴη οὔτε φύσει, οὔτε διδακτόν, ἀλλὰ θείᾳ μοίρᾳ παραγιγνομένη, ἄνευ νοῦ, οἷς ἂν παραγίγνηται (*virtus utique nec doctrina, neque natura nobis aderit; verum divina sorte, absque mente, in eum, qui illam sortitus fuerit*) [*Meno* 99e].

[4] φύσει.

[5] θείᾳ μοίρᾳ.

[6] οὐκ ἐφ' ἡμῖν γενέσθαι τὸ σπουδαίους εἶναι ἢ φαύλους (*in nostra potestate non est, bonos, aut malos esse.*) [*Ethica magna* I. 9 (or *Magna moralia* I. 9), 1187a 7].

[7] Πᾶσι γὰρ δοκεῖ ἕκαστα τῶν ἠθῶν ὑπάρχειν φύσει πως· καὶ γὰρ δίκαιοι καὶ σωφρονικοὶ [καὶ ἀνδρεῖοι] καὶ τἆλλα ἔχομεν εὐθὺς ἐκ γενετῆς (*singuli enim mores in omnibus hominibus quodammodo videntur inesse natura: namque ad justitiam, temperantiam, fortitudinem, ceterasque virtutes apti atque habiles sumus, cum primum nascimur.*) [*Nicomachean Ethics* 1144b 4; Schopenhauer omits καὶ ἀνδρεῖοι ('and courage') but offers for it in his Latin translation *fortitudinem*].

*Greeks*,[1] edited by Orelli, vol. II, p. 240. The same is given in Dorian dialect: 'For those virtues relying on reason and demonstration must be called sciences. Conversely, the ethical virtue, which is the best, is understood to be a habit of the soul's irrational part, on the basis of which we are regarded as possessing a specific moral nature, e.g., as being liberal, just, and temperate.'[2] If one surveys all the virtues and vices concisely summarized by Aristotle in his book *On Virtues and Vices*, then one will find that all are conceivable only as innate properties. Indeed, only as such can they be genuine; whereas, if they were assumed to be voluntary, as a result of rational deliberation, they would really amount to pretence and would be spurious; for that reason their persistence and reliability under the pressure of circumstances could not be counted upon at all. It is also no different with the virtue of loving kindness, which Aristotle, like all the ancients, ignores. Although retaining his sceptical tone, Montaigne says in a similar sense: 'Would it be true that, to be thoroughly good, we must be so through an occult, natural, and universal quality, without law, reason, or example?'[3] (bk. II, chap. 11). But Lichtenberg says it plainly: 'All virtue from deliberation is not worth much. Feeling, or habit, is the thing' (*Miscellaneous Writings*, 'Moral Observations'*). Yet even the original teaching of Christianity agrees with this view, since in the Sermon on the Mount itself, in Luke 6: 45, it says: 'the good person out of the good treasure of his heart produces good, and the evil person out of evil treasure produces evil,'[4] following the two previous verses, in which the matter is presented in a metaphorical explanation of the fruit that always turns out in accordance with the tree.

251

---

[1] *Opusculis Graecorum sententiosis et moralibus, edente Orellio.*

[2] Τὰς γὰρ λόγοις καὶ ἀποδείξεσιν ποτιχρωμένας ἀρετὰς δέον ἐπιστάμας ποταγορεύεν, ἀρετὰν δέ, τὰν ἠθικὰν καὶ βελτίσταν ἕξιν τῶ ἀλόγω μέρεος τᾶς ψυχᾶς, καθ' ἅν καὶ ποιοί τινες ἦμεν λεγόμεθα κατὰ τὸ ἦθος, οἷον ἐλευθέριοι, δίκαιοι καὶ σώφρονες. (*Eas enim, quae ratione et demonstratione utuntur, virtutes fas est, scientias appellare; virtutis autem nomine intelligemus moralem et optimum animi partis ratione carentis habitum, secundum quem qualitatem aliquam moralem habere dicimur, vocamurque v.c. liberales, justi et temperantes.*) [Stobaeus, *Anthology*, chap. I, § 77.]

[3] *Seroit-il vrai, que pour être bon tout-à-fait, il nous le faille être par occulte, naturelle et universelle propriété, sans loi, sans raison, sans exemple?* [Montaigne, *Essays.*]

[4] ὁ ἀγαθὸς ἄνθρωπος ἐκ τοῦ ἀγαθοῦ θησαυροῦ τῆς καρδίας αὐτοῦ προφέρει τὸ ἀγαθόν, καὶ ὁ πονηρὸς ἄνθρωπος ἐκ τοῦ πονηροῦ θησαυροῦ τῆς καρδίας αὐτοῦ προφέρει τὸ πονηρόν (*homo bonus ex bono animi sui thesauro profert bonum, malusque ex malo animi sui thesauro profert malum*).

However, it is Kant who had first completely clarified this important point in his great doctrine that, at the basis of the *empirical character*, an appearance, lies the *intelligible character*, which is the constitution of the thing in itself, of that appearance, presenting itself in time and in a plurality of actions, and which, therefore, is independent of space and time, of plurality and alteration. From this alone is the very astonishingly rigid unalterability of characters explicable, as is recognized by any experienced person, for virtue is innate and cannot be instilled by preaching, as has been proven insofar as reality and experience have always triumphantly opposed the promises of an ethics that wants to improve humans morally and to speak about a progress in virtue. If the character, as original, unalterable, were not thus, intractable to all improvement by means of correction of knowledge; if, moreover, as that insipid ethics maintains it, 'a constant progress toward the good' were thus possible—then, unless all the many religious institutions and efforts at moralizing have failed in their purpose, at least on average the older half of humanity would have to be significantly better than the younger half. But there is so little trace of this improvement, that, conversely, we would sooner hope for something good from the young than from the old, who have become worse through experience. To be sure, it can occur that one person in old age appears somewhat better and, again, another worse than he was in his youth, but what lies behind this is simply that in old age, as a result of mature and frequently correct knowledge, the character stands out more purely and clearly; whereas, in youth, ignorance, errors, and chimeras presented false motives at one moment and concealed real ones at another—for how this follows see that which is said in the preceding essay, p. [50 ff.] under 3.*—That among convicted criminals there are to be found many more young than old occurs because, when a tendency for such criminal actions exists in the character, it soon finds the opportunity to appear as a deed and reaches its goal, the galleys or the gallows, and, conversely, whoever could not be moved to have committed a crime during the opportunities of a long life, will not later easily be prompted to do so by motives. Thus the true reason for the respect paid to elders seems to me to be that an old man has stood the test of a long life and proven his integrity, for this is the condition of that respect.—As is consistent with this view, no one has ever been misled in real life by those promises of moralists; rather, one who has once proved himself to be bad is no longer trusted, and another who had once shown proof of magnanimity, even when everything else might have changed, is always viewed with confidence. 'Doing follows essence'[1] is a rich dictum of the scholastics: everything in the world works from its unalterable nature, which constitutes its essence, its *essentia*; so, too, it is with the human being. What one *is*, so will, so must one act, and the *liberum arbitrium indifferentiae* is an invention from the infancy of philosophy which has long been exploded and which a few old women in academic mortar-boards still like to drag around.

The three ethical fundamental incentives of humans, egoism, malice, compassion, are present in everyone in various and incredibly different proportions. Depending on these incentives, motives will work on a person and actions will result. On an egoistic character, only egoistic motives will have power, and neither motives appealing to compassion nor those appealing to malice will prevail against egoistic motives, and one of such character will no more sacrifice his interests to take revenge on his enemy than he will to help his friend. Another man who is highly responsive to malicious motives will frequently not shy away from his own great disadvantage to injure another. For there are characters who, in causing others to suffer, find a pleasure that outweighs their own equally great suffering: 'disregarding himself if only he can injure another'[2] (Sen[eca], *On Anger* I. 1). These characters proceed with passionate delight into a fight in which they experience just as many injuries as those they expect to inflict; indeed, they will with premeditation murder one who has caused them harm and immediately thereafter kill themselves to escape punishment, as experience frequently shows. Conversely, *goodness of heart* consists in the deeply felt, universal compassion for all living beings, but primarily for the human because responsiveness to suffering keeps in step with increase in intelligence; hence, humans' countless intellectual and physical sufferings have a much stronger claim to compassion than the pain of animals, which is only physical and, thus, less acute. Accordingly goodness of character will first restrain one from injuring another, whatever it may be, but then require one to help wherever another's suffering presents itself. And here, too, compassion can go as far as malice goes in the

___

[1] *Operari sequitur esse.*

[2] *dum alteri noceat sui negligens* [Seneca, *De ira*].

opposite direction, that is, so far that characters of rare goodness take another's suffering more to heart than their own, and, so, in sacrificing for another, suffer more than had the one whom they helped. Where several or even a great many are to be helped at the same time, they will, as the case requires, sacrifice themselves completely, as did Arnold von Winkelried. Joh. v. Müller* (*World History*,[1] Book 10, chap. 10) says of Paulinus, bishop of Nola in the fifth century during the Vandals' invasion of Italy from Africa: 'After he had used up all the wealth of the church and his and his friends' own fortunes as ransom money for prisoners, seeing the misery of a widow whose only son had been led away, he offered himself in the son's place for servitude. For those who were of age and had not fallen by the sword, were captured and taken to Carthage.'

In accord with this incredibly great, innate, and original difference, for the most part, someone will be stimulated only by *those* motives to which he has a prevailing responsiveness, just as *one* body reacts only to acids and another only to alkalis, and like the former, so, too, the latter cannot be changed. Philanthropic motives, which are such a powerful impulse for a good character, cannot as such move one who is responsive only to egoistic motives. If, however, one wishes to move such a person to philanthropic actions, then it can only happen through a delusion that the alleviation of another's suffering in some way *mediately* contributes to *his own advantage* (just as most moral theories are actually various attempts of this sort). But in this way his will is merely led by error, and not improved. For actual improvement would require that the entire nature of his responsiveness to motives be transformed; so, e.g., for one, another's suffering as such would no longer remain a matter of indifference; for a second, causing another's suffering would no longer be pleasurable; or for a third, improvement of his own well-being, even the slightest, would no longer outweigh and render ineffective all motives of a different kind. But this is more certainly impossible than being able to transform lead into gold. For it would require not just turning around a human heart in the body, but completely re-creating his deep, innermost essence. On the contrary, all that one might do is enlighten the *head*, correct the *insight*, bring a person to a more correct apprehension of that which is

---

[1] *Weltgeschichte.*

objectively present, of the true circumstances of life. But in this nothing else is gained than that the nature of his will reveals itself more consistently, clearly, decisively, expressing itself more genuinely. For, just as many good actions rest on the ground of false motives, on the well-meant delusions of a presupposition that in so doing one's own advantage will be achieved in this or in the next world, so, too, many misdeeds rest merely on false cognition of the circumstances of human life. The American penal system is grounded on this: it does not intend to improve the *heart* of the criminal, but merely to set his *head* right so that he arrives at the insight that work and honesty are a more certain, indeed, easier way to one's own prosperity than being a miscreant.

*Legality* can be compelled through motives, *morality* cannot: one can reform *acting*, but not actual *willing*, to which alone moral value pertains. One cannot change the goal to which the will strives, but only the path it takes. Instruction can change the choice of means, but not that of the ultimate ends in general: each person's will sets these ends in accordance with its original nature. One can show the egoist that by giving up little advantages, he will achieve greater advantage, or the malicious person that being the cause of another's suffering will bring him even greater suffering. But no one can be talked out of egoism or malice any more than the cat can be of its inclination to mousing. Even goodness of character, too, can be brought to a more consistent and complete expression of its essence by improved insight, by instruction about the circumstances of life, that is, by enlightening the head, e.g., by means of demonstrating the more remote consequences our doings have for others, how sometimes one or another action that we do not take to be bad can indirectly and eventually increase their suffering; similarly, by instruction in the harmful consequences of many well-intended actions, e.g., pardoning a criminal; and especially by instruction in the priority which 'harm no one'[1] generally takes over 'help everyone',[2] etc. In this regard there is certainly a moral education and an ethics that improves: but it does not go beyond this, and its limits are easy to perceive. The head is enlightened; the heart remains unimproved. That which is fundamental, that which is decisive, in the moral as well as the intellectual

---

[1] *neminem laede.*    [2] *omnes juva.*

256 and the physical, is *that which is innate*: artifice can generally only help. Each is what he is, so to speak, 'by God's grace', *jure divino*, θείᾳ μοίρᾳ.

> You are, in the end — *what you are.*
> Put on a periwig of a million ringlets,
> Put yard-long hose on your feet,
> *Indeed you are what you are.**

But I already hear the reader throw out the question: where are blame and merit to be found? — In answer to this, I refer to § 10. The answer, which would otherwise be given *here*, has already found its place because it is closely connected with Kant's theory of the coexistence of freedom and necessity. Please read again that which was said there. In conformity with what was said there, *operari* is entirely necessary when motives occur; therefore *freedom*, which is only announced through *responsibility*, can lie only in *esse*. Indeed, the reproaches of conscience primarily and ostensibly concern that which we *have done*, but actually and fundamentally that which we *are*, to which our deeds alone bear valid witness since they relate to our character as symptoms to disease. Thus with this *esse*, by which we *are*, blame and merit must lie. That which in others we either esteem and love or condemn and hate is not something perishable and alterable, but enduring, existing once and for all. It is what they *are*, and if we once change our minds about them, then we do not say that they have changed, but that we have been mistaken about them. Even so the object of our satisfaction and dissatisfaction with ourselves is that *which we are*, which we are irrevocably and which we remain. This even applies to the intellectual, indeed, to the physiognomic attributes. How, then, could blame and merit not lie in that which we *are*? — Our constantly becoming more acquainted with ourselves, the ever more complete *record of our deeds*, is *conscience*. Our actions are in the first instance the theme of conscience, and, indeed, these actions are those in which, because egoism or even malice governed us, we either gave no hearing to the summons of compassion,

257 which called upon us at least not to harm others and even to help and support them, or, instead, these actions are those in which, denying both egoism and malice, we have followed compassion's call. Both cases indicate the extent of the *distinction* we draw *between ourselves and others*. On *this distinction* ultimately rests the degree of morality

or immorality, i.e., of justice and loving kindness, as well as of their opposite. The recollection of our actions that are significant in this respect becomes ever richer, increasingly completing the image of our character, the true acquaintance with ourselves. From this, however, grows satisfaction or dissatisfaction with ourselves, with that which we *are*, according to whether egoism, malice, or compassion have prevailed, i.e., according to how much greater or lesser has been the distinction that we have made between our person and that of all others. In any case, we judge others according to the same standard, coming to know their character empirically, just as we do our own, only less completely, but in this case, what appears as praise, support, and esteem, or censure, indignation, and contempt, is announced by self-judgement as a satisfaction or a dissatisfaction, which can go so far as qualms of conscience. That even the reproaches that we apply to others are only *in the first instance* directed at the deeds, but *actually* at the unalterable character, and that virtue or vice are seen as inherent, enduring qualities, many of the commonly encountered forms of speech verify, e.g., *'Jetzt sehe ich, wie du bist!'*[1]—'I have been mistaken about you.'—'Now I see what you are!'—'There, that's the kind of person you are!'[2]—'I am not such a person!'—'I am not the man, who would be capable of deceiving you', and similar forms; and further: 'persons of excellent disposition;'[3] also in Spanish, 'well-born';[4] in Greek, 'of noble birth', 'well-born'[5] for virtuousness, virtue; in Latin 'a friend of noble mind',[6] etc.

Therefore, conscience is conditioned by reason, since only by means of reason is a clear and cogent recollection possible. It lies in the nature of the thing that conscience first speaks *afterwards*, which is why it is also called the *judging* conscience. *Beforehand* it can only speak in a figurative sense, namely indirectly, since from memory of similar cases, reflection infers future disapprobation of a deed which is planned for the first time.—This is as far as the ethical fact of conscience goes: it itself remains a metaphysical problem, which does not immediately belong to our task; however, it will be touched upon in the last chapter.—That *responsiveness* to the motives of selfishness, malice, and compassion, upon which the entire moral

258

---

[1] [Schopenhauer translates this in English in the third example.]
[2] *Voilà donc, comme tu es!*     [3] *les âmes bien nées.*     [4] *bien nacido.*
[5] εὐγενὴς, εὐγένεια.     [6] *generosioris animi amicus.*

worth of humankind rests, so greatly differs among different humans, agrees perfectly with the recognition that conscience is a familiarity, originating only by means of deeds, with our own, unalterable character, something neither to be explained by something else, nor to be achieved through instruction and, thus, neither originating in time, nor alterable, nor even dependent on chance, but innate, unalterable, and not to be explained further. Accordingly, the course of anyone's life itself, with all its various activities, is nothing more than the external clock-face of that inner, original mechanism, or it is the mirror in which the nature of anyone's own will, which is his core, can only become apparent to his intellect.

Whoever takes the trouble to think through correctly what is said here and in the aforementioned § 10 will discover in my grounding of ethics a consistency and well-rounded completeness, which all others are missing, and also an agreement with the facts of experience, which they have even less. For only truth can thoroughly agree with itself and with nature; in contrast, all false fundamental views internally conflict with themselves and externally with experience, which at each step enters its silent protest.

That the truths presented here in the conclusion especially fly directly in the face of many firmly rooted prejudices and errors, particularly of a certain prevalent kindergarten morality, I am well aware, though without remorse and regret. For first, I do not speak here to children, nor to the people, but to an enlightened academy whose purely theoretical question is directed to the ultimate, fundamental truths of ethics, and who also expect a serious answer to a most serious question; and secondly, I am of the opinion that there can be neither privileged, nor useful, nor even harmless errors, but that any error institutes infinitely more harm than good. — If in contrast, one would like to make existing prejudice into the measure of truth or the boundary-stone that one's exposition may not overstep, then it would be more honest to give up philosophical faculties and academies: for what is not so, should also not appear so.

# TOWARD THE METAPHYSICAL EXPLANATION OF THE URPHENOMENON* OF ETHICS

## § 21
### *Understanding this Supplement*

IN the preceding I have demonstrated the moral incentive to be a fact and have shown that from it alone can arise disinterested justice and genuine loving kindness, the two cardinal virtues on which everything else rests. This is sufficient for the grounding of ethics, insofar as ethics must necessarily be supported by something factually and demonstrably present, be it now given in the external world or in consciousness, if one does not want, like many of my predecessors, merely to arbitrarily accept an abstract proposition and derive from it ethical prescriptions, or, like Kant, to proceed in the same way with a mere concept, that of *law*. The task set by the Royal Society appears to me to have been satisfied by this, since the question is directed to the foundation of ethics and does not also require a metaphysics in order to ground this foundation. Meanwhile, I see quite well that the human mind still does not find ultimate satisfaction and comfort in this. Just as at the end of any research and any real science, so the human mind now stands here before an urphenomenon, which indeed explains everything comprehended under it and resulting from it, but itself remains unexplained and lies before us like a riddle. Thus here, too, the demand for a *metaphysics* presents itself, i.e., for an ultimate explanation of the urphenomena as such, and when they are taken collectively, of the world. Now this demand also raises the question of why that which exists, and which is understood, is as it is and is not otherwise, and how the character of the appearance, which presents itself, proceeds from the essence in itself of things. Indeed, in ethics the need for a metaphysical basis is all the more pressing, since philosophical as well as religious systems are in agreement that the ethical significance of actions would at the same time have to be a metaphysical one, i.e., one reaching beyond the mere appearance of things, and so, beyond all possibility of experience as well, and, consequently, one which would have to stand in strict relation to the

entire existence of the world and the fate of humankind, since the
ultimate point at which the meaning of existence altogether comes
to an end would undoubtedly be ethical. This latter is also proved
by the undeniable fact that with the approach of death, any person's
train of thought, whether he had adhered to religious dogma or not,
takes a *moral* direction, and he takes pains to account for the course
of his entire life from a *moral* point of view. On this, the testimony of
the ancients carries special weight, since they are not under Christian
influence. So I mention that we find this fact already expressed in
a passage, which Stobaeus has preserved for us (*Anthology*, chap. 44,
§ 20), ascribed to the ancient law-giver Zaleucus, however, according
to Bentley and Heyne,* originating from a Pythagorean: 'one must
have in view that point of time as the end comes near and one must
leave life. For all, when they are about to die, are seized by remorse,
remembering the injustice they committed, and wish that each time
they had acted justly.'[1] Likewise, to recall a historical example, we see
262 Pericles* on his deathbed, not wanting to hear of all his great deeds, but
only that he had never caused a citizen grief (Plut[arch]* in *Pericl[es]*).
But now to juxtapose a very different case, I recall from the report of
testimonies before an English jury that a rough, 15-year-old Negro
youth, aboard a ship, dying of an injury received in a brawl, hastily
had all his comrades called nearby to ask them whether he had ever
wronged or offended any of them: he found great peace in the denial.
Experience generally teaches that the dying wish to be reconciled
with everyone prior to death. Familiar experience gives another sort
of proof of our proposition: the author would gladly accept a reward
for intellectual achievements, if only he could get it, even if these
achievements are the greatest masterpieces in the world, yet almost
anyone who has accomplished something of moral excellence refuses
all reward. This is especially the case with great moral deeds, when,
e.g., someone has saved the life of another or even many, endanger-
ing his own. As a rule, even if he is poor, he absolutely refuses reward
because he feels it would detract from the metaphysical worth of

---

[1] Δεῖ τίθεσθαι πρὸ ὀμμάτων τὸν καιρὸν τοῦτον, ἐν ᾧ γίγνεται τὸ τέλος ἑκάστῳ τῆς
ἀπαλλαγῆς τοῦ ζῆν. Πᾶσι γὰρ ἐμπίπτει μεταμέλεια τοῖς μέλλουσι τελευτᾶν, μεμνημένοις
ὧν ἠδικήκασι, καὶ ὁρμὴ τοῦ βούλεσθαι πάντα πεπρᾶχθαι δικαίως αὐτοῖς. (*Oportet ante
oculos sibi ponere punctum temporis illud, quo unicuique e vita excedendum est: omnes enim
moribundos poenitentia corripit, e memoria eorum, quae injuste egerint, ac vehementer optant,
omnia sibi juste peracta fuisse.*)

his action. Bürger* provides us with a poetic presentation of this process at the close of his song of the worthy man. But in reality, too, it most often turns out this way, and many times I came across it in English newspapers.—These facts are universal and occur regardless of religion. On account of this undeniable ethical-metaphysical tendency of life, no religion in the world could get a foothold without giving some sort of explanation in this sense, since by means of its ethical side, religion has its hold on a people's minds. Religion lays its dogma at the basis of its moral incentive, which any person can feel, yet still not understand, and binds the dogma so closely to the incentive that the two seem to be inseparable; indeed, priests take pains to pass off unbelief and immorality as one and the same. Based on this, the believer considers the unbeliever to be identical with the morally bad, as we have already seen, in that expressions such as godless, 263 atheistic, unchristian, heretic, etc., are used as synonyms for morally bad. The matter is made easy for religions since, starting from *faith*, they may absolutely demand faith in their dogma, even through threats. But here philosophical systems do not have such an easy game; thus, one will find on investigation of all systems that both the grounding of ethics and its point of connection with a given metaphysics are generally in an extremely bad way. Yet the demand that ethics be supported by metaphysics is inevitable, as I have already confirmed in the introduction through the authority of Wolf[f] and Kant.

However, now the problem of metaphysics is by far the most difficult of all problems occupying the human mind, so that many thinkers regard it to be absolutely insoluble. In the present case, there is for me still an added, quite special disadvantage that the form of a separate monograph causes; namely, that I may not proceed from a determinate metaphysical system, to which I, perchance, subscribe, because I would either have to present it, which would be far too complicated, or I would have to assume it as given and certain, which would be most awkward. From this, again, it follows that I may use the synthetic method as little as in the preceding, but I may only use the analytic, i.e., I may not proceed from the grounds to the consequence, but I have to go from the consequence to the grounds.* However, this demanding requirement to proceed without presupposition and to start from the standpoint common to all, and from no other, has already made my exposition of the foundation of ethics so very difficult that I now look back on it as on a feat difficult to carry out, one which is analogous to when one has done something in mid-air which otherwise is usually only accomplished on a firm footing. But now, finally, when the question of the metaphysical explanation of the basis of ethics is broached, the difficulty of proceeding without presuppositions becomes so overwhelming that I see as the only way out to turn to quite general sketches, more to provide allusions than explanations, to indicate here the way which leads to the goal, but not to follow it to the end, and in general, only to say a very small part of that which under other circumstances I would have produced. With this proceeding, however, along with the grounds I presented, I refer to the fact that the actual task has been completed in the previous sections; consequently, that which I provide here is supererogatory,[1] a *supplement* provided and to be taken at your discretion.

## § 22

## *Metaphysical Basis*

THUS we must now leave the firm ground of experience, which up to now has supported all of our steps, in order to seek the ultimate theoretical satisfaction where experience cannot possibly reach. We will be fortunate, if by only a pointing finger or a fleeting glance we can get some measure of comfort. However, what should not forsake us is the honest way of proceeding which we followed up to now: we will not, following the way of so-called post-Kantian philosophy, fall into a reverie, serve up fairy tales, impress through words, and try to kick sand in the reader's eyes, but our promise is a little, offered honestly.

That which, up to here, was a ground of explanation, now itself becomes our problem: specifically, the natural compassion innate and ineradicable in any human, which compassion has been given to us as the only source of *non-egoistic actions*, to which, however, moral worth exclusively belongs. The methods of many modern philosophers treat the concepts of *good* and *evil* as *simple*, i.e., concepts neither requiring nor amenable to explanation, and, then, for the most part, speak quite mysteriously and reverentially of an '*idea of the good*' out of which they make the support of their ethics or at least a cloak

---

[1] *opus supererogationis.*

for their inadequacy.[1] It is necessary for me to interject here the explanation that these concepts are anything but simple, much less given *a priori*; rather, they are expressions of a relation and created by everyday experience. Everything that is consistent with the striving of a particular individual will is called *good* with reference to this will—good food, good roads, a good omen—the opposite is called *bad*, or concerning living beings, *evil*. In just the same respect, a person, who by virtue of his character, is disinclined to hinder another's striving, but insofar as he can reasonably do so, is favourable and helpful, a person who, thus, does not injure others, but rather, offers help and support when he can, will be called by them *a good person*; hence, the concept of *good* is applied to him from the same relative, empirical, viewpoint situated in the passive subject. But if we now investigate the character of such a person, not merely with reference to others, but with reference to himself, we know from the preceding that we have recognized a quite immediate participation in the well-being and woe of another as the source of that compassion from which the virtues of justice and loving kindness arise in him. But if we return to that which is essential in such a character, we will undeniably find that *he makes less of a distinction between himself and others than do most*. In the eyes of a malicious character, this *distinction* is so great that he takes immediate pleasure in another's suffering, which, therefore, he seeks without further personal advantage, indeed, even against it. In the eyes of the egoist, the same *distinction* is still great enough that he would use great harm to another as a means to achieving a slight advantage for himself. Thus, for both of these there is a broad chasm, a vast *distinction*, between the *I*, which is limited to its own person, and the *Not-I*, which encompasses the rest of the world: 'the world may perish, if only I be safe'[2] is their maxim. In contrast, for the good person, this *distinction* is in no way as great; indeed, through the actions of generosity it appears to be suspended because here another's well-being demands the cost of one's own; 266

---

[1] 'The concept *of the good*, in its purity, is a *primary concept*, an *absolute idea*, the content of which loses itself in infinity.' [Friedrich] Bouterweck [or Bouterwek (1766–1828) philosopher of aesthetics and one of two professors of philosophy during Schopenhauer's period of study at Göttingen], *Practical Aphorisms* [*Praktische Aphorismen*], p. 54.
One sees that he would prefer to make out of the simple, indeed, trivial concept of *good* a gift from the gods [Διίπετής] in order to be able set it up as an idol in the temple. [Schopenhauer's note.]

[2] *pereat mundus, dum ego salvus sim.*

thus, another's I is made equal to one's own: and where *many* others are to be saved, his own I will be completely sacrificed for them, since the individual gives up his life for the many.

Now the question arises whether the latter apprehension of the relation between one's own and another's I, which lies at the basis of actions of good character, is erroneous and rests on a deception? or whether, instead, this is the case with the opposing apprehension on which egoism and malice stand? —

This apprehension, lying at the basis of egoism, is strictly justified *empirically*. According to experience the *distinction* between one's own person and another's person appears to be an absolute one. The difference of space that separates me from another also separates me from his well-being and woe. — Against this, however, it should first be noted that the cognition which we have of our own selves is in no way exhaustive and clear to its ultimate ground. Through the intuition which the brain carries out on the data of the senses, thus mediately, we recognize our own body as an object in space, and through inner sense, we recognize the continuous series of our striving and acts of will originating on the occasion of external motives, and, finally we recognize the various movements of our own will, weaker or stronger, to which all inner feelings can be traced. That is all: for cognizing itself is not cognized in turn. In contrast, the actual substrate of this whole appearance, our inner *essence in itself*, that which wills and cognizes itself, is not accessible to us: we merely see the outward; the inner is dark. Accordingly the cognition which we have of ourselves is in no way complete and exhaustive; moreover, it 267 is very superficial, and for the greater, indeed, the essential part, we are unknown to ourselves and a riddle, or, as Kant says: the I recognizes itself only as appearance, not as that which it may be in itself. According to that other part that falls within our cognition, each person is completely different from the other, but from this it still does not follow that this is also the case with regard to the great and essential part, which remains cloaked and unknown to anyone. Thus, for this there remains at least a possibility that it be one and identical in all.

On what rests all plurality and numerical difference of beings? — On space and time: only through these is plurality possible, since the many can only be thought of and represented as either next to each other or after one another. Now because many of the same type are *individuals*, I call space and time, in this regard, that which makes *plurality* possible, the principle of individuation,[1] without concern for whether this be the exact sense in which the scholastics took this expression.

If among the information which Kant's marvellous profundity has given the world, there is *anything* undoubtedly true, then it is the *Transcendental Aesthetic*,* thus the doctrine of the ideality of space and time. It is so clearly grounded that it has not been possible to raise any apparent objection to it. It is Kant's triumph and belongs among the very few metaphysical doctrines that can be considered as actually proven and as true conquests in the field of metaphysics. Thus, according to this doctrine, space and time are forms of our own intuitive faculty, belonging to this faculty and not to things cognized through this faculty; thus, they could never be a determination of things in themselves; rather, they belong only to the *appearance* of them, which appearance, as such, is only possible for us through consciousness of the external world bound by physiological conditions. But if *time* and *space* are foreign to the thing in itself, i.e., the true essence of the world, then, too, *plurality* is necessarily so; consequently, in the countless appearances of the sensory world, the thing in itself can only be one, and only that one and identical essence can manifest itself in all these. And conversely, that which presents itself as *many*, hence, in time and space, cannot be the thing in itself, but only an *appearance*. But this appearance, as such, exists merely for our consciousness, which is limited by all sorts of conditions, and indeed, depends on an organic function, and is not outside of consciousness.

268

This doctrine, that all plurality is only apparent, that only one and the same truly existing essence is present and identical in them all and manifests itself in all individuals of this world, no matter how endless the number in which, successively and next to one another, they present themselves; this doctrine certainly precedes Kant; indeed, one might say this doctrine has been present for all time. For it is first of all the principal and basic doctrine of the oldest book of the world, the sacred *Vedas*, the dogmatic part of which, or, rather, the esoteric doctrine, is given in the *Upanishads*.[2] We find that great doctrine on almost every page of this book; it is repeated tirelessly in countless

---

[1] *principium individuationis.*
[2] The authenticity of the *Oupnek'hat* [1801–5] has been challenged on the grounds that some marginal glosses had been appended by Muhammadan copyists and got into

variations and explained through various metaphors and similes.
That, likewise, this doctrine lies at the basis of the wisdom of Pythagoras is certainly not to be doubted, even from the scanty reports of his
philosophy which have reached us. It is well known that almost the
entire philosophy of the Eleatic school* is contained in this doctrine.
Later the Neo-Platonists were pervaded by it, since they taught that,
'because of the unity of all things, all souls are one'.[1] We see this doctrine unexpectedly appearing in Europe in the ninth-century Scotus
Erigena,* who, inspired by it, took pains to dress it in the forms and
expressions of the Christian religion. Among the Muhammadans
we again find it as the inspired mysticism of the Sufis. But in the
Occident, Jordanus Brunus* had to suffer a humiliating and agonizing death because he could not resist the urge to proclaim its
truth. Moreover, we also see the Christian mystics, against their
will and intent, caught up in this doctrine whenever and wherever
it appeared. Spinoza's name is identified with it. Finally in our day,
after Kant had demolished the old dogmatism and the world stood
terrified before the smoking ruins, this knowledge was again awakened through the eclectic philosophy of Schelling, who, amalgam-
ating the teachings of Plotinus, Spinoza, Kant, and Jakob Böhme
with the results of contemporary natural science, hastily composed
a complete piece to temporarily satisfy the pressing need of his
contemporaries and then played it with variations. As a result, this
knowledge achieved general currency among the learned of Germany
and, indeed, is almost universally disseminated even among the

the text. Except that its authenticity was completely vindicated by the Sanskrit scholar
F. H. H. Windischmann (the son) in his *Sankara, or Concerning the Sacred Literature
of the Veda* [*Sancara, siva de theologumenis Vedanticorum*], 1833, p. xix; as well as by
Bochinger, *On the Contemplative Life of the Hindus* [*De la vie contemplative chez les
Indous*], 1831, p. 12.—Through comparison of the most recent translations of individual
Upanishads by Rām Mohan Roy, Poley, and even that of Colebrooke, as also the most
recent by Röer, even the reader unfamiliar with Sanskrit can clearly convince himself
that the one by [Abraham Hyacinthe] Anquetil [-Duperron], which is a strictly literal
translation into Latin carried over from the Persian of the martyr for this teaching,
Sultan [Mohammed] Dara Shikoh, is based on a more accurate and complete understanding of words; and that, in contrast, those others for the most part have helped themselves
by fumbling and guessing; therefore they quite certainly are much less accurate.—One
may find more about this in the second volume of *Parerga* [*and Paralipomena*], chap. 16,
§ 184. [Schopenhauer's note.]

[1] διὰ τὴν ἑνότητα ἀπάντων πάσας ψυχὰς μίαν εἶναι (*propter omnium unitatem cunctas
animas unam esse*) [Plotinus (c.203–269 CE), *Enneads* IV. 9].

merely educated.[1] The sole exception are present-day university philosophers, who have the difficult task of working to oppose so-called
*pantheism*, in the course of which they are placed in great need and
perplexity in their deep anxiety, now grabbing onto the most wretched
sophisms, and again to the most bombastic phrases, in order to tack
together some sort of decorous disguise in which to dress a favourite
and mandatory spinning-wheel philosophy. In short, the one-and-all[2]
was at all times the jest of fools and the endless meditation of the wise. 270
Yet the strict proof of it can be adduced only from Kant's doctrine, as
was shown above, although Kant never had done so himself, but like
a clever orator, gave only the premises, leaving for the listener the joy
of the conclusion.

Hence, if plurality and separateness belong only to *appearance*, and
if it is one and the same essence that presents itself in everything
living, then that apprehension which suspends the distinction
between I and Not-I is not in error. Rather it must be the opposite
that is in error. We also find this latter indicated by Hindus with
the name *Māyā*, i.e., illusion, deception, phantasm. It is the former
view that we have found lying at the basis of the phenomenon of
compassion, indeed, have found compassion to be the real expression
of this view. This view, then, would be the metaphysical basis of
ethics, and it would consist in the fact that *one* individual immediately
recognizes in *another* himself, his own, true essence. Thus, as a result,
practical wisdom, doing right and doing good, would coincide exactly
with the most profound teaching of the most far-reaching theoretical
wisdom, and the practical philosopher, i.e., the just, the benevolent,
the generous person, would express through his deed the same knowledge that is just the outcome of the theoretical philosopher's greatest thoughtfulness and most laborious inquiry. Meanwhile moral
excellence stands higher than all theoretical wisdom, which is always

---

[1] On peut assez longtemps, chez notre espèce,
Fermer la porte à la raison.
Mais, dès qu'elle entre avec adresse,
Elle reste dans la maison,
Et bientôt elle en est maîtresse.

'It is true that with our species the door can for a long time be closed to reason but as
soon as it adroitly enters it remains in the house and soon becomes the mistress there.'
Volt[aire 'Letter to Saurin' 10 Nov. 1777]. [Schopenhauer's note.]

[2] ''Εν καὶ πῆν.

just a patchwork and reaches its goal through the slow path of inferences which the other reaches with a single stroke, and the one who is morally noble, even if he is so very lacking in intellectual excellence, reveals through his action the deepest knowledge, the highest wisdom, and shames the most gifted and learned if through their deeds they reveal that this great truth indeed remains foreign to their hearts.

'Individuation is real: the principle of individuation[1] and the distinction among individuals, resting on the same, is the order of the thing in itself. Each individual is a being fundamentally distinct from all others. In my own self alone I have my true being; everything else, in contrast, is Not-I and foreign to me.'—This is the knowledge, to the truth of which flesh and bone bear witness, the knowledge which lies at the basis of all egoism, and of which every unloving, unjust, or malicious action really is the expression.

'Individuation is merely appearance, originating by means of space and time, which are nothing more than the forms of all objects conditioned by my cerebral, cognitive faculty; thus, plurality and distinction of individuals, too, exists as mere appearance, i.e., only as my *representation*. My true, inner essence exists in everything living just as immediately as it makes itself known only to me in my self-consciousness.'—This knowledge, for which in Sanskrit the formula *tat-twam asi*,* i.e., 'that thou art', is the standing expression, is that which bursts forth as *compassion* on which, therefore, rests all genuine, i.e., disinterested, virtue, and of which every good deed is the real expression. Ultimately, this knowledge is that to which any appeal to leniency, to loving kindness, to mercy instead of justice conforms, for such an appeal is a reminder of the respect in which we are all one and the same essence. In contrast, egoism, envy, hate, persecution, harshness, revenge, *Schadenfreude*, cruelty refer to that other knowledge and are content with it. The emotion and joy, which we feel on hearing about, still more on seeing, and most of all on our own performing a noble action, most profoundly rests on the fact that it gives us the certainty that beyond all plurality and distinction of individuals, which the principle of individuation[2] presents to us, lies a unity of individuals, which truly exists, indeed, is accessible to us, since after all, it appeared as actual fact.

---

[1] *principium individuationis.*     [2] *principium individuationis.*

Depending on whether one adheres to one or the other way of cognizing, between being and being appears what Empedocles* called love[1] or strife.[2] But whoever is inspired by strife,[3] were he, in his hostility, to fathom the deep recesses of his most-hated adversary, to his astonishment, he would there find himself. For just as we place ourselves in all the persons who appear to us in a dream, the case is just the same when we are awake—even if it is not so easy to comprehend. But *tat-twam asi.* 272

The prevalence of one or the other of these two ways of knowing shows itself not merely in individual actions, but in the whole manner of consciousness and mood, which, therefore, in a *good* character is so essentially different from that of the *bad.* The *latter* everywhere feels a thick partition between himself and everything outside himself. To him, the world is an *absolute Not-I*, and his relation to it is a naturally hostile one; thus, the keynotes of his mood are odiousness, distrust, envy, *Schadenfreude.*—In contrast, the good character lives in an external world homogeneous with his essence: to him, others are not Not-I, but 'I once more'. Thus, his natural relation with everyone is friendly: in his innermost being, he feels himself related to all beings, immediately participates in others' well-being and woe, and confidently presupposes the same participation on their part. From this grows a profound inward peace and that confident, calm, contented mood because of which everyone near him feels good.—The evil character in distress does not put his trust in the assistance of others. If he calls to them, he does so without confidence; if he receives assistance, he accepts it without true gratitude because he can scarcely conceive of it as other than the effect of others' foolishness. For then, he is still incapable of recognizing his own in another's essence even after it had given evidence of itself through unambiguous signs. Actually, that which is shocking about all ingratitude is due to this. This moral isolation in which he essentially and inevitably finds himself, lets him readily fall into despair.—The good character will appeal for others' assistance with just as much confidence as he is aware of his willingness to give his to them. For, as was said, to the one, humankind is Not-I; to the other, 'I once more'.—The magnanimous one, who pardons his enemies and returns good for evil, is sublime

---

[1] φιλία.    [2] νεῖκος.    [3] νεῖκος.

and receives the highest praise because he recognizes his very own essence, too, where it was decidedly denied.

Any quite purely benevolent deed, any completely and truly disinterested help that, as such, has as its exclusive motive the distress of another, if we explore it to its ultimate ground, is actually a mysterious action, a practical mysticism, insofar is it ultimately arises from the same cognition which comprises the essence of all genuine mysticism, and is truly explicable in no other way. For, that someone would even give alms, without thereby having the most remote purpose other than that the need which oppresses the other be lessened, is only possible insofar as he recognizes that it is he himself who now appears to him in the sorrowful form, that his own essence in itself might again be recognized in another's appearance. Therefore in the previous part I have called compassion the great mystery of ethics.

Whoever goes to his death for his fatherland has become free of the deception which restricts his existence to his own person: he extends his own being to his countrymen, in whom he lives on, indeed, in the future generations for whom he works—for which reason he considers death as the blink of an eye which does not interrupt vision.

He for whom all others were always Not-I, indeed, who fundamentally took only his own person to be truly real, and who in contrast actually viewed others as phantoms in whom he recognized only a relative existence insofar as they were means to his ends or could have opposed these ends, so that an immeasurable distinction, a deep chasm between his person and all those Not-I remained, who thus existed exclusively in his own person, sees in death all reality and the entire world perishing with his self. Conversely, he, who in all others, indeed, in everything that has life, saw his own essence, saw himself, whose existence, therefore, is fused with the existence of everything living, loses only a small part of his existence through death: he endures in all others, in whom he had always recognized and loved his very essence and his self, and the deception disappears which separated his consciousness from that of the rest. On this, though not completely, yet for the most part, might rest the distinction between the manner in which especially good and predominantly bad people receive their hour of death.

In all centuries poor truth has had to blush because she is paradoxical, and in fact, it is not her fault. She cannot assume the form of universal error which has been enthroned. So, sighing, she looks up to her tutelary god, time, who waves victory and fame to her, but the stroke of whose wings is so long and slow that the individual perishes in the meantime. So I, too, am very well acquainted with the paradox that this metaphysical explanation of the ethical urphenomenon must pose for those educated in the Occident, those who are accustomed to other sorts of groundings of ethics; however, I cannot do violence to the truth. Instead, considering this, all that I may do is prove through quotation how thousands of years ago that metaphysics of ethics was already the fundamental insight of Indian wisdom, a wisdom to which I point back as did Copernicus to the cosmic system of the Pythagoreans, supplanted by Aristotle and Ptolemy. In the *Bhagavad-Gita,*\* Book 13, 27–8, it says, in A. W. v. Schlegel's translation: 'He who sees a supreme lord in all living things, never perishing when they perish, sees truly.—He who sees the same lord present everywhere, will not harm himself through his own fault: then he hastens to the summit.'[1]

With these allusions to the metaphysics of ethics I must let it be, although there remains here still a significant step to take. But this presupposes that one would go even a step further in *ethics*, which I may not do because in Europe ethics fixes its highest goal in the doctrine of right and doctrine of virtue, and what goes beyond this is neither known nor admitted. Thus to this necessary omission may be ascribed the fact that the outline of the metaphysics of ethics presented here still does not allow us, even from a distance, to see the keystone of the entire edifice of metaphysics or the actual coherence of the divine comedy.[2] This, however, lies neither in the task nor in my plan. For one cannot say everything in a single day, nor should one answer more than one is asked. 275

In seeking to advance human knowledge and insight, one will always feel the resistance of the times like that of a load one must drag, a load which presses heavily on the ground, defying all effort. For despite the prejudice, one must comfort oneself with the certainty that one has the truth on one's side, and that as soon as her ally, time, is united with her, she is completely assured of victory, if not today, then tomorrow.

---

[1] *Eundem in omnibus animantibus consistentem summum dominum, istis pereuntibus haud pereuntem qui cernit, is vere cernit.—Eundem vero cernens ubique praesentem dominum, non violat semet ipsum sua ipsius culpa: exinde pergit ad summum iter.*

[2] *Divina Commedia.*

# JUDGEMENT
## OF THE ROYAL DANISH SOCIETY OF SCIENCES

To the question proposed in the year 1837, 'Are the source and basis of moral philosophy to be sought in an idea of morality that resides immediately in consciousness* and in an analysis of the remaining basic moral concepts that arise out of it, or in another cognitive ground?' only one writer attempted a response, whose study, written in German and prefaced by the words: 'Preaching morals is easy, grounding morals is[1] hard,' we were unable to judge worthy of the prize. For, omitting what had been asked first and foremost, he thought that the task was to set up some principle of ethics, so that he placed the part of his study where he expounded the nexus between the ethical principle proposed by him and his metaphysics only in an appendix, which he presented as more than had been required, while the theme itself demanded the kind of investigation in which the nexus between metaphysics and ethics would have been considered first and foremost. But when the writer attempted to show that the basis of ethics consists in compassion, he neither satisfied us with the form of his discussion, nor in fact proved that this basis is sufficient; rather, he was forced to admit the opposite himself. Nor should it go unmentioned that several supreme philosophers of recent times were so indecently mentioned, that it caused just and grave offence.[2]

---

[1] The Academy added this second, 'is' of its own means in order to provide an example of Longinus' lesson (*On the Sublime* 39 [4]) that by adding or removing *one* syllable all the energy of a sentence can be destroyed. [Schopenhauer's note.]

[2] **Judicium**
**Regiae Danicae Scientiarum Societatis.**

*Quaestionem anno 1837 propositam, 'utrum philosophiae moralis fons et fundamentum in idea moralitatis, quae immediate conscientia contineatur, et ceteris notionibus fundamentalibus, quae ex illa prodeant, explicandis quaerenda sint, an in alio cognoscendi principio', unus tantum scriptor explicare conatus est, cujus commentationem, germanico sermone compositam et his verbis notatam:* Moral predigen ist leicht; Moral begründen ist schwer, *praemio dignam judicare nequivimus. Omisso enim eo, quod potissimum postulabatur, hoc expeti putavit, ut principium aliquod ethicae conderetur, itaque eam partem commentationis suae, in qua principii ethicae a se propositi et metaphysicae suae nexum exponit, appendicis loco habuit, in qua plus quam postulatum esset praestaret, quum tamen ipsum thema ejusmodi disputationem flagitaret, in qua vel praecipuo loco metaphysicae et ethicae nexus consideraretur. Quod autem scriptor in sympathia fundamentum ethicae constituere conatus est, neque ipsa disserendi forma nobis satisfecit, neque reapse, hoc fundamentum sufficere, evicit; quin ipse contra esse confiteri coactus est. Neque reticendum videtur, plures recentioris aetatis summos philosophos tam indecenter commemorari, ut justam et gravem offensionem habeat.*

# EXPLANATORY NOTES

## ABBREVIATIONS

Academy Edition    *Kant's Gesammelte Schriften*, ed. the Royal Prussian (later German) Academy of Sciences (Berlin: Georg Reimer, later Walter de Gruyter, 1900– )

*CPr.R*            Kant's *Critique of Practical Reason*

*CPu.R*          Kant's *Critique of Pure Reason*

*GMM*            Kant's *Groundwork of the Metaphysics of Morals*

*SW*              Schopenhauer, *Sämtliche Werke*, 4th edn., ed. Arthur Hübscher, 7 vols. (Mannheim: F. A. Brockhaus, 1988)

[*title page*]: the Greek epigraph means: 'Truth is great, and it will prevail' (1 Esdras 3: 12).

## PREFACE TO THE FIRST EDITION

5   *a posteriori basis*: in *The World as Will and Representation*, vol. II, trans. E. F. J. Payne (New York: Dover, 1966), 122 [*SW* vol. III, p. 133], Schopenhauer explains his somewhat unusual use of *analytic* and *synthetic*: 'The analytic method goes from the facts, the particular, to the propositions, the universal, or from consequents to grounds; the other method [synthetic] proceeds in the reverse direction. Therefore it would be much more correct to name them the *inductive and deductive methods*.'

     *my principal work*: Schopenhauer is referring to *The World as Will and Representation*.

     *On the Will in Nature*: in this work Schopenhauer attempted to show how scientific theories supported his thesis that what we recognize in ourselves as will is that which is expressed in all natural phenomena. He analysed the natural sciences to show how they lead to his metaphysics and argued that his metaphysics completes the scientific image of the world by explaining that which is presupposed and unexplainable by science. Schopenhauer believed that his metaphysics of the will provides a comprehensive explanation of the totality of experience.

6   *this academy*: Schopenhauer uses 'society' and 'academy' interchangeably.

11   *as safely established*: by 'the *negative* part' Schopenhauer is referring to his extensive critique of Kant's ethics in the second chapter of *On the Basis of Morals*.

11　*any metaphysics*: for Schopenhauer's use of the terms *analytic* and *synthetic* see note to p. 5.

12　*will not help us*: by 'us' Schopenhauer here refers to himself and the Danish Academy. Schopenhauer refuses to tell the reader where the error lies, but his fear is that the perceptive reader will nonetheless detect the failing. Then, too, the Danish Academy should have been embarrassed to have failed to 'catch the scent of the rotted spot'.

　　*the Gentleman*: 'Gentleman' here is Schopenhauer's English. The reference to Don Juan is to Act II, Scene 17 of Mozart's *Don Giovanni*. In jest, Don Giovanni invites to a banquet the statue of the Commendatore, Donna Anna's father, whom he has killed. The statue comes, but refuses to eat. Yet the statue then invites Giovanni to dine with it. Giovanni grasps the statue's hand in acceptance. The statue does not release Giovanni, but demands that he repent. When Giovanni repeatedly refuses, he is carried off to hell. Schopenhauer cites this scene in *The World as Will and Representation*, vol. II, p. 452 [*SW* vol. III, p. 517], *On the Will in Nature*, 142 [*SW* vol. IV, p. 143], and *Parerga and Paralipomena*, trans E. F. J. Payne, 2 vols. (Oxford: Clarendon Press), vol. II, p. 388 [*SW*, vol. VI, p. 413].

14　*the human will*: Schopenhauer recognized four fundamental incentives for all human actions. In this essay he discusses three: egoism (a desire for one's own well-being), compassion (a desire for another's well-being), and malice (a desire for another's woe). In *The World as Will and Representation*, vol. II, p. 607 [*SW*, vol. III, p. 697], Schopenhauer articulated a fourth incentive, 'a desire for one's own woe'. He explained that he did not discuss this in *On the Basis of Morals* because the essay was written 'in the spirit of the philosophical ethics prevailing in Protestant Europe', thereby implying that such a discussion would neither be welcomed nor understood by the Royal Danish Society. In a letter to Johann August Becker (10 December 1844), Schopenhauer claimed that this unnamed fourth driving-force had ascetic and not moral value. For Schopenhauer, to have moral value, an action must bear on one's relation with another (see p. 211); whereas, an ascetic desire bears only upon the self. See *Arthur Schopenhauer: Gesammelte Briefe*, ed. Arthur Hübscher (Bonn: Bouvier Verlag Herbert Grundmann, 1987), 221.

　　*supreme philosophers*: throughout Schopenhauer uses the Latin for *supreme philosopher*. We give the English without further note.

　　*Fichte and Hegel*: Johann Gottlieb Fichte (1762–1814) was a German philosopher and professor of philosophy at the universities of Jena and Berlin. He was propelled to fame when his anonymously published *Critique of All Revelation* (1782) was mistaken as Kant's fourth *Critique*. Schopenhauer was drawn to Berlin to hear Fichte, but after enduring his lectures in the winter term of 1811–12, quickly judged that Fichte's philosophy, which was called the 'doctrine of science' (*Wissenschaftslehre*) was already 'empty of science' (*Wissenschaftsleere*). The German philosopher Georg

Wilhelm Friedrich Hegel (1770–1831) had just assumed the important chair of philosophy at the University of Berlin when Schopenhauer's *The World as Will and Representation* appeared in 1818. Schopenhauer blamed Hegel for the failure of his own philosophy to gain an audience, for at the time Hegel was Germany's most influential philosopher. When Schopenhauer became an unsalaried lecturer (*Privatdozent*) in 1820 at Berlin, he had the audacity to schedule his first and only convened lecture course at the same time as Hegel's. He drew five students to Hegel's 200, failed to complete the term, and blamed Hegel for his academic failure. It is curious to note that Schopenhauer mentions Hegel only once in *On the Basis of Morals* (see p. 160).

19 *spinning-wheel philosophy*: the translators are indebted to Günther Zöller for this translation of *Rockenphilosophie*.

20 *foundations of natural science*: the phrase is literally the title of Kant's *Metaphysical Foundations of Natural Science* (1786).

21 *and act disdainfully*: in quoting here, Schopenhauer transposes *Faust*, I. 2177–8. See *Goethe's Faust*, trans. Walter Kaufmann (New York: Doubleday, 1961). A student, *Frosch* (Frog), speaks to his buddies as they try to identify the mysterious strangers who join them for a drink. The strangers, of course, are Faust and the devil himself.

22 *than is imagined*: before quoting this passage, Schopenhauer explains that he has translated it into German 'for the benefit of the German reader'. We provide Locke's original English from *An Essay Concerning Human Understanding*, IV. 20. 18 (ed. Peter H. Nidditch (Oxford: Oxford University Press, 1975), 719).

24 *the false*: Goethe, *Maximen and Reflexionen*, II. 84.

*the common brow*: Friedrich Schiller (1759–1805), 'Die Ideale', stanza 9.

25 *Zoilus...Aristarchus*: Zoilus, Greek grammarian and rhetorician (400–320 BCE), known for his caustic criticism of Homer and Plato. The name Zoilus came to be generally used of a spiteful and malignant critic. Aristarchus of Samothrace (217–*c*.145 BCE), Greek scholar, librarian at Alexandria, is credited with reliable texts of Homer that survive. His name is the origin of the term *aristarch*, used to indicate a caustic literary critic.

*respectable schwanz*: Schopenhauer provides *Zagel* and *Schwanz*, both of which have a double meaning: 'tail', or slang for 'penis'.

27 *Enceladus nor Typhoeus*: in Greek mythology, during the battle between the gods and the giants, Athena tossed the island of Sicily after the fleeing Enceladus. Typhoeus, the first son of Gaia and Tartarus, was a giant with a hundred heads which sounded the calls of various beasts.

28 *at an end*: in Virgil's *Aeneid* (II. 77), the Greek Sinon, who pretends to have deserted the Greek forces, is let into Troy. Sinon gains the Trojans' trust and convinces them that the huge wooden horse at the city gate is an offering of the Greeks, who had abandoned the siege.

## PREFACE TO THE SECOND EDITION

30 *my principal work*: The World as Will and Representation.

31 *a hole in the earth*: Schopenhauer alludes to *Metamorphoses*, XI. 146–93, in which Ovid tells the story of King Midas' having received the ears of an ass for preferring the music of Pan's reeds to Apollo's lyre.

32 *as you deserve*: Zahme Xenien, V. 1315, 1316.

*goes without saying*: see *Über die vierfache Wurzel des Satzes vom zureichenden Grunde: Eine philosophische Abhandlung*, in *SW*, vol. I, § 20, pp. 48–9 (*On the Fourfold Root of the Principle of Sufficient Reason*, trans. E. F. J. Payne (La Salle, Ill.: Open Court, 1974), 73–4).

## ON THE FREEDOM OF THE WILL

33 *Prize Essay on the Freedom of the Will*: see Note on the Text and Translation for a discussion of the differing titles.

[*Epigraph*]: 'freedom is a mystery.' Arthur Hübscher attributes this motto to Claude-Adrien Helvetius (1725–71), *De l'esprit* (1758); see '*La liberté est un mystère*', *Schopenhauer Jahrbuch*, 45 (1964), 26–30.

35 *attach to such things*: these adjectives might better be translated variously, e.g., '*clear* skies', '*open* view', '*clean* air'. However, the German adjective *frei* (free) is in each case suitable, serving Schopenhauer's point that the colloquial language indicates physical freedom.

36 *free choice of the will*: unless otherwise noted, for 'free choice of the will' Schopenhauer uses *liberum arbitrium*. In translating *liberum arbitrium*, we follow Günther Zöller. In his initial translation (above) of the society's question, Schopenhauer rendered the Latin phrase *liberum arbitrium* simply as 'freedom'.

39 *by oneself*: see Immanuel Kant, *CPu.R*, A 445/B 473. Many modern editions, including English translations of this work, will give the pagination for its first edition (1781) as 'A' and its second edition (1787) as 'B'. In 1837 Schopenhauer convinced the editors of the first collected edition of Kant's works, Johann Karl Friedrich Rosenkranz and Friedrich Wilhelm Schubert, that there were significant differences between the two editions and that the second edition introduced numerous contradictions that mitigated against Kant's original radicalism and commitment to idealism, not all evidence of which Kant struck from the second edition. After Schopenhauer sent Rosenkranz a careful collation of the first edition and fifth edition (which was identical to the second), the editor agreed with Schopenhauer's judgement, choosing to publish the *Critique of Pure Reason* in its first edition and relegating to an appendix the alterations and additions found in the second. This 'Rosenkranz' edition to which Schopenhauer refers later in the present essay is *Immanuel Kant: Sämmtliche Werke*, 12 vols. (Leipzig: Leopold

Voss, 1838–42). In vol. II, pp. xi–xiv, extracts from Schopenhauer's letters are published. For Schopenhauer's letters to these editors and for his collation, see Schopenhauer, *Gesammelte Briefe*, 165–74.

40 *conscientia*: Schopenhauer recognizes that the Latin term *conscientia* encompasses the ordinary English senses of both 'conscience' and 'consciousness'.

53 *the supposed antinomy*: see *CPu.R*, A 444 ff./B 472 ff. An antinomy is a pair of contradictory propositions—*thesis* and *antithesis*—with each proposition following from allegedly valid arguments. In this work Kant detailed four antinomies, and Schopenhauer is referring to the third. The *thesis* is: 'causality in accordance with laws of nature is not the only one from which all the appearances of the world can be derived. It is also necessary to assume another causality through freedom in order to explain them.' The *antithesis* is: 'There is no freedom, but everything in the world happens solely in accordance with laws of nature.' Schopenhauer rejected the proof for the thesis since it presumed that a causal series has an unconditioned beginning; see *The World as Will and Representation*, vol. I, pp. 497–8.

59 *Mimosa . . . muscipula*: *Mimosa pudica*, still commonly called 'sensitive plant,' responds to touch. The German name for this plant is 'Rührmichnichtan'—the 'touch-me-not' plant. The leaves of the *Hedysarum gyrans* (now *Codariocalyx motorius*), known as the 'telegraph' or 'semaphore' plant, perceptibly rotate. *Dionaea muscipula* is the infamous Venus's flytrap.

70 *Vacherot*: Victor Cousin (1792–1867), French philosopher and historian, author of the work Schopenhauer has cited above, *Cours d'histoire de la philosophie*.

74 *Apollo and Thersites*: while Apollo was beautiful, Thersites was the ugliest, most obnoxious and loud-mouthed complainer among the Greeks at Troy. In the *Iliad*, Book II, Odysseus beats Thersites for his complaining, and in the lost *Aithiopis* Achilles kills him.

*Herodotus*: (*c*.480–*c*.320 BCE), Greek historian, frequently referred to as the 'father of history'.

76 *of the first edition*: this addition from the second edition of the present work shows that Schopenhauer hoped to have a second edition of *Parerga and Paralipomena*. However, he died before he could produce this. The page reference Schopenhauer gives here is to the 1851 edition. See *Sämmtliche Werke*, ed. Hübscher, vol. VI, § 118, p. 247.

*which he himself committed*: the French philosopher and writer Jean-Jacques Rousseau (1712–78) discusses this incident in his autobiography, *Confessions* (1781–8).

79 *knowledge and instruction*: Antoninus Pius (86–161 CE), Marcus Aurelius Antoninus (121–80 CE), Publius Aelius Hadrian (76–183 CE), and Titus Flavius Vespasianus (9–79 CE), Caius Julius Caesar Germanicus, infamously known as 'Caligula' (12–41 CE), Nero Claudius Caesar (37–68 CE), and Titus Flavius Domitianus (51–96 CE) were Roman emperors.

79  *Seneca*: Lucius Annaeus Seneca (*c*.4 BCE–65 CE) the Roman philosopher, statesman, poet, philosopher, and orator.

*Velleius Paterculus*: (*c*.19 BCE–after 30 CE), a historian who wrote a *Roman History* (*Historia Romanae*).

*Cato*: Marcus Porcius Cato, opponent of Caesar and Stoic philosopher (95–46 BCE): in what immediately follows Schophenhauer refers to Thomas Hobbes, the English philosopher and political theorist (1588–1679) and Joseph Priestley (1733–1804), an English chemist, clergyman, and philosopher. The essay of Friedrich Wilhelm Joseph von Schelling (1775–1854) to which Schopenhauer refers in this note is titled *Philosophical Inquiries into the Essence of Human Freedom* (1809). Schopenhauer counted Schelling, along with Hegel and Fichte, as one of the three pestilential sophists whose pseudo-philosophy despoiled the rare insights of Kant. As a young man Schopenhauer closely studied Schelling, and of the three aforementioned afforded him the slight praise of considering him the most gifted, attributing some value to his philosophy of nature.

81  *and living grows*: Goethe, 'Daimon'.

82  *Buridan*: the theologian and philosopher John Buridan (*c*.1295–1360) was a student of William of Occam, the fourteenth-century philosopher best known for 'Occam's razor'. Buridan's best-known work, *Sophismata*, first appeared in 1489.

83  *Bayle*: Pierre Bayle (1647–1706), whose historical and critical dictionary included comments on Buridan's ass.

85  *second sight*: here Schopenhauer gives the English 'second sight' for the German 'zweiten Gesicht'.

88  *that I brought up above*: see p. 78.

*Great Ethics . . . Eudemian Ethics*: *Ethica magna* [or *Magna moralia*] I. 9–18 and *Ethica Eudemia* II. 6–10.

89  *On Fate*: *De fato*, *c*.45 BCE.

*more or less clearly*: Chrysippus (*c*.280–208 BCE): philosopher, considered by some to be the founder of Stoicism. Diodorus Cronus of Iasos (*c*.300 BCE) of the Megarian school.

*dialogue of the dead*: Lucian (*c*.120–80 CE) Greek orator and satirist.

*Septuagint*: the Greek version of the Hebrew Old Testament translated from *c*.250 BCE on.

90  *Nemesius*: (*c*.400 CE), Syrian Christian Neo-Platonist philosopher.

*Pelagius*: (*c*.360–431 CE), Christian theologian who argued that grace is not necessary for salvation.

*Retractions, Book I, chapter 9*: Schopenhauer cites Augustine's *Retractions: Argumento in libros de lib. arb. ex Lib. I, c. 9 Retractionum desumto*. Because some editors of the *Retractions* combine Book I, chapters 5 and 6 of the

*Retractions* into one, as chapter 5, in some editions of the *Retractions* the comment to which Schopenhauer refers will appear in Book I, chapter 8. For a discussion, see *Saint Augustine: The Retractions*, trans. Sr. Mary Inez Bogan, RSM, The Fathers of the Church: A New Translation, vol. 60 (Washington, DC: Catholic University of America Press, 1968), p. xix.

91 *Argument*: Schopenhauer refers to Augustine's *Retractions* (see previous note).

*Manicheans*: a Persian religious movement led by Mani (216–77 CE), considered a heresy by the Catholic Church because Manicheans asserted a dualism of equal powers of good and evil pervading the universe.

92 *Vanini*: Lucilio Vanini (1584–1619); his *Amphitheatre of Eternal Providence* was published in 1615.

94 *Hume*: David Hume, Scottish philosopher and historian (1711–76), wrote 'Of Liberty and Necessity' as chapter 8 of his *An Enquiry Concerning Human Understanding* (1748).

*Vaucançonian automaton*: Jacques de Vaucançon (1709–82), a French engineer, built a mechanical duck capable of quacking and chewing grain.

95 *in a strange hand*: Academy Edition, vol. V, p. 100.

*to think of it*: Academy Edition, vol. V, p. 103.

96 *aseity*: from the Latin *a se*, 'from onself', refers to the self-originated nature of God, depending on and derived from nothing else.

*Spinoza . . . ethics*: Baruch Spinoza (1632–77), Dutch philosopher whose *Ethics* was first published immediately after his death. Schopenhauer may have admired Spinoza's intellectual integrity, but despite striking points of agreement with Spinoza's philosophy, he rejected what he saw as Spinoza's pantheistic optimism.

98 *De cive*: (1642), published in English as *Philosophical Rudiments Concerning Government and Society* (1651).

100 *Philosophical Necessity*: The Doctrine of Philosophical Necessity Illustrated serves as the appendix to Priestley's *Disquisitions Relating to Matter and Spirit* (1777). Priestley refers to Dr David Harley (1705–57), an English philosopher and physician.

102 *Voltaire*: assumed name of François-Marie Arouet (1694–1778), French philosopher and author, one of Schopenhauer's favourite writers.

103 *Even for a metaphysical purpose . . . as any other natural occurrence*: Schopenhauer cites the opening sentence of *Idea for a Universal History with a Cosmopolitan Purpose* (*Idee zu einer allgemeinen Geschichte in weltbürgerliche Absicht*, 1784).

*Critique of Pure Reason*: the fifth edition of Immanuel Kant's *Kritik der reinen Vernunft* was 1799. Here and subsequently Schopenhauer cites the first and fifth editions: these correspond to the A and B pagination respectively.

103 *Critique of Practical Reason*: Kant's *Kritik der praktischen Vernunft* (1788), Academy Edition, vol. V, p. 99.

. . . *pages 224–231*: *CPu.R*, Academy Edition, vol. V, pp. 94–100.

104 *Body and Soul*: *Leib und Seele* by Johann Eduard Erdmann (1805–92), German historian and philosopher.

105 *The boys are masters of the course*: Goethe, *Parabolic*, no. 7, line 8.

*Jakob Böhme*: (1575–1624), German cobbler, merchant, and famous mystic.

106 *Condillac*: Etienne Bonnot de Condillac (1715–80), French Catholic philosopher.

*Maine de Biran*: François Pierre Maine de Biran (1766–1824), a French philosopher and popularizer of Locke.

107 *with them for hours*: Friedrich Schiller, *The Death of Wallenstein*, Act II, Scene 3.

108 *be this so*: with these lines (*Twelfth Night*, I. v.), Olivia, a rich countess, resolves to reject a suitor.

109 *I am not as guilty . . . I would murder others*: 'Arrival of Troops from Bombay and Madras.—', *The Times*, 2 July 1845, p. 5 col. B. Schopenhauer translated into German Gomez's words as reported in *The Times*. We provide the English of the *Times* article; however, the emphases are Schopenhauer's.

*Schiller's Wallenstein*: *Death of Wallenstein*, Act II, Scene 3.

111 *in the Rosenkranz*: *CPr.R*, Academy Edition, vol. V, p. 106.

120 *Nicomachean Ethics III. 2*: Hübscher cites *Eudemian Ethics* II. 7 and 9, 1223 and 1225; for the *Nicomachean Ethics*, Hübscher cites III. 2.1110 ff. In modern editions, 1110 occurs in III. 1.

*when lewd debaucheries lead to horrible illness*: on his return from his second trip to Italy in 1825 it is probable that an illness Schopenhauer suffered was due to his indiscretions, but he was never eaten by a bear.

## ON THE BASIS OF MORALS

121 *On the Basis of Morals*: see Note on the Text and Translation for a discussion of the differing titles.

[*Epigraph*]: *Über den Willen in der Natur*, *SW* vol. IV, p. 140. Schopenhauer actually put it: 'Moral-Predigen leicht, Moral-Begründen schwer ist'—'moral-preaching easy, moral-grounding is difficult', a rather more stylistically interesting construction. See also Schopenhauer's note on p. 276.

123 *conscience*: for the Latin term *conscientia* we have chosen 'conscience'. In translating the Royal Society's Latin introduction to the question, Schopenhauer chooses the German *Gewissen*, or 'conscience'; however,

in translating the question itself, Schopenhauer chooses first *Bewußtein*, 'consciousness', but adds parenthetically, *Gewissen*, 'conscience'.

125 *Meister*: Johann Christian Friedrich Meister (1758–1828), a professor of law and author of *Lehrbuch des Naturrechts* (*Textbook on Natural Law*) (1809).

126 *parrhesia*: meaning 'to speak freely, candidly', a classical rhetorical figure noted, among other places, in the *Rhetorica ad Herennium* IV. 36–7. 48–50 (in Latin, *licentia*), and in Quintilian's *Institutio Oratoria* IX. 2. 27.

*Christian Wolf[f]*: (1679–1754), perhaps the most significant German philosopher between Leibniz and Kant, was a professor of mathematics at the University of Halle. In 1723, because of his reputation and influence as a significant proponent of Enlightenment philosophy, he was dismissed from his position by the Pietist-dominated authorities. He went to the University of Marburg, where he became Professor of Mathematics and Philosophy. On the intervention of Friedrich II (Friedrich the Great), in 1740 he returned to the University at Halle.

*Preface*: GMM, Academy Edition, vol. IV, p. viii.

127 *built from the ground up*: see note to p. 5, *a posteriori basis*.

*urphenomenon*: the coinage translates the German *Urphänomen*. In both German and English the prefix *ur-* occurs in other combinations to indicate something primordial, primitive, original—something as a source, something non-derivative. The prefix is used here to indicate more specifically a source from which related phenomena are derived, but which is itself not derivable from or explicable by other physical phenomena. At § 21, p. 259, Schopenhauer explains: 'an urphenomenon, which indeed explains everything comprehended under it and resulting from it, but itself remains unexplained and lies before us like a riddle . . . the demand for a *metaphysics* . . . for an ultimate explanation of the urphenomena as such, and when they are taken collectively, of the world.' It is possible that Schopenhauer derived the idea of an urphenomenon from Goethe's *On the Theory of Colours* (1810), where Goethe argued that lightness and darkness were the *urphänomene* for colours. (But Schopenhauer found the phenomena of lightness and darkness not to be urphenomena, because they could be accounted for by states or modifications of the eye, and thus, by physical phenomena.) The translators recognize this term as a coinage, although perhaps not without precedent.

128 *Better is . . . vain striving*: Ecclesiastes 4: 6.

*von Zimmermann*: Johann Georg Ritter von Zimmermann (1728–95), Swiss philosopher and physician; his *Observation on Solitude* was published in 1756.

*loving kindness*: the German is *die Menschenliebe*, literally 'love of humankind', most often translated as 'philanthropy'. For Schopenhauer the capacity is much broader than the modern sense of charitable action and is a capacity of some higher animals as well as humans. What is more, the object of this loving kindness is not just humans, but also other animals.

131 *Garve's . . . Ethics*: Christian Garve (1741–98), Professor of Philosophy at Leipzig. Reference is to his *Uebersicht der vornehmsten Principien der Sittenlehre, von dem Zeitalter des Aristoteles an bis auf unsere Zeiten* (Breslau: W. G. Korn, 1798).

*Stäudlin's History of Moral Philosophy*: Karl Friedrich Stäudlin (1761–1826), Professor of Theology at Göttingen; reference is to his *Geschichte der Moralphilosophie* (Hannover, 1822).

*Columbus's egg*: an idea or discovery that in retrospect seems simple: attributed to various origins, including (probably apocryphally) Christopher Columbus, who was alleged to have won a wager that he could balance an egg on its end. He was said to have accomplished this task by slightly crushing the bottom of an egg to make it stand upright.

135 *. . . moral investigation*: *GMM*, Academy Edition, vol. IV, p. 392.

*new edition prepared by Rosenkranz*: see note to p. 39.

136 *pp. 223–231*: *CPr.R*, Academy Edition, vol. V, pp. 94–100.

*pp. 438 ff.*: *CPu.R*, Academy Edition, A 532/B 560–A 558/B 586.

*p. 54*: *GMM*, Academy Edition, vol. IV, p. 426; Schopenhauer adds emphasis on the phrase, '*ought to happen, even if it never happens*'. The phrase πρῶτον ψεῦδος is from Aristotle's *Prior Analytics* II. chap. 18, 66a, 16.

*petitio principii*: to 'beg the question' is to assume one's conclusion as a premise for one's argument.

*Who told you*: for 'you' in this and the following two questions Schopenhauer uses the plural *familiar* German form, *euch*. In this context, the choice is condescending.

137 *thou shalt (sic) not lie*: the biblical form 'thou shalt' has its German equivalent in 'du sollt', whereas, Schopenhauer's contemporary form would be 'du sollst', more equivalent to 'you should'.

138 *Decalogue*: i.e. the Ten Commandments.

*R., p. 16*: *GMM*, Academy Edition, vol. IV, p. 397.

139 *contradictio in adjecto*: a term of craft for Schopenhauer, attributing a quality to a noun such that the attributed quality contradicts the meaning of the noun. Rhetorically, this is usually an oxymoron or paradox, such as the ever-tasty 'jumbo shrimp'.

*On Understanding*: in a footnote Schopenhauer provides a German translation of Locke's English, mis-citing the source slightly: it is *An Essay Concerning Human Understanding*, Book II, chap. 28, § 6.

141 *sixth and seventh sections*: Schopenhauer referred to the sections, indicated by §, as *Paragraphen*, 'paragraph'.

142   *The Metaphysical First Principles . . . p. 230*: i.e. Part II of Kant's
      *Metaphysics of Morals*, Academy Edition, p. 386.

      *. . . p. 57*: *GMM*, Academy Edition, vol. IV, pp. 422 and 429.

      *Cleopatra . . . Arria*: Cleopatra, Egyptian queen (66–30 BCE), was a
      favourite of Julius Caesar and Mark Antony; she is traditionally said
      to have committed suicide not with a knife, but by sleeping with an asp;
      Marcus Cocceius Nerva (15–98 CE), Roman emperor 96–8 CE; Arria
      Caecina, wife of Paetus, committed suicide in 42 CE.

143   *Tissot*: Simon André Tissot (1728–97), a Swiss physician in Lausanne, author
      of *A Treatise on the Diseases Produced by Onanism* (1758; English trans. 1832).
      See C. Rosenberg and C. Smith-Rosenberg (eds.), *The Secret Vice Exposed!
      Some Argument Against Masturbation* (New York: Arno Press, 1974).

144   *p. 142*: *CPr.R*, Academy Edition, vol. V, p. 31; although Schopenhauer
      marks this as a direct quote, it is a loose paraphrase.

      *p. 5*: *GMM*, Academy Edition, vol. IV, p. 389.

      *it must not borrow . . . from anthropology*: Academy Edition, vol. IV, p. 389;
      Schopenhauer interjects that which is in parentheses without note.

      *every rational being*: *GMM*, Academy Edition, vol. IV, p. 425; Schopen-
      hauer adds emphases.

145   *only because of this*: Schopenhauer here paraphrases and quotes without
      attribution Kant's *GMM*, Academy Edition, vol. IV, p. 425 (second
      edition, p. 59 and Rosenkranz, p. 52).

146   *rational soul . . . just rational*: *anima rationalis . . . anima sensitiva . . . anima
      vegitativa*: likely an allusion to distinctions (discussed in Aristotle's *On
      the Soul* [*De anima*], Book II, chap. 2) among the types of souls possessed
      by living beings. The vegetative soul (*anima vegitativa*), sometimes also
      translated as nutritional soul, is typically ascribed to plants and concerns
      the capacity to receive nutrition, grow, and reproduce. The sensitive
      soul, or animal soul (*anima sensitive*), includes the capacity for sense per-
      ception, desire, and motion. The rational soul, or human soul (*anima
      rationalis*), is capable of reason and reflection. These souls are arranged
      in a hierarchy corresponding to the type of living being which possesses
      them. They are such that all higher forms have the properties of the
      lower, but not vice-versa.

147   *p. 228*: *CPr.R*, Academy Edition, vol. V, p. 97.

      *p. 18*: *GMM*, Academy Edition, vol. IV, p. 398.

148   *two pointed epigrams*: 'Scruple of Conscience': 'Gladly I serve my friends,
      but alas I do it with pleasure, | Hence I am plagued with doubt that
      I am not a virtuous person.' 'Decision': 'Sure, your only resource is to try
      to despise them entirely, | And then with aversion to do what your duty
      enjoins you.' Trans. A. B. Bullock, cited in H. J. Paton, *The Categorical
      Imperative: A Study in Kant's Moral Philosophy* (Philadelphia: University
      of Pennsylvania Press, 1971), 48.

148  *p. 211*: CPr.R, Academy Edition, vol. V, p. 84; Schopenhauer adds emphasis.

  *p. 257*: CPr.R, Academy Edition, vol. V, p. 118; Schopenhauer makes lexical and syntactic changes but preserves the meaning of the quoted material.

  *p. 18*: GMM, Academy Edition, vol. IV, p. 398.

  *fear of the gods: deisidämonie*, the Greek δεισιδαιμονία, transliterated.

  *p. 19*: GMM, Academy Edition, vol. IV, pp. 399–400.

  *the maxim which one obeys*: Schopenhauer offers here an unconventional interpretation of Kant's understanding of the source of moral worth. Kant claims that actions possess moral worth if they are done out of duty. One could say the *intention* is *to do one's duty*. Maxims, however, if they are capable of becoming universal laws, specify duties and delineate moral right and wrong. See GMM, Academy Edition, vol. IV, pp. 397–402 and 421–3.

149  *p. 20*: GMM, Academy Edition, vol. IV, p. 400.

  *p. 28*: GMM, Academy Edition, vol. IV, p. 406.

  *p. 29*: GMM, Academy Edition, vol. IV, p. 407; Schopenhauer paraphrases here and by the German grammatical construction indicates it as such, despite the quotation marks.

  *p. 50*: GMM, Academy Edition, vol. IV, pp. 408 and 419.

  *p. 21*: GMM, Academy Edition, vol. IV, p. 402.

  *core of the poodle*: in early modern Germany black poodles were considered to be consorts of the devil. In Goethe's *Faust* the learned Doctor Faust takes in a stray black poodle, actually Mephistopheles in disguise. In Part I Mephistopheles is tortured as Faust debates aloud how to translate the opening line of John's Gospel. After taking various fantastic shapes, as Faust conjures, at line 1323 Mephistopheles finally transforms into a travelling scholar, at whose appearance Faust says: 'So that was the core of the poodle.'

150  *a fortuitous union of Poverty and Plenty*: Schopenhauer is echoing a famous myth Socrates retells from Diotima in the *Symposium* at 203b, in which Poverty conceives Eros of drunken Plenty, who is a lot like Socrates himself.

152  *p. 53*: GMM, Academy Edition, vol. IV, p. 425.

  *p. 44*: GMM, Academy Edition, vol, IV, p. 419.

  *p. 45*: GMM, Academy Edition, vol. IV, pp. 419–20.

  *Reinhold*: Carl Leonhard Reinhold (1758–1823), Professor of Philosophy at Jena and later at Kiel, the first great popularizer of Kant's philosophy.

153  *p. 830 of the fifth edition*: CPu.R, Academy Edition, A 802/B 830

  *(Schiller)*: *The Philosophers*, line 24.

is laid out in Rosenkranz's preface to ... Kant's works: see note to p. 39.

154 *Diderot had Rameau's nephew say . . . (Goethe's translation, p. 104):*
Rameau's Nephew: A Dialogue (1769) by Denis Diderot (1713–84), the
French Enlightenment philosopher, art critic, mathematician, and poet.

'I have frequently observed . . . what is best': Georg Christoph Lichtenberg
(1742–99), wit and satirist; from his *Miscellaneous Writings*, Göttingen,
vol. I (1844), 169.

*of which the following is a clearer presentation*: GMM, Academy Edition,
vol. IV, pp. 402–4.

*p. 147*: CPr.R, Academy Edition, vol. V, p. 34.

155 *Hutcheson*: Francis Hutcheson (1694–1747), Scottish philosopher who
wrote *A System of Moral Philosophy* (1755).

*p. 8*: GMM, Academy Edition, vol. IV, p. 391.

157 *p. 223*: CPr.R, Academy Edition, vol. V, p. 94.

*p. 230*: CPr.R, Academy Edition, vol. V, p. 99.

*'you can: for you ought'*: the exact wording is not from Kant, but has a
tradition from Schiller, 'The Philosophers', *Xenien* 383; however, see
CPr.R, Academy Edition, vol. V, pp. 31 and 159.

*apagogic*: a means of disproving a claim by demonstrating that maintain-
ing the claim would lead to absurd consequences; sometimes known as
*reductio ad absurdum*.

*p. 163*: CPr.R, Academy Edition, vol. V, p. 47.

*p. 164*: CPr.R, Academy Edition, vol. V, p. 49.

*Fichte . . . p. 49: System of Moral Theory following the Principles of the
Science of Knowledge (System der Sittenlehre nach den Principien der
Wissenschaftslehre)* (Jena and Leipzig: 1798).

159 *p. 8*: CPr.R, Academy Edition, vol. V, p. 49.

*Jacobi*: Friedrich Heinrich Jacobi (1743–1819), an opponent of the
Enlightenment, well known for launching a controversy with the
eminent philosopher Moses Mendelssohn concerning Lessing's being a
'Spinozist' and for accusing Fichte of being an atheist.

*pulverize*: the verb here (*zermalmen*) echoes the words of Moses
Mendelssohn, who called Kant 'the all-pulverizing' ('alles zermalmenden
Kant'), *Early Morning Hours, or Lectures on the Being of God (Morgenstunden
oder Vorlesungen ueber das Dasein Gottes)* (1785).

160 *Cloudcuckooland*: in Aristophanes, *Birds* 819, the comic heroes plan to
found a utopia in the sky called 'Cloudcuckooland'.

164 *as it stands in the first edition*: Schopenhauer here is probably referring
to the *CPu.R*, 'The Second Book of the Transcendental Dialectic',
A 341–A 367.

165 *De la Forge*: Louis de la Forge, a seventeenth-century French physician;
in *Parerga and Paralipomena*, vol. I, p. 49, Schopenhauer recommends

the work of de la Forge as evidence of how the flaws of Descartes' system are unwittingly worked out by his followers.

166   *Phaedo*: 99a ff.

*On the Power of the Imagination . . . 13*: (*Della forza della fantasia*) by Ludovico Antonio Muratori (1672–1750), Italian historian.

*Act only according to . . . all rational beings*: Schopenhauer here paraphrases various statements of the categorical imperative in *Groundwork of the Metaphysics of Morals*. The most well-known statement of Kant's categorical imperative can be found in the Academy Edition, vol. IV, p. 421.

168   *p. 24*: *GMM*, Academy Edition, vol. IV, p. 403.

*p. 49*: *GMM*, Academy Edition, vol. IV, p. 422.

*p. 50*: *GMM*, Academy Edition, vol. IV, p. 423.

*p. 192*: *CPr.R*, vol. V, p. 69.

*Metaphysical First Principles of the Doctrine of Virtue, § 30*: Academy Edition, p. 453.

*p. 67*: *GMM*, Academy Edition, vol. IV, p. 437.

169   *a hypothetical imperative*: a categorical imperative applies without condition, e.g., 'Thou shalt not lie'—no ifs, ands, or buts. A hypothetical imperative allows such conditions as, 'If you wish to avoid God's wrath, thou shalt not lie'.

*Wordsworth*: *Memorials of a Tour in Scotland*, XI, 'Rob Roy's Grave'. Wordsworth's stanza reads: 'For why?—because the good old rule | Sufficeth them, the simple plan, | That they should take, who have the power, | And they should keep who can.'

170   *p. 60*: *GMM*, Academy Edition, vol. IV, p. 424.

171   *at the head of this division*: i.e. the division of duties to oneself from the duties to others.

*p. 48*: *GMM*, Academy Edition, vol. IV, p. 422.

*. . . p. 57*: *GMM*, Academy Edition, vol. IV, pp. 422 and 429.

172   *p. 55*: *GMM*, Academy Edition, vol. IV, p. 427.

*p. 56*: *GMM*, Academy Edition, vol. IV, p. 428.

*'Metaphysical First Principles of the Doctrine of Virtue', § 16*: Academy Edition, p. 442.

*§ 17*: Academy Edition, p. 443.

173   *pariahs, chandalas, and mlechchas*: three terms drawn from Hinduism: a *pariah* is a low-caste agricultural labourer, hence, a social outcast; a *chandala* is the offspring of a high-caste woman and a low-caste man, hence, an abomination; a *mlechcha* is a foreigner who does not speak Sanskrit, and hence has no protection under Hindu law.

*Act in such a way . . . simply as a means*: *GMM*, Academy Edition, vol. IV, p. 429.

175   *p. 60*: *GMM*, Academy Edition, vol. IV, p. 431.

     *p. 62*: *GMM*, Academy Edition, vol. IV, p. 433.

176   *Kant celebrates* . . . *p. 62*: *GMM*, Academy Edition, vol. IV, pp. 433 ff.

177   *p. 66*: *GMM*, Academy Edition, vol. IV, p. 436.

     *So right . . . just in time*: Goethe, *Faust*, Part I, ll. 1995–6.

     *p. 97*: *GMM*, Academy Edition, vol. IV, p. 461.

178   *p. 52*: *GMM*, Academy Edition, vol. IV, pp. 389 and 425.

     *p. 44*: *GMM*, Academy Edition, vol. IV, p. 419.

     *p. 45*: *GMM*, Academy Edition, vol. IV, p. 420.

180   συνείδησις: both the Latin *conscientia* and the Greek συνείδησις mean either 'conscience' or 'consciousness'.

     *Court of the Star Chamber*: Schopenhauer actually names the *Vehmgericht*, a secret tribunal in Westphalia which came into prominence in the thirteenth century as a court intended to ensure conformity to church doctrine. An analogy for English readers is to the Court of the Star Chamber.

182   *that, 'but if through his conscience . . . indeed the accuser would lose every time'*: 'Metaphysical First Principles of the Doctrine of Virtue', Academy Edition, p. 438.

     *here*: i.e. in 'Metaphysical First Principles of the Doctrine of Virtue', Academy Edition, pp. 439–40.

184   *pp. 561–582 of the fifth edition*: *CPu.R*, Academy Edition, pp. A 533–554, B 561–582.

     *pp. 224–231*: *CPr.R*, Academy Edition, vol. V, pp. 94–100.

     *Holbach*: the *Système de la nature* (1770) of the French philosopher Paul Henri Dietrich, baron d'Holbach (1723–89).

187   *Porphyry*: (232–305 CE), Neo-Platonist philosopher, pupil and biographer of Plotinus.

     *Stobaeus*: Joannes Stobaeus (*c*.5th century CE), a Neo-Platonic, author of the *Anthology* or *Florilegium*, a collection of philosophical sayings of 500 Greek authors, published in Leipzig by Teubner in Greek as *Anthologion* (1855) and in Latin as *Florilegium* (1855–7).

189   *the doctrine of empty science*: see note to p. 14.

194   *Sextus Empiricus*: a second-century CE Greek physician and philosopher whose writings are our main source for the sceptical philosophy of Pyrrhon (*c*.360–*c*.270 BCE).

195   *theory of pre-occupation*: the legal theory that one can gain possession of property by occupying it.

197   *d'Alembert*: Jean le Rond d'Alembert (1717–83), French philosopher and mathematician, one of the encyclopaedists.

198   *To be honest . . . of ten thousand*: Schopenhauer cites, in English, *Hamlet*, II. ii. 178–9.

198 *you shall kindle no fire . . . throughout your habitations*: Exodus 35: 3.

202 *The German word Selbstsucht . . . connotation of sickness*: in the compound *Selbstsucht*, the German noun *Sucht* carries the primary meaning of 'passion', 'mania', 'rage', or 'craze'. Archaically, it means 'sickness' or 'disease'.

205 *Schadenfreude*: this German word indicates a malicious joy or pleasure taken in another's misfortune. Hereafter it will be used in this sense in the text, in italics as a foreign borrowing.

206 *Milton's Pandemonium*: *Paradise Lost*, I. 756 ff.

208 *Arnold von Winkelried*: legendary Swiss hero who, in the Battle of Sempach (1386), is alleged to have rescued his Swiss compatriots by throwing himself against the spears of the Austrian enemy.

214 *the three fundamental incentives*: see note to p. 14.

   *Plato*: *Republic* 584b ff.

215 *Cassina*: Ubaldo Cassina (1736–1824), Italian moral philosopher at the University of Padua. Schopenhauer also refers to the German translation by Karl Friedrich Pockels (1757–1810). Although he was fluent in Italian, Schopenhauer likely used the Pockels' translation and had it in his library: *Analytischer Versuch über das Mitleiden* (Hannover, 1790). In English the title would be translated as 'Analytic Investigation of Compassion'.

220 *she*: Schopenhauer's reference to justice as 'she' follows Pausanias in Plato's *Symposium*. Pausanias uses the Greek terms here to distinguish between two female goddesses of love, two Aphrodites: the common, or vulgar (πάνδημος) at 180d and the heavenly (οὐρανία) at 181b.

   *Hugo Grotius*: (1583–1645), Dutch scholar, lawyer, and statesman, author of *De Iure Belli ac Pacis* (*The Law of War and Peace*, 1625).

   *Give to each his own*: cf. Plato, *Republic* 331e.

226 *Ask me no question, and I'll tell you no lies*: Schopenhauer cites the maxim in English, providing a German translation in a footnote.

227 *that of the Marquis Posa . . . Gerusalemme liberata II. 22*: Friedrich Schiller, *Don Carlos*, Act V, Scene 3; *Gerusalemme liberata* is an epic poem by Torquato Tasso (1544–95).

   *At Kant's suggestion*: see Kant, *The Metaphysical Principles of Virtue*, Academy Edition, p. 429.

228 *three others selected unsuitably*: the other three classical cardinal virtues are courage, wisdom, and moderation.

229 *Veda . . . Purāna*: the *Veda* forms the four basic collections of Hindu scripture; the *Dharmaśāstra* is a collection of Hindu rules governing society, among which the most famous are the law-codes of Manu; the *Itihāsa* is a collection of early Hindu literature comprising legends, myths, poems, and the like, associated with epics, and *Purāna* are Sanskrit verses giving mythological accounts of ancient times.

231 *Calderón*: Pedro Calderón de la Barca (1600–81), Spanish playwright, a dominant figure in Spain's Golden Age of the theatre.

233 *Wollastone*: William Wollaston (1659–1724), English moral philosopher and deist, author of the highly popular *The Religion of Nature Delineated* (1722).

*Hutcheson*: see note to p. 155.

*Adam Smith*: (1723–90), Scottish moral philosopher and political economist, author of *The Theory of Moral Sentiments* (1759) and *The Wealth of Nations* (1776).

235 *Guebres*: followers of Zoroastrianism, a religion of the prophet Zarathustra originating in Persia (now Iran), sometimes claimed to be the first religion to postulate a duality of forces, good and evil.

236 *St Bartholomew's . . . Alba*: the Duke of Alba [Alva] was the title of Fernando Alvarez de Toledo (1508–82), a Spanish general and conqueror of Portugal; governor of the Netherlands. The Saint Bartholomew's Day Massacre, 24–5 August 1572, was the onset of murders of thousands of French Huguenots by Catholics, beginning in Paris on the feast day of St Bartholomew.

240 *Boileau*: Nicolas Boileau-Despréaur (1636–1711), French poet; the quotation is from his *Satire* VIII. 165.

241 *a canting zootomist*: in a letter to Julius Frauenstädt (12 Sept. 1852) Schopenhauer identifies the unnamed animal anatomist as Rudolph Wagner (1805–64), a physiologist and anthropologist, professor at Erlangen and Göttingen. Schopenhauer also refers to Wagner in another letter to Frauenstädt on 15 October 1852. See *Gesammelte Briefe*, ed. Hübscher, pp. 294 and 296–7.

242 *Sanyassi*: a Hindu ascetic who renounces the world, including all ties to family and any permanent residence, instead wandering, subsisting on alms, dedicated solely to the goal of *mokṣa*, or liberation.

243 'cold superstition': from Hermann Ludwig Heinrich, prince of Pückler-Muskau (1785–1871), *Letters of a Dead Man*.

246 *p. 257*: CPr.R, Academy Edition, vol. V, p. 118.

247 *Mandeville*: Bernard Mandeville (1670–1733), author of *The Fable of the Bees: or, Private Vices, Publick Benefits* (1714).

248 *the Chinese accept five cardinal virtues*: the 'five constants' (*wu-ch'ang*), i.e., whatever ought to be constantly upheld, are (1) *jen* (given by Schopenhauer as *sin*): humaneness, benevolence, compassion, empathy, sympathy; (2) *yi*: appropriateness, justice, fairness; (3) *li*: observing rights and customs, i.e., all forms of civilized behaviour; (4) *chih*: wisdom, knowing, intelligence, discerning; and (5) *hsin*: mutual trust, i.e., both trustfulness and trustworthiness.

249 *Phocion*: (c.402–318 BCE), an Athenian military commander-in-chief.

249 *Pañcatantra*: an Indian collection of stories intending to teach moral and other lessons, compiled in about the fifth century CE.

*Lessing, too, said in a letter . . . all sorts of magnanimity*: the citation is to *Lessings Werke* (Leipzig, 1867), vol. X, p. 249; Gotthold Ephraim Lessing (1729–81), German dramatist and critic.

251 *Lichtenberg . . . 'Moral Observations'*: new edition (Göttingen, 1844): vol. I, p. 142.

252 *in the preceding essay . . . under 3*: see pp. 54 ff. above.

254 *Joh. v. Müller*: Johannes von Müller (1752–1809), Swiss theologian, philologist, historian, and statesman.

256 *. . . Indeed you are what you are*: Goethe, *Faust*, Part I, ll. 1806–9; the emphases are Schopenhauer's.

259 *Urphenomenon*: see note to p. 127.

260 *according to Bentley and Heyne*: Zaleucus (*c.*650 BCE), renowned as a law-giver of Greece; Richard Bentley (1662–1742), English classical philologist and textual critic; Christian Gottlob Heyne (1729–1812), German classical philologist.

*Pericles*: (493–429 BCE), celebrated Athenian orator and politician.

*Plut[arch]*: (46–125 CE), Graeco-Roman statesman and historian.

261 *Bürger*: Gottfried August Bürger (1747–94), German poet.

*from the consequence to the grounds*: see note to p. 5.

265 *Transcendental Aesthetic*: Schopenhauer here refers to the 'Transcendental Aesthetic', the first part of the 'Transcendental Doctrine of Elements' from Kant's *Critique of Pure Reason*.

266 *the Eleatic school*: early- to mid-5th century BCE Greek pre-Socratic philosophers, followers of Parmenides of Elea, noted for their tendency towards monism, a belief that the universe is but a single substance.

*Scotus Erigena*: Johannes Scotus Erigena (*c.*810–877 CE), Irish philosopher at the court of Charles the Bald, much influenced by Neo-Platonism.

*Jordanus Brunus*: Latinized form of Giordano Bruno (1548–1600), the Italian philosopher, scientist, and Dominican whom the church burned at the stake as a heretic because he accepted Copernican astronomy. Schopenhauer unsuccessfully tried to secure a contract for a Latin translation of Bruno's *On the Cause, the Principle, and the One* (*Della causa, principio ed uno*), and in *The World as Will and Representation*, vol. I, § 67, he says of Bruno's fate: 'So died Socrates and Giordano Bruno, and so did many a hero of truth meet his death at the stake at the hands of priests.'

268 *tat-twam asi*: one of the 'great sayings' found in the *Chāndogya Upanishad*, meaning that ultimate reality (*Brahman*) is immanent in the self (*ātman*) of all beings.

269 *Empedocles*: (5th century BCE), pre-Socratic physician and philosopher who viewed love and hate as two primal forces exemplified in the cosmos.

271 *Bhagavad-Gita*: the Sanskrit 'Song of the Lord', a section from Book 6 of the *Mahābārata*, one of the most revered and influential Hindu texts. Schopenhauer cites the translation by August Wilhelm von Schlegel (1767–1845), philologist, poet, and translator, one of the most important of the early German Romantics.

272 *immediately in consciousness*: the Latin *conscientia* includes both the English meanings 'consciousness' and 'conscience' as Schopenhauer recognizes; see p. 40 above.

# INDEX

*The Oxford World's Classics Website*

**www.worldsclassics.co.uk**

- Browse the full range of Oxford World's Classics online

- Sign up for our monthly e-alert to receive information on new titles

- Read extracts from the Introductions

- Listen to our editors and translators talk about the world's greatest literature with our Oxford World's Classics audio guides

- Join the conversation, follow us on Twitter at OWC_Oxford

- Teachers and lecturers can order inspection copies quickly and simply via our website

**www.worldsclassics.co.uk**

American Literature

British and Irish Literature

Children's Literature

Classics and Ancient Literature

Colonial Literature

Eastern Literature

European Literature

Gothic Literature

History

Medieval Literature

Oxford English Drama

Poetry

Philosophy

Politics

Religion

The Oxford Shakespeare

A complete list of Oxford World's Classics, including Authors in Context, Oxford English Drama, and the Oxford Shakespeare, is available in the UK from the Marketing Services Department, Oxford University Press, Great Clarendon Street, Oxford OX2 6DP, or visit the website at www.oup.com/uk/worldsclassics.

In the USA, visit www.oup.com/us/owc for a complete title list.

Oxford World's Classics are available from all good bookshops. In case of difficulty, customers in the UK should contact Oxford University Press Bookshop, 116 High Street, Oxford OX1 4BR.

| | |
|---|---|
| HORACE | The Complete Odes and Epodes |
| JUVENAL | The Satires |
| LIVY | The Dawn of the Roman Empire |
| | Hannibal's War |
| | The Rise of Rome |
| MARCUS AURELIUS | The Meditations |
| OVID | The Love Poems |
| | Metamorphoses |
| PETRONIUS | The Satyricon |
| PLATO | Defence of Socrates, Euthyphro, and Crito |
| | Gorgias |
| | Meno and Other Dialogues |
| | Phaedo |
| | Republic |
| | Selected Myths |
| | Symposium |
| PLAUTUS | Four Comedies |
| PLUTARCH | Greek Lives |
| | Roman Lives |
| | Selected Essays and Dialogues |
| PROPERTIUS | The Poems |
| SOPHOCLES | Antigone, Oedipus the King, and Electra |
| STATIUS | Thebaid |
| SUETONIUS | Lives of the Caesars |
| TACITUS | Agricola and Germany |
| | The Histories |
| VIRGIL | The Aeneid |
| | The Eclogues and Georgics |
| XENOPHON | The Expedition of Cyrus |

Bhagavad Gita

The Bible  Authorized King James Version
*With Apocrypha*

Dhammapada

Dharmasūtras

The Koran

The Pañcatantra

The Sauptikaparvan (from the
  Mahabharata)

The Tale of Sinuhe and Other Ancient
  Egyptian Poems

The Qur'an

Upaniṣads

ANSELM OF CANTERBURY  The Major Works

THOMAS AQUINAS  Selected Philosophical Writings

AUGUSTINE  The Confessions
On Christian Teaching

BEDE  The Ecclesiastical History

HEMACANDRA  The Lives of the Jain Elders

KĀLIDĀSA  The Recognition of Śakuntalā

MANJHAN  Madhumalati

ŚĀNTIDEVA  The Bodhicaryàvatàra

Travel Writing 1700–1830

Women's Writing 1778–1838

WILLIAM BECKFORD       Vathek

JAMES BOSWELL          Life of Johnson

FRANCES BURNEY         Camilla
                       Cecilia
                       Evelina
                       The Wanderer

LORD CHESTERFIELD      Lord Chesterfield's Letters

JOHN CLELAND           Memoirs of a Woman of Pleasure

DANIEL DEFOE           A Journal of the Plague Year
                       Moll Flanders
                       Robinson Crusoe
                       Roxana

HENRY FIELDING         Jonathan Wild
                       Joseph Andrews and Shamela
                       Tom Jones

WILLIAM GODWIN         Caleb Williams

OLIVER GOLDSMITH       The Vicar of Wakefield

MARY HAYS              Memoirs of Emma Courtney

ELIZABETH INCHBALD     A Simple Story

SAMUEL JOHNSON         The History of Rasselas
                       The Major Works

CHARLOTTE LENNOX       The Female Quixote

MATTHEW LEWIS          Journal of a West India Proprietor
                       The Monk

HENRY MACKENZIE        The Man of Feeling